IFIP Advances in Information and Communication Technology   668

Editor-in-Chief

IFIP – The International Federation for Information Processing

IFIP was founded in 1960 under the auspices of UNESCO, following the first World Computer Congress held in Paris the previous year. A federation for societies working in information processing, IFIP's aim is two-fold: to support information processing in the countries of its members and to encourage technology transfer to developing nations. As its mission statement clearly states:

> IFIP is the global non-profit federation of societies of ICT professionals that aims at achieving a worldwide professional and socially responsible development and application of information and communication technologies.

IFIP is a non-profit-making organization, run almost solely by 2500 volunteers. It operates through a number of technical committees and working groups, which organize events and publications. IFIP's events range from large international open conferences to working conferences and local seminars.

The flagship event is the IFIP World Computer Congress, at which both invited and contributed papers are presented. Contributed papers are rigorously refereed and the rejection rate is high.

As with the Congress, participation in the open conferences is open to all and papers may be invited or submitted. Again, submitted papers are stringently refereed.

The working conferences are structured differently. They are usually run by a working group and attendance is generally smaller and occasionally by invitation only. Their purpose is to create an atmosphere conducive to innovation and development. Refereeing is also rigorous and papers are subjected to extensive group discussion.

Publications arising from IFIP events vary. The papers presented at the IFIP World Computer Congress and at open conferences are published as conference proceedings, while the results of the working conferences are often published as collections of selected and edited papers.

IFIP distinguishes three types of institutional membership: Country Representative Members, Members at Large, and Associate Members. The type of organization that can apply for membership is a wide variety and includes national or international societies of individual computer scientists/ICT professionals, associations or federations of such societies, government institutions/government related organizations, national or international research institutes or consortia, universities, academies of sciences, companies, national or international associations or federations of companies.

More information about this series at https://link.springer.com/bookseries/6102

Olivia McDermott · Angelo Rosa ·
José Carlos Sá · Aidan Toner (Eds.)

Lean, Green and Sustainability

8th IFIP WG 5.7
European Lean Educator Conference, ELEC 2022
Galway, Ireland, November 22–24, 2022
Proceedings

 Springer

Editors
Olivia McDermott (iD)
University of Galway
Galway, Ireland

Angelo Rosa (iD)
LUM University "Giuseppe Degennaro"
Casamassima, Italy

José Carlos Sá (iD)
Instituto Superior de Engenharia do Porto
Porto, Portugal

Aidan Toner (iD)
University of Galway
Galway, Ireland

ISSN 1868-4238   ISSN 1868-422X   (electronic)
IFIP Advances in Information and Communication Technology
ISBN 978-3-031-25743-8   ISBN 978-3-031-25741-4   (eBook)
https://doi.org/10.1007/978-3-031-25741-4

This Springer imprint is published by the registered company Springer Nature Switzerland AG
The registered company address is: Gewerbestrasse 11, 6330 Cham, Switzerland

Preface

In this proceedings, we share the papers that were presented at the 8th European Lean Educator Conference (ELEC 2022), which was hosted face to face in Galway, Ireland, during November 22–24, 2022. This year's conference was special in that it was sponsored by the International Federation for Information Processing (IFIP) for the second time in its history, having been organized in close collaboration with the IFIP Working Group 5.7 Special Interest Group (SIG) on the Future of Lean Thinking and Practice. The conference was organized by the University of Galway, Ireland.

The ELEC community is dedicated to fostering knowledge exchange within academia as well as between academic institutions and industry, which we believe is especially important. As such, ELEC 2022 provided a platform for professors, teachers, trainers, and coaches from academia, industry, and public sector organizations to share their knowledge and experiences and learn from one another.

ELEC conferences distinguish lean thinking as a broad management and operations improvement philosophy, fully grounded in science and supported by a continually growing set of methods, techniques, and tools. Given that this year's conference theme was 'Lean, Green and Sustainability', ELEC 2022 made a special effort to highlight the role of lean and green as well as sustainability concepts in the emerging digital lean manufacturing paradigm.

This volume includes the 28 full papers that were presented at ELEC 2022. The papers were double-blind peer-reviewed to ensure quality and went through a rigorous editing and 'redline' review to ensure conformance to the standards of ELEC. We had 42 presentations at the conference of which 28 were academic paper submissions.

We thank the many experienced Lean authors and academics who submitted academic papers and guaranteed a high quality of submissions and acceptances. To name but a few of these academics, they included Angelo Rosa, José Carlos Sá, Daryl Powell (ELEC 2021 chair), Ton van Kollenburg (ELEC 2023 chair), José Dinis Carvalho (ELEC 2019 chair) and Matteo Rossini (ELEC 2020 chair), and their extended faculty members, who ensured and authored high-quality submission.

Thanks also to the reviewer team who reviewed several papers each and redlined areas for improvement and gave feedback to ensure high standards and aid decisions.

We thank the academics from various Irish educational institutions who worked closely with their industry-based MSc and PhD Lean students to ensure that firstly those high-achieving student thesis/final papers were edited to a high academic standard before submission to the ELEC system and secondly that Irish Lean industry practice was represented and showcased at ELEC 2022.

The topics which emerged at ELEC 2022 were:

- Lean & People
- Lean in Healthcare
- Lean 4.0
- Lean in Manufacturing

- Lean Learning in the Digital Era
- Lean in Services
- Lean, Green & Sustainability

In addition to the technical program, ELEC 2022 featured five keynote talks:

- Daryl Powell (SINTEF Manufacturing AS), 'Lean & the Green Economy: The Promise of a Waste Free Society';
- Richard Keegan (Trinity College Dublin), 'Is Lean Operational Excellence Useful Today?';
- Rose Heathcote (University of Buckingham), 'The Sustainable Enterprise: Delivering a Better Kind of Value';
- Richard Dawson (UPMC Medical Group), 'Creating a Culture of Service Excellence in Healthcare'.
- Stuart Nelson (University of Galway) 'Leadership in Lean'.

On behalf of the Conference Committee, we would like to thank all contributors for the high standard of work presented at ELEC 2022. This of course would not have been possible without the support of our International Scientific Committee and reviewers, so we would also like to thank these members for their efforts in reviewing and selecting the papers to be presented at ELEC 2022.

To conclude, we hope that ELEC 2022 stimulated the exchange of both research results and practical experiences to enhance the state of the art of lean thinking and practice.

November 2022

Olivia McDermott
Angelo Rosa
José Carlos Sá
Aidan Toner

Organization

Conference Chair

Olivia McDermott — University of Galway, Ireland

Program Chair

Angelo Rosa — LUM University "Giuseppe Degennaro", Libera Università Mediterranea di Bari, Italy

Conference Co-chairs

José Carlos Sá — Instituto Superior de Engenharia do Porto, Portugal
Aidan Toner — University of Galway, Ireland

International Advisory Board

Constantin May — Ansbach University of Applied Sciences, Germany
Pia Anhede — Revere AB, Sweden
Joakim Hillberg — Revere AB, Sweden
John Bicheno — University of Buckingham, UK
Christoph Roser — University of Applied Sciences, Karlsruhe, Germany
Jannes Slomp — HAN University of Applied Sciences, The Netherlands
Dinis Carvalho — Universidade do Minho, Portugal
Monica Rossi — Politecnico di Milano, Italy
John Shook — Lean Global Network, Boston, USA

International Scientific Committee

Erlend Alfnes — Norwegian University of Science and Technology, Norway
Jos Benders — Norwegian University of Science and Technology, Norway
Dinis Carvalho — Universidade do Minho, Portugal
Eivind Arne Fauskanger — University of South-Eastern Norway, Norway
Peter Hines — Waterford Institute of Technology, Ireland
Poul Houman Andersen — Aalborg University, Denmark
Olivia McDermott — University of Galway, Ireland
Torbjørn Netland — ETH Zurich, Switzerland
Daryl John Powell — SINTEF Manufacturing AS, Horten, Norway
Eivind Reke — SINTEF Manufacturing AS, Trondheim, Norway
Christoph Roser — University of Applied Sciences, Karlsruhe, Germany

Matteo Rossini	Politecnico di Milano, Italy
Henrik Saabye	Velux, Denmark
José Carlos Sá	Instituto Superior de Engenharia do Porto, Portugal
Jannes Slomp	HAN University of Applied Sciences, The Netherlands

Reviewers

Aidan Toner	University of Galway, Ireland
Olivia McDermott	University of Galway, Ireland
Mary Butler	Atlantic Technological University, Sligo, Ireland
Paul Butler	Department of Education, Ireland and University of Galway, Ireland
Ratri Parida	Guildhall School of Business and Law, London Metropolitan University, UK
Shane McHugo	White Swell Medical Device Manufacturing, Ireland
John Donovan	Atlantic Technological University, Sligo, Ireland
Fionnuala Farrell	Atlantic Technological University, Sligo, Ireland
John Noonan	University of Limerick, Ireland
Mary Ní Fhlathartaigh	Universidade do Minho, Portugal
Deirdre Barrow	Atlantic Technological University, Sligo, Ireland
Daryl John Powell	SINTEF Manufacturing AS, Norway
José Carlos Sá	Instituto Superior de Engenharia do Porto, Portugal
Brian Galli	Hofstra University, USA
Angelo Rosa	LUM University "Giuseppe Degennaro", Libera Università Mediterranea di Bari, Italy

Contents

Lean in Manufacturing

Lean Learning in the Digital Era

Lean and People

Is There Such a Thing as a Lean Philosophy?

Joop de Zwart[✉]

Avans University of Applied Sciences, Breda, The Netherlands
jg.dezwart@avans.nl

Abstract. The word 'philosophy' has been regularly used within the context of Lean thought. For example, Liker [1] insists that a long term *philosophy* is required in order to become a Lean organization, while Bicheno and Holweg [2] use the word as the title of a chapter to describe what they consider to be the essence of Lean thought.

However, what does this all have to do with philosophy? Philosophy – viewed as an academic discipline – is not the same as the philosophies used in the discussions about Lean. For Lean educators it could be interesting to reflect philosophically upon Lean thought. In this paper it shall be explored what happens if you approach Lean thought from a philosophical perspective. The use of the singular can be misleading: there are different ways to approach Lean thought, so in this paper is described how philosophy can be used to reflect upon Lean thought both from the *inside out* and from the *outside in* and demonstrated examples of the *inside out* approach. This study has implications for further research and is of relevance for Lean (education) practitioners. This paper is built upon the hypothesis that (philosophical) reflection upon Lean thought is relevant because it can improve both Lean practices and the in-depth knowledge of the methods applied in practice.

Keywords: Lean philosophy · Lean thought · Lean essence · Critical lean thought

1 Introduction

If there is no chapter about Lean philosophy in books on philosophy, does that automatically mean that there is no such thing as Lean philosophy? Some authors do write about Lean philosophy [2] or production philosophy [3, 4], but then philosophy is used in a specific way, and that is not the way philosophers tend to use the word. It is more to indicate that Lean thought is a more or less consistent set of vocabulary and methods. This use of philosophy is an everyday use of the word, as one can also say that organizations or persons have a certain philosophy [5]. This everyday use of the word is just a small part of what philosophy is all about.

Philosophy, as a specific discipline, is most commonly defined as the art of asking questions, most introductions on philosophy agree about that [6, 7]. The philosopher 'is putting into words an amazement or sense of wonder' [8]. A currently popular Dutch

© IFIP International Federation for Information Processing 2023
Published by Springer Nature Switzerland AG 2023
O. McDermott et al. (Eds.): ELEC 2022, IFIP AICT 668, pp. 3–13, 2023.
https://doi.org/10.1007/978-3-031-25741-4_1

book on philosophy [9] has as its subtitle 'guide to asking good questions'. What's different then to for example the 5W1H-approach, also known as the Kipling questions [10] or the '5 times why' method, which are also about asking questions and deep learning [11]?

Philosophical questioning tends to focus upon fundamental issues in reality. For example, in Lean thought, the idea of 'respect for people' [12] can be philosophically addressed by asking what *respect* means and what its boundaries are. Or one could ask why respect for people should be limited to people? Asking questions philosophically – and in the case of *respect* ethically – means that one wonders about certain things in reality and that seeks to clarify the concepts (like respect) and critically examining the scope and limits of a concept (*why should respect be limited to people?*). Magee [7] emphasises that this attempt to clarify concepts is concerned with subjects that are of great practical importance, but at the same time can be very problematic. The concepts of Lean thought are indeed of practical importance but can be ambiguous at the same time. Respect looks familiar at first sight, but when one looks a bit closer it can appear quite ambiguous. In the remainder of this paper other concepts will be addressed that also seem familiar, but, when investigated more thoroughly, reveal surprising insights.

What's the use of a philosophical approach towards Lean thought? Questioning Lean thought philosophically (or critically) may have several results. Firstly, the concepts used so often by Lean practitioners are questioned from time to time which deepens the understanding of them and prevents a sloppy use of them and provides newcomers in the field with an up-to-date vocabulary. Secondly, the critical questions about the concepts in use give even experienced professionals a possibility to update their conceptual library. In the example of 'respect for people', sustainability issues or societal dynamism like the changing attitude towards gender issues can give the concept 'respect for people' a new content or provide arguments to rename it to 'respect for life'.

Approaching Lean philosophically in general can be done in two ways: from the inside out and from the outside in. The approach is *inside out* if one takes Lean thought and digs into the Lean concepts philosophically, by asking questions. It is the approach also used by Griseri [5], when, in the first part of his book, he questions phenomena like 'organisations', 'work' and 'leadership'. One does not need a certain philosophical vocabulary, but rather certain methods of questioning. It is *outside in* when the starting point is taken in philosophy and from that point Lean thought is questioned. So, in this respect lean thought is the inside and philosophy the outside. Jones and Ten Bos [13] call this approach towards, in their case, organisation studies, 'injections of philosophy'. Authors try to take a certain philosophical concept to enrich Lean thought. This paper focuses on the inside out. This is primarily because of the lack of space to perform both exercises. The outside in approach requires elaborations of specific philosophic topics, while the inside out approach starts from concepts that are familiar to Lean practitioners.

2   Method: How to Approach Lean Philosophically

This paper searches to explore some Lean concepts from the inside out. The method is based upon what Griseri [5] did. In his *Introduction to the philosophy of management* he explains his project in the following manner: 'this book looks, not at the thinking that goes on *in* management (…) but rather at the thinking *behind* management. What is the basis of our understanding of what organisations are'. Most simply put, in this paper 'Lean thought' replaces 'management': What thinking lies behind Lean thought? What is the basis of our understanding about what Lean thought is? That means that Lean thought is examined in a way which seeks to further clarify it.

The other approach, outside-in, starts from philosophy and then questions Lean thought. Koskela and Kagioglou [14, 15] performed such an exercise twice, when they examined production and management through the lens of metaphysics. They did so in order to understand better how Lean thought differs from much of the managerial literature and practices traditionally used. Previously, the example of ethics was mentioned, which is also a branche of philosophy. In other words, the outside in approach starts from the questions that are traditionally asked by philosophers and then examines Lean thought through that lens. In this paper the inside out approach is elaborated on, and further research will explore the outside-in approach.

The inside out approach can be performed in roughly two ways. Firstly, Lean thought is questioned in order to find certain characteristics that can be considered to be *its essence*. Where the five times why method seeks to understand a certain problem thoroughly, philosophical investigation seeks to do that with Lean thought itself. If one studies the body of literature about Lean thought (e.g. meta analysis like Van Kollenburg and Kokkinou [16]), combined with practical application like the ones performed by students at the author's University of Applied Science, can one distinguish one or more essential features that help to understand Lean thought? And can one thus develop a better understanding why it is so notoriously difficult to really establish something like a Lean culture?

Secondly, a familiar Lean concept will be questioned, in this paper that will be customer value. The method used can be referred to as 'conceptual archaeology'. In this method one takes the present concept – customer value – and starts digging in the source material where it originally comes from. Then the original is re-read in order to see what was meant in the original work and whether or not interesting features have been lost somewhere along the way. An example of such a conceptual archaeology was done on corporate social responsibility (CSR), which led to the conclusion that much of the richness of the original reflections about CSR was lost in translation [17]. Basically this process is a similar to 'Chinese Whispers', the children's play where the first child in a row whispers a phrase in the ear of the second child, the second to the third and so on until the last child has to repeat the sentence out loud, to see what's left of the original phrase.

Books on Lean thought in general will pay attention to the concept of customer value. Womack and Jones [12] made it one of the five basic principles and also in Liker's pyramid [1] it is hugely important. But Womack, Jones and Liker got it from Toyota. And Toyota got it from Henry Ford. What happens if one returns to the original work by Henry Ford, mentioned by Ohno [18]?

So in this paper the inside out approach searches for the answers to two questions:

1. Is there something essential behind Lean thought?
2. What can we learn from Henry Ford about customer value?

3 Results 1: About the Essence of Lean Thought

Many authors have given definitions of Lean or main characteristics of it. Of course, there is the pyramid by Jeffrey Liker [1], there are the five elements of Lean thinking by Womack and Jones [12] or the 25 characteristics named by Bicheno [2], there is A3 thinking what John Shook [19] proposes to be the key to the system. Recently van Kollenburg and Kokkinou [16] performed a literature study into the definitions and characteristics (which apparently added up to 736!). Each analysis has in common that one of the essential aspects of Lean thought is the idea of continuous improvement. Therefore, I want to further elaborate on that in order to illustrate the thinking behind Lean thought.

During my career as a Lean educator, at a faculty of a Dutch university of Applied Science specifically concerned with the construction industry, it became clear that it is by no means self-evident to establish a culture of continuous improvement. Of course, every student has to start from scratch in his or her learning career, but the same seems to be the case for the organisations where the students do their internships. The number of organisations that seek to apply Lean thought and continuous improvement is much larger that the number of organisations that succeed in establishing a culture where continuous improvement is part and parcel of company practices. The continuous improvement of many construction companies seems to exist solely of the internship assignments of the students they host.

Why was it so difficult to establish a culture of continuous improvement? The procedures aren't rocket science, so what seems to be the problem? In one of his books on (societal) transitions, the Dutch author Jan Rotmans mentions the paralyzing effect of a stationary view of reality. Transitions need a more dynamic view of reality and a more dynamic way of organising. Rigid blueprint structures or project approaches should be abandoned in favour of more organic approaches to change [20]. And that does not come natural. Change has to be trained constantly, he claims, referring to the German philosopher Peter Sloterdijk [20].

Transition, continuous improvement, learning organisations; they all have at least two things in common: they share a high appreciation of change, of learning, of dynamism. And they share the awareness that it is notoriously difficult to achieve such a thing. And I think that touches upon something behind Lean thought: a stationary or at least linear view of reality that dominates over a dynamic view of reality. And one could argue that this is deeply rooted in (Western) thought.

One of the philosophers that asked attention for this stationary aspect of Western thought was Martin Heidegger (1889–1976). One of his hypotheses was that Western thought has had a tendency to objectify reality. In de Zwart [17] this is summarised in four characteristics, one of them being an inclination to Truth. The capital T hints at the absolute status of truth. Western thought, or modern thought, seeks for Truth. It has done so in religion, where God was the highest of beings, and is has done so in the era of the Enlightenment, where universal knowledge became the ideal of science. The title of the movie about the life of the famous scientist Stephen Hawking says it all: 'a Theory of Everything' was the positivist ideal. The German Philosopher Karl Jaspers (1883–1969) called this belief in science scientific superstition (*wissenschaftliches Aberglaube*, [21]).

The idea of Truth comes with an absolute preference of stability over instability. Instability even means chaos. In medieval times, God was not just a little higher than his creatures, he was the 'higher than anything that could be thought' (Anselm of Canterbury), the ultimate and absolute being of beings. There could not be more than one creator, that would make God less perfect and this perfection was eternal. That already was the case with Plato, who could not stand the idea that the reality as we perceive it, with its diversity and temporality was all there was to it. There must exist something behind reality which is perfect, he claimed: his world of ideas, stable and eternal [6, 7].

The era of the Enlightenment in the end seems to have been secularised, famously coined 'the death of God' by Nietzsche ((1844–1900), the famous aphorism about the death of God is taken from *Human all too Human*), but that does not mean that the preference of universal and stable truths had diminished as well, as the title of the aforementioned movie already indicated. Science also seeks for universally applicable laws and methods and in philosophy post-modern thinkers that are critical of the idea of fixed truths are easily being accused of relativism. Dostoyevski's famous quotation: 'if God is dead, than everything is allowed' (in the novel *'The Brothers Karamazov'*, 1880) hints at the consequences of the loss of certainty, of stable truths, at least in the realm of morality.

Koskela and Kagioglou [14] likewise distinguish between *substance* and *process* metaphysics and conclude 'first, that it is the inappropriate metaphysical choice that is at the root of many of the problems of production, and, secondly, that the neglect of explicit metaphysical considerations has effectively concealed this situation'. I would go further than that: for many people there is not just a choice, but a struggle. It is extremely hard to move away from a certain way of perceiving reality. Change is not perceived neutrally, it is threatening, it is *normatively* inferior to stability. To put it more in Lean terms: the idea of a standard procedure as a point of departure for improvement, rather than a definitive conclusion of a search for a one best practice is extremely hard to accept if one has a strong inclination to stable and fixed truths.

So the first result of examining a concept like continuous improvement leads to the awareness of a rather fundamental barrier for people to adopt continuous improvement practices: people might hesitate, because a world with no end to change seems chaotic and threatening. To quote Nietzsche: 'man is something that must be overcome', which is a fragment taken from his *'Thus Spoke Zarathustra'*, originally published in 1883. This last quotation brings me to a second result of this exercise: what is it that has to be overcome?

Continuous improvement leans upon the idea that one carefully examines a problem. The five times why and the DMAIC procedures presuppose a thorough and cautious approach to a problem, as does the A3 problem solving process. During the years as a Lean educator, I found it interesting to see that the favourite research method seems to be the interview. Rarely students (and the professionals who coach them) choose for themselves to measure a problem. They often choose to approach a problem by means of interviews, collecting opinions – how valuable these may be – instead of measuring facts. It takes effort to take the step towards measuring a problem.

What we've learned from neuro scientists is that there is a distinction between type 1 and type 2 thinking [22]. Type 1 thinking is intuitive and prefers to jump to conclusions. It is the kind of thinking that is required outside in dangerous situations: it is more successful to mistake a stone for a lion than vice versa. Based upon superficial knowledge quick decisions have to be made.

Type 2 thinking is the more sophisticated type of thinking: reflective, analytic, scientific. It is the kind of thinking that is quite modern, compared to the type 1 way of thinking. Type 1 thinking is connected to the older parts of the brain, seen from an evolutionary point of view, while type 2 thinking belongs to the more recently developed parts of the brain, like the frontal cortex.

Because type 1 thinking is rooted in the oldest, most primitive parts of the brain, it is a very strong way of thinking. Many people absolutely trust in their intuitions, in their first impressions, although scientific research has proven that this way of thinking is not at all reliable. The frontal cortex has quite a difficult task overruling the quick and superficial conclusions of the primitive parts of the brain. It takes training and certainly doesn't come by itself to be critical, reflexive, scientific.

Lean thought, with its thorough approach to problem solving, belongs to the realm of type 2 thinking. One has to be prepared to postpone one's conclusions and really try to figure out the facts behind a problem. Many people absolutely don't like to do such a thing as postponing their conclusions and do thorough research into a problem and its causes.

So, is the thinking behind Lean thought a kind of thinking that is difficult to practice, simply because it does not fit with the most deeply rooted thinking routines? Continuous improvement, with its slow procedures, belongs to the realm of the part of the brain that developed most recently, and that has difficulty overruling the habits of type 1 thinking.

During the centuries, a number of writers have written about the struggle between these types of thinking, without knowing about neuro sciences. An example from ancient philosophy is Plato describing in his Faidros [23] the soul (*psyche*) as a chariot, with a rational part of the soul being the charioteer, who has to control the other, less rational parts of the soul. Of course, this looks like what we encounter for example in Christian tradition; here it is sufficient to say that it seems that what has been discovered scientifically about the brain, already was preluded by many ancient thinkers, and also Nietzsche [24] seemed to have an understanding of this paradoxical characteristic of the brain when he claimed that 'man is something that must be overcome'.

In a very brief manner I tried to show how the thinking in Lean thought might differ from the thinking behind it, with the Lean principle of continuous improvement as a starting point.

4   Results 2: Customer Value

The second research question concerns the lean concept of customer value, so some roots of lean thought are examined in order to see what can be learned from them. For that purpose one of the roots shall be especially looked at, namely Henry Ford's famous book *'Today and Tomorrow'* [25] The reason that Ford [25] was chosen is a result of 'philosophy as conceptual archaeology', where one tries to trace back a concept as far as possible. When one reads Ohno's Toyota Production System [18], one of the important sources from within Toyota, one automatically stumbles upon some of the sources he uses, among which Henry Ford ('*I, for one, am in awe of Ford's greatness*', writes Ohno where he also explicitly quotes Today and Tomorrow).

After reading Ohno, the author immediately started reading Ford, and was struck by some very 'Toyota-ist' passages. Of course that shouldn't have been a surprise, because Ohno already wrote how much he admired this work and that much of his own thought was already present in Today and Tomorrow. In this paper there is no intention to simply summarise Ford, but to read it with a specific Lean concept in mind, which is customer value.

Actually, Ford never mentions 'customer value', but instead uses 'service power' on several occasions. But what does that add to reading for example Womack and Jones, who claim that customer value is one of the key components of their five-step approach to Lean thought? They approach value from their perspective, which is a (positive) construction of a way of thinking that can be characterised as Lean. They analysed Toyota in order to find the key to their success. Doing that, something got lost which originally was present in the work of Ford: a criticism of practices of his times.

Ford was very critical about some practices in his days: the attitude towards 'big business' and the financial markets. At the very beginning of '*Today and Tomorrow*' he states: '*Big business is not about money power: it is service power*' (p. 9), and '*the test of the service of a corporation is in how far its benefits are passed on to the consumer*' (p. 17). He considered that a too dominant position of financial institutions was a threat to the service power of the corporation. Management that is pressurised by financial goals (both interest and dividends) loses attention for the service power of the company ('*pressed from above for interest and dividends, pushed from below to grant more money for less work, he had small chance to give service*', p. 23).

It seems that Ford was even more radical in his ideas than his successors: although he mentions many of the wastes that have become classics in lean thought, interest and dividend haven't made it to the list of wastes that seriously threat customer value. Of course, Lean thought has always been critical about profit as an end, which can explicitly be traced back to Ford: '*the profit motive (…) is really not practical at all, because (…) it has as its objectives the increasing of prices to the consumer and the decreasing of wages*' (p. 25). This has made it to Lean literature, but his opinion about '*absentee dividend takers*' is much less apparent.

Another example of Ford's critique of '*the profit motive*' can be found in the chapter about his ideas about wages: '*the right price is the lowest price an article can steadily be sold for. The right wage is the highest wage an employer can steadily pay*' (p. 140). This is exactly opposite of the profit motive, where wages are always to be reduced. Ford's idea of the profit motive looks a lot like the Marxist critique of capitalism with its infinite tendency to cut wages in favour of the shareholders. Ford calls that the old theory of wages, in which wage depends of bargaining power: '*the old theory, which still persists in business, is that the rate of wages depends on the bargaining power of the worker as against the monopoly power of the employer. Under that theory, both sides lost*' (p. 138).

Time and time again, one finds critical remarks like the aforementioned that are completely the opposite of what later thought about the function of a corporation would emphasize. Think of someone like Milton Friedman who in 1970 criticised CSR authors with the (in)famous article *'The only responsibility of the corporation is to increase its profits'* [26], a plea for the profit motive of which Ford wrote: *'the face of business is bowed towards the stockholder and not towards the customer, and this means a denial of the primary purpose of industry'* (p. 215). And again: *'industry is not money – it is made up of ideas, labour and management, and the natural expression of these is not dividends, but utility, quality, and availability'* (p. 215). In this chapter Ford is highly critical about a capitalist society where shareholder value is the ultimate goal of the corporation. Money is just a commodity, and if that is out of sight, Ford foresees great problems, because *'money will get itself ahead of service'* (p. 213).

Next to the criticism of financial institutions, Ford already introduces the idea of waste as a threat to customer value: *'a man cannot be paid high wages for standing around waiting for tools. Nor, which amounts to the same, can the public be served'* (p. 92) Waiting is directly connected to the 'service power', or rather the loss of it. The same goes for *'stooping to the floor'* (p. 92), excess movement, Ford already calls it a waste.

Some of the 'classic' wastes can already be found in Fords Today and Tomorrow, so that does not really add to the understanding of wastes. Re-reading Ford is, from the perspective of the wastes, not revolutionary. It is amazing to see how these ideas were already present in 1926. In the case of his criticism of the financial markets, the sensation is more profound: it provides interesting arguments to add profit to the list of wastes! That would mean that this conceptual archaeology led us to a ninth waste!

5 Discussion and Conclusion

This paper is a first step towards something like a Lean philosophy. Two questions were asked as examples of how one can approach Lean thought philosophically. When one asks questions about Lean thought and tries to discover what could be the thinking behind Lean thought, it becomes clear that certain habits are not easily turned around. Lean thinking requires an attitude that is by no means evident to the way humans are used to think and work. The reflection upon the concept continuous improvement showed that Western thought seems to prefer a static concept of truth. This means that if one searches for improvement, that will be a quest for one best way of doing things, and the very idea of improvement being eternally provisional seems appalling.

The brain also objects to the slow and reflexive methods of continuous improvement. This helps Lean educator to pay attention to the adaptation of Lean principles. Many students (and professionals alike) try to rationalize their almost natural hesitation towards Lean thought. It is important to be aware of deeply rooted aversions that function as mental barriers in educational processes. Some students are eager to adopt innovative ways, but many must go to greater difficulty to achieve such a thing.

In the first part of this paper only one exercise was executed to show what happens if one searches for thinking behind concepts like continuous improvement. Further analyses are required to analogously shed light upon other Lean principles.

The second part of the paper was dedicated to another way of doing philosophy about Lean thought: conceptual archeology. Using again one concept – customer value – Ford (1926) was re-read and thus Ohno's statement that much of the principles applied at

Toyota are already there to be found was verified. This demonstrated that reading Ford showed that some principles present there were (at least partly) forgotten. The critical attitude towards capital as an end instead of a means is even more sharply present in Ford that in later works on Lean thought.

Is this exercise taking philosophy seriously? Shouldn't that be about fundamental questions like knowledge, righteousness, morality, existence? As a specific and specialized academic discipline, philosophy does not seem interested in something like Lean thought and its concepts. More specific disciplines, like philosophy of management or philosophical practice, could be more suitable for reflections about Lean thought. At the other hand, if philosophy is about asking questions about important things in life or in reality, is Lean thought not one of them? People spend much of their time in organisations and trying to improve organisational practices seems a modern time way of thinking about the good life.

Does such a philosophical approach take Lean thought seriously? One of the positive aspects of Lean is that seems to have a certain no-nonsense approach to improvement. Go to the gemba and see what is going on there. Does this paper propose to leave the gemba and retreat in a library? It certainly does not! The philosophical approach seeks to think about Lean thought and see what can be learned from that, in order to improve Lean practices. If one is aware of the barriers that may exist between people and their possibilities to continuously change, it may be easier to coach them.

Furthermore, we must not forget that Lean concepts have a certain background, and an approach that wants to apply the concepts immediately, may forget to reflect upon the backgrounds of the concepts. If Lean thought has to do with a thorough analysis of a problem at hand, why should that not apply to Lean thought itself? If one asks five times why on the gemba, why not do that to the method itself? This paper is built upon the hypotheses that 1) thorough elaboration of the methods used will improve the practical use of them, and 2) that returning to the classics of a debate can improve one's understanding of the thinking behind it. Doing that, one may even be rewarded with insights that can be excitingly new.

Lean thought has become a rather complex body of knowledge. It takes effort to understand the concepts that are so familiar to Lean practitioners. Returning time and time again to the basic concepts 1) helps newcomers to adapt to the professional standards required and 2) helps experienced professionals not to take any of them for granted. Furthermore, in the times we live in, with many transitions at hand on a macro level (e.g., circular economy, sustainable energy), we shall need the ideas of continuous improvement, of Lean thought to implement the many changes that we will encounter. A deeper understanding of what these principles are and why it can be so difficult to implement them, can help improving practices on a micro level in order to achieve transitions on a macro level. But it may be necessary to reflect upon the connection between the two levels. Lean thought must then perhaps be reconsidered and refined as well, and philosophy can help to bridge the societal level and the organisational level. Chapters like the last one in Van Kollenburg's [11], about Lean thought and the 21st century challenges, should perhaps be granted a more equal position next to the more traditional Lean methods, which now make up the largest part of the book.

Although there is not a Lean philosophy as such, other than the everyday use of it, and there is not a chapter on Lean thought in philosophy books, that doesn't mean that there cannot be a Lean philosophy. Philosophical methods can be applied to deepen the understanding of the thinking behind Lean, and about the clarification of the concepts used in the Lean body of knowledge. In this paper an exercise to show the above was carried out. Many such exercises are waiting to be performed.

References

1. Liker, J.K.: The Toyota Way. McGraw-Hill, New York (2004)
2. Bicheno, J., Holweg, M.: The Lean Toolbox. The Essential Guide to Lean Transformation. PICSIE books, Buckingham (2009)
3. Koskela, L: Application of the new production philosophy to construction. CIFE Technical report, 72. Stanford University, Stanford (1992)
4. Bertelsen, S, Koskela, L: Construction Beyond Lean: a new understanding of Construction Management. In: Proceedings International Group for Lean Construction (2004)
5. Griseri, P.: An Introduction to the Philosophy of Management. SAGE, London (2013)
6. Aufenanger, J.: Filosofie. Prisma, Utrecht (1994)
7. Magee, B.: Het Verhaal van de Filosofie. Areopagus, Amsterdam (1998)
8. Kaulingfreks, R.: The Uselessness of Philosophy. In: Jones, C, Ten Bos, R., Philosophy and Organization. Routledge, New York (2007)
9. Wiss, E.: Socrates op Sneakers. Filosofische gids voor het stellen van goede vragen. Ambo/Anthos, Amsterdam (2020)
10. Kipling, R.: Just So Stories. MacMillan, London (1902)
11. Van Kollenburg, T.: Lean Green Belt – improvement as practical skill in the 21st century. Learning Lean, 's- Hertogenbosch (2021)
12. Womack, J.P., Jones, D.T.: Lean Thinking. Zeist, Lean Management Instituut (2011)
13. Jones, C., Ten Bos, R.: Introduction. In: Jones, C., Ten Bos, R., Philosophy and Organization. Routledge, New York (2007)
14. Koskela, L, Kagioglou, M.: On the metaphysics of production. In: 13th Annual Conference of the International Group for Lean Construction, 19–21st July 2005, Sydney, Australia. (Unpublished) (2005)
15. Koskela, L, Kagioglou, M.: On the metaphysics of management. In: Proceedings IGLC-14, July 2006, Santiago, Chile. IGLC, pp. 1–13 (2006)
16. Van Kollenburg, T., Kokkinou, A.: What comes after the transformation?. In: Powell, D.J., Alfnes, E., Holmemo, M.D.Q., Reke, E. (eds) Learning in the Digital Era. ELEC 2021. IFIP Advances in Information and Communication Technology, vol. 610. Springer, Cham (2021). https://doi.org/10.1007/978-3-030-92934-3_26
17. De Zwart, J.G.: Corporate Social Responsibility, an Interpretative Practice. Rediscovering CSR through the hermeneutic philosophy of Gianni Vattimo. Radboud University, PhD thesis, Nijmegen (2016)
18. Ohno, T.: Toyota Production System. Beyond Large-Scale Production. CRC Press, Boca Raton (1988)
19. Shook, J: Managing to Learn; het A3-managementproces: problemen oplossen, overeenstemming bereiken, mentoren en leiden. Lean Management Instituut, Zeist (2016, original English edition: 2008)
20. Rotmans, J.: Omarm de Chaos. De Geus, Amsterdam (2021)
21. Jaspers, K.: Der philosophische Glaube angesichts der Offenbarung. Piper, München (1962)
22. Heijltjes, A.: Kritisch leren Denken. Avans University of Applied Science, Breda (s.d)

23. Plato, translated into Dutch by Warren, H, Molegraaf, M: Faidros. Bert Bakker, Amsterdam (1998)
24. Nietzsche, F.: Aldus sprak Zarathustra, translated into Dutch by Oranje, W. Boom, Amsterdam/Meppel (1996)
25. Ford, H.: Today and Tomorrow. BN Publishing, Hawthorne (2012, 1926)
26. Friedman, M.: The Social Responsibility of Business is to Increase its Profits. New York Times, New York (1970)

The Role of Lean Management Practices in the Valorisation of Neurodiverse People in Production

Matteo Zanchi$^{(\boxtimes)}$, Paolo Gaiardelli , and Giuditta Pezzotta

Department of Management, Information and Production Engineering, University of Bergamo,
Viale Marconi 5, Dalmine, BG, Italy
{matteo.zanchi,paolo.gaiardelli,giuditta.pezzotta}@unibg.it

Abstract. Increasing awareness on the widespread presence of people with neurodiverse traits among manufacturing companies has been orienting Lean managers to understand how to ease the inclusion of such individuals to working environments. Neurodiversity, intended as atypical neurological developments due to natural variations of the human brain, is not a marker of neurological diseases, but rather of a different way the brain works. As such, people with neurodiverse traits possess a set of strengths and weaknesses that are not common among other workers, thus resulting in significant advantages for production effectiveness. This paper aims to understand how Lean Management techniques may unleash the full potential of neurodiverse people, enhancing their key assets and limiting their weak points, by putting into relation, from a human factor perspective, each tool with the neurodiversity they deal with, in a dedicated framework.

Keywords: Lean management · Neurodiversity · Human factors

1 Introduction

The growing awareness regarding the wider presence of neurodiverse conditions among the population such as Attention Deficit and Hyperactivity Disorder (ADHD), autism and dyslexia, which have an overall prevalence oscillating between 16% and 16.6% worldwide [1], has led to the question in recent times as to whether the current working environments are inclusive in respect of the people affected by such conditions.

A more accommodating workplace may in fact support neurodiverse people in the execution of different activities with a lower degree of stress and anxiety, often generated by specific tasks that may put these people in discomfort. However, working environments are not usually designed for the needs of neurodiverse people who, consequently, are substantially excluded from the labour market. For example, it is only in the US, that the percentage of working age people affected by neurodiverse condition amounts to 37%, as compared to 79% of neurotypical individuals [2].

Whenever an attempt is made to render the working place more inclusive, Lean methodology can be considered as a possible way to pursue this mission [3]. Derived

O. McDermott et al. (Eds.): ELEC 2022, IFIP AICT 668, pp. 14–22, 2023.
https://doi.org/10.1007/978-3-031-25741-4_2

from the Japanese tradition, Lean Management methodology puts the human factor in the spotlight, as underlined by the Hitozukuri ("the art of doing people well") and provides its effectiveness, by leveraging on people inclusion.

Given this premise, the inclusivity aspect typical of the Lean methodology has not yet been proven for neurodiverse people, with particular reference to the capability of each Lean practice to actually concur to the creation of a more supportive environment. The aim of this paper is, therefore, to understand which benefits different Lean techniques may bring to the working conditions of neurodiverse people, from a human factors perspective.

Following this brief introduction, the paper proceeds with the explanation of the methodology used for the research (Sect. 2) and a summary description of the theoretical background concerning human factors on the workplace, neurodiversity and Lean techniques (Sect. 3). Following, three relationship maps linking neurodiversity and lean methodologies are shown, within which each connection is contextualised in the light of any specific human factor inferred from literature (Sect. 4). Last in this report, Sect. 5 provides a final picture about the obtained results, in addition to clues and hints for further research on the topic.

2 Methodology

From a methodological point of view, the research was led throughout two different phases. The first of which consisted of a literature review regarding three main streams of research, respectively: i) the expression of neurodiversity in the workplace, as it can be useful to identify strengths and weaknesses of neurodiverse people in a typical manufacturing environment [4]; ii) the redaction of a comprehensive set of Lean tools and practices that may influence the work environment which in turn affects the performances of neurodiverse people; and lastly iii) the provision of a complete set of human factors related to the field of production, which may serve to properly frame the mentioned effects on the work sphere of the neurodiverse operator. Web of Science and Google Scholar were the two main databases used to collect relevant papers on the topics under exploration.

On the basis of the themes found in literature, three relationship maps (one for each neurodiversity) were then drafted by three scholars participating in the research, to depict whether the Lean practices could contribute to the creation of a more accommodating working environment in respect of workers with neurodiverse traits. The impact of such techniques was, in particular, placed in the context of those human factors that mostly reflect the set of strengths and weaknesses characteristic of each specific neurodiversity.

Then, the proposed maps were tested and validated by interviewing a Lean expert with both theoretical and practical knowledge. Interviews were carried out through semistructured sessions to avoid excessive limitations to the discussion of such a vast and multi-thematic subject.

3 Theoretical Background

3.1 Neurodiversity

The term 'neurodiversity', coined by Judy Singer in 1998 [5], generally refers to the varied spectrum of conditions underlying a different cognitive functioning of human beings. Although over the years the term neurodiversity has often been associated with a pathological condition, it actually implies an atypical neurological development, but merely as a natural variation of the human brain that is not characterised by an actual neurological deficit [1]. Whereas in a neurotypical subject cognitive scores, measured in relation to the dimensions of verbal skills, working memory, visual skills and processing speed, fall within a tolerance of one or two standard deviations from the average IQ (Intelligent Quotient) value, delineating a relatively flat cognitive profile; in neurodiverse individuals, scores vary significantly beyond this threshold, delineating peaks and troughs in correspondence of the respective strengths and weaknesses, thus forming a 'spiky' profile specific to each neurological condition.

The following analysis focuses on the three neurodiversity statistically most present in the population, each one characterised by a set of work-related difficulties and strengths [1]:

- **ADHD.** With a prevalence around 5% among the worldwide population, attention deficit hyperactivity disorder manifests itself, from early childhood onwards, with an evident difficulty in concentrating or working on the same task for a prolonged period of time, and a range of behaviours displaying hyperactivity and impulsivity. Despite these cognitive conditions, individuals affected by ADHD possess an elevated creative thinking [6] as well as a heightened visual-spatial reasoning [7];
- **Autism.** With a prevalence of 1.6% globally, autism is a neurodevelopmental condition characterised by difficulties in social and communicative interaction, sensory apathy, as well as the presence of narrow interests and an obsessive desire to maintain one's environment and living habits [8]. The strengths possessed by autistics include a strong memory ability [9], innovative thinking and detail observation [10];
- **Dyslexia.** With an incidence up to 10% of the global population, dyslexia is a specific reading disorder that manifests itself with a difficulty in decoding text. Nonetheless, people affected by dyslexia possess normal levels of intelligence [11] and also own a strong orientation towards entrepreneurialism [12], a strong sense of creativity and cognitive control [13], as well as visual reasoning skills [14].

3.2 Lean Tools

Existent literature distinguishes Lean Management (LM) practices as "hard" and "soft" [15], where the former includes a set of distinctive technical tools used to improve production processes, the latter more related to the managerial perspective [16]. In order to be fully effective, a Lean approach should be implemented considering both aspects, so that the effect of each one will be magnified by the other [17].

Table 1 reports the breakdown of the different identified LM categories into specific tools described in both from a theoretical and practical literature perspective.

Table 1. Breakdown of Bortolotti [16] LM practices in single LM tools

Type of practice	LM practice	LM tools
Hard	Set-up time reduction	SMED
	Just-in-time delivery by suppliers	Kanban, Just In Sequence (JIS) & Junjo Sequence
	Equipment layout for continuous flow	VSM, Spaghetti chart, 5S, Yamazumi chart, Cell-design, Chaku-chaku
	Kanban	Heijunka box, Kanban & Milk run, Water spider & Mizusumashi
	Statistical process control	Jidoka, Ishikawa, Andon, Kamishibai, Poka-Yoke
	Autonomous maintenance	TPM
Soft	Small group problem solving	Brain storming, 5 whys, Genchi Genbutsu, A3 sheets
	Training employees	Job enlargement, Job enrichment, Coaching kata, OPL
	Top management leadership	Hoshin Kanri, Walk the floor (Genchi Genbutsu), Challenge, Teamwork (Scrum meeting), Respect, Kaizen mind
	Supplier partnership	Trust, Open communication, Close interaction (involvement)
	Customer involvement	Gemba walking, Stand-up meetings, Obeya room, Catchball approach
	Continuous improvement	PDCA/SDCA, «Make it ugly» (Kintsugi), Hansei, Shu-Ha-Ri

3.3 Human Factors

Whenever an attempt is made to implement a Lean approach within a company, putting the focus on human factors involvement and motivation is almost imperative [18]. The sole application of Lean tools, without considering the role of people in delivering value to customers, is indeed not enough for organisations to achieve a proper conversion that traces a Lean logic [19].

Existent literature defines human factors as *"all physical, psychological, and social characteristics of the humans, which influence the action in sociotechnical systems"* [20]. In order to get an overall picture of how human factors from the Industry 4.0, production and logistics areas can influence work tasks, a list of 27 human factors, belonging respectively to the physical, cognitive and organisational areas, was identified [21].

Table 2. List of physical, cognitive and organisational human factors [21]

Category	Human factor
Physical	Working postures
	Materials handling
	Repetitive movements
	Workplace layout
	Risk of accident
	Fitness for duty
	Reactivity
	Perception
	Available time/Rapidity/Time pressure
Cognitive	Memory
	Decision-making
	Complexity (reasoning and parallel tasks)
	Skilled performance/Experience
	Human error probability
	Work stress
	Training
Organisational	Policies
	Processes formalisation
	Communication
	Crew resource management/Leadership
	Teamwork
	Proactivity
	Self-management
	Telework

4 Discussion

Based on evidence put forward in current literature and the wealth of experience possessed by the three researchers participating in the project on the LM subject, three relationship maps were created. Each map was drafted for a specific neurodiversity (autism, ADHD and dyslexia), to give a proper illustration of how LM practices exert influence on the physical, cognitive and organisational human factors referring to neurodiverse workers.

During the assessment phase, the impact of each single "LM Tool" was considered among the entire list of human factors available. A score of +1 was assigned in case of positive effect of the LM tool on the considered human factor, −1 for all the circumstances where some kind of disadvantages were instead showing, and 0 whenever there were both pros and cons to the implementation of the considered technique. For all the other cases where no meaningful effects were feasible, no score was given.

The results have then been grouped according to the categorisation previously described in Tables 1 and 2.

Tables 3, 4 and 5 report, for each relation, the number of interactions found between the "LM Practice" and the HF (human factor) of interest, as well as the overall evaluation about the impact of such tools, being positive or negative, the latter reported in brackets across the different tables.

Table 3. Impact of LM tools on human factors (HF) – Autism[1]

LM practices	Physical HF	Cognitive HF	Organisational HF
Set-up time reduction	2 (− − −)	/	/
Just-in-time delivery by suppliers	2 (− − −)	5 (+ +)	2 (+ + +)
Equipment layout for continuous flow	8 (+ + +)	8 (+ +)	1 (=)
Kanban	/	3 (+ + +)	2 (+ + +)
Statistical process control	12 (+ + +)	7 (+ + +)	4 (+ + +)
Autonomous maintenance	2 (+ + +)	/	/
Small group problem solving	1 (− − −)	5 (− − −)	3 (− − −)
Training employees	2 (− − −)	5 (+)	/
Top management leadership	1 (− − −)	3 (− − −)	1 (− − −)
Supplier partnership	/	/	/
Customer involvement	1 (− − −)	5 (− − −)	3 (− − −)
Continuous improvement	/	3 (+)	/

With regard to autism, cognitive HFs are the most affected by LM Practices (44 total interactions) corresponding, though, to an unremarkable overall benefit. Physical HFs are, in fact, the ones receiving most of the benefits from a LM implementation program. Speaking of "LM Practices", instead, "Statistical Process Control" tools overall show the highest influence, both in terms of number of relations found and efficacy; meanwhile "Supplier partnership", "Set-up time reduction" and "Customer involvement" show the lowest efficacy, whether in terms of relations found or negative impact.

In terms of ADHD, cognitive HFs still present the highest number of interactions (44) but, this time, organizational HFs are, overall, the mostly positive influenced by such tools. Referring to Lean practices, "Statistical Process Control" tools still affect neurodiverse workers to the greater extent (22), even though the realms of the most

---

[1] Legend: (+ + +) and (− − −) for "strong positive or negative feedback"; (+ +) and (− −) for "mild positive or negative feedback"; (+) and (−) for "slight positive or negative feedback"; (=) for "neutral feedback"; / for "no interaction".

Table 4. Impact of LM tools on human factors (HF) – ADHD (See footnote 1)

LM practices	Physical HF	Cognitive HF	Organisational HF
Set-up time reduction	2 (– – –)	/	/
Just-in-time delivery by suppliers	2 (– – –)	5 (+)	2 (=)
Equipment layout for continuous flow	8 (=)	8 (– –)	1 (+ + +)
Kanban	/	3 (+ + +)	2 (=)
Statistical process control	12 (+ +)	7 (+ + +)	3 (+ + +)
Autonomous maintenance	2 (– – –)	/	/
Small group problem solving	1 (+ + +)	5 (+ + +)	3 (+ + +)
Training employees	2 (+ + +)	5 (+)	/
Top management leadership	1 (+ + +)	3 (+ + +)	1 (+ + +)
Supplier partnership	/	/	/
Customer involvement	1 (+ + +)	5 (+ + +)	3 (+ + +)
Continuous improvement	/	3 (–)	/

beneficial LM tools belong to "Small group problem solving" and "Customer involvement" categories. "Supplier partnership" practices do not affect HFs of people affected by ADHD, while "Set-up time reduction" and "Autonomous maintenance" ones bring the most disadvantages to these people.

Table 5. Impact of LM tools on human factors (HF) – Dyslexia (See footnote 1)

LM practices	Physical HF	Cognitive HF	Organisational HF
Set-up time reduction	2 (– – –)	/	/
Just-in-time delivery by suppliers	2 (– – –)	5 (+)	2 (=)
Equipment layout for continuous flow	/	2 (+ + +)	1 (+ + +)
Kanban	/	3 (+ + +)	2 (=)
Statistical process control	5 (+ + +)	6 (+ + +)	4 (+ + +)
Autonomous maintenance	/	/	/
Small group problem solving	1 (– – –)	5 (– – –)	3 (+ + +)
Training employees	/	3 (+ + +)	/
Top management leadership	1 (– – –)	3 (– – –)	1 (+ + +)
Supplier partnership	/	/	/
Customer involvement	1 (– – –)	5 (– – –)	3 (+ + +)
Continuous improvement	/	3 (+ + +)	/

Similarly to what has been said for ADHD, even for dyslexia, cognitive HFs have the highest number of interactions (35), just like organizational HFs are, overall, the mostly positive influenced by such tools. "Autonomous maintenance" practices, especially in the form of Total Productive Maintenance (TPM), do not affect dyslexic people in any way, meanwhile "Set-up time reduction" techniques are the worst impacting. On the other hand, "Statistical process control" are the most influential (15) as well as the most beneficial tools.

5 Conclusion

The relationship charts provided throughout the paper provide insights on how Lean Manufacturing practices may play a role in supporting neurodiverse individuals on the workplace, a topic that has not been covered yet in current literature. It is evident, from the results of the research, that not all Lean tools have a beneficial effect among the entire range of human factors detected but are rather effective in dependence to the specific neurodiversity. Autism, ADHD and dyslexia have, in fact, different clinical manifestation on people suffering from these conditions and, consequently, they require a different treatment on the workplace.

Still, although the relationship charts may provide a useful insight on how a more accommodating working environment can be created for neurodiverse people, it is important to consider that results have only been validated by a Lean expert, with a deep theoretical and practical knowledge, but limited to this only topic. A need for a further validation, provided this time by an expert in the field of neurodiversity, is therefore required, as well as a final assessment on the workplace to definitively consolidate the relations found.

References

1. Doyle, N.: Neurodiversity at work: a biopsychosocial model and the impact on working adults. Br. Med. Bull. **135**(1), 108 (2020)
2. Krzeminska, A., Austin, R.D., Bruyère, S.M., Hedley, D.: The advantages and challenges of neurodiversity employment in organizations. J. Manage. Organ. **25**(4), 453–463 (2019)
3. Mascarenhas, R.F., Pimentel, C., Rosa, M.J.: The way Lean starts–a different approach to introduce Lean culture and changing process with people's involvement. Procedia Manuf. **38**, 948–956 (2019)
4. Brinzea, V.M.: Encouraging neurodiversity in the evolving workforce: the next frontier to a diverse workplace. Sci. Bull.-Econ. Sci. **18**(3), 13–25 (2019)
5. Singer, J.: Odd people in: the birth of community amongst people on the autistic spectrum: a personal exploration of a new social movement based on neurological diversity. Honours Dissertation, University of Technology, Sydney (1998). www.neurodiversity.com.au/lightd ark.htm
6. White, H.A., Shah, P.: Uninhibited imaginations: creativity in adults with attention-deficit/hyperactivity disorder. Pers. Individ. Differ. **40**(6), 1121–1131 (2006)
7. Grant, D.: The psychological assessment of neurodiversity. In: Pollak, D. (ed.). Neurodiversity in Higher Education, pp. 33–62. Wiley-Blackwell, Chichester (2009)
8. Volkmar, F.R., Lord, C., Bailey, A., Schultz, R.T., Klin, A.: Autism and pervasive developmental disorders. J. Child Psychol. Psychiatry **45**(1), 135–170 (2004)
9. Meilleur, A.A.S., Jelenic, P., Mottron, L.: Prevalence of clinically and empirically defined talents and strengths in autism. J. Autism Dev. Disord. **45**(5), 1354–1367 (2015)

10. Armstrong, T.: The Power of Neurodiversity: Unleashing the Advantages of Your Differently Wired Brain (Published in Hardcover as Neurodiversity). Da Capo Lifelong Books (2011)
11. Kirby, P.: A brief history of dyslexia. Psychologist **31**(3), 1–3 (2018)
12. Logan, J.: Dyslexic entrepreneurs: the incidence; their coping strategies and their business skills. Dyslexia **15**(4), 328–346 (2009)
13. Leather, C., Hogh, H., Seiss, E., Everatt, J.: Cognitive functioning and work success in adults with dyslexia. Dyslexia **17**(4), 327–338 (2011)
14. Von Karolyi, C., Winner, E., Gray, W., Sherman, G.F.: Dyslexia linked to talent: global visual-spatial ability. Brain Lang. **85**(3), 427–431 (2003)
15. Fotopoulos, C.B., Psomas, E.L.: The impact of "soft" and "hard" TQM elements on quality management results. Int. J. Qual. Reliabil. Manage. **26**(2), 150–163 (2009)
16. Bortolotti, T., Boscari, S., Danese, P.: Successful Lean implementation: organizational culture and soft Lean practices. Int. J. Prod. Econ. **160**, 182–201 (2015)
17. Rodríguez, D., Buyens, D., Van Landeghem, H., Lasio, V.: Impact of Lean production on perceived job autonomy and job satisfaction: An experimental study. Hum. Factors Ergon. Manuf. Serv. Industr. **26**(2), 159–176 (2016)
18. Gaiardelli, P., Resta, B., Dotti, S.: Exploring the role of human factors in Lean management. Int. J. Lean Six Sigma **10**(1), 339–366 (2019)
19. Liker, J.K.: The Toyota Way: 14 Management Principles from the World's Greatest Manufacturer. McGraw-Hill Education (2004)
20. Stern, H., Becker, T.: Concept and evaluation of a method for the integration of human factors into human-oriented work design in cyber-physical production systems. Sustainability **11**(16), 4508 (2019)
21. Cimini, C., Lagorio, A., Pirola, F., Pinto, R.: How human factors affect operators' task evolution in Logistics 4.0. Hum. Factors Ergon. Manuf. Serv. Industr. **31**(1), 98–117 (2021)

Barriers to Performance Measurement Systems Effectiveness

Flávio Cunha(⊠), José Dinis-Carvalho, and Rui M. Sousa

Department of Production and Systems, Algoritmi Centre, School of Engineering, University of Minho, Campus of Azurém, 4800-058 Guimarães, Portugal
id10046@alunos.uminho.pt, {dinis,rms}@dps.uminho.pt

Abstract. In many organizations, it is common to find performance measurement systems (PMS) whose practical utility turns out to be very limited due to several factors/barriers. The purpose of this paper is to identify and categorize the main barriers to the effectiveness of PMS, and to explore how they can be eliminated or, at least, how their impact can be mitigated. A systematic literature review, using PRISMA methodology, is carried out to identify which factors are most frequently referred to as barriers to the effectiveness of PMS, due to their negative influence in terms of implementation, continued use or maintenance of these systems. Those barriers are grouped and classified into categories according to their similarities. The initial findings point out to 19 types of barriers (e.g. inappropriate indicators, lack of employee involvement and lack of connection to the strategy) divided into six categories. Then, cause-effect relationships between barriers should be explored and investigated, in order to identify interdependencies that can further influence the effectiveness of the PMS. From a perspective of continuous improvement, after identifying the most common barriers, as well as the existing cause-effect relationships, solutions and methodologies should be suggested that could help to mitigate or eliminate the impact on the effectiveness of the organizations' PMS.

Keywords: Performance measurement system · Key performance indicators · Continuous improvement · Operational excellence · Lean production

1 Introduction

The collection and analysis of data on the current state of a production unit allows the starting point for improvement to be described and represented and enables the analyst to identify where the focus should be placed [1]. Performance data is a particular important type of data that is crucial to drive and manage performance improvement, but using and maintaining a PMS (Performance measurement system) in an effective way can be quite a challenge. PMS is defined by Neely et al. [2] as a group of metrics used to quantify the efficacy and efficiency of actions. Bititci [3] defines the creation and implementation of a PMS as the process of defining targets, developing a group of performance metrics, collecting, analyzing, reporting, interpreting and acting on performance data. Although

© IFIP International Federation for Information Processing 2023
Published by Springer Nature Switzerland AG 2023
O. McDermott et al. (Eds.): ELEC 2022, IFIP AICT 668, pp. 23–29, 2023.
https://doi.org/10.1007/978-3-031-25741-4_3

there are several models of PMS, their implementation, use and maintenance continues to fail. McCunn [4] states that 70% of the performance measurement initiatives fail. Therefore, it becomes extremely important to identify why PMS fail and which are the barriers to PMS effectiveness, so those failure modes can be eliminated or mitigated in order to improve the chances of success of a PMS.

2 Methodology

A systematic literature review (SLR) was selected as methodology to help on identifying the main barriers to PMS effectiveness. The SLR was performed accordingly to the steps described by PRISMA (Preferred Reporting Items for Systematic Reviews and Meta-Analyses) methodology [5]. Firstly, a search for scientific articles and book chapters was performed on Scopus and Web of Science databases. The research was performed using "performance measurement" as a keyword, in publications cited in five or more articles and from the areas of study of Engineering, Management, Business, Social Sciences and Computer Sciences. From this, 1787 publications were obtained from Scopus and 1728 from Web of Science.

After removing duplicates 2808 publications remained. A filtering was conducted by analyzing the title and the keywords, and 2550 publications were removed in this step. On the 258 publications obtained, the abstract was analyzed and 176 were removed. The remaining publications were read and analyzed and 31 were included in the analysis of the barriers to PMS effectiveness.

The barriers to PMS effectiveness described in the literature were classified into six categories (system, data, technology, indicators, people and culture) and types of barriers. The results of this classification are described in the findings section.

3 Findings

After classifying the barriers found on the literature according to the proposed categories and types of barriers, the results obtained are presented in Table 1. This table presents all types of barriers organized by categories, as well as the references where the barriers were identified.

Table 1. Summary of categories, subcategories and references

Category	Types of barriers	References
Indicators	Inappropriate indicators	[6–24]
	Lack of balance of indicators	[11, 18, 19, 25]

(continued)

Table 1. (*continued*)

Category	Types of barriers	References
	Too many indicators (complexity)	[8, 19, 21, 22]
System	Communication system	[9, 19, 23, 25]
	Complexity	[4]
	Lack of connection to strategy	[4, 7, 12, 14, 17–20, 22, 26–28]
	Lack of use for improvement	[11, 17, 24, 25, 28–30]
	Problems in defining objectives/goals	[11, 21]
	Unclear system	[4, 9, 12, 16–19, 21, 25, 30–32]
People	Employee involvement	[8–10, 16, 17, 19, 20, 24, 28, 29, 32, 33]
	False expectations	[34]
	Lack of resources or expertise	[4, 7, 10, 13, 30, 35]
	Not understanding the indicators	[9, 16, 19, 20, 22, 25]
Culture	Blame culture	[4, 9, 15, 16, 19, 24–27, 30, 31, 34]
	Lack of rewards/compensations	[14, 19]
	Top management commitment	[4, 7, 10, 13, 16, 17, 19, 25, 28, 32]
Technology	Inadequate IT tools	[9, 23, 31]
	Time and resources required	[4, 7, 8, 13, 17, 20, 26–28, 32, 34, 35]
Data	Difficulty in collecting, analyzing and presenting data	[6, 7, 9, 13, 18, 19, 22, 26–28, 33]

4 Discussion

As simple and visual way of presenting the barriers to PMS effectiveness found, an Ishikawa diagram was used. In Fig. 1 is represented the Ishikawa diagram where in the main spines are the categories and in the smaller spines of each main spine are the types of barriers identified. In front of each category and type of barrier identified is the frequency which each one is referred in the literature.

Of the several types of barriers found in the literature, some are referred more frequently than others. The categories, types of barriers and the frequency with which they are referred are presented in Graph 1.

The fact that the indicators used are not appropriate is the most referred type of barrier in the literature. After this type of barrier the most referred ones are: lack of employee involvement; unclear system; difficulty in collecting, analyzing and presenting data; and, lack of connection to the strategy.

There can be a cause-effect relationship between several of the barriers identified making it more complex. For example, the fact that there is a blame culture in the organization can cause a lack of involvement from the employees, resulting in resistance

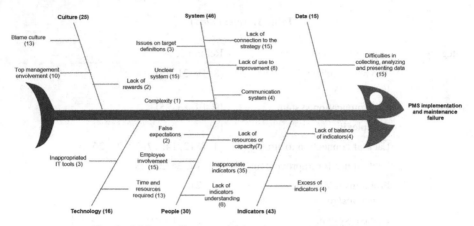

Fig. 1. Ishikawa diagram with barriers to PMS effectiveness

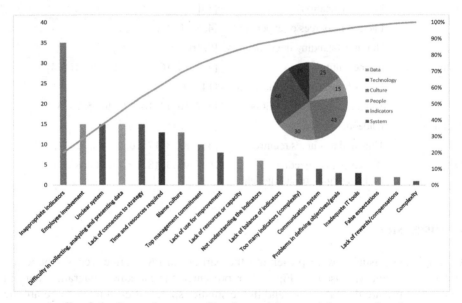

Graph 1. Categories, types of barriers and frequency they are referred

to an effective use of the PMS. The ineffectiveness of a PMS can be caused by a single barrier or by the combination of several.

5   Conclusion

As discussed previously the relation between the barriers identified can be complex. The failure of a PMS can result from one or from the combination of several of the barriers identified. Therefore, in order to maximize the odds of achieving an effective PMS, the cause-effect relationships between barriers should be investigated and methodologies and techniques that eliminate or mitigate the barriers should be developed and used.

As future investigation, all the recommendations that emerge as way to eliminate or mitigate the barriers to PMS effectiveness, could be transformed in to methodologies that can be grouped in a model, a guide allowing to properly implement, use and maintain a PMS.

The barriers identified in this research were obtained through a systematic literature review that composes a secondary data source. The barriers found should be validated through the collection and analysis of data from a primary source.

Acknowledgements. This work has been supported by FCT – Fundação para a Ciência e Tecnologia within the R&D Units Project Scope: UIDB/00319/2020.

References

1. Imai, M.: Gemba Kaizen, 2nd edn. McGraw-Hill (1997)
2. Neely, A., Gregory, M., Platts, K.: Performance measurement system design: a literature review and research agenda. Int. J. Oper. Prod. Manag. **15**(4), 80–116 (1995). https://doi.org/10.1108/01443579510083622
3. Bititci, U.S.: Managing Business Performance: The Science and the Art. Wiley, Hoboken (2015)
4. McCunn, P.: The balanced scorecard...the eleventh commandment. Manag. Account. **76**(11), 34–36 (1998). https://www.proquest.com/trade-journals/balanced-scorecard-eleventh-commandment/docview/195676560/se-2?accountid=39260
5. Moher, D., Liberati, A., Tetzlaff, J., Altman, D.G., Group, T.P.: Preferred reporting items for systematic reviews and meta-analyses: the PRISMA statement. PLoS Med. **6**(7) (2009). https://doi.org/10.1371/journal.pmed.1000097
6. Brown, M.G.: Keeping score: using the right metrics to drive world-class performance. Qual. Resour. (1996)
7. Charan, P., Shankar, R., Baisya, R.K.: Modelling the barriers of supply chain performance measurement system implementation in the Indian automobile supply chain. Int. J. Logist. Syst. Manag. **5**(6), 614–630 (2009). https://doi.org/10.1504/IJLSM.2009.024794
8. Nudurupati, S.S., Bititci, U.S., Kumar, V., Chan, F.T.S.: State of the art literature review on performance measurement. Comput. Ind. Eng. **60**(2), 279–290 (2011). https://doi.org/10.1016/j.cie.2010.11.010
9. Okwir, S., Nudurupati, S.S., Ginieis, M., Angelis, J.: Performance measurement and management systems: a perspective from complexity theory. Int. J. Manag. Rev. **20**(3), 731–754 (2018). https://doi.org/10.1111/ijmr.12184
10. Şerban, R.-A., Herciu, M.: Performance management systems – proposing and testing a conceptual model. Stud. Bus. Econ. **14**(1), 231–244 (2019). https://doi.org/10.2478/sbe-2019-0018
11. Schneiderman, A.M.: Why balanced scorecards fail. J. Strateg. Perform. Meas. **2**(11), 6–11 (1999)
12. Dixon, J.R., Nanni, A.J., Vollmann, T.E.: The new performance challenge (1990)
13. Sousa, S.D., Aspinwall, E.M., Guimarães Rodrigues, A.: Performance measures in English small and medium enterprises: survey results. Benchmarking Int. J. **13**(1/2), 120–134 (2006). https://doi.org/10.1108/14635770610644628

14. Watts, T., McNair-Connolly, C.J.: New performance measurement and management control systems. J. Appl. Account. Res. **13**(3), 226–241 (2012). https://doi.org/10.1108/096754212 11281308
15. Wouters, M., Wilderom, C.: Developing performance-measurement systems as enabling formalization: a longitudinal field study of a logistics department. Account. Organ. Soc. **33**(4–5), 488–516 (2008). https://doi.org/10.1016/j.aos.2007.05.002
16. Zairi, M.: Measuring Performance for Business Results. Springer, Heidelberg (1994)
17. de Waal, A.A., Counet, H.: Lessons learned from performance management systems implementations. Int. J. Product. Perform. Manag. **58**(4), 367–390 (2009). https://doi.org/10.1108/ 17410400910951026
18. Franceschini, F., Galetto, M., Maisano, D.: Management by Measurement: Designing Key Indicators and Performance Measurement Systems. Springer, Heidelberg (2007). https://doi. org/10.1007/978-3-540-73212-9
19. Franco, M., Bourne, M.: Factors that play a role in 'managing through measures. Manag. Decis. **41**(8), 698–710 (2003). https://doi.org/10.1108/00251740310496215
20. Ghalayini, A.M., Noble, J.S.: The changing basis of performance measurement. Int. J. Oper. Prod. Manag. **16**(8), 63–80 (1996). https://doi.org/10.1108/01443579610125787
21. Giovannoni, E., Maraghini, M.P.: The challenges of integrated performance measurement systems: integrating mechanisms for integrated measures. Account. Audit. Account. J. **26**(6), 978–1008 (2013). https://doi.org/10.1108/AAAJ-04-2013-1312
22. Hatten, K.J., Rosenthal, S.R.: Why-and how-to systematize performance measurement. J. Organ. Excell. **20**(4), 59–73 (2001). https://doi.org/10.1002/npr.1108
23. Lohman, C., Fortuin, L., Wouters, M.: Designing a performance measurement system: a case study. Eur. J. Oper. Res. **156**(2), 267–286 (2004). https://doi.org/10.1016/S0377-2217(02)009 18-9
24. Neely, A., Bourne, M.: Why measurement initiatives fail. Meas. Bus. Excell. **4**, 3–7 (2000). https://doi.org/10.1108/13683040010362283
25. Meekings, A.: Unlocking the potential of performance measurement: a practical implementation guide. Public Money Manag. **15**(4), 5–12 (1995). https://doi.org/10.1080/095409695 09387888
26. Bourne, M.: Researching performance measurement system implementation: the dynamics of success and failure. Prod. Plan. Control **16**(2), 101–113 (2005). https://doi.org/10.1080/ 09537280512331333011
27. Bourne, M., Neely, A., Platts, K., Mills, J.: The success and failure of performance measurement initiatives: perceptions of participating managers. Int. J. Oper. Prod. Manag. (2002). https://doi.org/10.1108/01443570210450329
28. Bourne, M.: Handbook of Performance Measurement. GEE Publishing (2004)
29. Bourne, M., Neely, A., Mills, J., Platts, K.: Why some performance measurement initiatives fail: lessons from the change management literature. Int. J. Bus. Perform. Manag. **5**(2–3), 245–269 (2003). https://doi.org/10.1504/ijbpm.2003.003250
30. Kennerley, M., Neely, A.: A framework of the factors affecting the evolution of performance measurement systems. Int. J. Oper. Prod. Manag. **22**(11), 1222–1245 (2002). https://doi.org/ 10.1108/01443570210450293
31. Bititci, U., Garengo, P., Dörfler, V., Nudurupati, S.: Performance measurement: challenges for tomorrow. Int. J. Manag. Rev. **14**(3), 305–327 (2012). https://doi.org/10.1111/j.1468-2370. 2011.00318.x
32. Townley, B., Cooper, D.J., Oakes, L.: Performance measures and the rationalization of organizations. Organ. Stud. **24**(7), 1045–1071 (2003). https://doi.org/10.1177/017084060302 47003
33. Simons, R.: Control in an Age of Empowerment. Harvard Business Review Press (1995)

34. Gabris, G.T.: Recognizing management technique dysfunctions : how management tools often create more problems than they solve. Public Product. Rev. **10**(2), 3–19 (1986). https://doi.org/10.2307/3380448
35. da Costa, M.L.R., de Souza Giani, E.G., Galdamez, E.V.C.: Vision of the balanced scorecard in micro, small and medium enterprises. Sist. Gestão **14**(1), 131–141 (2019). https://doi.org/10.20985/1980-5160.2019.v14n1.1505

An Analysis of Agile Coaching Competency Among Practitioners

Leigh Griffin[1,2]([✉]) and Arjay Hinek[1]

[1] Red Hat, Raleigh, USA
{lgriffin,ahinek}@redhat.com
[2] South East Technological University, Waterford, Ireland

Abstract. A key approach used by improvement specialists is that of Coaching. Coaching is described as a power tool for organisations looking to transition towards, and sustain, a new way of working. That new way of working, is often described as an Agile or Lean mode of work, with Agile being the progenitor of Lean. Agile is not alone in promoting the role of the coach, with Lean having similar roles identified as a cornerstone of mindset immersion. However, there is no accepted industry definition of what a process improvement Coach is, with a leading reference mode adopted informally. This outlines a core Competency Framework to capture the holistic skills required to become a competent Coach and is not specific about levels of mastery to attain the various competencies outlined. The model, being imprecise, is not backed by academic literature and aligns with noted observations about competency modelling being typically derived by less methodologically rigorous consultants who were not researchers. Despite this, the role of the Agile Coach has become an accepted and formative piece of a teams strategy and can derive success when deployed appropriately. In this paper, we will explore the deficiencies in the established competency model and propose a theoretically grounded competency model for Agile Coaches to act as a reference for Agile Coaches.

Keywords: Agile · Coaching · Competencies · Lean

1 Introduction

According to [1], the predominant approach to a methdology to build software is known collectively as Agile, a progenitor of Lean, and hence, from the perspective of this paper, is used interchagenably as a concept for the paradigm of process improvement. The implementation of any process improvement within Agile or Lean, hinges on a number of key inputs as noted in [2]. The culture, environment, knowledge of the team and the attitude of management are key inputs to the success of any transformation. They are also the key inputs to fostering the Continuous Improvement (CI) mindset, a cornerstone of both Lean and Scrum, with the latter having lost that perspective of wanting to improve beyond the visible gap generated as the motivation was not there, largely from a risk perspective and from a sense of status quo retention. A challenge

© IFIP International Federation for Information Processing 2023
Published by Springer Nature Switzerland AG 2023
O. McDermott et al. (Eds.): ELEC 2022, IFIP AICT 668, pp. 30–37, 2023.
https://doi.org/10.1007/978-3-031-25741-4_4

therefore exists to ignite the CI mindset and progress the team towards a new way of working. That new way of working needs to be a reversal towards embracing the philosophy behind improvement. Mechanically, adoption is a simple case of following rules, tools and guidance. Mentally, where all process improvement specialists want their teams to get to, a different approach is required. A key tool used by improvement specialists is that of Coaching as a power tool for organisations looking to transition towards a better way of working. Agile Coaching Institute [3] has formed a Competency Framework, which tries to capture the holistic skills required to become a competent Agile or Lean Coach which will be explored in this paper.

2   The Growing Role of Agile Coaching

A key approach used by improvement specialists is that of Coaching. Agile Coaching is described within [4] as a power tool for organisations looking to transition towards, and sustain, an Agile way of working. The paper by [4] goes on to capture the growth of it and indeed reinforces the key role it plays in success. Agile is not alone in promoting the role of the coach, with Lean having similar roles identified as a cornerstone such as the work of [5]. Coaching is predominantly forward facing and helps individuals and teams to break down barriers and progress towards a goal. Indeed when deployed within companies that use concepts such as Key Performance Indicators to metricize and reinforce goals and progression, coaching can become a force multiplier. As discussed in [6], if the individual goals are tied closely to goals of the entire organisation, it can be layered into the success of the individual on their own journey of understanding. Coaching can help companies hit those goals and is a cornerstone of transformational leadership [7] and an engagement accelerator [8]. Yet, the authors of [2], supported by insights from [9], explore the reasons why long lasting change is difficult to attain for Lean companies. That change, which is defined by implementations that have a lasting impact, has a 10% success rate, with this statistic further backed by similar findings by several academics, most notably [10] and [11]. Agile transformations have no such long term, sustained improvement benchmarks due to the immaturity of the approach when compared to Lean. Yet Agile, has embraced the Coaching approach and despite the ingredients of successful sustained transformation in play, it did encounter a paradigm shift that it was ill prepared for. The Covid-19 pandemic has seen extensive research by [12–15] and [16] who all had a common denominator of the process improvement gap no longer being sustainable and regressing in many cases due to a shift in working practices forced by the pandemic. This insight is provoking an analysis on the role of the Coach in both Agile and Lean transformations to allow for sustainable transformation and in particular what competencies do they need to bring in order to enact such change. The Agile Coaching Institute has outlined a core Competency Framework [3] which is visible in Fig. 1 which tries to capture the holistic skills required to become a competent Agile Coach. This is the main reference competency framework for Agile Coaches and the basis of the seminal work by [17], with minimal research in the academic literature dedicated to such a topic. It is accepted by practitioners and has spawned alternative models such as the one published by the Lean Agile Institute [18] which is attempting to tailor the model towards Enterprise coaching. Given the prevalence of the model, this review will focus on pertinent literature of key competencies encompassed by the framework. Specifically, Facilitation, Teaching and Coaching will be explored as the most applicable and transferable skills, with a complimentary discussion on the core knowledge of Lean and Agile as well as the role of Mentoring rounding out the literature review.

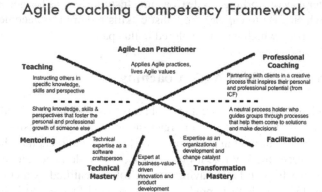

Fig. 1. Agile coaching competency framework courtesy of agile coaching framework [3]

3   The Current Challenge

It is clear that the breadth of competencies and the ability to master even elements of the competency matrix require a dedicated amount of commitment. With coaching emerging as a growing field of interest for teams looking to begin transformational journeys in how they work [19], the danger is that the role is being treated as a panacea. The body of academic research behind this area is currently light, as it is predominantly a practitioner driven role, with the leading framework by [3] derived from practitioners rather than academics. It is one which has gained widespread adoption and spawned multiple variants such as [18] to adapt to new and emerging domains.Companies, and motivated career facing individuals, want to obtain what [20] derived as career best workers and that is underpinned by what [21] deemed quality centric validation, one which certifications, to identify the capstone achievement of mastering a particular skill, brings. Career best workers help move a company towards what [22] describes as stated enterprise objectives. Those objectives are tied to maturing the company towards a new position, which [2] noted has multiple stages of maturity, with the competitive advantage and the adoption of systemic change within the company occuring over a longer period of time. [23] complements this by exploring that the knowledge, culture and buy in of everyone can help achieve those higher levels of maturity and key tools and approaches are needed to complement it. Change agents, which coaches are, can be an internal factor, something that [19] looks at as a cyclic form of change that can help magnify other changes and ultimately create the critical mass. With such a complex depth to consider, both for the role of the coach, and the state of the organisation, the hidden competencies, which [24] deemed to be difficult to acquire, are crucial to identify. They hold the key to sustained success in the role the person plays in an organisation and indeed where the organisation is looking to move towards. This is the challenge that prompted a round of interviews with practicing Agile Coaches to assess their view on the competencies they possess.

3.1 A Survey of Self Identifying Agile Coaches

For the survey, an anonymous survey approach was pursued to both maximise privacy conditions for the respondents and to avoid any stigmatising of information dissemination that respondents might feel when answering questions, which is an approach noted in [25]. The anonymous nature also aligns with the General Data Protection Regulation [26], ensuring no personally identifiable information is disclosed or retained. With ethical considerations at the forefront of the design and execution of the survey the 5 key principles that [27] described are therefore satisfied, ensuring that this part of the study avoids any ethical quandaries. A survey was designed which aimed to explore how Agilists, the generic term for people working in Agile centric roles, view themselves as coaches as well as their own qualifications. Key industry certifications such as ScrumMaster, Certified Team Coach (CTC), Certified Enterprise Coach (CEC) and ICF accreditation were captured. Initial questions were asked in order to gain insight into how practitioners are approaching the career of a Coach and to understand the continuous improvement mindset which the literature indicates should be present in practitioners in a Lean and Agile environment. The questions additionally are attempting to gain insight into how coaching happens in industry, as in many cases, coaching, as a discipline, can occur in many settings. The latter part of the survey asked the subjects of the survey how they and their team(s) or client(s) viewed their own abilities against the coaching competencies as defined in [3].

3.2 Initial Findings

An initial examination looking at the qualifications each respondent had, with respect to where they ranked themselves on their Coaching Ability and where they were on their Journey can be seen in Table 1.

Of note here is the similarity in Coaching ability recorded by participants who identify as a coach, with no qualifications, and with respondents who have an formal title of a coach. Not surprisingly, the ICF and CTC/CEC results have the highest ability for Coaching and Journey recorded. 47% of respondents had formal certifications and 53% of respondents have no qualifications to validate their skills from a quality perspective and overall, of that group, with no qualifications, 62% have no intention of attaining coaching accreditation within the next 12 months. A Correlation anlaysis was performed to examine how Coaching ability related to the various masteries captured in the Coaching Competency framework. A reasonable correlation exists between Coaching rating and both Transformational Mastery (0.46) and Business Mastery (0.42). Business and

Table 1. Coaching Ability and Journey ranking from survey respondents where n = 143

Intersection	n = 143	Coaching	Journey
Identify as an Agile Coach, have no qualifications and no plans	22%	7.90	7.20
Formal Title includes Agile Coach	29%	7.90	7.54
No Formal Coaching Qualifications	53%	7.14	5.97
ScrumMaster Qualification only	11%	6.00	6.00
ICF Qualification or CTC/CEC Qualification	7.7%	8.80	8.18
ACC Qualification only	26%	7.50	6.80
ACC and ICF Qualifications	3.5%	9.20	8.00
Future Plans for ICF Accreditation	7.7%	7.277.5	7.27
Future Plans for CTC Accreditation	17.5%	7.56	7.04

Transformational Mastery also have a reasonable correlation at 0.567. A regression analysis was carried out with Coaching Ability declared a dependent variable and the remainder of the Agile Coaching Framework designated the predictor variables. The model is indicating that 66.8% of the variability on Coaching ability can be attributed to the predictor variables that make up the remainder of the framework. A significant percentage of influence on coaching ability is thus undocumented and an open question of what else could be impacting coaching ability and knowledge? Additionally, this model shows us that for every increase in ability in the key competency areas of Facilitation (.198), Mentoring (.379) and Teaching (.183), the corresponding increase, denoted in brackets, on Coaching ability occurs. This is showing a potential conflation of ability by improving related skills.

4   Towards a New Model

Having considered the insights and after careful analysis of the relevant pertinent literature, an initial model was created which can be seen in Fig. 2.

The model outlines five key competencies. Influencer was selected to help create a disambiguation between the role of a Facilitator and that of an Influencer. With the conflation of Facilitation and Coaching, the change to influencing speaks more to the language of leadership of which [28] describes as being a key learning style for coaches to adopt. Continuous Learning is a cornerstone of the principles behind the learning organisation and represents the awareness that the pursuit of new knowledge and approaches is rarely ever completed. [29] discussed the need for a flexible minsdset to change, a mindset that is necessary for the integration of new ideas into the wider system. With coaches being a driver of organisational change, [30] examined the need for empowered self development centered around continuous learning, with the ability to self recognise behaviors and thus coach more favorable outcomes in their engagements. Advocate was chosen to represent the need for the coach to project out the mindset of both Agile and Lean centric concepts. The final competencies were retained from the original analysed

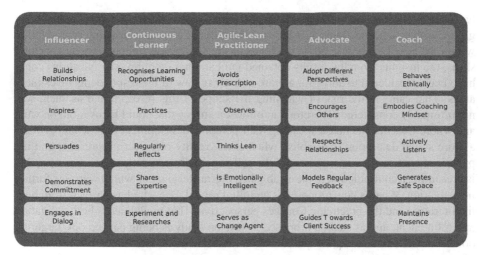

Fig. 2. Initial proposed competency model

model due to the need to quantify that the blend of coaching is Agile-Lean centric, and hence being a practitioner of such is mandatory. Coaching, being at the heart of the model, is included with the subtle word changing to Coach, to project the role of the Coach rather than the act of Coaching. For each of the competencies, a set of complementary behaviors are presented to help people evaluating the model to identify attitudes, personality traits and actions that help to predict the competency levels maturation that they may have attained. As [31] notes the term behavioral competencies are used to help make individuals successful in their roles by establishing demonstrable examples. Where competencies describe the broad expectations of the role, behaviors identify the act of doing.

5 Conclusion and Future Work

Irrespective of titles, a significant percentage of Agilists identify as a coach within their teams. Having a coaching qualification is not a barrier to this self identification and despite the continuous improvement mindset being a hallmark of Agility and indeed Coaching as a profession, there are a significant number of Coaches unwilling to continue their journey of learning. This is in contradiction to the established literature, for example, the works of [23] and [2] talk extensively towards continuous improvement as a mindset and the need to bring new ideas, tools and learnings to bear on problems as companies mature through their adoption of Lean. Indeed, [32] notes that a key role is becoming teachers, with the unstated assumption being that the competency is there to teach the subject matter at hand. That gap and the interpretation of the results can some-what be attributed to the certification levels of the respondents of the survey. 47% of respondents had formal certifications and as [21] described, certifications provide quality assurance, particularly in the field of computing and become a validator for base skills. While that can explain a viewpoint that the certification is a capstone of sorts, 53% of respondents have no qualifications to validate their skills from a quality perspective and overall, of that group, with no qualifications, 62% have no intention of attaining coaching accreditation within the next 12 months. While the focus of the survey was deliberately on coaching skills, the insights from the results obtained indicate that more broader questions could have been considered to allow for a more holistic review of the respondents investment areas. That came at the risk of widening the scope of this research and as such, was not ultimately considered. Therefore, a follow on survey that could focus more on what and where Coaches intend on spending their personal development time would provide a more sound data point to establish whether the reality of career progression and the pursuit of continuous improvement of the self is actually occuring or not. For now, this is presenting a contradiction to the established literature, and one which warrants further investigation. What is now proposed is an initial model, one which is derived from both the literature and the practicing Coaches perspective. That model needs both validation and refinement, and as such, a proposed follow on study is being carried out, targeting domain experts with adaquate qualifications to iterate on a more informed model.

References

1. Dingsøyr, T., Nerur, S., Balijepally, V., Moe, N.B.: Journal of Systems and Software **85**(6), 1213 (2012). Special Issue: Agile Development
2. Hines, P., Taylor, D., Walsh, A.: Total Qual. Manag. Bus. Excell. **31**(3–4), 389 (2020)
3. ACI (2021). https://agilecoachinginstitute.com/agile-coaching-resources/
4. Stray, V., Memon, B., Paruch, L.: (2020)
5. Gørtz, K.: Coaching, lean processes, and the concept of flow, pp. 299–315 (2015)
6. Parmenter, D.: Key Performance Indicators (KPI): Developing, Implementing, and Using Winning KPI's. Wiley, Hoboken (2019)
7. Arthur, C., Lynn, A.: Transformational leadership and the role of the coach, pp. 187–202 (2016)
8. Lai, F.Y., Tang, H.C., Lu, S.C., Lee, Y.C., Lin, C.C.: SAGE Open **10**(1), 2158244019899085 (2020)
9. Stone, K.: Int. J. Lean Six Sigma **3**(2), 112 (2012)
10. Bateman, N.: Sustainability ... a guide to ... process improvement (2001)
11. Amrik, S., Adrian, E.: Int. J. Oper. Prod. Manag. **14**(11), 35 (1994)
12. Griffin, L.: Implementing lean principles in scrum to adapt to remote work in a Covid-19 impacted software team, pp. 177–184 (2021)
13. Cucolas, A.A., Russo, D.: ArXiv (2021)
14. Neumann, M., Bogdanov, Y., Lier, M., Baumann, L.: The Sars-Cov-2 Pandemic and agile methodologies in software development: a multiple case study in Germany. In: Przybyłek, A., Miler, J., Poth, A., Riel, A. (eds.) LASD 2021. LNBIP, vol. 408, pp. 40–58. Springer, Cham (2021). https://doi.org/10.1007/978-3-030-67084-9_3
15. Marek, K., Wińska, E., Dąbrowski, W.: The state of agile software development teams during the Covid-19 pandemic. In: Przybyłek, A., Miler, J., Poth, A., Riel, A. (eds.) LASD 2021. LNBIP, vol. 408, pp. 24–39. Springer, Cham (2021). https://doi.org/10.1007/978-3-030-670 84-9_2
16. Butt, S.A., Misra, S., Anjum, M.W., Hassan, S.A.: Agile project development issues during COVID-19. In: Przybyłek, A., Miler, J., Poth, A., Riel, A. (eds.) LASD 2021. LNBIP, vol. 408, pp. 59–70. Springer, Cham (2021). https://doi.org/10.1007/978-3-030-67084-9_4

17. Adkins, L.: Coaching Agile Teams: A Companion for ScrumMasters, Agile Coaches, and Project Managers in Transition. Addison-Wesley (2010)
18. LAI (2020). https://www.leanagileinstitute.org/post/enterprise-agile-coaching-competency-framework
19. Jalagat, R.: Int. J. Sci. Res. (IJSR) **5**, 1233 (2016)
20. Baartman, L., Bruijn, E.: Educ. Res. Rev. **6**, 125 (2011)
21. Abazi, B., Hajrizi, E.: IFAC-PapersOnLine **51**(30), 336 (2018). 18th IFAC Conference on Technology, Culture and International Stability TECIS 2018
22. Tekez, E.K., Ta̦sdeviren, G.: Proc. Comput. Sci. **100**, 776 (2016)
23. Bhasin, S., Burcher, P.: J. Manuf. Technol. Manag. **17**(1), 56 (2006)
24. Kwok, J., Wong, M., Ng, P.: Public Adm. Policy **17**, 74 (2014)
25. Murdoch, M., et al.: BMC Med. Res. Methodol. **14**(25027174), 90 (2014)
26. GDPR (2018). https://gdpr-info.eu
27. Smith, D.: (2003). https://www.apa.org/monitor/jan03/principles
28. Berg, M., Karlsen, J.: Int. J. Knowl. Learn. **13**, 356 (2020)
29. Palaima, T., Skarzauskiene, A.: Balt. J. Manag. **5**(3), 330 (2010)
30. London, M., Smither, J.W.: Hum. Resour. Manage. **38**(1), 3 (1999)
31. Albino, G.: SAGE Open **8**(2), 2158244018780972 (2018)
32. Senge, P.: The Fifth Discipline. Doubleday/Currency (1990)

Lean in Healthcare

Implementation Experiences of Lean Organization in Healthcare for Apulian Hospitals: A Longitudinal Interview In-Depth Study

Angelo Rosa[1], Giuliano Marolla[1], and Olivia McDermott[2]($\boxtimes$)

[1] Department of Management, Finance and Technology, LUM University, Casamassima, Italy
[2] College of Science and Engineering, University of Galway, Galway, Ireland
Olivia.McDermott@universityofgalway.ie

Abstract. The purpose of this study is to explore how representatives of the pilot projects teams and dissemination practitioners, belonging to several hospitals in Apulian hospitals in Italy experienced the implementation of Lean over 3 years. An exploratory and qualitative design was drawn based on data triangulation from semi-structured interviews, documentation analysis relating to Lean implementation and direct observation. The main implementation drivers of the methodology in hospitals were increasing patient value and improving workplace well-being. The panel highlighted three pivotal implementation stages: introduction, spontaneous and informal dissemination, and strategic-level implementation. Critical success and failure factors emerged for each of these stages. During the introduction, expert training and coaching from an external consultant are among the most impactful factors in the success of pilot projects, while time constraints and the adoption of process analysis tools are the main barriers to implementation. However, the absence of managerial expertise to support implementation and organisational constraints, such as departmental organisational structure, do not allow for systemic adoption of the methodology.

Keywords: Lean healthcare · Organisational models · Critical success and failure factors · Longitudinal analysis · Lean adoption phases

1 Introduction

The continuing and steady rise in healthcare costs, the increasing demand for care and assistance, and the high variability in operational performance have prompted national and local healthcare organisations to explore new ways to increase the level of service quality for patients and, more generally, to enhance value for healthcare stakeholders [1, 2]. Lean management is recognised as one of the most effective managerial paradigms for improving operational performance and reducing waste [2, 3]. Nowadays, many testimonials and articles discuss the benefits of implementing Lean projects in primary and support healthcare processes [1, 4–6]. However, the literature shows that due to a lack

O. McDermott et al. (Eds.): ELEC 2022, IFIP AICT 668, pp. 41–53, 2023.
https://doi.org/10.1007/978-3-031-25741-4_5

of skill in managing internal and external contextual factors and critical failure factors, many organisations experience failures or under-optimised performance when implementing Lean at the systemic level [7–9]. Developing the skills needed to implement the paradigm at the systems level requires great organisational and managerial efforts from healthcare organisations [8, 9]. In this scenario, an important role can be played by healthcare agencies, which through programmes for the introduction and dissemination of Lean, can encourage and assist the adoption of the paradigm by healthcare organisations [10, 11]. Thus, how Lean diffusion programs promoted by healthcare agencies facilitate the adoption of the paradigm is still an issue to be explored. In presenting the experiences of several Apulian hospitals staff that were involved in the Lean introduction and dissemination program- 'Lean Lab'- promoted by the Apulia Regional Strategic Agency for Health and Social Care (AReSS), this article aims to explore issues related to the Lean implementation in multiple healthcare organisations. The study aims to answer the following questions:

Rq.1 What factors drove the regional initiative's success or failure?
Rq.2 How have Lean Lab participants experienced the Lean introduction and dissemination in their organisations?
Rq.3 How have hospitals managed Lean implementation over time?

A qualitative research methodology was used to assess the effectiveness of the Lean strategic introduction and dissemination programme. It consists of data analysis from semi-structured interviews, AReSS reports describing the design and implementation of the 'Lean Lab', internal hospital reports on Lean adoption and direct observation. The article comprises four sections, discussed in the following order: literature review, research methodology, results, discussion, and conclusion.

2   Literature Review

Lean is a management paradigm that integrates approaches and methods focused on employee empowerment and continuous process improvement [12]. The paradigm was born and developed in the manufacturing sector and was later adopted by other sectors in the late 1990s [13]. Over the past two decades, the healthcare sector's adoption rate has grown at a very high rate [1, 14]. The great interest of healthcare organisations in this paradigm is due to the numerous testimonies of the benefits achieved in patient pathways support processes and related to the organisation's work environment [6, 14, 15]. As widely demonstrated in the literature, implementing Lean in primary healthcare processes improves risk and safety performance, promotes multidisciplinary learning, enhances vertical and horizontal communication and facilitates the creation and adoption of standard work. Improvements related to supporting processes include increasing resource availability (e.g., operating rooms, diagnostic laboratories, maintenance activities), reducing waste in transportation and travel (e.g., drug logistics, space arrangement, layout), organisational flexibility and reducing excess processes (e.g., referral activities, discharge administrative activities), and cost performance [5, 6]. Although the methodology seems to be increasingly popular in the health sector, a closer investigation of how it is implemented reveals that, in most cases, it is merely applied at the level of stand-alone clinical or support processes [1–6]. This form of implementation, also called micro-level implementation, is typical of organisations that are introducing the paradigm or have a low level of maturity in their deployment [7, 16, 17]. Organisations aiming to exploit the full value o f Lean are required to disseminate and adopt its concepts at every organisational level and apply them systemically [17, 18]. Key characteristics of systemic or meso-level implementation include the continuous improvement culture deeply rooted in the organisation, consensus-based decision-making systems, the use of improvement-oriented project management systems, high staff maturity in the use of Lean tools, regular evaluation of improvement programmes, formalised Lean management systems and alignment between strategic and operational Lean objectives [1, 19]. Prior to the Lean introduction, critical failure factors refer to organisational barriers during the Lean dissemination phase [21, 22]. Among the hindering factors related to the internal context and most critical to consider is the inability to manage benchmark activities [21, 23]; the silo logic affecting both organisational functions and clinical specialities [7, 23]; the lack of confidence toward methodology [7–9]; the absence or ineffectiveness of communication systems [7, 9]; the inability to manage multidisciplinary teams [7, 21]; and, most importantly, the total lack of project management skills [6–8].

Furthermore, the successful implementation of Lean is largely determined by the organisation's ability to understand stakeholder value and optimise processes in relation to it; in this perspective, knowledge and interpretation of the external context is a key determinants in defining effective implementation strategies [9, 12]. With regard to critical failure factors, the most discussed and common ones include lack of investment in training and education; lack of time resources; lack of managerial and staff commitment; poor leadership; ineffective communication system; poor alignment between strategic objectives, main goals and goals of Lean projects [2, 7]. Other failure factors discussed in the literature refer to a lack of project management skills, structural constraints, unclear Lean implementation roadmap, inadequate data collection system, lack of performance measurement systems and lack of dissemination agents [2, 7]. Overcoming these barriers requires significant organisational efforts [2, 8, 18]. Some authors discussed the role that local, regional or national health agencies could play in supporting health organisations to overcome barriers and constraints to successful paradigm implementation [11, 24]. The main success factors of multi-organisational Lean deployment initiatives undertaken by agencies include stakeholder involvement in programme development; long-term strategic planning; effective communication with stakeholders to raise awareness of continuous improvement in healthcare; the ability to motivate organisations to embark on the implementation journey; defining a clear vision of objectives; developing a training and implementation support programme; and testing and improving the programme over time.

3 Research Methodology

3.1 Case Description

In order to better contextualise the research methodology and the results obtained, this section discusses the role of the AReSS agency, the objective of the 'Lean Lab' programme and its implementation framework.

The Apulia Strategic Regional Agency for Health and Social Care (ARess) was established by Regional Law No. 29 on July 24, 2017. It is a technical-operational agency established to support the definition and management of social and health policies of the Apulia Region. The agency identified Lean as a useful methodology for responding to this goal while simultaneously reducing waste and improving working well-being in Apulian healthcare organisations. Therefore, AReSS proposed to the ten Apulian local healthcare authorities (USLs) to collaborate in order to co-design a strategic plan for the development and implementation of the Lean paradigm at the regional level. The USL is the set of facilities, offices and services organised in a given geographical area through which municipalities provide health care to citizens in accordance with the principles and objectives of the National Health Service. Within its area of responsibility, the USL is called upon to perform the various tasks of prevention, diagnosis, treatment, rehabilitation and forensic medicine as a whole. During 2018, the program was developed through collaboration between the AReSS and a scientific committee composed of senior managers from the Apulian USLs and representatives of physicians and nurses from those organisations. The programme framework is based on the model of "The Productive Ward" implemented by the NHS and is developed considering the contextual factors of Apulian healthcare policies. At the end of 2018, the programme was defined in detail and was named 'Lean Lab' (Fig. 1).

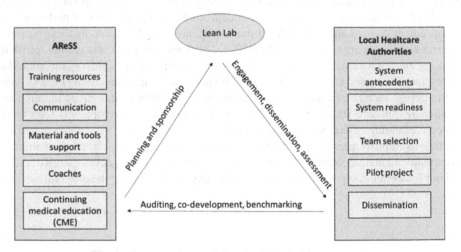

Fig. 1. Framework describing the 'Lean Lab' programme

3.2   Study Setting and Design

Based on the research by Dannapfel et al. [11], this article aims to investigate the impact of 'Lean Lab' - the AReSS strategic Lean dissemination programme - on adopting Lean in Apulian healthcare organisations. In contrast to the research by Dannapfel et al. [11], the research focuses on the lived experience of the pilot project participants - subsequently referred to as dissemination practitioners - of the organisations involved. The research covers three 'Lean Lab' operative phases over almost four years. The first phase concerns Lean introduction in the first year, while the second and third phases are related to Lean dissemination phases in Apulian healthcare organisations over the second and third years. As the 'Lean Lab' is a 5-year strategic programme, the study's results cannot cover the entire period of the programme. In order to ensure the validity of the qualitative study, multiple data sources and data collection methods are used. Through the use of triangulation methodology [25], data are analysed by the researchers. The authors conducted the interviews and recorded the responses. Interviews were administered to each of the 52 participants in the first operational phase of the programme over 6 months. The first interview focused on the early experiences of introducing the paradigm through a pilot project, and the second on the dissemination phase in organisations they belong. During the second operative phase of the programme, the 52 participants are called disseminator practitioners as their role changes from learners and executors of the pilot projects to trainers, Lean leaders, and coaches of the subsequent projects implemented in healthcare organisations. The interviewees come from one of the ten USLs in the Apulia region. The interviews were structured to reveal experiences according to the macro determinants of Lean implementation success proposed by the Model for Understanding Success in Quality (MUSIQ) [20]. The macro-factor is the external environment, organisation, quality improvement team and micro-system.

4   Results

The results are organised in paragraphs discussing the participants' experiences of the operational phases of piloting, testing, and dissemination. They also include perceptions regarding programme support activities. The second set of interviews was conducted before the activation of the reinforcement phase. The dissemination practitioners acted as Lean disseminators within their organisations and participated in the auditing and review phases of the Lean Lab. The results are aggregated per group of participants. Each participant group is assigned a label Gx where X range from 1 to 10.

4.1   Piloting and Testing Phase

Approximately 100 applications for the piloting and testing programme were received (equally distributed among the USLs). The communication campaign for the Lean Lab programme was instrumental in understanding the opportunities arising from the methodology and overcoming mistrust of the methodology (G_{1-10}). The most motivating factors of the communication campaign included training credits and the description of external contextual factors, such as the results of benchmarking activities against other territorial organisations and the presentation of healthcare policies aimed at improving waste and optimising stakeholder value (G_{1-10}). In addition, the opportunity to participate in a five-year strategic programme highly supported by the directorates and learn about projects from other regions represent another motivating factor ($G_{1-3, 6, 8-10}$). $G_{2-4, 6-10}$ stressed that the communication campaign allowed them to reconsider the Lean paradigm. They viewed it as a mere and exclusive tool to reduce costs and increase productivity at the expense of occupational well-being. $G_{1-2, 9-10}$ emphasised the importance of effective communication of the implementation modalities and the operational and strategic objectives of the programme. All groups highly appreciated the modalities of carrying out the piloting and testing phase. The theoretical training hours are also considered fundamental for better understanding the methodology and introducing the Lean tools. $G_{2, 5, 7-8}$ claimed that through the serious games and testimonies, their concerns regarding the difficulty of implementation were allayed. Other elements strongly valued by all the participants were the subdivision of the training and implementation phases of the Lean projects ($G_{2, 5, 8-10}$), the chance to define the application areas of the project with experts and managers ($G_{2-4; 7-8, 10}$); and the time allocated to run the Lean project ($G_{4-6, 10}$). All groups completed the project implementation sub-phase. At the end of the follow-up phase, all but two projects returned better results than expected ($G_{1-7, 10}$). Goal setting and outcome evaluation were conducted jointly with the project coach. Goals were set to be clear, challenging and measurable (G_{1-10}). Here are some outcomes settled and achieved: increase in the percentage of surgery for hip fracture; lead time reduction of the oncology patient pathways for chemotherapy. All groups emphasised the difficulty of collecting data during the patients' pathway (adoption of standard data collection tools, Gemba Walk) and independently using mapping tools such as the visual stream map or demand map (G_{1-10}). $G_{4, 5, 8, and 10}$ stated that working on the project was very stressful regarding the time they spent on it. Most project activities were carried out outside working hours without the executors being paid overtime. $G_{1, 2, 6, and 9}$ reported the commitment of the managers who provided the material resources (printing, blackboards, brainstorming and meeting rooms) and technical-managerial support (historical data collection, management control, data analysis) was central to the success of their project. Among the most interesting pieces of evidence to note are: that all groups reported that they achieved more than they expected and that all of them understood the importance of finding and addressing chronic structural problems instead of dealing with them reactively (G_{1-10}). The groups particularly appreciated the final follow-up meeting and celebration phases (G_{1-10}). While the former enabled an effective exchange of ideas among the groups ($G_{1-6; 8}$), the latter further motivated participants through prestige-based reward systems ($G_{2-7; 9-10}$).

4.2 Dissemination Phases

The members of the ten groups that participated in the first operational phase were appointed as dissemination practitioners and have been involved in the programme communication activities and the programme review and improvement phase. The directors of the USLs involved dissemination practitioners in carrying out peer-to-peer training courses and witnessing the success of the projects implemented within their organisations. Although many dissemination practitioners valued the initiative, they complained about the lack of time to conduct the training activities ($G_{1-7; 9-10}$). Another issue related to outreach activities was the absence of a formal mission statement by the directorates and voluntary course participation ($G_{2-5; 7; 8; 10}$). The celebration phase of the previous year's projects and the Lean Award were the strongest motivating factors for participation in the programme ($G_{1-7; 10}$). All other motivational factors related to the first operational phase were re-confirmed (G_{1-10}). In the 2nd phase, applications exceeded 600. The directors of each USL selected doctors and nurses from departments other than the participants in the piloting and testing phase.

In the dissemination phase, three groups were involved in each USL (153 participants). The selection method took into account feedback from dissemination practitioners. They stated that the methodology, due to the proximity among colleagues, spread naturally and spontaneously in departments where Lean projects have been implemented ($G_{2-7; 10}$). By involving other colleagues, several dissemination practitioners implemented multiple Lean projects in their departments even before the start of the dissemination phase ($G_{1, 3, 5-7, 10}$). While some of these projects, mostly conducted with the kaizen blitz method, have yielded satisfactory results, others have failed ($G_{1', 3, 5-7, 10}$). The lack of management involvement in implemented projects has frequently been pointed out by dissemination practitioners ($G_{1-3, 5, 7-9}$). In particular, although fully skilled in using mapping tools, internal coaches could not manage multidisciplinary teams or employ complex data and analysis models. As of the end of the project implementation sub-phase, 26 projects had achieved the planned results, while 4 had failed. The successful projects focused on patient value (20), improving the resource management of the organisation (4) and improving the quality of the working environment (2). Lack of commitment and support from leadership and management, which is essential to undertake a project involving external organisations, was the main critical failure factor of the failed projects ($G_{1, 3, 6, 7}$). At the end of the first dissemination phase, the dissemination practitioners highlighted several problems: many participants complained about a lack of time to devote to projects ($G_{1-7, 10}$); although the directorates show great interest, they often do not support or facilitate project implementation ($G_{1-3, 5, 7-10}$). Several USLs have activated an internal Lean Award to stimulate implementing Lean projects ($G_{1, 6-8, 10}$). Spontaneous Lean projects were applied to clinical pathways. In one USL, a Lean project was conducted to improve administrative activities related to booking outpatient visits and patient care continuity (G_4). Perceptions of the training, project execution and Lean award sub-phases of the second dissemination session are the same as those of the first session (G_{1-10}).

However, some dissemination practitioners brought up a need concerning the management of the dissemination activity ($G3-8; 10$). In their opinion, as the number of projects was growing rapidly, organisations should have set up a dedicated structure to monitor and support the projects ($G3-8; 10$). In the 2nd phase, micro implementations increased in all USLs (G_{1-10}) (Table 1). However, although the number of projects increased, the project failure rate increased more than proportionally. Moreover, organisations were no longer able to govern the dissemination process. In those USLs where the Lean Award was not introduced, many projects were implemented without being communicated to management (G_{2-5}). Dissemination practitioners pointed out that, as the number of projects increased, priority management and resource allocation conflicts have risen ($G_{1-7, 10}$). In addition, there were cases in which the increase in the performance of certain patient pathways (in terms of execution time, waiting time, saturation of resource capacity utilisation and quality perceived by patients) was counterbalanced by a reduction in the performance of other processes that shared the same resources ($G_{1, 5-7, 10}$). Although dissemination was spontaneously arising, and maturity in the use of the tools was growing, organisations could not govern implementation at the meso level (G_{1-10}). The lack of a dedicated structure to drive Lean dissemination, management involvement, and clear, formalised strategies are considered the main barriers to meso implementation ($G_{1-6, 8-10}$). Thus, in preparation for the operational phase of the reinforcement, many dissemination practitioners discussed with management setting up pilot control rooms to support and monitor the spread of Lean in selected organisations ($G_{1-4, 6, 8-10}$). Although the directorates had planned to test such a solution with AReSS during the 'Lean Lab' programme planning, they seemed hesitant about it. The concern was that assigning resources to control and monitor the paradigm's dissemination might negatively impact organisational performance and, above all, generate internal conflicts ($G_{3-4, 6, 8-10}$). The perception of dissemination practitioners was that managers not experiencing project implementation could not understand the need for this type of facilitation ($G_{1-4, 6, 8-10}$). In May 2022, none of the USLs had a control room or had established an operation manager team (G_{1-10}). Therefore, in the review phase (January - April 2020), dissemination practitioners emphasised the importance of primarily management staff participating in the reinforcement phase.

The publication of the National Outcome Plan System, covering the initial year's 1st-year deployment, confirmed the great improvements achieved in patient pathways where Lean projects had been implemented.

Table 1. Lean dissemination in Apulian USLs

	Year	Internal coach	Internal training hours	No internal training courses	Staff trained by an internal trainer	Lean projects detected	Internal lean award success		Dedicated structure to monitor & support the projects	
							Yes	No	Yes	No
USL1	2019	0	0	0	0	1	1	1	N	N
	2020	5	30	2	11	9	8	3	N	N
	2021	21	30	2	18	11	8	2	Y	N
	2022*	51	30	2	24	6	4		Y	N
USL1	2019	0	0	0	0	1	1		Y	N
	2020	5	40	2	21	5	4	1	N	N
	2021	20	40	2	25	8	8		N	N
	2022*	50	40	2	26	6	4	2	N	N

(*continued*)

Table 1. (*continued*)

	Year	Internal coach	Internal training hours	No internal training courses	Staff trained by an internal trainer	Lean projects detected	Internal lean award success		Dedicated structure to monitor & support the projects	
							Yes	No	Yes	No
USL2	2019	0	0	0	0	1	1		N	N
	2020	5	20	1	15	8	8		N	N
	2021	21	32	1	10	9	6	4	N	N
	2022*	51	32	1	12	6	5	1	N	N
USL3	2019	0	0	0	0	1	1		N	N
	2020	5	30	2	14	5	5		N	N
	2021	21	36	2	16	9	6	3	N	N
	2022*	51	36	2	18	6	5	1	N	N
USL4	2019	0	0	0	0	1	1		N	N
	2020	5	32	2	17	5	4	1	N	N
	2021	20	36	2	25	7	5	2	N	N
	2022*	50	36	2	24	9	7	2	N	N
USL5	2019	0	0	0	0	1	1	1	N	N
	2020	5	20	1	15	4	4		N	N
	2021	20	20	1	11	6	6		N	N
	2022*	50	32	2	18	8	7		N	N
USL6	2019	0	0	0	0	1	1		N	N
	2020	7	36	2	31	7	7		Y	N
	2021	22	28	2	33	11	9	2	Y	N
	2022*	52	28	2	31	5	5		Y	N
USL7	2019	0	0	0	0	1	1		N	N
	2020	5	40	2	22	5	5		N	N
	2021	20	40	2	20	8	7	1	N	N
	2022*	50	40	2	32	10	8	2	N	N
USL8	2019	0	0	0	0	1	1		N	N
	2020	5	16	1	18	6	6		Y	N
	2021	20	16	1	24	10	8	2	Y	N
	2022*	50	16	1	14	8	6	2	Y	N

(*continued*)

Table 1. (*continued*)

	Year	Internal coach	Internal training hours	No internal training courses	Staff trained by an internal trainer	Lean projects detected	Internal lean award success		Dedicated structure to monitor & support the projects	
							Yes	No	Yes	No
USL9	2019	0	0	0	0	1	1		N	N
	2020	5	32	2	32	7	7		N	N
	2021	20	60	4	54	8	7	1	N	N
	2022*	50	60	4	60	11	7	4	N	N
USL 10	2019	0	0	0	0	1	1		N	N
	2020	5	32	2	25	8	8		Y	N
	2021	20	32	2	31	12	10	2	Y	N
	2022*	50	32	2	25	9	6	3	Y	N

*Period: January - May 2022.
**In some USLs, the number of projects implemented may differ from those shown.

5 Discussion

The results from the study provide clear answers to the research questions. With regard to the determinants of the success or failure of the regional Lean Lab programme, co-design with the organisations involved and communication of the objectives and methods of implementation were among the most decisive factors in increasing and sustaining motivation among potential participants and eliminating barriers related to mistrust of improvement methodologies. The communication campaign was also important in spreading the potential of Lean and familiarising potential participants with the concept of the value and the importance of external contextual factors. These results confirm what has been reported by Dannapfel et al. [11] and Morrow et al. [26].

Furthermore, from an operational point of view, the training and coaching were instrumental in the paradigm introduction and dissemination phase at the micro level. The celebration and the Lean Award sub-stages were other elements of great value in the programme's success. Recognition of employee involvement is instrumental in aiding lean program success [27]. While the assignment of witnessing, coaching and communication tasks to the dissemination practitioners during the operational phases allowed them to gain experience in both the use of tools and project management, the workload assigned was also negatively evaluated because it was not recognised as working time. In summary, although the dissemination practitioners were willing to take on the assigned roles, the difficulties they experienced in relation to time availability were a major obstacle. However, it is crucial to remember that the role of the dissemination practitioners was decisive for dissemination.

Even though the operational phases took place from May to December each year, organisations were always engaged in the micro-implementation and dissemination phase of Lean. This increased the speed of dissemination and increased employee involvement.

About the implementation experiences within the organisations, the success and celebration of the pilot projects was the key trigger for activating the dissemination process. However, as reported by the practitioners, dissemination occurs more easily in units with at least one junior or senior Lean coach, while it is null or slow where there is no staff skilled in the methodology. In addition, some Lean tools, such as simulation or data-taking models, cannot be easily used by doctors and nurses. Thus, experienced coaches are needed to perform these tasks. Managers' commitment is a critical factor in the experience of dissemination practitioners during the introduction and dissemination phases. Facilitation activities of management and internal initiatives such as the Lean Award are concrete elements of management commitment.

On the other hand, the lack of management commitment is a failure factor of both micro- and meso- implementation. Based on the study's findings, even though organisations have shown great capacity in planning and implementing the introduction and dissemination phases of Lean, they have not managed the latter phase to its fullest extent. As a result, it has become a spontaneous and natural phenomenon rather than strategically organised. When the number of projects and their failure or sub-optimisations realised increased, organisations could not adopt project management systems or consider introducing dedicated structures for monitoring and controlling the strategic implementation of the paradigm. This was due to fears and a lack of strategic vision on the part of management and is a failure factor in many Operational Excellence initiatives.

6   Conclusion

In conclusion, the regional 'Lean Lab' plan strongly impacted the introduction and dissemination of the programme methodology. In turn, the organisations empowered the doctors and nurses who participated in the programme to take the lead in disseminating the methodology. After two years, organisations are still unable to implement Lean on a meso level, although many of their employees have reached a high level of maturity in handling Lean tools. It is critical for successful meso implementation that management is strongly committed and embraces Lean from a strategic point of view. The creation of a control room or team committed to project management and dissemination governance should be the main tool to support management in this regard. Further research will study further the impact and progress of Lean in hospitals since this study.

References

1. Rosa, A., Marolla, G., Lega, F., Manfredi, F.: Lean adoption in hospitals: the role of contextual factors and introduction strategy. BMC Health Serv. Res. 21(1), 1–18 (2021)
2. Marolla, G., Rosa, A., Giuliani, F.: Addressing critical failure factors and barriers in implementing Lean Six Sigma in Italian public hospitals. Int. J. Lean Six Sigma 13(3), 733–764 (2022). https://doi.org/10.1108/IJLSS-01-2021-0018

3. Graban, M.: Lean Hospitals: Improving Quality, Patient Safety and Employee Satisfaction, 1st edn. Productivity Press, London (2008)
4. McDermott, O., Antony, J.: Lean Six Sigma as an enabler for healthcare operational excellence in COVID-19. In: Six Sigma for Healthcare & Leadership. Purdue University Press Journal, Purdue University, Indiana, 26–27 June (2021)
5. McDermott, O., et al.: Lean Six Sigma in healthcare: a systematic literature review on challenges, organisational readiness and critical success factors. Processes **10** (2022). https://doi.org/10.3390/pr10101945
6. McDermott, O., et al.: Lean Six Sigma in healthcare: a systematic literature review on motivations and benefits. Processes **10** (2022). https://doi.org/10.3390/pr10101910
7. Brandao De Souza, L., Pidd, M.: Exploring the barriers to Lean health care implementation. Public Money Manag. **31**(1), 59–66 (2011)
8. Radnor, Z., Burgess, N., Sohal, A.S., O'Neill, P.: Lean in healthcare: views from the executive. In: European Operations Management Association Conference, Cambridge, 3–6 July (2011)
9. Al-Balushi, S., Sohal, A.S., Singh, P.J., Al Hajri, A., Al Farsi, Y.M., Al Abri, R.: Readiness factors for Lean implementation in healthcare settings – a literature review. J. Health Organ. Manag. **28**(2), 135–153 (2014)
10. Radnor, Z.: Implementing Lean in health care: making the link between the approach, readiness and sustainability. Int. J. Ind. Eng. Manag. **2**(1), 1–12 (2011)
11. Dannapfel, P., Poksinska, B., Thomas, K.: Dissemination strategy for lean thinking in health care. Int. J. Health Care Qual. Assur. **27**(5), 391–404 (2014)
12. Morrow, E., Griffiths, P., Maben, J., Jones, S., Robert, G.: The Productive Ward: Releasing Time to Care-Learning and Impact Review. NHS Institute for Innovation and Improvement, London (2010)
13. Robert, G., Sarre, S., Maben, J., Griffiths, P., Chable, R.: Exploring the sustainability of quality improvement interventions in healthcare organisations: a multiple methods study of the 10-year impact of the productive ward: releasing time to care programme in English acute hospitals. BMJ Qual Saf. **29**(1), 31–40 (2020)
14. Womack, J.P., Jones, D.T.: Lean Thinking. Simon & Schuster, London (2003)
15. Suàrez-Barraza, M.F., Smith, T., Dahlgaard-Park, S.M.: Lean service: a literature analysis and classification. Total Qual. Manag. Bus. Excell. **23**(3/4), 359–380 (2012)
16. Chiarini, A., Bracci, E.: Implementing Lean Six Sigma in healthcare: issues from Italy. Public Money Manag. **33**(5), 361–368 (2013)
17. Joosten, T., Bongers, I., Janssen, R.: Application of Lean thinking to health care: issues and observations. Int. J. Qual. Health Care: J. Int. Soc. Qual. Health Care/ISQua **21**(5), 341–347 (2009)
18. Hassle, P., Nielsen, P.A., Edwards, K.: Application of Lean manufacturing in hospitals- the need to consider maturity, complexity, and the value concept. Hum. Factors Ergon. Manuf. Serv. Ind. **26**(4), 430–442 (2016)
19. Antony, J., Lancastle, J., McDermott, O., Bhat, S., Parida, R., Cudney, E.A.: An evaluation of Lean and Six Sigma methodologies in the national health service. International Journal of Quality & Reliability Management, vol. ahead-of-print No. ahead-of-print (2021)
20. Kaplan, H.C., Provost, L.P., Froehle, C.M., Margolis, P.A.: The model for understanding success in quality (MUSIQ): building a theory of context in healthcare quality improvement. BMJ Qual. Saf. **21**(1), 13–20 (2012)
21. McIntosh, B., Sheppy, B., Cohen, I.: Illusion or delusion – Lean management in the health sector. Int. J. Health Care Qual. Assurance **27**(6), 482–492 (2014)
22. Feng, Q., Manuel, C.: Under the knife: a national survey of six sigma programs in US healthcare organisations. Int. J. Health Care Qual. Assur. **21**(6), 535–547 (2008)

23. Glasgow, J.M., Caziewell, S., Jill, R., Kaboli, P.J.: Guiding inpatient quality improvement: a systematic review of Lean and Six Sigma. Jt. Comm. J. Qual. Patient Saf. **36**(12), 533–540 (2010)
24. Coronado, R.B., Antony, J.: Critical success factors for the successful implementation of six sigma projects in organisations. TQM Mag. **14**(2), 92–99 (2002)
25. Coles, E., et al.: The influence of contextual factors on healthcare quality improvement initiatives: what works, for whom and in what setting? Protocol for a realist review. Syst. Rev. **6**, 168 (2017)
26. Morrow, E.M., Robert, G., Maben, J., Griffiths, P.: Implementing large-scale quality improvement – lessons from the productive ward: releasing time to caret. Int. J. Health Care Qual. Assur. **25**(4), 237–253 (2012)
27. McDermott, O., Antony, J., Sony, M., Looby, E.: A critical evaluation and measurement of organisational readiness and adoption for continuous improvement within a medical device manufacturer. 1–11 (2022). https://doi.org/10.1080/17509653.2022.2073917

Care Simplifiers': Students Contributing to Optimal Healthcare

Stephanie Monfils[✉] and Alinda Kokkinou

AVANS University of Applied Science, Breda, The Netherlands
sl.monfils@avans.nl

Abstract. The present paper documents the joint project of several hospitals in the Netherlands and Avans University of Applied Sciences to improve healthcare through the concept of "Care Simplifiers". "Care Simplifiers" is a concept that challenges hospital employees to improve their working situation. Students play an important role in this concept, because they are actually working on simplifying care processes, and are challenged to implement their proposed improvements during a 20-week internship period. Their efforts contribute to increasing the quality of care and alleviating work pressure for employees.

This approach can be implemented as part of a university curriculum and in a diversity of contexts other than healthcare. The present paper therefore describes how the "Care Simplifiers" project is setup, what the learning outcomes are for the students, what support is provided, what the benefits are for both parties, and concludes with lessons learned and best practices.

Keywords: Teaching · Internship · Lean · Healthcare

1 Introduction

Due to the aging of the population, the demand for care continues to rise in the Netherlands [1]. This is due to the convergence of several demographic trends. First, the number of elderly people is increasing significantly, as people are getting older. Second, they have increasingly complex care needs, partly because treatment options are increasingly effective [2]. The pressure on the entire healthcare system is exacerbated by a declining labour force, leading healthcare professionals to experience an increasing workload [3]. This manifests in several bottlenecks, such as long waiting lists for inpatient admissions [4] and a lack of outpatient facilities [5]. As a result, after patients are medically ready, they remain in the hospital unable to move on to an outpatient facility. This increased pressure on the healthcare system may be at the expense of the quality of care.

To cope with the challenges mentioned above, the Care Simplifiers concept was created in 2019. Care simplifiers is a joint cooperation of several hospitals in the Netherlands and Avans University of Applied Sciences to improve healthcare. It challenges hospital employees to improve their work-situation. The aim for the involved hospitals is to learn from each other in order to meet the increasing demand for care. Students

O. McDermott et al. (Eds.): ELEC 2022, IFIP AICT 668, pp. 54–60, 2023.
https://doi.org/10.1007/978-3-031-25741-4_6

play an important role in this concept. During a 20-week internship period, students work on simplifying care processes, and are challenged to implement their proposed improvements. Their efforts contribute to increasing the quality of care and alleviating work pressure for employees.

"Care Simplifiers" is an example of an industry-university cooperation (IUC). IUCs offer many benefits for both industry partners and universities. Industry partners pursue IUC as a way to acquire new knowledge and thereby create competitive advantage [6]. They benefit from highly qualified human resources such as researchers or students and access to knowledge and technology [7]. The success of IUC collaborations hinges on diverse factors, summarized as institutional, relationship and output factors [7]. Relevant institutional factors include resources (time, staff), structure, processes and control mechanisms. Relationship factors include communication, commitment, trust, culture, team expertise, and a clear role for leadership [6, 7]. Ideally, good personal relationships allow for the formation of sustainable linkages between organizations and universities. Output factors include objectives, knowledge and technology transfer.

In the context of the "Care Simplifiers" concept, the most important knowledge transfer occurs in the area of Lean. Lean management is a continuous improvement methodology that uses a customer perspective to identify and eliminate non-value-added activities [8]. The simplicity of its approach and tools fuelled its popularity and it has now been applied to a variety of industries beyond the automotive industry. In the context of healthcare, the implementation of Lean has been shown to improve hospitals performance in terms of productivity, cost efficiency, clinical quality, patient safety, and patient satisfaction [9].

The purpose of this paper is to demonstrate how the "Care Simplifiers" concept can be used in the context of IUC as a vehicle for learning for students, and continuous improvement for organisations. We describe how the "Care Simplifiers" concept is setup in the context of the educational curriculum (learning outcomes and support provided) and provide an overview of the research in which students are improving productivity in healthcare through simplifications in existing practices. The internship assignments were very diverse and each student worked on their own assignment in different departments in hospitals. By examining what their contribution has been in terms of learning outcomes for both student and healthcare professional, lessons learned and best practices are compiled and disseminated to improve healthcare productivity.

2 Collaboration Avans and Participating Hospitals

Before going into detail about some of the best practices, a brief description of one of the participating hospitals will be given as well as the students from Avans University of Applied Sciences that participate in the Care Simplifiers concept.

In order to shape the concept Care Simplifiers, collaborations have been established with various healthcare institutions such as Erasmus MC, Rivas Zorggroep, Jeroen Bosch Ziekenhuis and Amsterdam UMC. Of these relationships, Amphia has become a sustainable partner. Amphia is a top clinical training hospital located in the South of the Netherlands with branches in Breda, Oosterhout & Etten-Leur. Amphia aims to provide patients with the best medical and nursing care in Breda and the surrounding area and to keep everyone in the region as healthy as possible. To achieve this, Amphia works closely together with care providers in the region and pays a lot of attention to training, education and research [10].

Students joining the Care Simplifiers programme are Avans university of Applied Sciences in their third or final year of study. In response to a vacancy published within the various Avans programs, students send a letter of application directly to Stephanie Monfils, lecturer in business administration at the Avans Academy Associate degree program. She is connected to the concept as researcher and project leader. She collects all requests and helps assess whether a potential assignment is suitable for the student. Stephanie conducts the first round of introductory interviews with the students and then the second round of interviews is scheduled with the healthcare institution.

During the interviews, attention is given to the following characteristics: is the student coachable, communicative, driven, entrepreneurial and inquisitive? Does the student feel like exploring a research question in more depth if it is not concrete enough? The students' motivation to apply is also important. Furthermore, it can be an advantage if (s)he has an affinity with healthcare. After the two rounds of interviews, a final selection of students is made by mutual agreement. So far, mainly Avans students from the Business Administration programs are doing internships as part of the Care Simplifiers. In addition, students from Healthcare Technology program have also made valuable contributions to healthcare simplification.

The first two weeks of the students' internships consist of an intensive onboarding program. The students attend introductory presentations, get a tour of the hospital building and visit the departments. This is followed by all the formalities such as getting a badge, getting an uniform, getting to know the departmental team-leader and other stakeholders. They are also asked to read specific handbooks and to familiarize themselves with general information of the department they will be interning in. In this way, they get to know a whole new side of the hospital. Finally, the program is completed by attending meetings, shadowing nurses on day shifts, and occasionally also during evening shifts. From a methodology perspective, students use the DMAIC method to shape their research. DMAIC is the acronym for Define, Measure, Analyze, Improve and Control [11]. This research method is a structured problem solving method of Six Sigma and aims to improve and optimize business processes.

During the internship students' progress is closely monitored. Each student works with a team-leader of the department and is asked to find ways to simplify the work of the healthcare professionals. To this end, students research disruptions in (a part of) a care process and map out what can be improved. In order to thoroughly understand processes and gather information, students shadow various stakeholders such as nurses, physician assistants, medical specialists and logistics services. Students are individually supervised by business partners of the Hospital Control Center (HCC) from the department Process Improvement & Innovation. The supervisors are all Black or Green Belt certified.

Once every two weeks, progress meetings are organized. During these meetings, students give a status-update to the team-leaders and other stakeholders such as the internship supervisors from Avans. The feedback obtained from all those involved ensures that the student can make the right adjustments and take the right steps in the follow-up trajectory. The 20-week internship culminates in a final presentation and an internship report where students detail how they contributed to the simplification of care processes. The internship report describes how they actually have implemented their improvement and what results they have achieved.

The collaboration also takes place within the walls of Avans University of Applied Sciences by offering lessons in A3-Lean, a tool to structure the thinking behind the problem-solving. This class is provided to both the participating students in the Care Simplifiers concept as well as the healthcare professionals of Amphia. The lectorate Improving Business, in cooperation with the Lean Certification Platform, offers students the opportunity to obtain a Lean Green Belt certificate during their internship. With a Green Belt certificate, students can demonstrate their ability to solve problems at the departmental level of the hospital. The chances of the students obtaining their certificate are high, because during the internship at the hospital they can properly apply and put into practice their Green Belt knowledge and skills.

3   Introduction

Between August 2019 and June 2022, 28 students have started a Care Simplifiers Internship assignment at one of three different healthcare institutions. As from September 2022 six students started a Care Simplifiers Internship assignment at two different healthcare institutions. A review of the content of the assignments, and of the student experiences highlighted some commonalities.

3.1   Process Improvements

The majority of the internship assignments were (and are) about turnaround time. For example "How can the turnaround time in the department be reduced from 3.7 days to 1.88 days?" Or, "How can the discharge process be designed more effectively such that patients can be discharged before noon?". A second distinguishable category of assignments was (and is) about the use of materials. For example "How can we reduce the loss of patient alert-bands during the admission process in the nursing unit?" or, "How can the outpatient clinic be designed with a lower carbon footprint, such that fewer materials are wasted?".

The simplifications implemented aimed (and aim) to reduce workload, increase productivity and improve patient care. A good example of this is the research of student Mila de Rooijen. She investigated incorrect supplies in patient rooms. The problem arose that nurses in the Nursing Department too often misplaced materials in the patient rooms. This concerned patient-specific supplies, such as bandages and incontinence materials. As a result, staff were losing a lot of time walking around to get supplies elsewhere. Mila improved the replenishment process in collaboration with Housekeeping, Logistics and a number of nurses. As a result of her project, all drawers were given a standard layout and a visual representation was made of what and how much should be in each drawer. The number of misfires decreased by 65% and the number of minutes lost decreased by 74%.

3.2 Change Management

Students achieve even more than process improvement only. A care simplification process hinges on good collaboration among process participants. If there is resistance to a change, it is crucial to bring parties together and listen to each other. Creating common ground is difficult but students are able to address these types of issues during their internship.

This is for example illustrated by the internship assignment of Sam Braken, student of the Technical Business Administration program. Her assignment was to investigate and improve the procedure of defective and incomplete optiscans and optiseats. Optiscan and optiseat are wireless alarm systems to prevent dangerous situations for patients. In this assignment, a problem arose in the lending process of nursing materials. The nurses often missed the devices. Sam revealed that the collaboration between the clinic, medical technology department and technical management was difficult. Because of conflicting interests between the various parties and because of the multitude of parties involved, she exposed that the lending process was made unnecessarily complex. By first paying attention to the people-side, mutual frustrations diminished, which improved the working relations. New working arrangements could then be made.

3.3 Benefits for Students' Personal Development

The results are not only valuable to the healthcare institution. For students, participation in the Care Simplifiers concept is also meaningful. One student states: "The fact that we were actually able to implement a change that benefits the hospital makes me feel fulfilled." Or a comment of another student: "The best part was the implementation, the feeling that my research has produced a result and I was able to contribute".

The complexity of the hospital makes it clear that it is very important for a student to have communication skills. During the internship period, students grow in their role as project leaders, directing research, putting theory into practice and implementing the healthcare simplification. Student Maurice Dilisse states: 'Without social and communication skills, I am convinced that you will not get very far in the hospital. You will have to connect with your stakeholders to gather information and actually be able to improve processes'. And student Sam comments: 'Creating common ground was quite difficult. However without this conversation, the implementation would not succeed either'. She concludes with: 'I learned an incredible amount about stakeholder management in such a large organization'.

4 Lessons Learned

This approach can be implemented as part of a university curriculum and in a diversity of contexts other than healthcare. The following lessons learned have been identified that may be of use to those interested in setting up a similar programme.

1. **Continuity in supervision**
   Involving the same supervisors (university and hospital) over time ensures a warm relationship between hospital and university, an important success factor for IUC [7]. A dedicated practice supervisor within the organization must be appointed. He or she acts as the first point of contact for the students and can refer them to staff in the organization relevant to the student's research. In case of problems with students the practice supervisor can reach out to a familiar liaison within school. Close cooperation between practice and educational institution ensures that any problems are quickly resolved.

2. **Internship assignments: Let employees take part in developing and formulating internship assignments that are carried out by students**
   While assignments so far have been formulated alternatively by hospital supervisors and people on the work floor, the latter ones seem more successful. When assignments are formulated by people on the work floor, attention is paid to priorities that play a role in the department. Because employees contribute in this process, commitment from the stakeholders is high and the project is supported by the employees [12, 13]. Their proximity to students helps to overcome barriers and can lead to sustainable solutions. The side effect is that the (success) stories of the assignment spreads like an oil slick to other departments [13].

   This also illustrates the internship of student Pien Kuijpers. The nurses were facing a high workload in the Internal Medicine nursing unit. Pien implemented the Christmas tree. Every nurse in the department was allowed to hang a Christmas ball in the Christmas tree with a wish for improvement to reduce the work pressure in the department. Because the solutions for reducing work pressure were put forward by the group of nurses, there was broad support for the improvement proposals. The nurses were positively surprised that they were being listened to. In order to secure the initiative, the proposal was made to also link other holidays to the nurses' wishes for improvement and to examine the extent to which her initiative could be applied hospital-wide.

3. **Student Competencies**
   Certain students competencies have so far been found to lead to better results. Students should be proficient in interviewing, presenting and analyzing data. In addition, students should be able to apply the following Lean tools as well; an A3 to present visually, a fishbone diagram to identify root causes, an impact/effort matrix to rank improvement-ideas and 5S to implement improvement-ideas and a project plan to stay on track. These tools and competencies are not context specific, as they are equally important in contexts other than the concept of Care Simplifiers and can thus be transferred to another context.

4. **Training of health care professionals at Avans**
   Boundaries between the professional field and educational institutions are blurring. Studying is increasingly taking place in professional practice, close to social developments. This cross-pollination has a motivating effect and strengthens the learning capacity of all parties [6, 7]. Students, teachers and healthcare professionals help shape the process of knowledge acquisition. The progress meetings are in fact learning meetings in which students, teachers, researchers and health professionals learn with and from each other. To get even more benefit from each other, employees

should also be trained in skills on Lean at Avans university of applied science [9, 12].

5. **Logistics**
Due to the high workload of both supervising parties, regular progress meetings with all stakeholders need to be scheduled in advance. Ideally this should be done at the start of the internship program. The practice supervisor should be the initiator of these meetings. These types of process and monitoring measures, ensure that the IUC is successful [7].

5   Conclusion

The present paper provides a concrete example of a successful IUC involving several hospitals and Avans university of applied sciences. The "Care Simplifiers" concept provides the setting for the IUC to have a clear objective and successful knowledge transfer between the organizations involved [7]. The "Care Simplifiers" allows students to gain knowledge about Lean, and experience its application in a real world, high-stakes setting.

Declarations.   We state hereby that this project is not funded and there is no conflict of interest.

References

1. Woittiez, I., Ras, M., Eggink, E., Verbeek-Oudijk, D.: Vraag naar publieke zorg zal extra stijgen door achterblijven aanbod informele hulp. TSG - Tijdschrift voor gezondheidsweten-schappen 99(2), 47–53 (2021). https://doi.org/10.1007/s12508-021-00295-x
2. van der Sande, R., Rikkert, M.G.M.O., Westendorp, R.G.J., van Weel, C.: Advies Onderzoek medische zorg aan ouderen. In het bijzonder ouderen met multiple en complexe problematiek. GEEG 38, 41–43 (2007)
3. de Beer, J.A.A., Deerenberg, I.M., van Duin, C., Ekamper, P., van der Gaag, N.L., van Gaalen, R.I.A.: Bevolking 2050 in beeld: opleiding, arbeid, zorg en wonen. Netherlands Interdisciplinary Demographic Institute (NIDI)
4. Monitor Toegankelijkheid van Zorg: gevolgen van Covid-19. (NZa, 24 december 2021, 38 p.)
5. Monitor acute zorg 2020. (NZa, 19 april 2021, 16 p.)
6. Santoro, M., Gopalakrishnan, S.: The institutionalization of knowledge transfer activities within industry–university collaborative ventures. J. Eng. Tech. Manage. 17(3–4), 299–319 (2000)
7. Rybnicek, R., Königsgruber, R.: What makes industry–university collaboration succeed? A systematic review of the literature. J. Bus. Econ. 89(2), 221–250 (2018). https://doi.org/10.1007/s11573-018-0916-6
8. van den Heuvel, J., Does, R.J.M.M., de Koning, H.: Lean Six Sigma in a hospital. Int. J. Six Sigma Competitive Advantage 2(4), 377 (2006)
9. d'Andreamatteo, A., Ianni, L., Lega, F., Sargiacomo, M.: Lean in healthcare: a comprehensive review. Health Policy (2015)
10. Amphia.   https://www.amphia.nl/uploads/media/60a778d045633/amphia-strategienota-2017-2022-samen-gezonder-uw-gezondheid.pdf. Accessed 24 Sept 2022
11. Salentijn, W.: LEAN Six Sigma voor het Hoger Onderwijs (1e druk). Noordhoff (2017)
12. Drotz, E., Poksinska, B.: Lean in healthcare from employees' perspectives. J. Health Organ. Manag. 28(2), 177–195 (2014)
13. Radcliffe, E., et al.: Lean implementation within healthcare: imaging as fertile ground. J. Health Organ. Manag. 34(8), 869–884 (2020)

Analysis of the Relationship Between Knowledge Management and Lean Tools During Lean Implementation in Hospitals

Angelo Rosa[1], Giuliano Marolla[1]([✉]), and Olivia McDermott[2]

[1] Department of Management, Finance and Technology, LUM University, Casamassima, Italy
`Rosa@ibsc.it, marolla@lbsc.it`
[2] College of Science and Engineering, National University of Ireland, Galway, Ireland

Abstract. During the last two decades, lean healthcare has received increasing attention from both researchers and practitioners because it plays an imperative role in quality and safety clinical process improvement. Although there is much evidence of the positive results of the paradigm implementation at the micro level, only in few cases the methodology is implemented at meso level or improvements are observed at organizational level. Among the main factors leading to the failure of meso implementation is the lack of widespread knowledge of lean tools and concepts within the organization. The lean implementation process at the meso level require high efforts to manage the transfer, sharing, integration, and transformation of lean knowledge within the organization. Thus, many researchers have positively assumed knowledge management (KM) as a critical success factor of lean sustainability and meso implementation. Although, the relationship of KM and lean sustainability have gradually become a hot topic, few scholars have investigated this issue in healthcare sector. Based on literature review focusing on the key characteristics of the lean healthcare implementation process, this article aims to bring out the relationships between lean tools, KM and lean sustainability in hospital setting. Results provide some relevant insights for hospitals applying the lean paradigm namely: KM is a critical success factor in disseminating and sustaining lean methodology and lean knowledge degree is strongly influenced by the use of lean tools.

Keywords: Lean healthcare · Lean tools · Knowledge management

1 Introduction

Lean is a managerial paradigm that integrates principles, methods and techniques aimed at optimizing organizational processes. Its main purpose is to increase the value provided to end customers by systematically reducing waste [1]. Over the last two decades, the adoption of lean in healthcare has received increasing attention from both researchers and practitioners, as most scientific articles and direct testimonials highlight the effective application of the methodology results in increased value for both internal and external

O. McDermott et al. (Eds.): ELEC 2022, IFIP AICT 668, pp. 61–71, 2023.
https://doi.org/10.1007/978-3-031-25741-4_7

stakeholders of organizations and in operational cost reduction [2, 3]. The adoption of lean tools in healthcare processes improve clinical pathways lead times and quality performances, reduces transport and movement waste, as well as clinical risk, and simplifies communication and coordination practices [4]. These findings have led to a common consensus that lean tools are key drivers of lean implementation.

In the past, many researchers have argued that the lean philosophy is particularly suitable for healthcare organisations because its principles are intuitive and convincing and because doctors and technicians can easily master the main tools and methodologies [5]. However, in recent years, researchers have highlighted that the promise of an easy, pitfall-free implementation process and the existence of a tangible relationship between lean implementation and improved organizational performance is an oversimplification [5, 6]. In more detail, recent studies have shown that although healthcare organisations are successful in introducing lean into both single clinical and support processes they fail in the dissemination process of the methodologies at systemic level [7, 8]. This affects lean sustainability and consequently systemic (meso) implementation. Many researchers suggest that this phenomenon is due to the lack of or inability to use tools aimed at learning, knowledge dissemination and knowledge application [6]. Thus, the role of knowledge management (KM) in the successful deployment of lean in healthcare organizations is emerging as a prominent issue [6, 8].

Although the role of KM on lean sustainability is discussed through research in other sectors, it is not in healthcare. The study focuses on the themes of LM on Lean sustainability in healthcare.

The research questions (RQ's) are to ascertain:

RQ1; The effect of application of lean tools on lean sustainability.

RQ2: The effect of application of lean tools on Knowledge acquisition, Knowledge integration and on Knowledge application.

RQ3: the effect of Knowledge acquisition on knowledge integration and of Knowledge integration on knowledge adoption.

RQ4: The effect of knowledge acquisition, knowledge integration and knowledge adoption has on lean sustainability.

The paper is structured as follows: the following section shows the research methodology, in Sect. 3 the results and the theorized model are discussed; finally, Sect. 4 presents the discussion and the conclusion.

2   Methodology - Literature Review

A literature review was carried out in relation to the relationship between Knowledge Management and Lean sustainability with a specific focus on Healthcare. A systematic literature review (SLR) was utilized. Articles published between 2000 and 2021, using the full academic databases Web of Science and Scopus were searched. The search strategy followed the approach in Tranfield et al. [9] which seeks to create a reliable knowledge stock by synthesizing the relevant body of literature [9, 10]. The following search string was applied to search all the databases mentioned above: "Lean" AND "Knowledge Management", "Lean" AND "Knowledge acquisition" and "Lean" AND "Knowledge integration", "Lean" AND "Knowledge adoption" as well as "Lean Healthcare" AND "knowledge management". Table 1 provides a detailed listing of the inclusion/exclusion criteria. The references of the selected studies were manually checked to identify additional relevant studies that were missed in the database search. Grey literature (conference papers, magazine-related articles, workshops, books, editorials, prefaces) were excluded.

Table 1. Inclusion & Exclusion criteria for the SLR

Inclusion criteria	Exclusion criteria
Academic peer-reviewed journal articles books, magazine-related articles, etc.) related to Lean sustainability and Knowledge Management from a Healthcare viewpoint and other sectors Articles published in high quality relevant journals Articles published from 2000 to 2021	Grey literature (conference proceedings, dissertations, text Articles published in languages other than English and Italian Articles published before 2000 Articles published in non-refereed journals

The initial search identified 213 articles after which duplicates articles found were firstly removed, and the full text was retained if the abstracts stated that the study was related to Lean, Knowledge management and had a healthcare context. The four authors reviewed and independently assessed the eligibility for inclusion of the retrieved studies based on the search criteria Parameswaran et al. [11]. Inclusion agreement was solved by discussions and consensus among reviewers. This process yielded 50 studies for final inclusion at this stage of the review.

The analysis was conducted based on several observations in response to the research questions - Lean and Knowledge Management (knowledge acquisition, integration and adoption) and sustainability and the emerging themes in relation to the aforementioned topics were reviewed. Thus, for example, content analysis was used to comprehend the elements to be included in the factors under examination. In addition, the panel of four researchers discussed frequently to assess the interpretation of concepts as reported in the selected articles.

3   Results and Theoretical Model

The themes related to Lean tools, knowledge acquisition, integration and sustainability. Table 2 shows the factors and elements derived from literature review and the debate among researchers.

Researchers who have studied the lean transformation process of healthcare organizations have defined some specific steps in the implementation of the paradigm [18]. Each of these stages is characterized by several enabling factors and critical failure and success factors. Brandao de Souza and Pidd (2011) defined micro implementation as the condition in which a limited number of employees implements lean at the level of a single process at discrete times, while meso implementation is where the paradigm is implemented at the strategic level and the culture of continuous improvement spreads spontaneously within the organization [25]. As extensively demonstrated in the literature, the introduction and dissemination phases - belonging to micro implementation - are key factors in the implementation process as they largely affect the level of lean sustainability [6]. Sustainability refers to the widespread organisational consensus towards lean practices and tools and the employee commitment to embrace the culture of continuous improvement [22, 24]. The role of KM is to drive effectively the processes of knowledge

Table 2.   List of themes arising from the literature review

Construct	Items	References	Final items
Lean tools	Value Stream Map	Antony *et al.* (2018) [18]; Antony *et al.* (2019) [5]; Basu (2004) [13], Henrique and Godinho Filho (2020) [4]; Marolla *et al.* (2021) [8]; Parkhi, 2019 [14]	*Mapping tools*
	5S		5 s
	Root Cause Analysis		Root Cause Analysis
	Failure mode and effect analysis (FMEA)		*Total quality management tools*
	SMED tools		SMED tools
	Kanban		Kanban
	Assessment tools		Assessment tools
	Rapid improvement		*Kaizen blitz*
	Strategic tools		*Hoshin Kanri*
	Visual management tools		Visual management tools
Knowledge acquisition	Training course	Al Khamisi *et al.* (2019) [15]; Arumugam *et al.* (2013) [16]; Basu (2004) [13];Moreno-Luzon and Lloria (2008)[17]	*Internal training courses*
	Sharing of lean knowledge		Sharing of lean knowledge
	Kata coaching		Kata coaching
	Brainstorming		Brainstorming
	Employment of an external consultant or experts		*External training courses*

(continued)

Table 2. (*continued*)

Construct	Items	References	Final items
Knowledge integration	Lean tool promotion-related materials	Arumugam *et al.* (2013) [16]; Basu (2004) [13]; Grant (1996) [18]; Kaplan *et al.* (2012) [19]; Moreno-Luzon and Lloria (2008) [17]; McFadden *et al.* (2014) [20]	Lean tool promotion-related materials
	Lean assessment		Lean assessment
	Implementation of standard templates for project submissions (e.g., Report A3) Managing lean tools		Implementation of standard templates for project submissions (e.g., Report A3) *Common language*
Knowledge application	Decision-making models based on data from lean tools	Al Khamisi *et al.* (2019) [15]; Arumugam *et al.* (2013) [16]; Arumugam *et al.* (2016) [21]; Basu (2004) [13]	Decision-making models based on data from lean tools
	Building a lean authority system		Building a lean authority system
	Problem solving capability		Problem solving capability
	Groups of Lean experts acting horizontally across the organization		Groups of Lean experts acting horizontally across the organization
Lean sustainability	Employee involvement level	Al-Balushi *et al.* (2014) [22]; Assarlind *et al.* (2013) [23]; Henrique and Godinho Filho (2020) [4]; Papadopoulos *et al.* (2011) [24]; Kaplan *et al.* (2012) [19]	Employee involvement level
	Management sponsorship		Management sponsorship

(*continued*)

Table 2. (*continued*)

Construct	Items	References	Final items
	Management involvement		Management involvement
	Degree of spreading the culture of continuous improvement		Degree of spreading the culture of continuous improvement
	Processes improvements		Processes improvements

acquisition, integration and application of the tool and lean concepts within the organization [26–30]. Effective management of these steps results in increased confidence in the method and reduced organizational resistance to change. In addition, based on organisational characteristics, these phases allow the organization to assess the potential improvements achievable and designing the most effective processes for systematically adopting the paradigm [6, 18].

3.1 Lean Tools, Sustainability and Knowledge Management

During the introduction phase, running pilot projects is crucial to ensure that trainees gain experience using lean methodologies and tools and fully understand the fundamental concepts of the paradigm [25]. Many case studies show that the successful lean introduction is largely determined by the ability of the pilot projects teams to effectively apply lean tools [2, 14]. Successful pilot projects and their celebration motivate the organization to undertake additional improvement projects using lean tools. Moreover, the implementation of lean tools in the healthcare organizations has been shown to result in positive clinical and organizational outcomes [4, 18].

RQ: Hypothesis 1: The application of lean tools has a positive impact on lean sustainability.

Knowledge and maturity in using lean tools is a pre-requisite before proceeding with the other implementation phases [5, 6]. KM trigger with acquiring knowledge about the opportunities provided by lean tools, so an organization can interpret and assess that knowledge. Many authors discuss the role of the introduction phase as an organizational stimulus to acquire knowledge [19, 25]. In particular, the successful implementation of the tools during the pilot phases prompts organizations to foster knowledge exchange and provide internal training (in many cases by means peer teaching training courses) [19]. Discussions between the pilot projects participants and sharing experiences with other colleagues are other means of knowledge acquisition [6]. In the dissemination phase, the process of monitoring the appropriateness and effectiveness of the use of lean tools prompts organizations to set up kata coaching initiatives aimed at stimulating and fostering the transmission of tacit knowledge between employees [16, 21].

RQ: Hypothesis 2a: The application of lean tools has a positive impact on Knowledge acquisition.

Lean tools play an important role during the paradigm dissemination process by providing a common language and standard practices for improvement initiatives [8, 13]. The creation of a common knowledge base and the use of standard tools serves as a coordination mechanism in which organizations can more effectively utilize the valuable knowledge resources derived through improvement projects [20, 31]. Thus, the use of lean tools fosters the integration of lean knowledge within the organization.

RQ: Hypothesis 2b: The application of lean tools has a positive impact on Knowledge integration.

The implementation of lean tools not only offers a common approach to undertake improvement projects, but also produces a plethora of data allowing organisational weaknesses in process management to be exposed [20]. The data obtained and the evidence that emerges through the application of the tools can foster the establishment of decision-making models based on lean methodology and increase problem solving capacity within the organization [8, 16, 22]. When the dissemination phase is advanced and successful, healthcare organizations understanding the potential of lean tools and practices establish internal expert groups to support the methodology and/or embed a responsible "authority" in the organizational structure to support the paradigm over time [19]. As a result, the ability to apply lean knowledge increases.

RQ: Hypothesis 2c: The application of lean tools has a positive impact on Knowledge application.

3.2 Interaction Among Knowledge Management Dimensions

The effective dissemination process requires that lean knowledge is acquired, integrated, and applied within the organization. These three dimensions of knowledge are closely interrelated and mutually permeate each other [32]. Lean knowledge acquisition is the process of seeking, evaluating, and understanding the conceptual pillars and operational tools of the lean paradigm. The acquired knowledge represents the raw material through which the knowledge integration process can be activated [32]. Lean requires the application of sets of standard procedures, common thinking and language, and behaviours and culture oriented towards change and sharing. These elements are not typical of healthcare organisations; therefore, integration requires the creation of a common knowledge base through the acquisition of knowledge [19].

Hypothesis 3a: Knowledge acquisition has a positive impact on knowledge integration.

Knowledge integration has a significant influence on knowledge creation, allowing information to be incorporated and transformed into useful knowledge at every level of the organization [18, 23]. Thus, knowledge integration impacts the organization's capability to fully understand the value of lean and to act by effectively applying the concepts and tools of the methodology [15]. Antony et al. [12] explain that implementing lean-based decision- making models requires a deep focus on project management and lean evaluation systems; these practices require high levels of knowledge integration. Similarly, creating lean teams to support improvement projects without first encouraging the use of lean tools will result in a failure to adopt the methodology [6, 8].

Hypothesis 3b: Knowledge integration has a positive impact on knowledge adoption.

3.3   Knowledge Management and Sustainability

The role of knowledge is considered crucial during organizational transformation activities, whether they are oriented towards product, process or business innovation. Although there are many empirical studies assessing the impact of KM on performance goals of improvement practices or organizational models, there are very few studies discussing the role of KM on lean sustainability, particularly in healthcare. The most recent research evaluating the impact of KM on lean sustainability is by Zhang et al. (2020) who show the mediating role of KM between lean tools and lean sustainability, focusing on companies in Beijing, Tianjin and Weifang [27]. The authors considered the same three dimensions of knowledge adopted in this research and revealed that each dimension has a direct impact on the lean sustainability. Arumugam et al. [16] through the lens of goal theory and sociotechnical systems theory, show the mediating role of KM between the variables "challenging goal setting" and "adherence to the lean Six Sigma method" and the variable "success of Six Sigma projects". The authors specifically describe the elements of knowledge acquisition and adoption, while the processes of knowledge integration are assumed from a social rather than technical perspective. In previous research, Arumugan et al. [16] demonstrate the mediating role of the "learning behaviour" and "knowledge creation" variables among "Six Sigma resources (technical)" and "team psychological safety (social)" antecedent variables and the variable "success of Six Sigma process improvement projects". Reich et al. [33] demonstrate the effect of KM and Knowledge Alignment on achieving project management goals and business value in IT-enabled projects. In their research, the concept of Knowledge Alignment is reflective of knowledge integration concept.

From the results of these articles, the additional three hypotheses are formulated:

Hypothesis 4a: knowledge acquisition has a positive impact on lean sustainability;

Hypothesis 4b: knowledge integration has a positive impact on lean sustainability;

Hypothesis 4c: knowledge adoption has a positive impact on lean sustainability.

Figure 1 represents the theoretical model derived from the literature review.

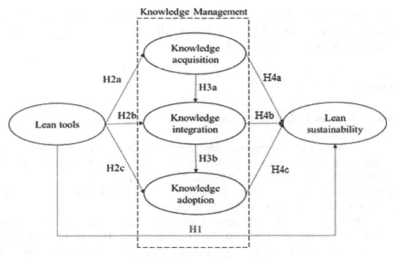

Fig. 1. Theoretical model

4 Discussion and Conclusion

The sustainability of lean plays a key role in the successful adoption of the paradigm within hospitals. High sustainability reduces the barriers to implementation and drives the spontaneous orientation of the organization to continuous improvement. The widespread application of lean tools within the organization has always been considered an enabler of sustainability, however, some researchers suggest that it happens because the tools stimulate and promote knowledge of the methodology. Thus, knowledge is considered a mediating variable between lean tools and sustainability. Based on this theory, a model has been hypothesized. The findings confirm the mediating role of KM between the tools and the sustainability of lean methodology. Moreover, the analysis clearly highlights the different importance of the stages of knowledge acquisition, integration, and application. In particular, widespread knowledge of lean tools encourages the adoption of project management systems, models for evaluating organizational capabilities and standardized procedures for improvement projects (e.g. Report A3, PDCA cycle, Kaizen Blitz, etc.). Although the hypothesis that knowledge integration positively influences system-wide adoption of knowledge is confirmed further analysis will test this.

The results of this study can provide policy makers and decision makers with some suggestions with respect to lean implementation. First, lean tools should be considered not only as best practices for conducting improvement projects but also, and more importantly, as a medium for creating, integrating, and applying knowledge. In addition, the importance of KM should be formally recognized and therefore driven within the organization. In order for knowledge integration to translate into an effective system of knowledge adoption, managers must be actively involved in this process and facilitate it by making decisions based on lean concepts, leveraging enabling factors such as the creation of a lean management authority or favouring the creation of cross-functional lean teams that act as operation managers.

The research study is characterized by a number of limitations, the first of which is that it is a model and requires testing. In light of these limitations, however, the study offers many insights for future research.

References

1. Womack, J.P., Jones, D.T.: Banish Waste and Create Wealth in Your Corporation. Free Press, NY (2003)
2. Bossone, E., et al.: Lean management approach for reengineering the hospital cardiology consultation process: a report from AORN "A. Cardarelli" of Naples. Int. J. Environ. Res. Public Health **19**, 4475 (2022). https://doi.org/10.3390/ijerph19084475
3. D'Andreamatteo, A., Iannia, L., Lega, F., Sargiacomo, M.: Lean in healthcare: a comprehensive review. Health Policy **119**(9), 1197–1209 (2015)
4. Henrique, D.B., Godinho, M.: A systematic literature review of empirical research in Lean and Six Sigma in healthcare. Total Qual. Manag. Bus. Excell. **31**(3–4), 429–449 (2020)
5. Antony, J., Sreedharan, R., Chakraborty, A., Gunasekaran, A.: A systematic review of Lean in healthcare: a global prospective. Int. J. Qual. Reliab. Manag. **36**(8), 1370–1391 (2019)
6. Rosa, A., Marolla, G., Lega, F., Manfredi, F.: Lean adoption in hospitals: the role of contextual factors and introduction strategy. BMC Health Serv. Res. **21**(1), 1–18 (2021)
7. Glasgow, J.M., Caziewell, S., Jill, R., Kaboli, P.J.: Guiding inpatient quality improvement: a systematic review of Lean and Six Sigma. Jt. Comm. J. Qual. Patient Saf. **36**(12), 533–540 (2010)
8. Marolla, G., Rosa, A., Giuliani, F.: Addressing critical failure factors and barriers in implementing Lean Six Sigma in Italian public hospitals. Int. J. Six Sigma (2012)
9. Tranfield, D., Denyer, D., Smart, P.: Towards a methodology for developing evidence-informed management knowledge by means of systematic review. Br. J. Manag. **14**, 207–222 (2003). https://doi.org/10.1111/1467-8551.00375
10. Yang, E.C.L., Khoo, C., Arcodia, C.: A systematic literature review of risk and gender research in tourism. Tour. Manag. **58**, 89–100 (2017)
11. Parameswaran, U.D., Ozawa-Kirk, J.L., Latendresse, G.: To live (code) or to not: a new method for coding in qualitative research. Qual. Soc. Work **19**, 630–644 (2020). https://doi.org/10.1177/1473325019840394
12. Antony, J., Palsuk, P., Gupta, S., Mishra, D., Barach, P.: Six Sigma in healthcare: a systematic review of the literature. Int. J. Qual. Reliab. Manag. **35**(5), 1075–1092 (2018)
13. Basu, R.: Six Sigma to operational excellence: role of tools and techniques. Int. J. Six Sigma Compet. Advant. **1**(1), 44–64 (2004)
14. Parkhi, S.S.: Lean management practices in healthcare sector: a literature review. Benchmarking **26**(4), 1275–1289 (2019)
15. Al, Y.N., Khan, M.K., Munive, J.E.: Knowledge-based lean six sigma system for enhancing quality management performance in healthcare environment. Int. J. Lean Six Sigma **10**(1), 211–233 (2019)
16. Arumugam, V., Antony, J., Kumar, M.: Linking learning and knowledge creation to project success in Six Sigma projects: an empirical investigation. Int. J. Prod. Econ. **141**(1), 388–402 (2013)
17. Moreno-Luzon, M.D., Lloria, M.B.: The role of non-structural and informal mechanisms of integration and coordination as forces in knowledge creation. Br. J. Manag. **19**, 250–276 (2008)
18. Grant, R.M.: Prospering in dynamically-competitive environments: organisational capability as knowledge integration. Organ. Sci. **7**(4), 375–387 (1996)

19. Kaplan, H.C., Provost, L.P., Froehle, C.M., Margolis, P.A.: The model for understanding success in quality (MUSIQ): building a theory of context in healthcare quality improvement. BMJ Qual. Saf. **21**(1), 13–20 (2012)
20. McFadden, K., Lee, J., Gowen, C., Sharp, B.: Linking quality improvement practices to knowledge management capabilities. Qual. Manag. J. **21**(1), 34–55 (2014)
21. Arumugam, V., Jiju, A., Linderman, K.: The influence of challenging goals and structured method on Six Sigma project performance: a mediated moderation analysis. Eur. J. Oper. Res. **254**(1), 202–213 (2016)
22. Al-Balushi, S., Sohal, A.S., Singh, P.J., Al, A., Al Farsi, Y.M., Al, R.: Readiness factors for lean implementation in healthcare settings – a literature review. J. Health Organ. Manag. **28**(2), 135–153 (2014)
23. Assarlind, M., Gremyr, I., Bäckman, K.: Multi-faceted views on a Lean Six Sigma application. Int. J. Qual. Reliab. Manag. **30**(4), 387–402 (2013)
24. Papadopoulos, T., Radnor, Z., Merali, Y.: The role of actor associations in understanding the implementation of Lean thinking in healthcare. Int. J. Oper. Prod. Manag. **31**(2), 167–191 (2011)
25. Brandao De Souza, L., Pidd, M.: Exploring the barriers to lean health care implementation. Public Money Manag. **31**(1), 59–66 (2011)
26. Davenport, T.H., Prusak, L.: Working Knowledge: How Organizations Manage What They Know. Harvard Business School Press, Boston (1998)
27. Zhang, B., Niu, Z., Liu, C.: Lean tools, knowledge management, and lean sustainability: the moderating effects of study conventions. Sustainability **12**(3), 956 (2020)
28. Barney, J.B.: Firm resources and sustained competitive advantage. J. Manag. **17**(1), 99–120 (1991)
29. Nonaka, I.: A dynamic theory of organizational knowledge creation. Organ. Sci. **5**(1), 14–37 (1994)
30. Marr, B., Schiuma, G.: Measuring and managing intellectual capital and knowledge assets in new economy organisations. In: Bourne, M. (ed.) Handbook of Performance Measurement. Gee, London (2001)
31. Zahra, S.A., George, G.: Absorptive capacity: a review, reconceptualization, and extension. Acad. Manag. Rev. **27**(2), 185–203 (2002)
32. Nonaka, I., von Krogh, G., Voelpel, S.: Organisational knowledge creation theory: evolutionary paths and future advances. Organ. Stud. **27**(8), 1179–1208 (2006)
33. Reich, B.H., Gemino, A., Sauer, C.: How knowledge management impacts performance in projects: an empirical study. Int. J. Proj. Manag. **32**(4), 590–602 (2014)

A Lean Approach for Reducing Downtimes in Healthcare: A Case Study

Stefano Frecassetti[(✉)] , Matteo Ferrazzi , and Alberto Portioli-Staudacher

Politecnico di Milano, Department of Management, Economics and Industrial Engineering,
Milano, Italy
stefano.frecassetti@polimi.it

Abstract. Lean Management is considered one of the most successful management paradigms for enhancing operational performance in the manufacturing environment. However, it has been applied throughout the years to several sectors and organisational areas, such as service, healthcare, and office departments. After the Covid-19 outbreak, increasing attention has been given to potential performance improvements in healthcare organisations by leveraging Lean. This paper intends to add further knowledge to this field by presenting a case study in a hospital. In this paper, a pilot project is presented carried out in a healthcare organisation. Lean methods were used to improve the operating room performance, particularly by reducing the operating room changeover time. The A3 template was used to drive the project and implement a new procedure using the Single Minute Exchange of Die (SMED) method. With the implementation of the new procedure, the changeover time between two different surgeries in the operating room was significantly reduced, together with a more stable and reliable process.

Keywords: SMED · Lean thinking · Healthcare · Changeover · A3

1 Introduction

With the outbreak of COVID-19, the efficiency of health institutions is under the public spotlight, thus leading to a growing interest towards improving the operational performance of hospitals and clinics. In particular, it has emerged that having a reliable and time-responsive operational process is fundamental, especially for hospitals. This means an increasing need for these organisations in guidance on how time and resources can be managed in an optimal way.

Among the other managerial strategies, Lean management is considered one of the most successful to achieve operational excellence [10]. Throughout the years, this theory's application to other fields has increased thanks to the increased awareness of the benefits given by Lean. In the literature, it is possible to find several examples in which Lean has been applied in other areas of manufacturing firms, such as offices [3]. Also, it is possible to find applications of Lean in sectors different from manufacturing, such as service [18] or healthcare [4, 13].

© IFIP International Federation for Information Processing 2023
Published by Springer Nature Switzerland AG 2023
O. McDermott et al. (Eds.): ELEC 2022, IFIP AICT 668, pp. 72–81, 2023.
https://doi.org/10.1007/978-3-031-25741-4_8

In fact, some papers showed how Lean techniques and tools have been applied in healthcare. These examples include the use of seven wastes or SMED and could be beneficial to improving performance and reducing downtimes [1, 2, 4, 7, 13]. Thus, the application of Lean in the healthcare environment has recently been topical due to the strong push that Covid-19 has given to healthcare organisation in improving their performance.

By knowing this, the aim of this paper is adding knowledge on how Lean tools can be implemented in a successful way in the healthcare sector. A case study will showcase how Lean has been introduced in a public hospital to reduce the changeover time of an operating room. This article will be organized into the following paragraphs: literature review, methodology, results, discussion, conclusions and limitations.

2 Literature Review

Lean management is one of the most diffused managerial paradigms in manufacturing environment for improving operational performance [10]. Its wide set of tools [16] has been applied across several areas of the manufacturing industry, ranging from the shop floor [15] to the offices [3]. Furthermore, in recent years, the implementation of Lean tools in other sectors has become common. In fact, thanks to the huge benefits that can be achieved through its implementation, a raising interest is raising in the way in which Lean tools can be implemented in other sectors.

In addition to this, some Lean tools as the A3 template can be easily used for driving improvement projects and as a reference for conducting pilot projects or introducing the Lean culture in a company [18]. Other Lean methods, like SMED, which was usually implemented for set-up optimization in manufacturing [15], have recently turned out to be a relevant method for reducing downtimes in other sectors. SMED could be particularly useful when there is a need to synchronise a set of activities and define a rigorous procedure [15] and healthcare sector is the case in point.

In the literature it is possible several examples of how Lean practices can be applied in the healthcare [1, 4, 7, 8, 12, 13]. Henrique and Godinho Filho 2020 [8] mapped the empirical research done in this field, highlighting the barriers and possible impact on performance. For instance, SMED method has been applied particularly in operating rooms [1, 7, 12] to reduce their set-up time (i.e., changeover time) thus leading to an improved efficiency of the room [11]. Other authors pointed out the factors needed to sustain lean improvements in the long term [9].

Thus, it is evident that there is still a lack of contributions on how Lean can be successfully implemented in healthcare [6]. In fact, some authors have pointed out how the focus is on the results of the Lean implementation rather than in the process [14]. By knowing this, it is interesting understand how Lean can be introduced for the first time to have an improvement replicable and sustainable in the long term [5, 9]. This is particularly relevant not only from the literature perspective, but also from the organisations' perspective which are struggling to find a way to successfully implement methodologies to better manage their time and resources.

3 Research Methodology

Coherently with the aim of the research is to demonstrate a successful implementation of Lean tools in the healthcare sector for improving operational performance, a case study will be presented. The methodology used here is the single case study [20], considered the most appropriate one to address the starting research objective. Even though this methodology has some limitations, for instance, [19] argued whatever is derived from a single case study is not statistically relevant and extendable to other contexts; however, others [17] said a single case study could add new knowledge for improving the current literature and for further research.

An improvement project aimed at the reduction of an operating room changeover time will be presented. By using the A3 template, the organisation was able to analyse their processes and address some issues that were causing inefficiencies in their operations. In particular, the operating room changeover process was reshaped using the Single Minute Exchange of Die (SMED) method.

This chapter will present the context related to the case study and the detailed methodology used to conduct it.

3.1 Case Study Context

The case study was conducted in a public hospital. The focus was on the main district of this hospital, in the operating block. In the last period, great emphasis was given to understanding the issues incurred in the management of the operating rooms.

In fact, in this organisation, there were poor operational performances which were causing issues in the management of the operating room. In particular, it was observed that several delays in the planned surgery were caused by a high and unstable timing of the changeover operations. This was directly translated into a low level of the main Key Performance Indicator (KPI) used for the performance monitoring in this hospital, the Overall (Operating) Room Effectiveness (ORE). The ORE is computed as the ratio of Surgical Time to effective opening time. Having this situation clearly in mind, the hospital decided to start a deeper analysis to understand the causes and implement improvements to improve their performance. A detailed description of this process will be depicted in the following section.

3.2 Case Study Deployment

Since the improvement project was driven using the A3 template, the case study will be described by using its structure. Thus, the eight sections of the A3 template will be presented. Also, the relationship of the sections with the PDCA (Plan-Do-Check-Act) cycle will be made explicit, as some other authors did [18].

- Step 1 – Plan: Problem Background
- Step 2 – Plan: Problem Breakdown
- Step 3 – Plan: Target Setting
- Step 4 – Plan: Root Causes Analysis
- Step 5 – Plan: Countermeasures Definition

- Step 6 – Do: Countermeasures Implementation
- Step 7 – Check: Results Monitoring
- Step 8 – Act: Standardise and Share Success

Some of these steps will be aggregated to explain the case study better.

Problem Background and Breakdown (Steps 1–2, Plan)

As stated above, the starting point of this study was the quite low level of ORE, which could be improved through changes in the current situation. The value of the ORE was around 50% overall across all the operating rooms. After an evaluation of the goodness of this indicator, it was noted that it includes many aspects and variables, so there was the risk that the results of the projects were not documented. The medical and surgical time, which cannot be analysed and controlled in-depth, strongly influences this wide indicator. Considering the little knowledge in the medical field from the people involved in the project, it was decided to go more in-depth in investigating a particular phase of the process. The part investigated was between the end of an intervention and the start of another one, that is not strongly linked to the medical part of the operation. This period is defined as the changeover time, and it was noted that the time used was too much.

Then, due to the scarce expertise in the organisation in conducting improvement projects, it has been decided to focus only on one room that could be used as a pilot project preparatory for further improvements. The Orthopaedic room was considered as the one to start for the pilot project. Specifically, after data analysis using the hospital's information systems, it was possible to evaluate the changeover time for this room. Historically, it was 27.46 min with a standard deviation of 11.86 min. After a Gemba walk in the operating block, there was clear room for improvement due to an unclear procedure and several lack in the definition of roles and responsibilities.

A process map was created to understand the process better and obtain a clearer overview of the whole process, as in Fig. 1.

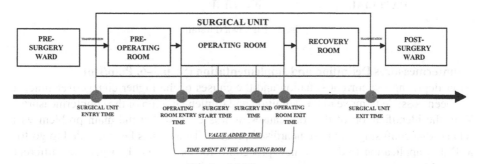

Fig. 1. AS-IS process

Target Setting (Step 3, Plan)

After all the analysis presented above, the hospital could identify a set of targets strongly related to the problem. As explained in the above section, the changeover time was the indicator to be monitored and improved, particularly in the Orthopaedic surgery room, which is considered the standard room to carry out the improvement project.

A decrease in the average changeover time was needed since by reducing this time, it is possible to save some precious minutes that could be employed in a valuable way. A reduction of 20%, going from 27.46 min to around 22 min, was set.

It was also important to reduce the standard deviation of the changeover time. This indicator also has a strong meaning since a low value tells us that the process is more reliable and repeatable. Here, the starting point was 11.86 min, and the target was 10.65, which is around a 10% reduction.

Root Causes Analysis (Step 4, Plan)

It has been decided to use the Ishikawa diagram to analyse the problem and identify the root causes. This tool has been used according to the original 4M (Men-Method-Machine-Material) classification. Several interviews and brainstorming with different stakeholders at all levels and direct observation have been conducted to obtain a clear and complete overview of the possible causes. Through its use, it has been possible to uncover several root causes directly linked to the problem under analysis, as represented in Fig. 2.

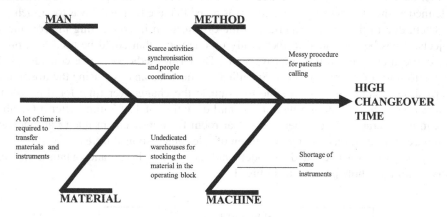

Fig. 2. Ishikawa diagram

Countermeasures Definition and Implementation (Step 5–6, Plan/Do)

After depicting the current situation and the causes of the higher changeover time, it has been possible to move to the definition and implementation of the countermeasures. With the identification of the root causes, it was evident that the main problem was related to a confusing and unstandardised process. Thus, it has been decided to go for a SMED application to define a new procedure for the change between two different surgical operations.

The new procedure has been developed, validated by all the medical staff, and approved by the hospital's management team. This double validation was needed to satisfy both the management of the hospital and the staff working on the operating room. In fact, on the one hand, the management wanted a simple, effective, and easily implementable procedure that could rapidly be understood and applied by all the actors involved in the changeover operations. On the other hand, medical validation was needed to know if the new procedure was feasible: a check was made on the constraints of timing and competencies of the activities. After this phase, the final procedure was developed and was ready to be implemented as in Fig. 3. The most relevant changes that impacted the changeover time have been some parallelisation of activities and anticipation of some others (e.g., the second patient preparation was done in parallel with the changeover time, thus leading to a longer operating room occupation in case of any delay or issue).

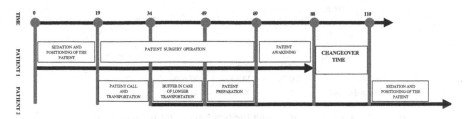

Fig. 3. New changeover procedure

Once the new procedure was developed, all the medical staff of the Orthopaedic surgery room (doctor, nurses, anesthetists) were informed and trained about the new procedure to get acknowledgement from them and minimise the risk of resistance to change.

Results Monitoring (Step 7, Check)

Two ways of monitoring were done simultaneously to be both time consistent and efficient in the analysis, focusing more in-depth on two aspects. A first check was done through direct observation in the operating block to verify if the procedure was understood and applied. A second check was on the time results, which were monitored with the data stored in the IT system of the hospitals, to understand if the performance was improved in terms of time.

The decision was to analyse the data four weeks after the implementation to have all the necessary data to spot problems and propose improvements to cope with them. Also, four weeks of analysis were considered sufficient for a reliable overview of the project's progress. The outcome of this phase will be presented accurately in the results section.

Standardise and Share Success (Step 8, Act)

After the four-week monitoring phase, a closing meeting was held to recap the improvements and formalise what was done. Thanks to this, it has been possible for the organisation to share with the management the success of the process and discuss the results, highlighting pitfalls and possible improvements that could be made, especially for the possible extension of this pilot project.

4 Results

Regarding the results, after the four-week monitoring phase, it has been possible to observe the weekly performance of the average changeover time and its standard deviation. The weekly fluctuation in terms of changeover time and its standard deviation is depicted in Figs. 4 and 5.

Weekly Performance (%)

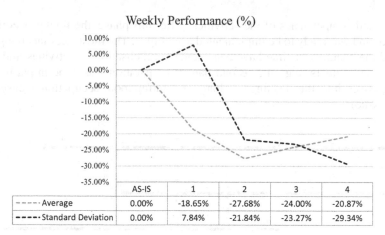

	AS-IS	1	2	3	4
- - - - Average	0.00%	-18.65%	-27.68%	-24.00%	-20.87%
- - - - Standard Deviation	0.00%	7.84%	-21.84%	-23.27%	-29.34%

Fig. 4. Weekly performance after the new procedure implementation (%)

Weekly Performance (minutes)

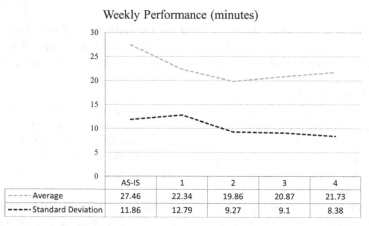

	AS-IS	1	2	3	4
- - - - Average	27.46	22.34	19.86	20.87	21.73
- - - - Standard Deviation	11.86	12.79	9.27	9.1	8.38

Fig. 5. Weekly performance after the new procedure implementation (minutes)

From the figures, it is possible to notice that the targets were achieved for all the weeks apart from the first one due to the newness of the countermeasure, which also worsened the standard deviation. Thanks to the intensive training and some corrective actions, it was then possible to reach the targets as shown in the figures. At first glance, it could seem that the improvement is of slight importance, but the effect of these upgrades must be considered from a larger perspective.

Considering the several changeovers during the day and the possible extension to the other operating rooms of this pilot project, this will lead not only to a mere improvement the changeover time. In fact, by taking as a reference a full day, when the operating time is around 8 h, a saving of about 8 min in a single changeover time could result in about 60 min saved, so the time needed for one more surgery. An improvement that could be even higher if extended to the whole set of operating rooms: in this way, it will be possible to enhance the daily surgery capacity of the operating block significantly, especially if combined with a change in the surgery planning logic.

Furthermore, other possible side effects of this project are a much more standardised way of working and a defined procedure, thus leading to less stressful working conditions for the doctors and nurses. Considering all these factors, it is possible to state that the new process certainly has higher reliability and stability.

5 Discussion

This case study shows a successful use of the SMED methodology in the healthcare sector. After the pilot project has finished, it was possible to highlight how the problem was solved, and the performance have improved significantly compared to the limited area of the project. It is also important to underline how using a Lean tool (SMED) driven by another Lean thinking tool (A3 template) was fundamental to address the problem, solve the issues and implement the right countermeasures to enhance the organisation's performance. Some possible hidden pitfalls and troubles were avoided thanks to the robust methodologies employed, and some examples are presented in the following lines.

The structured way in which the project has been carried out, i.e., using the A3 template, was fundamental to correctly spot the area to focus on and address the problem in a robust way. Furthermore, it has been fundamental to identifying the boundaries of the problem and setting the right targets to address it. Also, in a more advanced phase of the project, using tools such as the Ishikawa and the impact effort matrix, it has been possible to highlight the only causes causing the problem and link them with the possible countermeasures.

After seeing the results, it is necessary to stress the importance of a structured and prolonged monitoring phase characteristic of any project using the A3 template. During this step, the results are, at first glance, evaluated. The following are compared to the expected results. In case of any significant fluctuation or difference with the targets, corrective actions are deployed to improve performance in the following periods.

Also, if some possible hidden issues are discovered in the monitoring phase (e.g., in this case, potential interferences among medical staff or nurses), something in the countermeasures can be adapted, which could lead to a slight reduction in the performance.

Furthermore, this phase is fundamental to highlight all the possible failures, pitfalls and corrective actions that could be deployed in the following periods (i.e., after the monitoring) to sustain the change, thus preventing a worsening of the performance. This is particularly important in pilot projects such as the one under analysis, which with a high probability will be extended to similar but different operating rooms in the same organisation. Thus, these actions could be replied to and easily adapted to slightly identical situations.

6 Conclusions and Limitations

Firstly, knowing all these things, this paper confirms the results and adds further knowledge to the article dealing with the same topic, using Lean in healthcare to improve operating room changeover time [1, 7, 11]. This paper stressed the importance of using a standardised method (A3 template) to introduce Lean in environments where it was scarcely applied. By using this method, it is possible to successfully introduce Lean and its tools in a simple and replicable way. Through the use of this template, thanks to its robust structure, it is possible to set the basement for further improvement projects and could be used to address other improvement projects across the organisation.

Thus, this paper could be helpful for all the firms, managers, stakeholders, and practitioners working in the healthcare field who would like to improve their operational performance successfully using Lean methodologies. It could be useful also to other stakeholders not belonging to the healthcare sector who would like to see a unique way to redesign the SMED methodology (i.e., applying SMED in sectors where Lean is less applied). Lastly, this paper will enrich the existing literature dealing with the topics of Lean Management in the Healthcare sector, bringing a successful case study in which the implementation of the Lean techniques is addressed through the use of the A3 methodology.

This paper also has some limitations that need to be remarked on and explained here. The first limitation is related to the methodology chosen; being this a single case study, the results are difficult to generalise and can be influenced by the environment and the embedded characteristics of the organisation under analysis. Different effects can be expected in other organisations with different levels of Lean culture. This could have influenced the results of the project both in the negative (e.g., higher resistance compared to other organisations) and positive way (e.g., the increased commitment of some actors due to the innovativeness of the project); thus, is difficult to predict and extend the results in other similar organisations. Then, even if the monitoring has been done for four weeks, a long-term vision (e.g., one year or more) is missing. With the presence of a long-term perspective, it will be possible to also analyse the potential issues that arise in the long-term as well as how the Lean culture and methodologies can help in addressing them.

Thus, for future research, it will be interesting to proceed, for instance, by extending the size of analysis to other organisations, having a different Lean maturity grade or analysing the same topics from a long-term perspective, also using different methodologies.

References

1. Amati, M., et al.: Reducing changeover time between surgeries through lean thinking: an action research project. Front. Med. **9** (2022). https://doi.org/10.3389/fmed.2022.822964
2. Bharsakade, R.S., Acharya, P., Ganapathy, L., Tiwari, M.K.: A lean approach to healthcare management using multi criteria decision making. Opsearch **58**(3), 610–635 (2021). https://doi.org/10.1007/s12597-020-00490-5
3. Costa, F., Kassem, B., Staudacher, A.P.: Lean office in a manufacturing company. In: Powell, D.J., Alfnes, E., Holmemo, M.D.Q., Reke, E. (eds.) Learning in the Digital Era. IFIP Advances in Information and Communication Technology, pp. 351–356. Springer, Cham (2021). https://doi.org/10.1007/978-3-030-92934-3_36
4. Costa, F., Kassem, B., Portioli-Staudacher, A.: Lean thinking application in the healthcare sector. In: Powell, D.J., Alfnes, E., Holmemo, M.D.Q., Reke, E. (eds.) Learning in the Digital

Era. IFIP Advances in Information and Communication Technology, pp. 357–364. Springer, Cham (2021). https://doi.org/10.1007/978-3-030-92934-3_37

5. Curatolo, N., Lamouri, S., Huet, J.C., Rieutord, A.: A critical analysis of Lean approach structuring in hospitals. Bus. Process Manag. J. **20**(3), 433–454 (2014)
6. D'Andreamatteo, A., Iannia, L., Lega, F., Sargiacomo, M.: Lean in healthcare: a comprehensive review. Health Policy **119**(9), 1197–1209 (2015)
7. Guercini, J., et al.: Application of SMED methodology for the improvement of operations in operating theatres. The case of the Azienda Ospedaliera Universitaria Senese. Mecosan **24**(98), 83–203 (2016). https://doi.org/10.3280/mesa2016-098005
8. Henrique, D.B., Godinho Filho, M.: A systematic literature review of empirical research in Lean and Six Sigma in healthcare. Total Qual. Manag. Bus. Excell. **31**(3–4), 429–449 (2020)
9. Henrique, D.B., Filho, M.G., Marodin, G., Jabbour, A.B.L.D.S., Chiappetta Jabbour, C.J.: A framework to assess sustaining continuous improvement in lean healthcare. Int. J. Prod. Res. **59**(10), 2885–2904 (2020)
10. Holweg, M.: The genealogy of lean production. J. Oper. Manag. **25**(2), 420–437 (2007). https://doi.org/10.1016/j.jom.2006.04.001
11. Sales-Coll, M., de Castro, R., Hueto-Madrid, J.A.: Improving operating room efficiency using lean management tools. Prod. Plan. Control 1–14 (2021). https://doi.org/10.1080/09537287. 2021.1998932
12. Matos, I.A., Alves, A.C., Tereso, A.P.: Lean principles in an operating room environment: an action research study. J. Health Manag. **18**(2), 239–2577 (2016)
13. Portioli-Staudacher, A.: Lean healthcare. An experience in Italy. In: Koch, T. (ed.) APMS 2006. ITIFIP, vol. 257, pp. 485–492. Springer, Boston, MA (2008). https://doi.org/10.1007/978-0-387-77249-3_50
14. Rosa, A., Marolla, G., Lega, F., et al.: Lean adoption in hospitals: the role of contextual factors and introduction strategy. BMC Health Serv. Res. **21**, 889 (2021). https://doi.org/10.1186/s12913-021-06885-4
15. Rosa, C., Silva, F.J.G., Ferreira, L.P., Campilho, R.D.S.G.: SMED methodology: the reduction of setup times for Steel Wire-Rope assembly lines in the automotive industry. Procedia Manuf. **13**, 1034–1042 (2017)
16. Shah, R., Ward, P.T.: Lean manufacturing: context, practice bundles, and performance. J. Oper. Manag. **21**(2), 129–149 (2003)
17. Sunder, M.V., Mahalingam, S., Krishna, M.S.N.: Improving patients' satisfaction in a mobile hospital using Lean Six Sigma – a design-thinking intervention. Prod. Plan. Control **31**(6), 512–526 (2020)
18. Torri, M., Kundu, K., Frecassetti, S., Rossini, M.: Implementation of Lean in IT SME company: an Italian case. Int. J. Lean Six Sigma (2021)
19. Welsh, I., Lyons, C.M.: Evidence-based care and the case for intuition and tacit knowledge in clinical assessment and decision making in mental health nursing practice: an empirical contribution to the debate. J. Psychiatr. Ment. Health Nurs. **8**(4), 299–305 (2001)
20. Yin, R.K.: Case Study Research and Applications: Design and Methods, 6th edn. Sage, Los Angeles (2018)

Lean and Six Sigma Philosophies in Portuguese Laboratories

Andreia Craveiro[1], Vanda Lima[1], José Carlos Sá[2(✉)], Miguel Lopes[1],
Gilberto Santos[3], and José Dinis-Carvalho[4]

[1] CIICESI, ESTG, Instituto Politécnico do Porto, Rua do Curral, 4610-156 Felgueiras, Portugal
{8170003,vlima,aml}@estg.ipp.pt

[2] INEGI, ISEP, Instituto Politécnico do Porto, Rua Dr. António Bernardino de Almeida,
4249-015 Porto, Portugal
cvs@isep.ipp.pt

[3] Design School, Polytechnic Institute Cavado Ave, Vila Frescaínha S. Martinho, 4750-810
Barcelos, Portugal
gsantos@ipca.pt

[4] Production and Systems Department, School of Engineering, University of Minho, Campus de
Azurém, 4800-058 Guimarães, Portugal
dinis@dps.uminho.pt

Abstract. Increased consumer demand as well as increased competition, has led
organizations to need continuous improvement. The Lean and Six Sigma philosophies, widely applied in industry, have shown important results in terms of process
improvement, which has attracted the attention of many organisations, including
services.

This research aims to characterize the degree of knowledge and implementation of Lean and/or Six Sigma philosophies in Portuguese laboratories. Data
collection was carried out using a questionnaire applied to a population of laboratories, including clinical, testing and calibration laboratories, as well as accredited
and non-accredited laboratories. The results show that most laboratories are not
familiar with Lean and/or Six Sigma philosophies. Furthermore, it is noted that the
laboratories that have implemented these philosophies are those with the highest
number of employees and turnover.

Keywords: Lean · Six sigma · Lean six sigma · Portuguese laboratories

1 Introduction

With an increasingly globalized market, companies see as imperative the need to implement a culture of continuous improvement in order to cope with the constant volatility of
the market. In this context, Lean and Six Sigma philosophies, widely applied in industry,
have been adopted by services, given the positive results observed in organizations in
terms of process improvement [1–4].

The laboratory sector has also felt this competitive pressure from the market, and it
is urgent to maintain processes with a high level of flexibility and value creation [5].

© IFIP International Federation for Information Processing 2023
Published by Springer Nature Switzerland AG 2023
O. McDermott et al. (Eds.): ELEC 2022, IFIP AICT 668, pp. 82–92, 2023.
https://doi.org/10.1007/978-3-031-25741-4_9

More and more laboratories are faced with superior challenges associated with increased workload and cost reduction, and therefore there is a need to increase efficiency and quality levels [6].

This research aims to characterize the degree of knowledge and implementation of Lean and/or Six Sigma philosophies in Portuguese laboratories.

To accomplish this goal, a quantitative research methodology was used, with primary data collection through an online questionnaire addressed to Portuguese laboratories.

2   Literature Review

2.1   Lean Thinking

The foundations for Lean thinking can be attributed to Henry Ford (1913) for his implementation of a process flow that translated into low-cost mass production associated with employee involvement [7]. However, it was only in the 1950s, after the Second World War, that the Toyota Production System emerged in Japan, developed by Taiichi Ohno, on which the current principles associated with Lean thinking are based. The Toyota Production System focuses on waste reduction, thus working with the cost variable and leading to improved production efficiency and value creation for the customer. The Lean concept appeared only in the late 80's put forward by researchers from MIT - Massachusetts Institute of Technology. The worldwide divulgation arose from Womack, Jones & Roos in the first edition of in 1991 of their book "The machine that changed the world" [3, 4, 8, 9].

"Lean is the term used to describe a management philosophy and set of principles for the continuous improvement of any production process, focusing on eliminating waste and creating a better product from the customer's point of view" [7].

Lean Thinking is based on five fundamental principles [3, 4, 7, 8]:

1. Identify value - identify what value means from the customer's point of view in order to create value that is perceived by the customer as such;
2. Map the value chain - identify the sequence of actions and processes that enable value to be created for the customer;
3. Create a flow - promote a continuous flow of value-generating activities, ensuring that everything that does not add value to the process is eliminated
4. Establish Pull - producing only what is needed, when it is needed and in the quantity needed; production should be "pulled" by the customer, eliminating stocks
5. Seek continuous improvement - continuously seek improvement (kaizen) in the processes, in order to reduce costs, deadlines, errors, spaces and create new forms of value.

The goal of Lean thinking is the transformation of waste into value from the customer's perspective, where waste is something that does not add value to the final product or service and for which the customer is not willing to pay [3, 9, 10].

For the implementation of the Lean philosophy several tools can be used [3, 4, 11–15], among which we highlight: Value Stream Mapping, 5S, Visual management, Standardized work, Single Minute Exchange of Dies (SMED), Poka-Yoke, One piece flow production, Production balancing, Pull system, Kanban, Heijunka, Mizusumashi, Jidoka, Spaghetti diagram, Gemba (shop floor), Total productive maintenance (TPM), Organization of people in work cells, A3 Problem Solving and Kaizen (continuous improve- ment).

2.2 Six Sigma

The Six Sigma philosophy emerged in the 1980s at Motorola, with the objective of reducing the variation associated with the processes. Based on the work developed in Japanese companies, the creation and implementation of the first Six Sigma improvement program was promoted. Motorola achieved a significant increase in profits by reducing costs and process variation. Later, in the 1990s, General Electric, also reported impressive gains and savings after implementing several Six Sigma projects. The success of these companies led to increased global interest in this philosophy [1, 16].

Six Sigma is defined by General Electric as a "highly disciplined process that leads to the development and delivery of near-perfect products and services". The main tenet of Six Sigma is to be able to measure how many defects exist in a process, systematically figure out how to eliminate them, and get as close to zero defects as possible. To achieve Six Sigma Quality a process should produce no more than 3.4 defects per one million opportunities [16].

Six Sigma relates the variation in a process to customer requirements and a defect is any value that does not meet the customer's specifications [17]. According to the literature, the results obtained with the application of this philosophy in terms of defect reduction and process improvements are well known [18].

The Six Sigma philosophy is supported by a methodology, which is based on five phases: DMAIC- an acronym for Define, Measure, Analyze, Improve and Control - and focuses on existing processes to improve their performance [1, 17, 19].

In the process of implementing the Six Sigma philosophy, various quality techniques and tools are used, namely [12–14, 20–25]: Process capability analysis, Critical to Qual- ity tree (CtQ), Brainstorming, Deployment diagram, Gantt diagram, Failure Mode and Effects Analysis (FMEA), Six Sigma metrics, Project charter, House of Quality, Sigma- metrics method decision chart, Suppliers, Input, Process, Output, Custumers (SIPOC), Statistical Process Control (SPC), and Measurement Systems Analysis (MSA).

3   Method

A quantitative research methodology was used, based on a survey research strategy, and using an original, pre-tested, validated online questionnaire as a data collection instrument [26]. The online questionnaire was disseminated to Portuguese laboratories. Data collection was carried out through the Google Forms platform during October and November 2019.

The population consisted of 695 laboratories, including accredited/certified and non-accredited/certified clinical, testing, and calibration laboratories. A response rate of 15% was achieved, and the final sample comprised 106 laboratories. According to [26] in survey methodology studies the response rate tends to be around 10 to 20%.

The questionnaire design considered several aspects to ensure the consistency of responses, such as: the characteristics of the respondents, the structure of the questionnaire, the type, scales and number of questions, among others [26]. In order to avoid invalid questionnaires, facilitate data analysis and increase the objectivity of the answers, we chose to formulate mostly closed-ended and mandatory questions [27], using five-point Likert-type scales [28].

In the following sections descriptive and inferential analyses of the data are presented.

3.1 Population and Sample

In this section, the population and the sample are described.

Of the 695 laboratories included in the population, 9 (1%) are accredited clinical laboratories, 343 (50%) are accredited testing laboratories, 58 (8%) are accredited.

calibration laboratories, 120 (17%) are certified laboratories, and 165 (24%) are not ac- credited or certified laboratories (see Fig. 1).

Regarding the sample, 1 (1%) is an accredited clinical laboratory, 67 (63%) are accredited testing laboratories, 8 (8%) are accredited calibration laboratories, 15(14%) are certified laboratories, and 15 (14%) are not accredited or certified laboratories (see Fig. 1). As can be seen, the sample represents the population in an appropriate way.

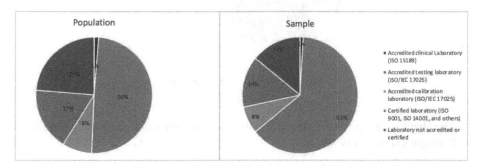

Fig. 1. Population and sample by laboratory type

Regarding the size of the laboratories (Table 1), there's a higher representation of laboratories with less than 30 employees (77%). Laboratories with 31 to 50 employees and with 51 to 100 employees represent (18%) of the sample (9% each category). Only 5% (5) are large-sized laboratories (more than 100 employees).

Table 1. Laboratories by size

Number of employees	N	%
101 to 250	5	5%
51 to 100	10	9%
31 to 50	10	9%
11 to 30	26	25%
1 to 10	55	52%
Total	**106**	**100%**

According to Fig. 2, the large majority of the laboratories in the sample (76%) have a turnover of up to €1 million. Only 2% of the laboratories have a turnover of more than €10 million.

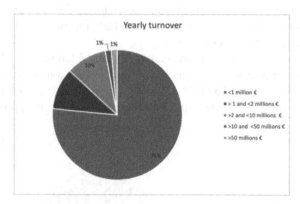

Fig. 2. Laboratories by turnover

The characterization of the sample allows us to conclude that it adequately represents the Portuguese laboratory sector.

4   Results

In this section the results obtained through the questionnaire are reported.

The questionnaire allowed us to understand if the laboratories were aware of and had applied the Lean and Six Sigma philosophies (see Fig. 3). Regarding the level of knowledge of Lean Thinking, 52% (55) of the laboratories were unaware of this philosophy. Similarly, it can also be seen that most laboratories are not familiar with Six Sigma (56%; 59 laboratories).

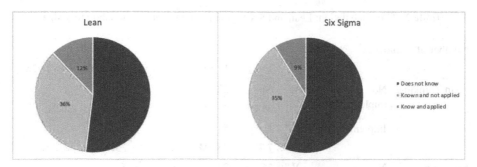

Fig. 3. Level of knowledge of the lean and six sigma philosophies

Taking into consideration the types of laboratories, it is the clinical and testing laboratories that have a higher level of unawareness of the two philosophies. On the other hand, calibration laboratories have the highest levels of knowledge.

The questionnaire allowed us to understand the reasons for not implementing Lean and/or Six Sigma philosophies. The main reasons pointed out were: (1) satisfaction with the management and quality systems already implemented in the laboratories; (2) lack of human resources; and (3) financial unavailability.

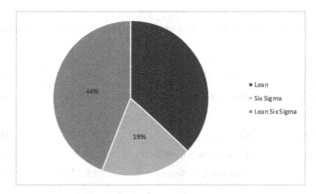

Fig. 4. Level of application of the Lean and/or Six Sigma philosophies

Of the 106 laboratories in the sample, only 16 have implemented at least one of the philosophies. Figure 4 shows that 37% (6) have implemented Lean Thinking, 19% (3) Six Sigma, and 44% (7) both philosophies (Lean Six Sigma).

The analysis by type of laboratory, allows us to see that the vast majority of laboratories 69% (11) are testing laboratories. It is also verified that 94% (15) of the laboratories that have at least one of the philosophies implemented are accredited and/or certified laboratories.

In order to understand if the implementation of Lean and Six Sigma philosophies are associated with the size and the turnover of the laboratories, we proceeded to a cross tabulation analysis.

Table 2. Cross tabulation: Lean and Six Sigma implementation and laboratory size

Number of employees				1 to 10	11 to 30	31 to 50	51 to 100	101 to 250
Lean Thinking	No implementation		N.º	54	22	9	6	2
			%	58.1%	23.7%	9.7%	6.5%	2.2%
	Implementation		N.º	1	5	1	3	3
			%	7.7%	38.5%	7.7%	23.1%	23.1%
Six Sigma	No implementation		N.º	55	23	8	7	3
			%	57.3%	24.0%	8.3%	7.3%	3.1%
	Implementation		N.º	0	4	2	2	2
			%	0.0%	40.0%	20.0%	20.0%	20.0%

Table 2 shows that the larger laboratories tend to be the ones that have implemented Lean and Six Sigma philosophies. This conclusion is corroborated by the chi-square tests and their symmetry measures, which reveal that there is a moderate and statistically significant association between the variables analyzed (see Table 3).

Table 3. Chi-Square tests and symmetric measures: Lean and Six Sigma implementation and laboratory size

Variables	Tests and measures	Value	Significance
Lean Thinking	Pearson Chi-Square	20.909[a]	< 0.002[b]
*			
Number of employees	Cramer's V	0.444	< 0.002[b]
	Contingency Coefficient	0.406	< 0.002[b]
Six Sigma	Pearson Chi-Square	15.141[a]	< 0.13[b]
*			
Number of employees	Cramer's V	0.378	< 0.013[b]
	Contingency Coefficient	0.354	< 0.013[b]

[a]5 cells (50.0%) have expected count less than 5.
[b]Monte Carlo significance: Based on 10000 sampled tables

Concerning the association between the implementation of Lean and Six Sigma philosophies and the turnover of the laboratories, it is also found that the larger ones tend to implement more these philosophies, especially regarding Lean Thinking (see Table 4).

Table 4. Cross tabulation: Lean and Six Sigma implementation and laboratory turnover

Turnover

			<1 M€	>1 to < 2 M€	>2 to < 10 M€	>10 to < 50 M€	50 M€
Lean Thinking	No implementation	N.º	49	5	4	0	0
		%	84.5%	8.6%	6.9%	0.0%	0.0%
	Implementation	N.º	3	2	3	1	1
		%	30.0%	20.0%	30.0%	10.0%	10.0%
Six Sigma	No implementation	N.º	50	5	4	1	1
		%	82.0%	8.2%	6.6%	1.6%	1.6%
	Implementation	N.º	2	2	3	0	0
		%	28.6%	28.6%	42.9%	0.0%	0.0%

Table 5 shows that there is a moderate and statistically significant association between the implementation of Lean and Six Sigma philosophies and turnover.

Table 5. Chi-Square tests and symmetric measures: Lean and Six Sigma implementation and laboratory turnover

Variables	Tests and measures	Value	Significance
Lean Thinking	*Pearson Chi-Square*	20.406[a]	<0.001[b]
*			
Turnover	Cramer's V	0.548	<0.001[b]
	Contingency Coefficient	0.480	<0.001[b]
Six Sigma	*Pearson Chi-Square*	13.141[a]	<0.019[b]
*			
Turnover	Cramer's V	0.440	<0.019[b]
	Contingency Coefficient	0.402	<0.019[b]

[a]6 cells (60.0%) have expected count less than 5.
[b]Monte Carlo significance: Based on 10000 sampled tables

5   Conclusion

Like what happens in the corporate environment, where these philosophies were primarily developed in large industrial companies, this study also found that in the laboratory environment, it was the laboratories with the largest size and turnover that implemented these philosophies. Of the 16 laboratories that implemented Lean e/or Six Sigma, only one did not belong to a larger corporate structure, and 76% had a turnover greater than 1 million Euros, quite different from the total sample where 76% of the laboratories had a turnover less than 1 million Euros. It should also be realized that, in the case of the number of employees, the laboratories that have implemented at least one of the philosophies have a larger number of employees, on average, almost double those that have not.

Since the Portuguese business environment is essentially characterized by micro, small, and medium-sized companies, which, despite playing an important role in the development of the country's economy, sometimes face some limitations inherent to the lack of resources, a more traditional management, and a lower degree of development, which may affect the need for initial investment in training, time, and human resources inherent to the implementation of Lean and/or Six Sigma philosophies.

From the data analysis it was found that the biggest limitations to the implementation of both philosophies were the lack of human resources, financial unavailability, and satisfaction with existing management and quality systems, which is in line with the already known characteristics of the Portuguese business environment. Also, the fact that only 14% of the laboratories in the sample are not accredited and/or certified may explain the satisfaction of most laboratories with the management and quality systems already implemented, and not moving towards Lean and/or Six Sigma philosophies.

This study contributes to increase the knowledge of Lean and Six Sigma philosophies at laboratory level. Research in Portugal has been focused on the application of Lean and Six Sigma philosophies in companies. The studies in laboratories are limited and usually address case studies. Therefore, this study contributes to an exhaustive diagnosis of the situation in Portugal, allowing the identification of opportunities for improvement in the sector.

This study also contributed to the construction of an original questionnaire that can be directly applied or adapted in future work within the scope of Lean and Six Sigma philosophies.

The main limitation of the study is related to the sample size. Although the response rate is acceptable [26], a larger sample size would have allowed for more robust statistical analyses.

In the future, it is suggested to use the questionnaire developed in this study in a larger sample of laboratories. It is also suggested that interviews be carried out in Portuguese laboratories with implemented Lean and/or Six Sigma philosophies, in order to understand the implementation approach, advantages and disadvantages, benefits and difficulties.

Research Funding. The work of the author Vanda Lima is supported by national funds, through the FCT— Portuguese Foundation for Science and Technology under the project UIDB/04728/2020.

References

1. Andersson, R., Eriksson, H., Torstensson, H.: Similarities and differences between TQM, six sigma and lean. TQM Mag. **18**(3), 282–296 (2006)
2. Dave, D.K., Murugesh, R., Devadasan, S.R.: Origin, principles and applications of lean six sigma concept: extractions from literature arena. Int. J. Serv. Oper. Manag. **22**(2), 123 (2015)
3. Neto, D.A.C., de Faria, A.C., da Silva, Í.B.: Utilizando o pensamento enxuto em um laboratório de controle biológico. Rev. Eletrônica Gestão e Serviços **6**(1), 1150–1169 (2015)
4. Oliveira, P.M.F.: Simulação Didática em Lean Thinking. Universidade de Aveiro (2013)
5. Berlitz, F.D.A.: Critical analysis of processes redesign experience in a clinical laboratory. J. Bras. Patol. e Med. Lab. **47**(3), 257–269 (2011)
6. Gras, J.M., Philippe, M.: Application of the six sigma concept in clinical laboratories: a review. Clin. Chem. Lab. Med. **45**(6), 789–796 (2007)
7. Collins, J., Wiersma, K.: Lean production principles can apply in the laboratory. Clin. Forensic Toxicol. News 1–8 (September 2008)
8. Womack, J., Jones, D.: Lean Thinking: Banish Waste and Create Wealth in Your Corporation. Free Press, New York (1996)
9. Womack, J., Jones, D., Roos, D.: The Machine That Changed the World: The Story of Lean Production–Toyota's Secret Weapon in the Global Car Wars That Is Now Revolutionizing World Industry. Free Press, New York (2007)
10. Halwachs-Baumann, G.: Concepts for lean laboratory organization. J. Med. Biochem. **29**, 330–338 (2010)
11. Liker, J.K., Meier, D.: The Toyota Way Fieldbook: A Practical Guide for Implementing Toyota's 4P's. The McGraw-Hill Companies, Inc., New York (2006)
12. Tague, N.R.: The Quality Toolbox, Second. ASQ Quality Press, Milwaukee (2005)
13. Sá, J.C., et al.: A model of integration ISO 9001 with Lean Six Sigma and main benefits achieved. Total Qual. Manag. Bus. Excell. **33**(2), 218–242 (2022)
14. Pereira, A.M.H., Silva, M.R., Domingues, M.A.G., Sá, J.C.: Lean Six Sigma approach to improve the production process in the mould industry: a case study. Qual. Innov. Prosper. **23**(3), 103–121 (2019)
15. Vaz, S., Morgado, L., Lima, V.: ISO9001 e Lean: Proposta de Modelo de Integração. Rev. TMQ - Tech. Methodol. Qual. **8**, 125–138 (2017)
16. Klefsjo, B., Bergquist, B., Edgeman, R.L.: Six sigma and total quality management: different day, same soup? Int. J. Six Sigma Compet. Adv. **2**(2), 162 (2006)
17. Winters-Miner, L.A., et al.: Root cause analysis, six sigma, and overall quality control and lean concepts. In: Practical Predictive Analytics and Decisioning Systems for Medicine, Elsevier Inc., pp. 143–164 (2015)
18. Elder, B.L.: Six sigma in the microbiology laboratory. Clin. Microbiol. Newsl. **30**(19), 143–147 (2008)
19. Silva, R.: Seis Sigma na Avaliação Externa da Qualidade em Laboratórios Clínicos. Universidade Nova de Lisboa (2013)
20. Bauer, J.E., Duffy, G.L., Westcott, R.: The Quality Improvement Handbook, Second. ASQ Quality Press, Milwaukee (2006)
21. George, M.L.: Lean Six Sigma for Service: How to Use Lean Speed and Six Sigma Quality to Improve Services and Transactions. McGraw-Hill Companies, Inc., New York (2003)
22. Westcott, R.T., Duffy, G.L.: The Certified Quality Improvement Associate Handbook, Third. ASQ Quality Press, Milwaukee (2014)
23. Westgard, S., Bayat, H., Westgard, J.O.: Analytical sigma metrics: a review of six sigma implementation tools for medical laboratories. Biochem. Med. **28**(2), 1–12 (2018)

24. Ferreira, C., Sá, J.C., Ferreira, L.P., Lopes, M.P., Pereira, T., Silva, F.J.G.: Lean DMAIC - a methodology for implementing the lean tools. Procedia Manuf. **41**, 1095–1102 (2019)
25. Fonseca, L., Leite, D., Lima, V.: Six Sigma methodologies: implementation and impacts on Portuguese small and medium companies (SMEs). Int. J. Qual. Res. **8**(4), 583–594 (2014)
26. Saunders, M., Lewis, P., Thornhill, A.: Research Methods for Business Students. Fifth edit. Pearson Education Limited, London (2009)
27. De Marconi, M.A., Lakatos, E.M.: Fundamentos de metodologia científica, 5ª edição. Editora Atlas SA, São Paulo (2003)
28. Passmore, C., Dobbie, A.E., Parchman, M., Tysinger, J.: Guidelines for constructing a survey. Fam. Med. **34**(4), 281–286 (2002)

Lean 4.0

Lean as a Facilitator for AGVs Implementation: A Case Study

Stefano Frecassetti(✉) ⓘ, Matteo Ferrazzi ⓘ, and Alberto Portioli-Staudacher ⓘ

Politecnico di Milano, Department of Management, Economics and Industrial Engineering, Milano, Italy
stefano.frecassetti@polimi.it

Abstract. The attention toward integrating Lean and Industry 4.0 (I4.0) has increased in the last few years. Nevertheless, the focus was mainly on how I4.0 can support Lean Management practices and how Lean tools can be digitalised through I4.0 technologies. Some authors have pointed out the need for further research on how Lean Management can support and benefit the introduction of Industry 4.0 technologies in firms. In particular, some authors supposed that Lean has a facilitating effect towards I4.0 implementations. This work aims to enrich the existing knowledge, stressing the support Lean Management can give to implementing I4.0 technologies. This article shows, through a case study conducted using the A3 framework, how Lean has been applied to reorganise a warehouse to facilitate the implementation of Automated Guided Vehicles (AGVs), showing the benefits of this approach.

Keywords: Lean · A3 · Warehouse Management · AGV · Digitalisation

1 Introduction

At the beginning of this century, digital technologies were widely introduced, on a global scale, substantially changing how companies behave. This was particularly true in the last decade when the evolution of technologies had become continuous and unstoppable, forcing companies to adapt to this rapidly changing environment. On the one hand, this helped businesses to survive and, on the other, to improve their performance. In fact, thanks to the development of Industry 4.0 (I4.0) and the introduction of digital technologies related to it on the shop floor, the presence of digital technologies in the industrial and manufacturing fields has risen. Another strong push for this change has resulted from the outbreak of Covid-19. This has encouraged firms to move in the digital direction.

To support this change, several scholars and practitioners have started studying how to implement these new technologies to exploit their capabilities successfully [7]. In particular, many "mature" managerial theories have been used to drive the firms' digitalisation. The outcome of this research has shown, in many cases, a double-sided synergetic effect, meaning that these theories can benefit companies' digital transformation but also that digital technologies can renew and enhance even more the benefits brought by these managerial theories [1, 6, 9].

O. McDermott et al. (Eds.): ELEC 2022, IFIP AICT 668, pp. 95–107, 2023.
https://doi.org/10.1007/978-3-031-25741-4_10

2 Literature Review

This synergetic effect is seen when digital technologies are integrated with Operational Excellence theories, especially with Lean Management [2]. Not an insignificant number of papers have been published in the past few years studying the integration of Lean with digital technologies and I4.0 [13, 17]. Several researchers have started studying how the practices of Lean Management impact different domains such as sustainability [12], digitalisation [5, 11], and the introduction of new technologies as the ones belonging to the Industry 4.0 paradigm [13, 17]. However, according to a study by Buer *et al.* [1], a great focus has been given to how the I4.0 and digitalisation phenomena support the application of Lean, particularly digitalising its tools. They also underlined the need for further research on how Lean Thinking can support the introduction of new and digital technologies in firms. In fact, even if some papers highlighted the issues that arise in the case of automation and the digitalisation of inefficient processes [3, 8], there is still much work to be done. This was also confirmed by Núñez-Merino *et al.* [9], where the highlighted research gap is related to how Lean principles can facilitate the introduction of I4.0 technologies.

It is evident that there is a strong need to address this gap in academia and the industry. Thus, this research will seek to add knowledge on this topic by answering the following research question:

"How can a Lean approach facilitate the introduction of Industry 4.0 technologies?"

This paper aims to contribute by adding knowledge on how Lean Management can help firms drive digital transformation and how a Lean environment is fundamental to implementing I4.0 technologies. This article is based on a single case study on a continuous improvement project carried out in a warehouse with the aim of improving its performance before the implementation of the two autonomous vehicles.

3 The Company

The company under analysis is a multinational company, a leader in the sector of inks and pigment production for various applications. This firm has always been characterised by a strong push for innovation from the customer side (i.e., adding several interesting and innovative features to their product, e.g., security features to fight fake products). This was also true from an internal perspective, where investments in innovative and digital technologies are regularly carried out to keep up with their operations. Among the several production plants established around the world, one situated in Italy started some years after the introduction of the Lean Management philosophy in their plants to improve operational performance. Thanks to the outstanding results obtained in previously conducted continuous improvement projects, the company has, this year, decided to start with another Lean implementation project. This project is mainly focused on warehouse management. In fact, within six months, the company will implement two new AGVs in the warehouse as part of its transition plan to an environment compliant with I4.0 technologies. This project was agreed upon to get a more streamlined environment before the AGV implementation solved some issues the company faced. The main Italian plant in which this case study is carried out is divided into two sites: A and B. Site A has more than 100 employees coping with more than 10,000 codes for raw materials and finished products.

In contrast, site B is the production plant responsible for realising some special products, with more than 150 employees dealing with more than 5,000 different codes. The focus of this case study is the on-site A warehouse. This is the most consequential warehouse in the plant since around 40% of the stocked products are delivered from there, and it is here that the AGV will be implemented soon.

4 Methodology

This case study is based on the A3 problem-solving tool [14], which has successfully driven continuous improvement projects in several firms, as demonstrated by several cases in the current literature [4, 10, 16]. A3 framework is also recognised as one of the most effective tools within the Lean philosophy [15]. The firm has decided to follow this model's steps throughout all the projects to identify issues, wastage and inefficiencies within their processes. This resulted in an effective and efficient problem resolution through the PDCA (Plan – Do – Check - Act) cycle. This structure will be followed in subsequent lines, and the eight sections of the A3 will be presented as subsections of the P-D-C-A.

4.1 Plan

In this section, all the actions belonging to the Plan part of the A3 model related to this project will be thoroughly described.

Problem Background
This continuous improvement project was mainly triggered by the need of the company to align its operations to a radical change in its warehouse, namely the upcoming implementation of two new AGV vehicles in the main warehouse. This deployment will bring substantial environmental changes, creating various opportunities and benefits, such as working cost reduction, improved productivity and retrieval time. Still, conversely, it was clear to the company that the current warehouse management was not optimal and ready for such a big change.

Starting from this pending structural change and analysing, at the same time, the dynamic and uncertain environment in which the firm operates, such as the Covid-19 pandemic and an expected increase in sales volumes by 10%, it was important to investigate the current situation of the warehouse. After some brief analysis, it was clear that there were some relevant issues regarding high space saturation and low operators' productivity, defined as the number of volumes in kilograms each operator can handle in a working day. The second problem was considered a consequence of bad management and will be solved by fixing the first one and then by introducing the AGVs.

Thus, tackling the first problem, related to high space saturation, the company reports a saturation of 91%, exceeding the threshold set at the corporate level. From this arose the need to reorganise and optimise the space within the warehouse by increasing the total number of pallet load (PL) positions while simultaneously facilitating the introduction of the new vehicles. Because of this, the project's first step was defined by the need to understand the source of complexity resulting from the warehouse layout, PL storage and lack of data. Therefore, several Gemba walks were conducted in the warehouse area to understand better how space and activities are organised.

Problem Breakdown

To have a clear understanding of the warehouse structure's criticalities and delve into the problem of space saturation, performing several Gemba walks turned out to be crucial for the firm, for the company was immediately clear that there were many issues in the current situation that needed to be fixed as soon as possible. Firstly, the distribution of the locations was not homogeneous, as the racks structures were not the same for all of them: in some aisles, the racks were engineered for storing three pallet loads per bay, while in others, only 2; then, some aisles have additional shelves to store other pallet loads while some others had not. Clearly, this situation was not good for implementing complex technology such as AGVs.

After other Gemba walks and deeper analysis, the firm could point out that other relevant issues were present relating to the codification of racks and data management: for instance, in a specific aisle, three columns were identified using the same code. Up until this point, this issue had not seemed to be a problem since the operator was only spending more time choosing the pallet to retrieve. Still, this would be a problem with AGVs implementation when they cannot behave like the operators. Furthermore, the presence of non-standard pallets, pallets of bigger size, had been detected in the racks, which can stock three pallet loads per bay, leading to the loss of one pallet placed for each non-standard pallet stored. This situation was causing trouble in inventory management; in fact, after comparing the data from the Gemba walks with those extrapolated from the firm information systems, a discrepancy between the two was highlighted. A low saturation was depicted by the information system (i.e., a higher number of free places available when they were actually occupied). This problem was relevant because when analysing data, the saturation appears wrongly. From the perspective of AGV implementation, the data coming from the systems must represent the environment faithfully.

Moreover, several structural constraints were found, such as the presence of the physical columns within the racks or in the middle of the aisles, which prevents the forklift from reaching the locations with the consequent loss of available pallet places. This forces the intervention of an operator, who must necessarily insert or move by hand, the goods stored on the ground-floor level to make maximum use of the space. This results in a major concern, particularly given AGV implementation, as the operator will no longer be able to enter the storage area, and products can be placed only on pallets. Lastly, several products which have been identified were then categorised as obsolete, thus considered as non-value-added items within the warehouse. These volumes reveal a problem for warehouse saturation, as they take away space from other products mostly requested by customers, which can represent a fruitful source of profit for the company.

After this phase, the company also decided to analyse the impact of the reduction of available pallet loads placed after the AGVs introduction. In fact, due to some embedded constraints of these vehicles, and if the current warehouse layout remains the same, certain aspects of the workspace need to be changed, thus reducing the available space. The outcome of the analysis showed a new condition with a saturation higher of almost one percentage point (i.e., 15 pallet loads places lost).

Thus, it was clear to the company that improving the current condition was absolutely necessary and needed to be done before implementing the new technology. This is especially true considering all of these problems were blocking the possibility of using different warehouse management policies, such as class-based storage (currently, the company is working with randomised storage, products are put in the first place available). Class-based storage could be optimal in this particular situation where some products are very often used, especially if compared to others. Furthermore, this bad management of the warehouse caused very low productivity of operators, which cannot be accepted with the AGVs because there will be the risk of not finalising the assigned mission. Since the AGV is more technologically advanced, it is more productive and precise but, at the same time, more rigid so mismanagement could lead to a decline in performance.

In this light, the company decided to rapidly proceed with the resolution of the issues, which impacted the saturation of the warehouse and was estimated as in the following Table 1:

Table 1. How current problems impact warehouse space

Problem	Impact on the total number of pallet locations
Unstandardised racks structure	6.20%
Physical columns and service room in the aisles	2.40%
The stock of obsolete products	7.13%
Unstandardised pallet loads	0.63%
The discrepancy between the Information System and the actual situation	1.35%

Target Setting

Concerning the target setting, the main objective is to lower the space saturation of the warehouse, both in the short-term and long-term view. The Key Performance Indicator (KPI) used to measure space saturation is calculated as follows:

$$Space\ Saturation = \frac{\#\ Occupied\ Pallet\ Locations}{Total\ \#\ of\ Available\ Pallet\ Locations\ in\ the\ Ware\ house}$$

Since the current performance resulted in a 91% space saturation, which exceeds the threshold set by the company, which is about 80%, the main idea is to work on both the numerator and the denominator, thus reducing the occupied locations and increasing the nominal value of the total places available in the warehouse, reaching the desired saturation as the target set by the firm within the implementation of the AGVs. This will also allow the company to change the storage and management policies, leading to the easier implementation of AGVs characterised by fewer problems and higher performance.

Root Cause Analysis

After the target definition, the root cause analysis was performed to investigate the causes of high space saturation further. The first tool used was the Ishikawa Diagram, which provided a general understanding and summary of the causes related to the problem. In contrast, a customised version of the FMEA was subsequently used to analyse that which influenced causes in terms of impact, visibility and importance, given AGV implementation. This allowed a study of those causes which have a greater overall impact on the identified high space saturation problem.

The outcome from the Ishikawa Diagram provided an overview of all factors impacting the space saturation of the warehouse. The traditional 5M categories were shaped and adapted to understand the problem under analysis better. In particular, the 5M were reshaped into three categories: Layout, Method and Information System. The main causes under these categories were:

- *Layout* – Structural ergonomics issues (columns in the middle of some aisles, old fire-fighting system, presence of a service room in the warehouse) and non- standardised rack structure
- *Method* – Reception of non-standardised pallet loads and stock of obsolete products
- *Information System* – Discrepancy between the information systems with the actually occupied pallet locations.

Taking into consideration the causes depicted in the Ishikawa Diagram, through a customised FMEA framework, it was possible to identify the overall impact of the causes related to high warehouse saturation. In particular, the parameters used to evaluate the effects of a cause were:

- *Severity:* An equivalent value is assigned according to the importance of the impact on space saturation. In particular, the severity determines the percentage of pallet locations lost for each cause concerning the total available warehouse locations.
- *Visibility:* also interpreted as detectability, this factor is evaluated based on how easy it is to identify the cause of the problem. More precisely, it can be seen through the Gemba walk that the value assigned is low; conversely is high if data analysis is required.
- *Importance in view of AGV implementation:* an assessment based on how relevant the problem will be when if not solved when the AGV will be implemented.

Following this analysis, each problem was evaluated according to the three parameters, and a Problem Priority Number (PPN) was computed as the product of the three factors (the higher the PPN, the higher the impact of the problem). In Table 2, it is possible to see the outcome of the FMEA with the most relevant causes.

Table 2. Amended FMEA for root causes' effect evaluation

Item and Function	Failure Mode	Effects	Severity (1–10)	Visibility (1–10)	AGV Importance (1–10)	Problem Priority Number (PPN)
Racks structure	Non-standardised dimensions	Loss of pallet locations	8	4	3	96
Structural ergonomics	Columns and service rooms in the middle of some aisle	Loss of pallet locations	5	1	3	15
Stocked products	Obsolete products	Loss of pallet locations	9	8	7	504
Reception of pallet loads	Non-standardised pallet dimensions	Loss of pallet locations	5	2	10	100
Information System data	The discrepancy with the actual data	Loss of pallet locations	2	6	7	84

Countermeasures Definition

Starting from the causes identified, five main countermeasures have been developed. For each of these, the impact and effort required for implementing fixes have been analysed to give the right prioritisation to the various solutions. To estimate the improvement (i.e., the impact), the FMEA has also been used in this case through the computation of a Countermeasures Priority Number (CPN). The CPN is the product of the three parameters mentioned above, but this time the impact of the problem was calculated considering its relevance with the implemented countermeasures. Then the PPN reduction is computed as the delta (PPN minus the CPN) has been calculated. Taking the highest delta value and holding it as the common denominator, the percentage of improvement of all other problems is calculated by classifying as low those values between 0–15%, medium those values between 16–49% and finally, high those values upwards from 50%. On the other hand, the effort has been qualitatively computed according to the time, costs and difficulty of implementation.

In Table 3, is it possible to see how the FMEA was used. The parameters used for evaluation are to be considered with respect to the future situation where the counter-measures will be fully implemented. At the same time, the proposed actions correspond to the problems having the same line in Table 2 (e.g., Line 1 problem – racks structure corresponds to Line 1 proposed action – change of racks).

Table 3. Amended FMEA for countermeasures' impact evaluation

Proposed Actions	New Severity (1–10)	New Visibility (1–10)	New AGV Importance (1–10)	Countermeasure Priority Number (CPN)	Delta – PPN Reduction
Racks change	1	1	1	1	95
External service room	2	1	2	4	9
Elimination of obsolete products + systematic and recurrent control on their level	4	4	7	112	392
Agreements with external suppliers	1	1	1	1	99
Periodical Gemba walks and comparison Information System data with shopfloor one	2	5	7	70	14

Afterwards, an economic evaluation of the costs and benefits was carried out to understand whether the money expenditures were worthwhile.

It is also important to say that the company studied two other countermeasures: the reallocation of the products according to a sort of class-based storage and the implementation of the AGV. These two have not been considered in the FMEA since their implementation was already agreed upon. Still, it is important to consider these since this project has been carried out in the light of AGV implementation. The results will estimate the overall impact after the full implementation. In particular, the new storage policy is developed through the Lean Warehousing approach using a crossed ABC-XYZ analysis to understand the optimal position for each product. A digital dynamic model has been preventively developed using a spreadsheet built to work in harmony with the company information system.

4.2 Do

The Do section only includes the part of the implementation of the countermeasure. In this case, the countermeasures are strictly related to warehouse structural and management changes; they will be physically done in the following months and mainly at the end of the year, simultaneously with the AGV implementation. The company board decided this due to convenience and functionality (i.e., in this period, the production department will operate at a reduced pace, and end-of-the-year inventories will be computed).

Countermeasures Implementation

The relevant company stakeholders have decided to implement all the countermeasures proposed. In spite of this, several factors influenced the application of the reported improvement planning. In particular, major structural and organisational changes are planned in view of the AGV implementation. Therefore, the countermeasure implementation was postponed until the project's conclusion was reached.

Nevertheless, following the method described above, a prioritisation order for the countermeasures has been developed; thus, Table 4 shows how the final order of countermeasures has been obtained.

Table 4. Countermeasures prioritisation

Problem	PPN	Countermeasure	CPN	Delta Improvement	Impact	Effort	Priority
Non-standardised racks structure	96	Racks change	1	95	Medium	High	2
Physical columns and service room in the aisles	15	External service room	4	9	Low	High	3
The stock of obsolete products	504	Obsolete elimination + recurrent check	112	392	High	Low	1
Nonstandardised pallet loads	100	Supplier agreement	1	99	Medium	Medium	2
The discrepancy between the Information System and the actual situation	84	Periodical Gemba walks and comparison	70	14	Low	Medium	3

After implementing these countermeasures, products will be reallocated, and AGV will be implemented. Hence, a Gantt chart has been designed to have a clear overview of what and when has to be done to implement the solutions successfully.

In the end, is it possible to summarise what the company has done to solve the problems to introduce the AGV in the following Fig. 1, where the project and its interaction with Lean are easily represented schematically.

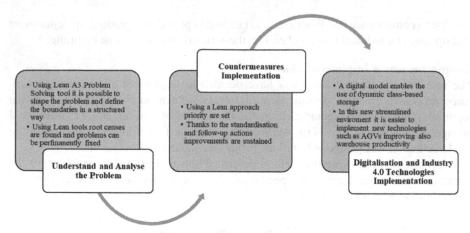

Fig. 1. Schematical representation of the approach used, and the benefits given by using a Lean approach

4.3 Check

The check phase is a very important step to understanding the success of the project through the measurement of the results and the comparison with the target. In this part, the expected results will be presented through a simulation of the expected environment after implementing the countermeasure.

Results Monitoring

Since the countermeasures will be implemented at the end of the year, there was a need to verify their effectiveness in another way. Therefore, a simulated estimation of the improvements in terms of space saturation has been done. Moreover, with all the countermeasures implemented (without AGVs and reallocation) and considering the KPI used for target definition, it has been registered as a positive impact. This impact is positive in the numerator, with a reduction of the occupied PLs location. The denominator will become bigger thanks to the increase in the nominal number of PL places in the warehouse. This will lead to an overall reduction of space saturation.

Overall, these improvements lead to a higher number of pallet locations available (127) and an expected decreased saturation level equal to around 14% points, thus meaning that the previously set target has been achieved. Also, from an economic perspective, the investments to be made to change the warehouse structurally were considered fair by the firm and the payback time corresponded to a few years.

After these implementations, the products will be reallocated according to a new storage policy, and the AGV will be done. This will allow the company also to improve productivity: a comparison has been made comparing the two storage policies (current policy vs the new policy developed through a Lean Warehousing approach), hypothesising the use of AGVs in both cases. An increase of more than 45% in productivity with respect to the current condition is expected after implementing both countermeasures, a new storage policy and AGVs. This will clearly lead to a significant decrease in retrieval time, stocking time and labour cost.

4.4 Act

This last phase is crucial for understanding if the project was successfully carried out and sharing its benefits. Moreover, possible improvements or extensions of the project are presented in this section.

Standardise and Share Success

This project has been recognised by the company's board as a very successful one and is fundamental for the proper AGV implementation in the warehouse. Thus, it will be considered a useful way to evaluate and introduce other potential technologies of I4.0. Furthermore, several learning points have been collected for the next implementation, future warehouse management, and further improvement projects.

Some of them are:

- Periodic Gemba Walks to check the alignment of the warehouse with the rules, policies and information systems.
- A systematic check of the product allocation according to the new storage model.
- Recurrent control of the possible obsolete products.

5   Conclusions

Even if the company was aware of the benefits of Lean projects conducted by the use of the A3 methodology, thanks to previous projects, this project corroborated the importance of systematic and recurrent use of the Lean approach. By using the A3, it is possible to tackle the issues constantly generated in every department by addressing the needed improvements. In this way, the companies can solve them and grasp the opportunities that new technologies can bring. In fact, thanks to this practical example, the company has confirmed the importance of applying Lean to their environment, especially when there is a need to introduce technologies related to I4.0.

From a broader perspective and to link the results with the current literature, this paper shows a successful and fruitful continuous improvement project aimed at introducing AGVs in a warehouse.

This work showcases an example of a company that understood the potential benefits of applying Lean before implementing digital technologies or I4.0. Thus it could be considered an example of how Lean supports I4.0. As shown in detail in the results section, the impact of the continuous improvement project is even greater when introducing new technologies. In fact, due to the rigidity embedded in automated vehicles, the current problems in the warehouse will be enhanced by their introduction. Thus, a Lean approach should be used in the environment where I4.0 technologies will be introduced. The implementation will be easier through a streamlined process using the right tools and methodologies, and the impact on firms' performance will be higher. On the other hand, this case shows that in a continuous improvement project, where Lean is correctly applied, the final introduction of I4.0 technologies boosts its results. Hence, it is possible to argue that the synergetic effect in this specific case study is bi- directional; Lean favours, in a tangible way, the introduction of I4.0 technologies, but the latter raises the effectiveness of the former.

In conclusion, Lean is a continuously evolving paradigm that is changing and adapting to different environments. Firms that want to embark on the digital journey must streamline their processes and start with a widespread introduction to the lean culture. By doing this, the effect brought by the innovation of I4.0 technologies will be even stronger, and the effectiveness of the Lean tools will be enhanced.

6 Implications, Limitations and Further Research

6.1 Implications

This paper showed the importance of spotting and addressing improvement points before implementing I4.0 technologies. In this sense, the A3 model is considered here as a tool that can be relevant for this purpose. Likewise, other Operational Excellence tools presented in this paper, such as FMEA and Ishikawa Diagram, are fundamental to analysing the current situation.

Thus, from a theoretical point of view, it is possible to state that this paper exhibits Lean's importance in the digital era. Few empirical studies have addressed how a Lean approach can facilitate the implementation of I4.0 technologies. From this study, Lean is considered an essential practice to be applied before I4.0, and furthermore, its facilitating effect has been showcased.

From a more practical viewpoint, the outcomes of this research could be useful for other firms or practitioners dealing with the same issues as a framework on how to proceed and which are the expected benefits of an improvement project like this one.

6.2 Limitations and Further Research

Even though this paper has added knowledge to the literature, and its outcome could be useful for other firms and practitioners, its main limitation lies in the methodology. In fact, the results of a single case study are hardly generalizable and extendable to other contexts or firms [16, 18]. Thus, the authors suggest taking this case study as a starting point for further research. This paper could be considered as a basis for further research using other methodologies; for instance, it could be extended by using a multiple-case study approach. Also, other methodologies could be employed (e.g., simulation) for having a quantitative estimation of the benefits obtained when Lean is implemented prior to digital or I4.0 technologies.

References

1. Buer, S.V., Strandhagen, J.O., Chan, F.T.S.: The link between industry 4.0 and lean manufacturing: mapping current research and establishing a research agenda. Int. J. Prod. Res. **56**(8), 2924–2940 (2018)
2. Costa, F., Portioli-Staudacher, A.: On the way of a factory 4.0: the lean role in a real company project. In: Rossi, M., Rossini, M., Terzi, S. (eds.) Proceedings of the 6th European Lean Educator Conference. ELEC 2019. LNNS, vol. 122, pp. 251–259. Springer, Cham (2020). https://doi.org/10.1007/978-3-030-41429-0_25

3. Kaspar, S., Schneider, M.: Lean Und Industrie 4.0 in Der Intralogistik: Effizienzsteigerung Durch Kombination Der BeidenAnsätze. Product. Manag. **20**(5), 17–20 (2015)
4. Kassem, B., Costa, F., Portioli-Staudacher, A.: JIT implementation in manufacturing: the case of Giacomini SPA. In: Rossi, M., Rossini, M., Terzi, S. (eds.) ELEC 2019. LNNS, vol. 122, pp. 273–281. Springer, Cham (2020). https://doi.org/10.1007/978-3-030-41429-0_27
5. Kassem, B., Staudacher, A.P.: Implementation of digital tools for lean manufacturing: an empirical analysis. In: Dolgui, A., Bernard, A., Lemoine, D., von Cieminski, G., Romero, D. (eds.) APMS 2021. IAICT, vol. 633, pp. 681–690. Springer, Cham (2021). https://doi.org/10. 1007/978-3-030-85910-7_72
6. Kolberg, D., Zühlke, D.: Lean automation enabled by industry 4.0 technologies. IFAC-PapersOnLine **48**(3), 1870–1875 (2015)
7. Liao, Y., Deschamps, F., Loures, E.D.F.R., Ramos, L.F.P.: Past, present and future of industry 4.0 - a systematic literature review and research agenda proposal. Int. J. Prod. Res. **55**(12), 3609–3629 (2017)
8. Nicoletti, B.: Lean and automate manufacturing and logistics. In: Prabhu, V., Taisch, M., Kiritsis, D. (eds.) APMS 2013. IAICT, vol. 415, pp. 278–285. Springer, Heidelberg (2013). https://doi.org/10.1007/978-3-642-41263-9_34
9. Núñez-Merino, M., Maqueira-Marín, J.M., Moyano-Fuentes, J., Martínez-Jurado, P.J.: Information and digital technologies of industry 4.0 and lean supply chain management: a systematic literature review. Int. J. Prod. Res. **58** (2020). https://doi.org/10.1080/00207543.2020. 1743896
10. Rossini, M., Audino, F., Costa, F., Cifone, F.D., Kundu, K., Portioli-Staudacher, A.: Extending lean frontiers: a kaizen case study in an Italian MTO manufacturing company. The Int. J. Adv. Manuf. Technol. **104**(5–8), 1869–1888 (2019). https://doi.org/10.1007/s00170-019-03990-x
11. Rossini, M., Cifone, F.D., Kassem, B., Costa, F., Portioli-Staudacher, A.: Being lean: how to shape digital transformation in the manufacturing sector. J. Manuf. Technol. Manag. **32**, 239–259 (2021). https://doi.org/10.1108/jmtm-12-2020-0467
12. Rossini, M., Portioli-Staudacher, A., Cifone, F.D., Costa, F., Esposito, F., Kassem, B.: Lean and sustainable continuous improvement: assessment of people potential contribution. In: Rossi, M., Rossini, M., Terzi, S. (eds.) Proceedings of the 6th European Lean Educator Conference. ELEC 2019. LNNS, vol. 122, pp 283–290. Springer, Cham (2020). https://doi. org/10.1007/978-3-030-41429-0_28
13. Rossini, M., Costa, F., Tortorella, G.L., Portioli-Staudacher, A.: The interrelation between industry 4.0 and lean production: an empirical study on European manufacturers. Int. J. Adv. Manuf. Technol. **102**(9–12), 3963–3976 (2019)
14. Sobek, D., Jimmerson, C.: A3 reports: tool for organizational transformation. In: 2006 IIE Annual Conference and Exhibition (2006)
15. Sobek, D.K.: Understanding A3 Thinking. CRC Press, Boca Raton (2008)
16. Torri, M., Kundu, K., Frecassetti, S., Rossini, M.: Implementation of lean in IT SME company: an Italian case. https://doi.org/10.1108/IJLSS-05-2020-0067
17. Tortorella, G.L., Fettermann, D.: Implementation of industry 4.0 and lean production in Brazilian manufacturing companies. Int. J. Prod. Res. **56**(8), 2975–2987 (2018). Author, F.: Contribution title. In: 9th International Proceedings on Proceedings, pp. 1–2. Publisher, Location (2010)
18. Yin, R.K.: Case Study Research and Applications: Design and Methods, 6th edn. Sage, Los Angeles (2018)

From Pain Points to Scale Points: Exploring Barriers to Lean Digital Transformation

Sagar Shinde[✉] [iD] and Kathryn Cormican[✉] [iD]

Enterprise Research Centre, School of Engineering, University of Galway, Galway, Ireland
s.shinde1@universityofgalway.ie

Abstract. Lean digital transformation (LDT) has gained momentum recently, with small and medium-sized enterprises (SMEs) eager to implement innovative digital solutions to enable scale and growth. However, LDT is not an easy endeavour and is fraught with challenges. Many organisations struggle to convert to a digitally-enabled business, finding it difficult to identify right-sized solutions that align with their needs or implement good management practices. This exploratory study aims to better understand the challenges and barriers to LDT in small and medium-sized enterprises. First, a comprehensive review of the extant literature was conducted to identify and classify these barriers. Second, empirical data was collected from key opinion leaders in the industry using structured interviews to capture real-world insights. Third, thematic analysis was conducted to isolate and categorise the constructs. These constructs then helped to design a survey which was circulated to relevant people in industry to elicit their opinions. The findings from this study add value to the SMEs by expanding the debate on lean digital transformation and will help organisations to identify barriers and levers toward more efficient business practices.

Keywords: Digital transformation · Lean · Strategy · People · Process · Technology · SMEs

1 Introduction

In the era of industry 4.0, small and medium enterprises (SMEs) are leaning towards the use of new technologies and digital products to increase optimisation, drive profits and grow. However, the move to a digitally enabled business leads to several challenges. For example, a lack of technology infrastructure [1, 2], a lack of relevant skills [3, 4] and complexity in integrating systems [5].

Kieviet [6] asserts that organisations must incorporate lean thinking into their operations to integrate digital technology effectively. LDT is based on lean concepts and business process improvement through the use of technology [7]. While lean enables organisations to achieve better customer value by reducing waste, lean digital focuses on maximising data usage and reducing digital waste. The aim is to achieve higher customer satisfaction and user engagement [5, 8]. Implementing lean digital transformation

O. McDermott et al. (Eds.): ELEC 2022, IFIP AICT 668, pp. 108–121, 2023.
https://doi.org/10.1007/978-3-031-25741-4_11

(LDT) as a mechanism to adopt digital tools effectively and efficiently is expected to give organisations a better chance of successful transformation towards efficiency.

Although LDT is lauded to benefit organisations, the process is complex. Not all projects are successful, and many organisations face challenges in implementing LDT initiatives [9]. Organisations, especially SMEs, find it difficult to implement digital solutions that help them to achieve customer value, operational efficiency and waste reduction [10]. Prior research suggests that SMEs face several barriers during their LDT. For example, Vogelsang et al. [1] conducted interviews with forty-six industry experts, which resulted in a list of common barriers in LDT, the greatest of which was a lack of relevant skills. According to Buvat et al. [11], more than 60% of companies lack the digital competencies to transform successfully into a digitally enabled organisation. In addition to technological barriers, Stentoft et al. [12] identified people and processes as major barriers. These categories strongly resonate with manufacturing SMEs, where the rate of adoption and LDT initiatives is slow [13]. In addition, cybersecurity threats and organisational processes are the foremost barriers related to LDT projects [13, 14]. Thus, previous analysis reveals that while there are many factors that impede LDT, they mainly comprise people, processes and technology-related issues.

Researchers are calling for a deeper analysis of this domain [15, 16]. A better understanding of these challenges can help design and take effective steps that address LDT challenges, thus improving SMEs' ability to transform to lean digital. Therefore, this research aims to better understand and classify SMEs' barriers in their journey toward lean digital transformation. The results are important as they provide a deeper understanding of the barriers to transformation and bring valuable insights from the real world to address critical challenges and offer practical suggestions for SMEs.

2 Literature Review

It is evident that three key constructs affect the LDT journey: people, process and technology-related issues. While these categories are by no means exhaustive or indeed mutually exclusive, they are factors that must be addressed as challenges and barriers to enabling LDT and deserve further scrutiny. The following sections synthesise the current literature relating to these factors.

2.1 People-Related Barriers

LDT projects centre around people. For example, Ashrafian et al. [7] emphasise that transformation always starts with senior business leaders agreeing on the LDT projects' goals. However, these goals are often poorly communicated within an organisation [5, 17]. In contrast, Verina and Titko [4] point out that an organisation can sometimes have a clear goal, but other 'people' factors are involved, for example, unmotivated employees who are not engaged in the process [18]. Other studies have identified the lack of relevant skills as a key challenge in LDT, which can lead to increased resistance to implementing modern technology [2, 3, 7, 15]. The summary of the studies mentioning people- related barriers is shown in Table 1.

Table 1. Overview of people-related barriers

Authors	Poor Leadership	Lack of Employee Motivation	Lack of skills
Kutnjak [17]	X		
Verina and Titko [4]		X	X
Erol et al. [18]		X	
Ashrafian et al. [7]	X		X
Karre et al. [19]	X	X	

2.2 Process-Related Barriers

LDT is considered a socio-technical phenomenon where people drive change by creating new processes [20, 21]. New technological introductions result in redefining business processes and operational structures [5]. However, prior research suggests that it is difficult to redefine processes. For example, Lichtenthaler [22] highlights that organisations often design processes around technology instead of customer behaviour. It leads to fragmented processes impeding LDT. To address this, Brozzi [23] points out that lean implementation requires an experienced expert to improve the flow of an organisation's processes, and consequently, the cost of hiring a professional in this domain can be a barrier for SMEs. In addition, small enterprises adopting technological transformation expose themselves to stiff competition from more prominent institutions using advanced technology. This results in a significant challenge to out-compete large organisations due to poor resource allocation [1]. Other studies suggest that inaccurate and disconnected utilisation of data leads to poor data collection and fragmented processes within and between the organisation, which is another key barrier to LDT [5, 20, 23, 24]. The summary of the studies discussing process-related barriers is shown in Table 2.

Table 2. Overview of process-related barriers

Authors	Poor integration of organisations process	Poor resource allocation	Poor data collection
Zezulka et al. [21]	X	X	
Romero et al. [5]	X		X
Lichtenthaler [22]	X		
Brozzi et al. [23]		X	X
Vogelsang et al. [1]	X	X	
Chan [24]		X	X

2.3 Technology-Related Barriers

Chan [24] asserts that technology transformations require an effective system that embraces large amounts of data. However, the lack of digital infrastructure in some SMEs required for managing and storing these large amounts of data hampers technological transformation. To implement new technologies organisations therefore require a roadmap for migrating from traditional technologies to modern technologies [25]. According to Borovkov et al. [2], organisations that are overly dependent on their old technologies, which have minimal automation of processes, are likely to find it very difficult to transform effectively towards digital as the latter relies on advancing and changing modern technologies. In addition, Julião and Gaspar [26] argue that traditional technologies can result in security breaches of confidential information. Furthermore, research suggests that old technologies cannot be relied on in a competitive market where advanced firms use modern technology [22, 24]. Thus, an organisation that does not-invest and upgrade existing technologies faces many challenges in their lean digital transformation journey [2, 18, 26, 27]. The summary of studies mentioning technology-related barriers is shown in Table 3.

Table 3. Overview of technology-related barriers

Authors	Lack of technology infrastructure	Lack of cybersecurity	Dependencies on legacy systems
Chan [24]	X		
Julião and Gaspar [26]		X	X
Borovkov et al. [2]			X
Weber & Studer [27]		X	X

3 Research Methods

This exploratory study aims to uncover emerging real-world challenges in lean digital transformation projects. This section begins by presenting a description of the research process used in the research.

3.1 The Research Process

Figure 1 presents an overview of the research process, followed by a description of the four stages of the research project.

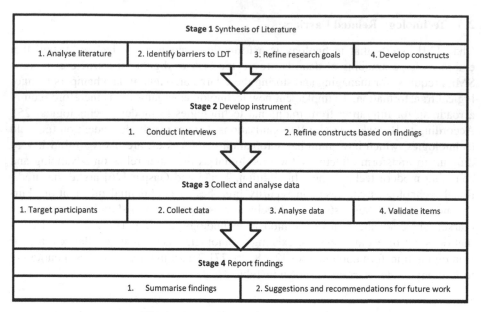

Fig. 1. Overview of the research process

3.2 Stage 1. Synthesis of the Literature

The first stage comprised a synthesis of the literature, which involved exploring prior work focusing on the barriers to LDT. The most relevant barriers to the implementation of lean digital projects were identified from the literature and classified into people, process and technology, forming the basis for the initial conceptual framework.

3.3 Stage 2. Develop Instrument

The second stage in the study involved developing an instrument to capture empirical data for this research. This involved conducting interviews with relevant industry experts who were associated with LDT projects. Five interviews were conducted to gain practitioners' insight into barriers to LDT implementation. The interview texts were transcribed using Nvivo. The study used a three-phase coding system advocated by Strauss and Corbin [28]. First, open coding was used to understand and identify key items. The second phase involved axial coding, where similar themes were grouped to form a higher category. The third phase involved linking categories and similar themes and removing irrelevant data to highlight relationships between items. The final themes were then used to develop the questionnaire in the following step. The details of the interviewees are shown in Table 5 (Table 4).

3.4 Stage 3. Collect and Analyse Data

The third stage involved the collection and analysis of empirical data. This step consisted of a questionnaire designed to measure relevant variables [29]. The questionnaire

Table 4. Profile of interviewees

Interviewee ID	Role	Company-size	Industry sector
INT1	Senior Leadership	Large	Industrial Automation
INT2	Senior Executive	Medium-sized	Electronics
INT3	Director	Medium-sized	Engineering
INT4	CEO	Small	Technology
INT5	Partner	Small	Technology

focused on capturing critical information regarding organisational barriers to lean digital transformation. Survey items were derived based on the themes from the literature and analysis of the interviews in the previous step. Every item was carefully designed (and refined through an iterative process) to measure specific elements of each parent factor in regard to LDT challenges [30, 31]. These factors comprised people- related barriers, process-related barriers, and technology-related barriers. Last, the survey was pre- tested with four industry professionals. Based on their feedback, ambiguous questions were amended. The survey was then pilot tested with a sample size of eight relevant industry people to test the structure and the coherence of the questions. Finally, the survey was distributed to 165 professionals through emails, LinkedIn contacts, industry networks and in-person events of which 58 responded.

The final stage involved the quantitative analysis of the data collected from the surveys. Pareto analysis was conducted using python (matplotlib and seaborn to visualise) to summarise the results into sections and subsections [32]. Pareto Analysis is used to identify the principle barriers to LDT. To perform this analysis, a bar chart was made of two main variables: the x-axis (barrier factors) and y-axis (count). The x-axis is used for plotting the different categories into which the data was broken down into (people, process and technology). The y-axis shows the number of the count for each specific category. The bars are ordered from the highest frequency to the lowest frequency, starting from left to right. Following the previous step, a line graph is used to depict the cumulative percentage of the total count number. Following the logic of the Pareto analysis, the analysis reveals that 80% of the challenges are due to 20% of the factors (x axis).

3.5 Stage 4. Report Findings

The last stage of the research design is to summarise and discuss findings, suggesting areas for future work and research limitations. The following section will present this fourth stage.

4 Findings and Discussion

This research and analysis suggest that people, processes, and technology are the key barriers to lean digital transformation. This section details participants' characteristics, identifies barriers and details how each barrier affects digital transformation based on the survey results.

4.1   Participant Characteristics

The survey targeted experienced professionals in Ireland. Of the 58 survey respondents, 79.3% were male, while 20.7% were female. Regarding age, 37.9% of respondents were between 31–40 years of age, 31% were between 21–30, 27.6% were between 41–50, and 3.4% were above 51 years of age. Regarding working experience, 43.1% of participants had worked for more than five years, 24.1% had been working for less than five years, and 32.8% had worked for more than ten years. In terms of their organisations, more than half of the respondents claimed their organisations were still at the start of their transformational journey (36.2%), while 36.2% said they were in the middle in comparison, 19% of respondents stated that their organisation had yet started the transformative process, while 8.6% stated they were already at the final stage of the transformation. The overview of the participant characteristics is shown in Table 5.

Table 5. Characteristics of research participants

Characteristics	Frequency	Percentage	Characteristics	Frequency	Percentage
Age (years old)			*Highest education*		
21–30	18	31.0%	Bachelors	29	50%
31–40	22	37.9%	Masters	27	46.6%
41–50	16	27.6%	Others	2	3.4%
More than 50	2	3.4%			
Gender			*Role*		
Male	46	79.3%	Engineer	20	34.5%
Female	12	20.7%	Management	24	41.4%
			Consultant	14	24.1%
Working experience (years)					
Less than 5 years	14	24.1%			
More than 5 years	25	43.1%			
More than 10 years	19	32.8%			
Total	58	100%		58	100%

4.2   Overview of Barriers to Lean Digital Transformation

According to Fig. 2, the first two factors on the cumulative line contribute to 68% of barriers. Overall, 32.8% of respondents considered process-related barriers to be the most difficult challenges to address, followed by people-related barriers (30.5%) and technology-related barriers (27.6%). These findings suggest that most respondents acknowledged the significance of having appropriate systems and infrastructure that support lean digital transformation. Meanwhile, 9.2% of respondents suggested that there are other barriers such as fear of the unknown and lack of experts than the three mentioned above. The following subsections explore each type of barrier in more detail.

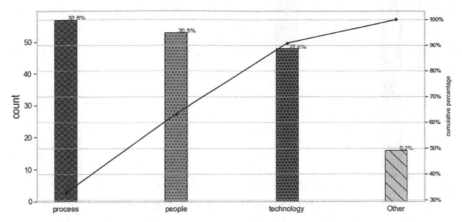

Fig. 2. Overview of barriers to lean digital transformation

4.3   People-Related Barriers

In this section, as depicted by the cumulative line in Fig. 3 below, the first two factors contribute to 68% of barriers. The survey results show that 35% of respondents claimed the lack of relevant skills as the top barrier to lean digital transformation, followed by poor leadership (33.2%), the lack of employee motivation (24.5%), and others (8.8%). The lack of relevant skills would impede any transformation since employees do not know what they must do during such a process [24]. In addition, Kutnjak [17] and Romero et al. [5] argue that leaders often communicate LDT goals poorly to their subordinates, indicating poor leadership. This result suggests that leadership is crucial in the success of LDT because leaders determine how communication within their team works.

This result is complemented by interview data, where INT1 respondents stated that "digital transformation starts at the top. The management at the top is responsible for disseminating the company's transformation vision. The message is sometimes lost when it reaches ground employees, creating a challenge for management". When the leadership fails to communicate digital transformation and its importance to their subordinates, these subordinates may not have the necessary motivation to engage in the process, thus helping to explain why 24.5% of respondents regarded the lack of motivation as one of the key barriers that impede LDT. When they lack such motivation, it would be hard to expect them to be willing to develop relevant skills or adapt to new technologies. Participant INT4 stated that "knowing your existing employees' capability and training them is important. Firms often include experienced professionals in management teams who need to change to have an innovative approach to projects." Participants INT3 and

INT5 further confirmed this argument by pointing out potential knowledge gaps in the lean digital transformation process.

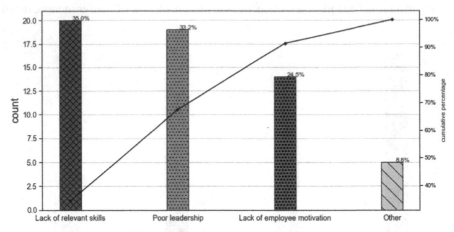

Fig. 3. Overview of people-related barriers

4.4 Process-Related Barriers

Regarding process-related barriers, depicted by the cumulative line in Fig. 4 below, the first two causes contribute to 75% of barriers. Overall, 45.5% of respondents argued that poor integration of their organisation's process is the main barrier to LDT initiatives. As Lichtenthaler [22] suggests, many organisations design their transformation procedure around technology rather than people, meaning they fail to integrate the process into their system. Meanwhile, 31.5% of respondents addressed poor resource allocation, and 22.8% regarded poor data collection as two key process-related barriers to LDT, while the remaining 1.8% identified other barrier forms such as unsure of the organisation process.

Brozzi et al. [23] suggest that organisations hire experienced professionals to help them implement their lean digital transformation initiatives. Without adequate experience, organisations will likely experience poor resource allocation and data collection. However, hiring qualified experts is expensive, which is why only organisations with a strong financial stature do so. That said, organisations are encouraged to focus on investing in the other two areas of people and technology. In this way, organisations can ensure they have the expected level of process that supports the LDT. The survey results also suggest that data collection and resource allocation are central to LDT. An adequate data collection capacity facilitates the transformation from manual data entry to an automated system. Meanwhile, an organisation's capacity to allocate its physical, material, and people resources determine how well it can embrace digital transformation initiatives. In this context, INT4 argued that start-ups have a better chance at embracing the transformation because "their flexibility leads to improved processes".

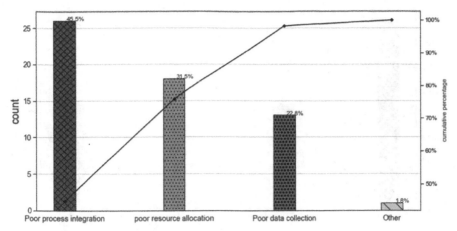

Fig. 4. Overview of process-related barriers

4.5 Technology-Related Barriers

In technology-related barriers, the first two causes contributed to 68% of barriers. Of respondents, 42.5% stated that the difficulty of moving from traditional systems towards automation impedes the implementation of lean digital transformation the most. Meanwhile, 23.4% of respondents chose a lack of IT infrastructure, 21.2% complained of the lack of security, and 14.9% identified other barrier forms such as lack of awareness of technology. Moving from manual practices to automated systems requires significant adjustments to how people do their day-to-day activities. For instance, they may no longer need to input data individually into the database. However, outdated and insufficient hardware and software may hamper such adjustments because no technology allows people to automate the system. Moreover, Borovkov et al. [2] claim that organisations that rely on old technologies would find it difficult to implement effective digital transformation. The interview data support the survey results with this. Participant INT5 also argued that "technology is the biggest factor for SMEs because organisations do not want to move from legacy systems".

Organisations need to consider building their people, processes, and technologies to succeed in adopting LDT initiatives. Moreover, these three development areas influence each other. For example, the lack of IT infrastructure may lead to the lack of qualified human resources since employees do not have adequate tools and facilities to develop their skills. Consequently, companies are incapable of delivering the required transformation process. An effective lean digital transformation requires organisations to build an adequate capacity in all those three areas to ensure they have the required infrastructure and resources for the process (Fig. 5).

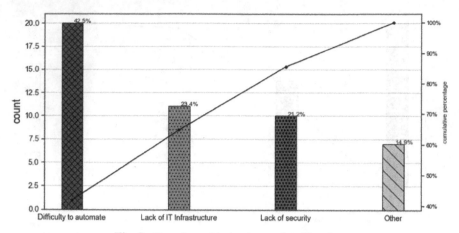

Fig. 5. Overview of technology-related barriers

5   Conclusions, Recommendations

In conclusion, the main challenges for LDT are related to people and processes, such as lack of skills, poor leadership, and poor integration of organisations' processes. Based on the findings from this study, the following recommendations are made for companies to develop their roadmap for LDT based on three steps.

5.1   People

Developing people and their skill sets can be achieved by training internal employees about lean concepts and digital transformation processes. Organisations can be encouraged to improve employee motivation and engagement internally by company experts or hire external experts to train and guide the teams through the entire process. The leadership team can enrol on courses related to lean digital transformation to familiarise themselves with the concepts.

5.2   Process

Organisations are encouraged to focus on assessing their current process gaps and start fixing those issues. For example, focussing on developing sustainable processes that can be easily integrated with other systems and online tools. In today's digital world, it is imperative to concentrate on generating, organising and analysing data. Hence, it is important to plan how data will flow through organisations' processes. There are several methods to remove challenges related to the process, such as fishbone analysis, root-cause analysis and creative thinking (design thinking) to develop innovative process designs.

5.3   Technology

Most respondents consider technology to be the easy part of the LDT journey. However, it depends from organisation to organisation and their planning to utilise different forms of technology. It is crucial to plan a roadmap for the organisation and pick technologies to help an organisation reach their goal. Sometimes, organisations choose old technologies due to cost factors, which can affect them negatively in the long term. In contrast, some organisations plan the roadmap and choose more expensive but advanced technologies at the start of their journey. This helps an organisation to pivot to other modern technologies if necessary. Organisations are encouraged to view technology infrastructure and cyber security as an investment.

6   Limitations and Future Research

The study's goal was to uncover insights into barriers to lean digital transformation in the specific context of SME organisations. Because of the importance placed on lived experiences of participants, a phenomenological approach was employed. The advantage of this method is its applicability to understanding social-technical systems, both from the qualitative and quantitative data generated. While this approach provides a broader spectrum for understanding the complex problem of a limited number of barriers regarding lean digital transformation, it is limited in the depth and generalisability of the results.

6.1   Research Limitations

This study examined complex social constructs by reducing them to several quantitative scale items. The scope of this study, limited to LDT and SMEs in Irish companies, therefore cannot take into account all possible antecedents and determinants of LDT adoption. Moreover, the findings indicate that SMEs do not approach people and process factors equally. Therefore, further in-depth analysis of each factor is required to understand how they impact SMEs and how they could overcome challenges and barriers while adopting LDT.

6.2   Future Research

Finally, the results of this study demonstrate a lack of relevant skills, poor integration of the organisation's process, and difficulty in moving to automation as top barriers to lean digital transformation by executives and senior management. It would be interesting and potentially quite valuable to further study people and process-related factors to understand the possible barriers to lean digital transformation philosophy. The results of this study offer a clear understanding of the barriers to lean digital transformation projects. Unfortunately, only employees from Ireland participated in the study. A multilevel analysis comprising various hierarchical samples with multinational companies might yield further intriguing results.

References

1. Vogelsang, K., Liere-Netheler, K., Packmohr, S., Hoppe, U.: Barriers to digital transformation in manufacturing: development of a research Agenda. In: Hawaii International Conference on System Sciences 2019 (HICSS-52) (2019). https://doi.org/10.24251/HICSS.2019.594

2. Borovkov, A., Rozhdestvenskiy, O., Pavlova, E., et al.: Key barriers of digital transformation of the high-technology manufacturing: an evaluation method. Sustain. Sci. Pract. Policy **13**, 11153 (2021). https://doi.org/10.3390/su132011153

3. Bakhtari, A.R., Kumar, V., Waris, M.M., et al.: Industry 4.0 implementation challenges in manufacturing industries: an interpretive structural modelling approach. Procedia Comput. Sci. **176**, 2384–2393 (2020). https://doi.org/10.1016/j.procs.2020.09.306

4. Verina, N., Titko, J.: Digital transformation: conceptual framework. In: Conference Contemporary Issues in Business (2019)

5. Romero, D., Flores, M., Herrera, M., Resendez, H.: Five management pillars for digital transformation integrating the lean thinking philosophy. In: 2019 IEEE International Conference on Engineering, Technology and Innovation (ICE/ITMC), pp. 1–8. ieeexplore.ieee.org (2019). https://doi-org.nuigalway.idm.oclc.org/, https://doi.org/10.1109/ICE.2019.8792650

6. Kieviet, A.: Lean Digital Transformation. Springer, Berlin, Heidelberg (2019). https://doi.org/10.1007/978-3-662-58517-7

7. Ameri, F., Stecke, K.E., von Cieminski, G., Kiritsis, D. (eds.): APMS 2019. IAICT, vol. 566. Springer, Cham (2019). https://doi.org/10.1007/978-3-030-30000-5

8. Angelopoulos, M., Kontakou, C., Pollalis, Y.: Digital transformation and lean management. Challenges in the energy industry of utilities. A review (2019)

9. Dossou, P.-E., Laouénan, G., Didier, J.-Y.: Development of a sustainable industry 4.0 approach for increasing the performance of SMEs. Processes **10**, 1092 (2022). https://doi.org/10.3390/pr10061092

10. Gupta, S., Sharma, M., Sunder, M.V.: Lean services: a systematic review. Int. J. Product. Perform. Manag. **65**, 1025–1056 (2016). https://doi.org/10.1108/IJPPM-02-2015-0032

11. Buvat, J., Solis, B., Crummenerl, C., et al.: The Digital Culture Challenge: Closing the Employee Leadership Gap (2017). Capgemini. https://www.capgemini.com/consulting. Retrieved 2020-02-32

12. Stentoft, J., Adsbøll Wickstrøm, K., Philipsen, K., Haug, A.: Drivers and barriers for Industry 4.0 readiness and practice: empirical evidence from small and medium-sized manufacturers. Prod. Plan. Control **32**, 811–828 (2021). https://doiorg.nuigalway.idm.oclc.org/. https://doi.org/10.1080/09537287.2020.1768318

13. Bailie, C.: Effectively harnessing data to navigate the new normal: overcoming the barriers of digital adoption. In: Offshore Technology Conference (2018). https://doi.org/10.4043/28699-MS

14. Lammers, T., Tomidei, L., Trianni, A.: Towards a novel framework of barriers and drivers for digital transformation in industrial supply chains. In: 2019 Portland International Conference on Management of Engineering and Technology, pp. 1–6 (PICMET). ieeexplore.ieee.org (2019). https://doi-org.nuigalway.idm.oclc.org/. https://doi.org/10.23919/PICMET.2019.8893875

15. Rossini, M., Dafne, C.F., Kassem, B., et al.: Being lean: how to shape digital transformation in the manufacturing sector. Int. J. Manuf. Technol. Manag. **32**, 239–259 (2021). https://doi.org/10.1108/JMTM-12-2020-0467

16. Ling, T.H., Shan, L.H.: Digital transformations and supply chain management: a Lean Six Sigma perspective. J. Asia Bus. Stud. **16**, 340–353 (2021). https://doi-org.nuigalway.idm.oclc.org/. https://doi.org/10.1108/JABS-10-2020-0415

17. Kutnjak, A.: Covid-19 accelerates digital transformation in industries: challenges, issues, barriers and problems in transformation. IEEE Access **9**, 79373–79388 (2021). https://doi-org.nuigalway.idm.oclc.org/. https://doi.org/10.1109/ACCESS.2021.3084801

18. Erol, S., Jäger, A., Hold, P., et al.: Tangible industry 4.0: a scenario-based approach to learning for the future of production. Procedia CIRP **54**, 13–18 (2016). https://doi.org/10.1016/j.procir.2016.03.162

19. Karre, H., Hammer, M., Kleindienst, M., Ramsauer, C.: Transition towards an industry 4.0 state of the LeanLab at Graz university of technology. Procedia Manuf. **9**, 206–213 (2017). https://doi.org/10.1016/j.promfg.2017.04.006

20. Dreyer, S., Olivotti, D., Lebek, B., Breitner, M.H.: Focusing the customer through smart services: a literature review. Electron. Mark. **29**, 55–78 (2019). https://doi.org/10.1007/s12 525-019-00328-z

21. Zezulka, F., Marcon, P., Vesely, I., Sajdl, O.: Industry 4.0–an introduction in the phenomenon. IFAC-PapersOnLine **49**(25) (2016). ISSNIP Biosignals Biorobotics Conf. https://doi.org/10.1016/j.ifacol.2016.12.002

22. Lichtenthaler, U.: Building blocks of successful digital transformation: complementing technology and market issues. Int. J. Innov. Technol. Manag. **17**, 2050004 (2020). https://doi.org/10.1142/S0219877020500042

23. Brozzi, R., D'Amico, R.D., Pasetti Monizza, G., Marcher, C., Riedl, M., Matt, D.: Design of self-assessment tools to measure industry 4.0 readiness. a methodological approach for craftsmanship SMEs. In: Chiabert, P., Bouras, A., Noël, F., Ríos, J. (eds.) PLM 2018. IAICT, vol. 540, pp. 566–578. Springer, Cham (2018). https://doi.org/10.1007/978-3-030-01614-2_52

24. Chan: Digital transformation in the era of big data and cloud computing. Int. J. Intell. Inf. Syst. (2020). https://doi.org/10.11648/j.ijiis.20200903.11

25. von Leipzig, T., Gamp, M., Manz, D., et al.: Initialising customer-orientated digital transformation in enterprises. Procedia Manuf. **8**, 517–524 (2017). https://doi.org/10.1016/j.promfg.2017.02.066

26. Julião, J., Calvete, G.M.: Lean thinking in service digital transformation. Int. J. Lean Six Sigma **12**, 784–799 (2021). https://doi.org/10.1108/ijlss-11-2020-0192

27. Weber, R.H., Studer, E.: Cybersecurity in the internet of things: legal aspects. Comput. Law Secur. Rev. **32**(5), 715–728 (2016). https://doi.org/10.1016/j.clsr.2016.07.002

28. Strauss, A., Corbin, J.: Grounded theory methodology: an overview. In: Denzin, N.K. (ed.) Handbook of Qualitative Research, pp. 273–285 (1994). https://psycnet.apa.org/home

29. Huselid MA (2018) The science and practice of workforce analytics: introduction to the HRM special issue. Hum. Resour. Manag. **57**, 679–684. https://doi-org.nuigalway.idm.oclc.org/. https://doi.org/10.1002/hrm.21916

30. Cormican, K., O'Sullivan, D.: Auditing best practice for effective product innovation management. Technovation **24**, 819–829 (2004). https://doi.org/10.1016/S0166-4972%2803%290 0013-0

31. Corry, S., Cormican, K.: Towards innovation in multinational corporation subsidiaries: development of an instrument to select and evaluate value driven strategies. Int. J. Innov. Technol. Manag. **14**, 25–33 (2019). https://doi.org/10.4067/S0718-27242019000100025

32. Hossen, J., Ahmad, N., Ali, S.M.: An application of Pareto analysis and cause-and-effect diagram (CED) to examine stoppage losses: a textile case from Bangladesh. J. Text. Inst. **108**, 2013–2020 (2017). https://doi-org.nuigalway.idm.oclc.org/. https://doi.org/10.1080/004 05000.2017.1308786

Lean Training as a Driver for Microbusinesses' Digital Transformation

Prabhjot Singh[1], Anuragini Shirish[2](✉), Anaya Kumar[2], and John O'Shanahan[3]

[1] Institut Mines Télécom Business School, Evry-Courcouronnes, France
[2] Université Paris-Saclay, Univ Evry, IMT-BS, LITEM, 91025 Evry-Courcouronnes, France
`anuragini.shirish@imt-bs.eu`
[3] LEAN BPI, Limerick, Ireland

Abstract. Lean management helps to increase the efficiency of microbusinesses by focusing on reducing costs, eliminating waste, and enhancing processes by focusing on customer needs. Practitioners believe that these Lean principles support digital transformation which has become increasingly important for small businesses due to high competition and the need to sustain their business. However, this assumption has not been empirically explored, little recent literature on Lean claims that it can influence digital transformation strategy. In this study, we conducted a focus group to uncover how Lean management programs impacted Microbusinesses' digital transformations. The results from the study reveal that Lean management is closely related to digital transformation efforts, and it enables microbusinesses to add capacity, reduce costs, optimize risks, innovate, and in some cases transform their organization.

Keywords: Lean principles · Lean management · Digital transformation · Microbusiness · Lean training · Digital strategy

1 Introduction

Lean management has played a key role in increasing the efficiency of numerous businesses by reducing costs, eliminating waste, and focusing on customer needs to drive process improvement. It helps decision-making by providing a data-based approach, highlighting the tracking of root cause. Lean is often considered as the best way to identify hidden problems and improvement opportunities [1]. Lean is said to facilitate digital transformation (DT) which has become essential nowadays for microbusinesses (MBs). Many companies have implemented lean and experienced the benefit of lean principles in their business. This is also true for microbusinesses, the backbone of our economies, as Lean helps them in identifying issues and areas for improvement. Through Lean management microbusinesses can improve productivity, sales, on-time delivery, product and service quality and facilitate business growth leading to increased employment.

Despite the large and diverse body of literature on Lean management, it has not addressed the impact of Lean on the implementation of a digital transformation strategy [2]. We focus on this gap and ask the following research question.

O. McDermott et al. (Eds.): ELEC 2022, IFIP AICT 668, pp. 122–142, 2023.
https://doi.org/10.1007/978-3-031-25741-4_12

RQ: To what extent do Lean principles contribute to digital transformation of micro businesses.

In order to answer the above research question, we undertook a focus group with a group of MB owner managers (MBOMs) from Ireland, who have previously used Lean management and are also undertaking DT efforts. We use ADROIT, a framework used to assess the value of digital innovations [3] as a theoretical lens for this study. ADROIT stands for: adding revenue or volume; differentiating or increasing willingness-to-pay; reducing costs; optimizing risks; innovating by generating and deploying knowledge and other capabilities; and transforming business models, priorities, and processes through a digital project. This study offers theoretical implications to digital transformation literature, as well as practical implications for MBs to apply Lean management principles in their digital transformation efforts.

2 Background Literature

2.1 Lean

The concept of Lean management is very popular among companies who are constantly looking for solutions to meet the challenges of competition, changing customer demands, and operational optimization. In fact, Lean methodologies are increasingly being applied [4]. The term "Lean" was coined by American businessman John Krafcik in his article "Triumph of the Lean Production System" in 1988, after observing Toyota's manufacturing system [5]. The term was further defined in 1996 by researchers James Womack and Daniel Jones, as a methodology relying on five main principles: "Specify value for each particular product, identify the value flow of each product, flow value uninterrupted, draw value from producers to customers and striving for perfection" [6]. Although Lean management has its roots in the Toyota production system, which was developed in Japan about 70 years ago, today this concept is widely adopted in various sectors worldwide [7].

Lean practices refer to a set of methods, processes, techniques, and tools aimed at continuously creating customer value and reducing product lead times [8]. Implementing Lean practices can improve operational performance for manufacturers [5, 9]. Lean manufacturing has emerged as an important operational management paradigm for organizations to achieve goals of improving quality, flexibility, and delivery while focusing on cost savings [5, 10]. Lean has been defined in numerous ways to highlight its various aspects. Table 1 lists key aspects of Lean definitions identified by authors.

To understand the Lean philosophy, it is essential to know the meanings of "effectiveness" and "efficiency". Effectiveness is the achievement of objectives, and efficiency is the time and resources dedicated to the achievement of objectives [1]. Lean's ultimate goal is to identify and eliminate all parts of the non-value-adding process. In this way, Lean manufacturing allows companies to respond more quickly to changing customer demands, leading to faster production and lower costs.

Figure 1 portrays the seven types of waste that Lean processes commonly aim to eliminate.

Table 1. List of lean definitions

Source	Lean definition
Christian Hohmann (2012) [1]	Lean is a system aiming to generate maximum added value at the lowest cost and as quickly as possible. It allows the use of the right resources
Worley & Doolen (2006) [11]	Lean is the systematic removal of waste by all members of the organization from all areas of the value stream
Karim & Arif-Uz- Zaman (2013) [12]	Lean process is an integrated socio-technical system whose main objective is to eliminate waste by concurrently reducing or minimizing supplier, customer and internal variability. Lean philosophy seeks to reduce waste anywhere in the company, optimize core resources and establish corporate culture dedicated to identifying and continuously fostering customer satisfaction
Al-Balushi, Sohal, Singh, Al Hajri, Al Farsi, & Al Abri (2014) [13]	Lean is a process reengineering philosophy composed of strategic guiding principles and a set of tools at the operational level. Lean is a system which requires less time, less human effort, less cost, less space, with fewer injuries, and less mistakes, to create an organization that accomplishes more and does these better

Lean promotes effectiveness and efficiency by doing things faster, better, and saving costs. It strives to eliminate waste and continuously improve the process [15]. To do this, everyone in the organization must always put the customer first and maximize customer value by reducing unnecessary waste constantly. Lean is a way of thinking and action that allows people to move their organization forward, improve performance and capacity and drive innovation. Lean helps ensure flexibility, responsiveness, efficiency, and innovation, enabling businesses to compete and gain an edge by continuously listening to their customers.

Researchers Womack and Jones [16] proposed a 5 step thought process to guide managers through a Lean transformation. These are as follows: identify value, map the value chain, create a seamless workflow, create a pull system and continuous improvement.

Many companies have utilized Lean training courses to grow sustainably and efficiently. In Ireland, for example, the *Lean for Micro program* was launched in 2015 by the Local Enterprise Offices to provide Lean training to micro enterprises. These Lean training programs train individuals to drive continuous improvement, harness time, effort and resources, bring significant benefits to their organization, increase productivity and competitiveness, and create the highest value for customers. In the current situation, it is undeniable that companies need to be more competitive by improving their productivity and efficiency. Lean practices are recognized as a key factor in improving

Source: Deloitte analysis.

Fig. 1. The seven kinds of waste [14]

efficiency and embracing MB innovation and technological change. Lean for Micro is designed to encourage MBs to adopt Lean business principles, build resilience, and be better at responding to market challenges and opportunities. Thus, Lean management is an approach to business management that supports ideas for continuous improvement. In fact, it's an ongoing effort to improve processes, products, and services. The Lean approach needs to constantly evolve over time to increase the overall efficiency of the organization. Some business advisors and lean consultants/mentors promote the use of digital technologies for such continuous improvement efforts through the use of Lean management. Consequently, Lean management is integrated with DT efforts of many MBs especially in the Irish context [17, 18].

2.2 Lean and Digital Transformation

In recent years, companies have been increasingly exploring new digital technologies and using their capabilities to create new value for their users [19, 20], that led information systems (IS) research to consider digital transformation as an important phenomenon. Slack et al. [21] describe digital transformation as a phenomenon that "encompasses the profound changes taking place in society and industries through the use of digital technologies". In response, organizations are forced to react to digital transformations and realign their strategies in order to take advantage of them [22] which affect people and processes both inside at the organizational levels and outside at the societal levels [23]. An overview of definitions from existing literature is depicted in Table 2.

The digital transformation of a company requires a fundamental organizational change [21], and reminds us that technology itself is "only part of the complex puzzle

Table 2. Digital transformation definitions

Source	Definition
European Commission (2019) [24]	Digital transformation is characterized by a fusion of advanced technologies and the integration of physical and digital systems, the predominance of innovative business models and new processes, and the use of certain smart products and services
OECD (2018) [25]	Digital transformation refers to the economic and societal effects of digitization and digitalization. Digitization is the conversion of analog data and processes into a machine-readable format. Digitalization is the use of digital technologies and data as well as their interconnection which results in new or changes to existing activities
Gruman (2016) [26]	The application of digital technologies to fundamentally impact all aspects of business
Schwertner (2017) [27]	The application of technology to build new business models, processes, software, and systems that results in more profitable revenue, greater competitive advantage, and higher efficiency
Fitzgerald et al. (2013) [28]	The use of new digital technologies (social media, mobile, analytics or embedded devices) to enable major business improvements (such as enhancing customer experience, streamlining operations or creating new business models)

that must be solved for organizations to remain competitive in a digital world." Similar results were reported by Kane et al. [1, 29] when discussing "technology fallacy" that revolve around the misunderstanding that solutions are likely to come from digital technology, as business challenges are driven by evolving digital innovation. Kane et al. [1, 29] also suggest that we need to shift our focus from technology to people when investigating digital transformations. They explain that people are inhibitors of digital transformation and place more importance on changing the culture to be more agile, risk tolerant, and experimental. Therefore, understanding processes around implementing, embedding, integrating, and evaluating digital technologies which transform business operations and business models are critical to sustaining a digital transformation process.

Integrating Lean into strategic thinking allows to fully leverage the potential of digital technologies to ensure that the digital transformations are actually helping add value and eliminate waste. Disconnected technology initiatives that lack a clear purpose will not get very far. Therefore, as stated in one of the core principles of Lean thinking, it is important to define the value intended to deliver to customers [9]. Both digital transformations and Lean principles are oriented towards creating value for customers, so we posit that these two concepts are interrelated [29]. Hence, we posit that digital transformation builds on and reinforces several pillars of the Lean philosophy: customer value, waste elimination, flexibility, agility, etc. The success of digital transformation may depend on the five dimensions that form the Lean transformation framework: purpose, process, people capabilities, management and leadership style, and mental models [1]. Thus, we believe that Lean management is a way to maximize customer value, and if it goes hand in hand with digital transformation, it can be effective for MBs.

2.3 Microbusiness and Digital Transformation

Microbusinesses are included in the SME sector; they represent the smallest businesses that exist. They operate on a small scale with less than 10 staff. Small and medium sized organizations represent more than 90% of all businesses, about 60–70% of employees, and 55% of GDP worldwide [30]. Microbusinesses face many challenges because of their size and owner led management. They often cannot scale their businesses [31]. Previously conducted research has shown that microbusinesses "work differently from large companies". Unlike large companies with complex applications and systems, microbusinesses may not necessarily use technology, or they may primarily use basic information and communications technology [32].

Every company needs to continuously evolve and look for ways to improve. This is especially relevant for microbusinesses' looking to enhance competitiveness and sustain their business. Lean thinking and practice are paramount to ensuring that microbusinesses are using all available resources to maximize results. This benefits the entire organization, from owners to employees as well as customers. According to prior literature, MBs are motivated by several external factors to participate in digital transformation efforts. These include the pandemic, income loss, and technological advancements [33]. However, the literature on microbusinesses does not focus on their digital transformation process and how lean might influence DT projects. In spite of this, policy makers support digital tools as having a lot of benefits for small and medium-sized businesses. Digitization reduces transaction costs and provides better access to information and communication. It can help microbusiness integration into global markets by reducing costs [25].

3 Theory and Method

3.1 The ADROIT Framework

For the purposes of understanding the impact of Lean management and Lean training on digital transformation strategy we employ the ADROIT framework on digital transformation [27, 34]. In his book Digital Intelligence, eminent scholar, Sunil Mithas explains that Digital Transformations enabled by information technology (IT) helps in creating sustainable competitive advantage by increasing the willingness to pay [34]. He explains the role of digital technologies for improving the competitive advantage through the framework called ADROIT This framework helps to analyze the value created by IT through six components: adding revenues or volume, differentiating or increasing willingness-to-pay, reducing costs, optimizing risks, improving industry attractiveness or innovating by generating and deploying knowledge and other resources and capabilities, and transforming business models and business processes. ADROIT delineates the role of IT in creating competitive advantage through five key drivers of sustainable economic value: volume, margins (through differentiating, reducing costs or improving industry attractiveness), optimizing uncertainty or risks in a competitive environment, improving resources and capabilities of an organization, and continuous transformation to shape and respond to a changing competitive landscape [34]. We use the ADROIT framework as a way to understand how Lean principles contribute to DT efforts.

3.2 Method

This research aims to understand the added value of Lean training for MBs engaging in a digital transformation journey. For this study, we focus on the Irish context. Irish MBs play an important role in the Irish economy in terms of stimulating innovation, employment, and growth. In Ireland, microbusinesses, with 1–9 employees, comprise over 90% of all businesses, but they are lagging behind in terms of digitalization- which puts their survival at risk [35]. Moreover, the Irish government undertook numerous policy level initiatives several years ago to promote Lean management amongst SMEs through their training programs. In fact, Ireland is at the forefront in equipping its businesses with Lean training, which aims to create a world leading Lean eco-system that brings significant impacts to businesses [36].

Since our research question is exploratory in nature, we use a qualitative approach using the focus group method to study the phenomenon of interest. We organized a focus group with 8 MB owner-managers (MBOMs) from the Irish MB ecosystem. Focus groups are usually conducted with sample size of 6 to 8 participants [37]) We conducted the session with two facilitators. The session lasted for 2 h and took place in the autumn of 2021. We recorded the session with permission ensuring anonymity of participation and transcribed it for further analysis. The participation in the focus group was voluntary. Our cohort of sample for focus group participants was gathered through consulting with a mentor associated with several Local Enterprise Offices in Ireland that run the Lean business improvement program. Mentors are professionals with several years of business experience who typically deliver business improvement programs to microbusinesses including Lean management training programs among other programs. In the mentoring process with MBs, a minority of mentors use and promote digital tools. All the focus group participants implemented Lean management in their businesses thanks to the 'Lean for Micro' training provided by LEOs. Since our sample group had experience with Lean methods, their responses and discussions are relevant to understanding how Lean management influences DT initiatives and training. The focus groups were guided by questions on the motivators and enablers for digital transformation as well as the challenges they have experienced. Table 3 shows the MBOMs demographics.

This research is based on a thematic analysis of the data collected via the focus group. We used manual coding [38]. For the purposes of understanding the impact of Lean management and Lean training on digital transformation strategy we employ the ADROIT framework on digital transformation. Our results are presented in the section below.

Table 3. Microbusiness participants' demographics

Participant code	Age range	Gender	Role	Sector	No. of employees	Lean training/implementation	Digital technology already implemented (Website, social media, mobile, data analytics, cloud, cloud for accounting)
P1	40–50	Female	Owner	Tertiary	5	Yes	Social media
P2	30–40	Female	Owner	Tertiary	4	Yes	Website presence, social media, mobile, data analytics cloud (excluding accounting, cloud)
P3	40–50	Male	Direct or	Secondary	5	Yes	Website presence, social media, cloud (excluding accounting) and cloud for accounting
P4	50–60	Male	Direct or	Secondary	4	Yes	Website presence, social media, mobile, cloud (excluding accounting) cloud for accounting
P5	50–60	Male	Owner	Tertiary	4	Yes	Website presence, social media, mobile, cloud (excluding accounting), cloud
P6	40–50	Male	Owner	Tertiary	1	Yes	Website presence, social media, mobile, cloud (excluding accounting), cloud for accounting

(*continued*)

Table 3. (*continued*)

Participant code	Age range	Gender	Role	Sector	No. of employees	Lean training/implementation	Digital technology already implemented (Website, social media, mobile, data analytics, cloud, cloud for accounting)
P7	50–60	Female	Manager	Tertiary	10	Yes	Website presence, social media, mobile, data analytics, cloud (excluding accounting), cloud for accounting
P8	40–50	Male	Owner	Secondary	9	Yes	Website presence, mobile, cloud (excluding accounting), cloud for accounting

4 Findings

4.1 Lean Trainings Helped Micro-businesses to Start Their Digital Transformation

From our data, we understand that Lean management is strongly linked to the digital strategy of microbusinesses, one can notice that the implementation of Lean methods helped them to start their journey of digital transformation. Thanks to Lean training the owners/managers implemented various digital tools to help them in their business processes. In addition, they raised awareness of the importance of staying competitive. As a result, they recognize that in order to remain competitive, they too should embrace digital transformation and make changes if they don't want to lose their clients to new or existing competitors. As a result of Lean training, they will be able to fully realize the benefits of deploying a digital strategy for their business, giving them the advantage to differentiate from their competitors. From the focus group, most managers/owners were very satisfied with the results from the Lean training that was initially subsidized by the government and therefore felt encouraged to continue the digital journey using their own resources and funding. The table below explains how micro-business owner- managers relate Lean and digital transformation. We have specifically outlined the influence of Lean management on the motivation to carry on the DT journey.

Table 4. Digital transformation motivators

Participant	Motivator	Illustrative Quotes
P8	Stay competitive and ensure the sustainability of their business	*"Due to digital transformation, anyone can do what we do... I'm very aware of that... But the way that our systems are, **the digital transformation that we've gone through with the Lean program in the last two years have helped us to stay connected and reach new businesses"***
P8	Differentiate from competitors	*"With Lean I'm not out trying to grow my business tomorrow morning. But to be the best. Yes. And I can definitely differentiate that very, very clearly in my own head. **What separates us from our competition is the digital transformation we've gone on to do**, and the motivation for that was to be the best"*
P2	Open to change	*"You need to be open to embrace new changes in the digital era to Continue"*
P7	Encourage to get more digital knowledge	*"When you get help from the government, like Lean programs it's great, they help you start the digital journey [...] Now, we are funding it ourselves, like, we pay for all our own digital learning"*

Table 4 portrays that Lean management training enables micro-businesses to build competitive advantages. The results of this analysis are presented using the ADROIT framework mentioned above in order to demonstrate that the implementation of Lean Management methods fits well within our chosen theoretical framework. Lean played a major role for MBs helping them to generate more revenues and add volume. It allowed them to increase willingness-to-pay of their products or services provided, reduce costs and optimize risks. Furthermore, Lean helped them improve industry attractiveness and innovate by generating knowledge and capabilities.

4.2 Lean Management Helps to Add Volume, Revenues, New Products, Customers When Fused with Digital Technologies

As a result of Lean training, micro-businesses were able to increase their output by streamlining and improving their processes. Prior to starting digital transformation efforts, microbusinesses needed to identify what process could be changed, in order to add value and identify what activities are not adding value. Furthermore, implementing Lean methodology allowed participants to grow their customer base by exploring new tools that helped them to increase their client reach, for example 'going online' proved very beneficial to increasing the number of orders. This enabled them to target a larger number of clients, across a broader geographical area, rather than being restricted to local customers. Moreover, they implemented digital communication applications during the Lean training, this was very useful in facilitating efficient communication between teams as well as with clients, again, increasing sales and in turn revenue. Below is a table that shows how MBOMs who attended Lean trainings or implemented Lean methods were successful in in adding volume, new products, customers, or channels as part of the firm's DT efforts.

Table 5. Lean benefits

Participant	Lean principle applied	Quotation
P8	• Create a seamless workflow • Create a pull system • Identify value	*"In Rowan most of the people are enthusiastic about any sort of digital transformation that helps in **improving what they do and that will increase output, like Lean**. And I think sometimes the issue can be identifying exactly what we want to do and then identifying the right solution and implementing it"*
P8	• Create a seamless workflow	*"The digital transformation that we've gone through in the last two years **have helped us to stay out of reach and gain clients**"*
P1	• Create a pull system • Create a seamless workflow	*"I really have to look at **getting online**. I need to look into that, maybe just with **different orders coming in from different areas, being able to kind of catch all of them**"*
P6	• Create a seamless workflow	*"It's definitely cost saving, [increases] **efficiency and revenue, and the network generates business**"*
P4	• Create a pull system • Continuous improvement	*"MMM (mentor) got us to embrace Evernote and came up with a very simple app for communication so that we had one point for messages to come from the office or from us and feed back to the office. **And hopefully stuff didn't get lost and we didn't lose sales,** and what we are working on at the moment is, we'd have three and a half thousand bits of equipment that would come back to us once a year for calibration, and it's managing that flow process and knowing where each piece of equipment is within that journey, is it on the way to the lab, is it in the lab, has it gone somewhere else for repair, back to the manufacturer"*
P2	• Create a pull system	*"**Revenue generation** is a kind of result or outcome of our digital processes"*

From Table 5 we can see that the most adopted Lean principles are: create a pull system and create a seamless workflow. Therefore, in order to increase volume, add customers and generate revenues companies need to ensure that the workflows remain smooth, and that they have cross- functional teamwork. The more stable the workflow, the faster and more efficiently the worker can process.

4.3 Lean Management Along with DT Efforts Enables MBs Increase Customer's Willingness to Pay and to Differentiate

Each of the sample companies had the opportunity to initiate a strategic digital initiative based on the Lean methodology, which allowed them to develop digital tools and streamline their processes, prompting them to get ahead of their competitors, or stay out of reach of new entrants. Furthermore, Lean enables microbusinesses to increase their willingness to pay, as they become more efficient in their processes. With Lean training, owners/managers can manage their activities better and operate quicker, that way they provide a better experience to their customers and in turn increase the willingness to pay. Additionally, it helps them expand their network and portfolio of clients.

Table 6 below shows verbatim responses from MBOMs regarding their experiences with Lean training and how it enabled them to differentiate and increase willingness to pay.

Table 6. Willingness to pay & Differentiation

Participant	Lean principle applied	Quotation
P8	• Continuous improvement	"Yes. Literally like, our goal is not to be like the richest company or anything like that. It's actually to be the best. And I can definitely differentiate that very clearly in my own head. What separates us from our competition is the digital transformation we've gone on to do, and the motivation for that was to be the best"
P4	• Create a seamless workflow • Create a pull system	"We were struggling and like some of the others, it was because emails were not being attended to, getting lost, messages between field staff and the office not being attended to, sales being lost. And that was our first step along, so MMM (a mentor) got us to embrace Evernote and came up with a very simple app for communication so that we had one point for messages to come from the office or from us and feed back to the office. Hopefully stuff **didn't get lost, and we didn't lose sales"**
P6	• Create a seamless workflow	"It's definitely a cost saving, [increases] **efficiency and revenue, the network generates business"**

(continued)

Table 6. (*continued*)

Participant	Lean principle applied	Quotation
P2	• Identify value • Continuous improvement	"The first objective was to make our business **more efficient**. The second thing is that so we can actually manage our business better. So that is financial planning, financial reporting. And staff management is just basically, I suppose, watching the figures. And the third thing is, this is really important for us, **delivering the best customer experience that we can, we're in a really competitive industry**. And we know from client feedback that they would value some of the digital processes that they would see on their end. We would use a lot of digital processes and **we're always on the lookout to make our current processes more efficient and better, but also looking out for more opportunities to.** Like It's quite addictive"

In Table 6, there is no emphasis on any particular Lean principle as different principles have been used by the participants in order to differentiate from the competition and increase clients' willingness to pay.

4.4 Lean Management Along with DT Efforts Allows MBs to Reduce Costs

Following the Lean trainings and mentorships, MBs were able to lower their costs- the result of streamlining processes in order to accomplish more in a shorter amount of time. Another way of reducing expenses with Lean is to use digital tools instead of traditional methods, for example, introducing online orders, incorporating a virtual planning system such as Calendly that allows them to book customers and virtually interact with them using a Zoom call, thus saving travel costs. The Table 7 below synthesizes the findings and provides illustrative codes:

Analyzing the Lean principles used in this table, we can say that there are indeed 2 principles that are mainly applied by MB for cost reduction, these are *identify value* and *continuous improvement*. Identifying value is a key step in microbusinesses' activities- by determining the value of every individual process they can differentiate between value-added and wasteful activities. The principle of continuous improvement helps MBs to lower their costs because its goal is to continuously improve each of the processes by focusing on strengthening the activities that generate the most value for customers while eliminating as much waste as possible and reducing waste leads to cost reduction. As Lean combined with digital technologies promotes efficiency, microbusinesses save money by not wasting effort on activities that do not add value to their business and are able to remain competitive.

Table 7. Cost reduction

Participant	Lean principle applied	Quotation
P7	• Mapping the value chain	*"I suppose the first thing was we used it to streamline our processes, and that had the **result of reducing costs** because we tried to become more efficient at extracting data and then analyzing that data"*
P6	• Mapping the value chain • Create a seamless workflow	*"We have implemented Calendly for booking customers in for meetings and doing a Zoom call meeting, which has been hugely **efficient on the cost and the time** of traveling to customers. **It's definitely cost saving, [increases] efficiency and a revenue, the network generates business**"*
P2	• Continuous improvement	***"Cost reduction** is a kind of result or outcome of our digital processes"*

4.5 Lean Management Along with DT Efforts Helps to Optimize Risk, Reduce Competitive Risk

Lean methodology results in reducing competitive risks and optimizing risks in general by using more effective digital tools. Indeed, by implementing digital solutions, owners/managers could better manage and analyze their data and therefore take informed decisions. With traditional methods they often analyzed data incorrectly or not precisely enough, which could induce risks for their businesses. Since digital tools improve overall data accuracy, they can reduce risks related to data management and analysis. Likewise, with communication tools, they can better organize business processes, for example the order taking process rather than taking orders via emails or on paper, which are more prone to mistakes than digital systems.

Furthermore, as explained in the previous result section, Lean management methods help micro businesses to remain competitive they are able to reduce their competitive risks and remain competitive by staying one step ahead of newcomers who engage in digital strategy as a means of entering the market Table 8 below synthesizes the finding and provides illustrative codes:

Table 8 demonstrates that for optimizing risks in the business there is no emphasis on any Lean principle in particular, they all partly contribute to reducing risk factors for MBs.

Table 8. Optimize risks

Participant	Lean principle applied	Quotation
P7	• Identify value	*"We had a lot of data but analyzing incorrectly **so we interrogated it better and then we could use the information we got out to perhaps influence any decisions we would make**. So, it was kind of analyzing the data which led to streamlining of some processes in terms of **how we dealt with that data previously**. And a lot of this would be monthly financial information- our key performance indicators. [Lean] helped us analyze that more quickly. And so that made us a bit **more efficient with that**"*
P8	• Map the value chain • Continuous improvement	*"A communication app into the office and to the two the guys on the field whose emails I always found them **confusing for everyone. Hundreds of emails flying around the place. No one really knows, there's no order to them... I kind of came up with this idea of a communication app** where it was no need for any please or thank you, you know. You just get to the point"*
P1	• Mapping the value chain • Create a seamless workflow	***"Afraid of missing sales or missing someone/ a call or missing a bride** [client] anything that helps. Any digitalization that helps that can only be a positive thing. I couldn't and I can't see myself being able to sleep at night or go on any further without knowing that there's some type of web[site] that will catch [these sales/calls]. So that feeling that you're going to miss something or that a bride is going to ring you and say, "what time can **I expect you with my flowers" and you're not going to have them ordered**. I mean, it has never come to anything like that, but I just kind of **feel that the safety nets have to be put in place**. And I just want to make it like having an **extra set of hands** watching out for you and kind of letting things move on to the next level"*

4.6 Lean Management Along with DT Efforts Favors Innovation by Generating Knowledge and Capabilities

Implementing Lean results in a change in business processes, it helps the microbusinesses to innovate. A growing number of companies utilize digital technology to perform their organizational and production functions. Thanks to Lean they improved their communication methods by using digital tools such as conference call applications- used for internal interactions as well as for dealing with customers. Employees are able to work remotely thanks to these communication tools, traditionally they worked in an office. However, they can now work from home or from any location.

Furthermore, pre-Lean, it was necessary for employees to perform a great deal of inefficient work, such as manually creating and operating Excel spreadsheets, these tasks weren't value- added. With Lean training, they have implemented integrated systems-which automate processes, freeing employees from tasks that waste time and that do not add value. The result is that they can devote more time to activities that require their intellect and knowledge, in turn saving them both time and money. They use digital tools like Docusign to get client signatures remotely. Table 9 below synthesizes the findings and provides illustrative codes:

Table 9. Digitalized process

Participant	Lean principle applied	Quotation
P7	• Mapping the value chain • Identify value	*"And we do a huge amount of our own internal meetings through Microsoft Teams, and we do a lot of our consultations, where we used to meet in person* and we do a lot of that remotely now as well. But I think the key thing for us is what we want to analyze next or what we want to do. How can we make things quicker? We are talking to a couple of people, and we do ask people we meet, and we do ask any of our advisors if they can *recommend people* and then we go and talk to them. And some turned out to be useful and others don't. So yes, I suppose *knowledge, integration and awareness of what's happening outside is important for us"*
P8	• Mapping the value chain	*"I went on the Lean program, and that was kind of the perfect fit, really, because I had a lot of ideas. And since then, the ideas I had, which was like, one was a communication app into the office and to the guys on the field whose emails, I always found them confusing for everyone I kind of came up with this idea of a communication app where it was, no need for any please or thank you, you know. You just get to the point. Say what you want to say. And then it's being actioned, done or closed"*

(continued)

Table 9. (*continued*)

Participant	Lean principle applied	Quotation
P6	• Identify value • Mapping the value chain • Create a seamless workflow	*"**With regard to how we communicate, it has made out lives much easier and also being able to work either from home** or in the office or, you know, sharing work on files at the same time without having to have a physical file. **We've implemented DocuSign for signatures for customers**. And we've implemented cloud solutions"*
P4	• Continuous improvement	*"**Skype has been around. Zoom has been around, Calendly links**, all that stuff. But partly my confidence to suggest those routes or to say this is the route we're going is one part of it. But the other part is definitely the public- **my customers' acceptance that we would be dealing this way has greatly improved"***
P2	• Mapping the value chain • Identify the value	*"So, you know, prior to having some of our integrated systems, **there was just a lot of kind of manual labor** that had to be done, you know, cutting and pasting from Excel into an excel file into another point. And you'd be doing that at 10–11 o'clock at night. **And you know, it's just some of the digital processes that we've brought in, mean that things work away in the background without always having to be physically involved in them. You're, free you know.** So that's great"*

From this table, we see that Innovation is closely related with *identifying the value* and *mapping* it. Indeed, it is crucial to understand what the clients need, because in Lean the value is in the problem that we are trying to solve for the customer (internal or external). After identifying the value, managers can seek digital tools that better meet the customer's needs. Mapping the value chain is also a key step, the company has to map its workflow including all the actions and people involved in delivering the final product to the customer. This enables identification of the process steps that are time consuming and do not add value and replace them with digitized processes.

4.7 Lean Along with DT Efforts Enables MBs to Transform Their Organization and Working Methods

As part of the Lean training, MBOMs learn how to eliminate tasks that are not of value to the business and introduce digital strategies for improving efficiency and streamlining processes. As an example, rather than traveling to each individual customer's location in person to gather information, creating an online platform that collects this information could save significant time and money. Lean management helps transform the business; at the same time, it opens the door for new opportunities by introducing various digital tools. Table 10 below synthesis the finding and provides illustrative codes:

Table 10. Transformation

Participant	Lean principle applied	Quotation
P7	• Mapping the value chain • Create a seamless workflow • Create a pull system	*"And we were also looking at it in terms of how we can do things quicker in terms of an automation of dictation and a few things like that and generating auto reports. **And we do a huge amount of our own internal meetings through Microsoft Teams, and we save a lot of our time with consultations where we used to meet in person, and we do a lot of that remotely now as well**. We need to produce a report and that report is used in court as evidence. But the question is how much of that can we **automate**. I'm just identifying the solution, whether that's dictation as we go and let somebody automatically type. And so that would be something we know we want to **automate**. We know we want to **make it more efficient**"*
P8	• Continuous improvement	*"Lean training, kind of **transformed my journey** in a way. I'm actually kind of dependent on certain technology at the moment to drive my business"*
P5	• Create a seamless workflow • Create a pull system	*"**We were a paper-based order taking system**. MMM (a mentor) developed an app for us, which allowed us to basically take our orders live in the shop. **They go directly back to the office and get started to be picked immediately**. Now we're developing a system for basically the component stock levels"*

4.8   Integrated Framework: Lean and Digital Transformation Strategy

The findings show the link between Lean principles and practices and DT practices of MBs. Figure 2 below synthesizes our findings using the ADROIT framework which initially is used to identify the role of IT in digital transformation efforts. We integrate Lean Principles to this framework and show the strength of its connection between each of the components of the framework. Thick blue lines signify stronger links and thinner blue lighter lines signify weaker links.

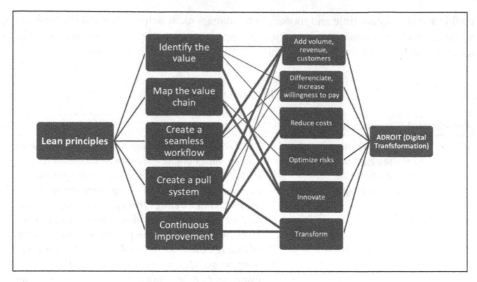

Fig. 2. Linking lean principles to digital strategy and transformation

5   Implications and Conclusion

This study contributes towards literature on Lean as well as digital transformation literature by extending it to include the microbusiness sector [39, 40]. In this study, we also present the link between the Lean principles and digital transformation by using the ADROIT framework, thereby demonstrating that Lean management does facilitate the process of digital transformation within microbusinesses. We also provide further validity to the ADROIT framework that has not been empirically tested in many studies in the past. In terms of practical implications, this study contributes to the microbusiness industry as it highlights the practical advantages of Lean management training and practices. This should provide further validity to policy makers continuing to provide Lean and Digital mentorships to MBs. The study also can be used by policy makers to encourage more MB owners/managers to enroll in the Lean training program if they wish to either begin or further their digital transformation process within the organization.

Implementing Lean management within MBs allows them to survive and sustain in the digital economy. Their contribution to the local and regional economy is significant, and digital transformation is crucial for their survival. Prior research on the factors enabling digital transformation efforts by microbusinesses have not been well studied [39]. The findings obtained from microbusiness owners/managers that experienced Lean methods implementation reveal that Lean, is in fact, very closely linked to digital transformation. Thus, we can see that Lean training helps MBs to start their digital transformation. Lean management and practices help to add volume, revenues and customers; it also enables microbusinesses to increase willingness to pay (of its customers) and to differentiate (product and services). Through Lean practices, costs are reduced, risks are optimized, and competitive risks are reduced. Moreover, Lean favors innovation by generating knowledge and capabilities and eventually enables microbusinesses to transform their organization and working methods. Most Lean principles play a significant role in driving efficiency as MBs embark of a DT journey.

References

1. Hohmann, C.: Lean Management: Outils, méthodes, retours d'expériences, questions/réponses: Editions Eyrolles (2012)
2. Antony, J., McDermott, O., Powell, D., Sony, M.: The evolution and future of lean Six Sigma 4.0. TQM J. (2022). (ahead-of-print)
3. Mithas, S., Murugesan, S., Seetharaman, P.: What is your artificial intelligence strategy? IT Prof. **22**(02), 4–9 (2020)
4. Ghosh, M.: Lean manufacturing performance in Indian manufacturing plants. J. Manuf. Technol. Manag. **24**(1), 113–122 (2013)
5. Krafcik, J.F.: Triumph of the lean production system. Sloan Manag. Rev. **30**(1), 41–52 (1988)
6. Womack, J.P., Jones, D.T.: Lean thinking: banish waste and create wealth in your corporation. Simon and Schuster (2003)
7. Charron, R., Harrington, H.J., Voehl, F., Wiggin, H.: The Lean Management Systems Handbook. CRC Press, Boca Raton (2014)
8. Shah, R., Ward, P.T.: Defining and developing measures of lean production. J. Oper. Manag. **25**(4), 785–805 (2007)
9. Womack, J.P., Jones, D.T., Roos, D.: The Machine that Changed the World: The Story of Lean Production. 1st Harper Perennial Ed., New York (1991)
10. Slack, N., Lewis, M., Bates, H.: The two worlds of operations management research and practice: can they meet, should they meet? Int. J. Oper. Prod. Manag. **24**(4), 372–387 (2004)
11. Worley, J., Doolen, T.: The role of communication and management support in a lean manufacturing implementation. Manag. Decis. **44**(2), 228–245 (2006)
12. Karim, A., Arif-Uz-Zaman, K.: A methodology for effective implementation of lean strategies and its performance evaluation in manufacturing organizations. Bus. Process. Manag. J. **19**(1), 169–196 (2013)
13. Al-Balushi, S.M., Sohal, A.S., Singh, P.J., Al-Hajri, A., Al Farsi, Y., Al-Abri, R.: Readiness factors for lean implementation in healthcare settings-a literature review. J. Heal. Organ. Manag. **28**(2), 135–153 (2014)
14. Digital lean manufacturing n.d. https://www2.deloitte.com/us/en/insights/focus/industry-4-0/digital-lean-manufacturing.html
15. Arnheiter, E.D., Maleyeff, J.: The integration of lean management and Six Sigma. TQM Mag. **17**(1), 5–18 (2005)
16. Womack, J.P., Jones, D.T.: Beyond Toyota: how to root out waste and pursue perfection. Harv. Bus. Rev. **74**(5), 140–151 (1996)
17. Lean Business Ireland [Internet]. [cited 2022]. https://www.leanbusinessireland.ie/funding-supports-overview/are-you-a-local-enterprise-office-client/lean-for-micro/
18. Lean Implementation In Micro & Small Enterprises: Book Of Cases 20202021
19. Bharadwaj, A., El Sawy, O.A., Pavlou, P.A., Venkatraman, N.V.: Digital business strategy: toward a next generation of insights. MIS Q. 471–82 (2013)
20. Carroll, N., Helfert, M.: Service capabilities within open innovation: revisiting the applicability of capability maturity models. J. Enterp. Inf. Manag. **2**, 275–303 (2015)
21. Vial, G.: Understanding digital transformation: a review and a research agenda. Manag. Digit. Transform. 118–144 (2021)

22. Hess, T., Matt, C., Benlian, A., Wiesböck. F.: Options for formulating a digital transformation strategy. MIS Q. Exec. **15**(2), 123–139 (2016)
23. Westerman, G., Bonnet, D., McAfee, A.: Leading Digital: Turning Technology into Business Transformation. Harvard Business Press, Brighton (2014)
24. Commission E.: Digital Transformation (2019). https://ec.europa.eu/growth/industry/policy/digital-ransformation_en
25. Statistics, O.: Stats.oecd.org. (2018). https://stats.oecd.org/Index.aspx?DataSetCode=ICT_
26. Gruman, G.: What digital transformation really means. InfoWorld. **18**(1), 1–3 (2016)
27. Schwertner, K.: Digital transformation of business. Trakia J. Sci. **15**(1), 388–393 (2017)
28. Fitzgerald, M., Kruschwitz, N., Bonnet, D., Welch, M.: Embracing digital technology: a new strategic imperative. MIT Sloan Manag. Rev. **55**(2), 1 (2014)
29. Kane, G.: The technology fallacy: people are the real key to digital transformation. Res. Technol. Manag. **62**(6), 44–49 (2019)
30. Arnold, C.: The foundation for economies worldwide is small business. In: International Federation of Accountants, Issues and Insights, 26 June 2019 (2019). https://www.ifac.org/knowledge-gateway/contributing-global-economy/discussion/foundation-economies-worldwide-small-business-0. Retrieved 25 Jan 2023
31. Zimmerman, M., Dunlap, D., Hamilton, III R.D., Hill, T., Chapman, E.A.: David versus goliath: strategic behavior of small firms in consolidated industries. J. Small Bus. Strateg. **13**(2), 56–74 (2002)
32. Bharati, P., Chaudhury, A.: Studying the current status of technology adoption. Commun. ACM **49**(10), 88–93 (2006)
33. Mandviwalla, M., Flanagan, R.: Small business digital transformation in the context of the pandemic. Eur. J. Inf. Syst. **30**(4), 359–375 (2021)
34. Mithas, S.: Digital Intelligence: What Every Smart Manager Must Have for Success in an Information Age. Third edition. Finerplanet (2015)
35. Bourke, J., Roper, S.: Micro-businesses in Ireland: from ambition to innovation. Cork University Business School (2019)
36. About Lean Six Sigma Courses - Who, What, & Where - Find out! (2021). https://www.leansixsigmatraining.ie/about/. Accessed 13 May 2021
37. Fern, E.F.: The use of focus groups for idea generation: the effects of group size, acquaintanceship, and moderator on response quantity and quality. J. Mark. Res. **19**(1), 1–13 (1982)
38. Saldana, J.: The Coding Manual for Qualitative Researchers. SAGE Publications Ltd., Thousand Oaks (2021)
39. Shirish, A., O'Shanahan, J., Kumar, A.: The enablers and inhibitors of digital transformation within the microbusiness sector in Irelan. In: UIIN 2022: University Industry Innovation Network Conference, Jun 2022, Amsterdam, Netherlands (2022). ⟨hal-03548215⟩
40. Shirish, A., Srivastava, S.C., Panteli, N: Management and sustenance of digital transformations in the Irish microbusiness sector: examining the key role of microbusiness owner-manager. Eur. J. Inf. Syst. Forthcoming

The Impact of Lean on Introduction of Industry 4.0 Technologies: A Longitudinal Study

Matteo Rossini[1]([✉]), Federica Costa[1], Alberto Portioli-Staudacher[1], and Guilherme Luz Tortorella[2]

[1] Politecnico di Milano, Milan, Italy
matteo.rossini@polimi.it
[2] University of Melbourne, Melbourne, Australia

Abstract. The purpose of this paper is to investigate the relationship/interaction between Lean and Industry 4.0. In particular, this research examines empirically the influence of Lean approach on industry 4.0 implementation in a longitudinal study. The research aims at understanding how the implementation of Industry 4.0 technologies changes during a time horizon of 3 years in companies with different level of Lean implementation. A survey has been selected to develop the longitudinal study, since it allows discovering the progression of Lean and Industry 4.0 implementation in several different plants, giving a general overview of the situation.

Keywords: Lean · Industry 4.0 · Longitudinal study

1 Introduction

In the last decade, the rise of industry 4.0 (i4.0) technologies has increased the research effort into how Lean and digital technologies may cooperate to achieve better performance [1]. Recently, research indicates that these two domains tend to co-exist in manufacturing companies, challenging the idea that they are incompatible, and probed a significant and strong correlation between Lean and factory digitalization [2, 3].

In the most recent years, one of the main points concerning Lean and digitalization developed in the literature is the fact that Lean is a enabler to develop Industry 4.0 [4]. Lean approach generates a fertile condition for i4.0 higher adoption levels, prepares the field for implementation of new technologies, and reduce sthe risk of digitalization of wastes when Lean practices are extensively implemented in the company [5, 6].

However, the facilitating or enabling effect of Lean on introduction of I4.0 technologies in factories is still an open debate [7, 8].

This research focuses on this debate, addressing the following research question: How is the integration between Lean and Industry 4.0 evolving over the years in manufacturing companies?

In order to answer to this research question a survey-based longitudinal study has been performed.

O. McDermott et al. (Eds.): ELEC 2022, IFIP AICT 668, pp. 143–147, 2023.
https://doi.org/10.1007/978-3-031-25741-4_13

2 Methodology

The longitudinal study shows a comparison between the recent situation (2021) and the one related to 2018.

A survey is the selected strategy to develop the longitudinal study since it allows to discover the progression of Lean and Industry 4.0 implementation in several different plants, giving a general overview of the situation [9].

In order to follow the research strategy defined, a questionnaire has been developed. The questionnaire has been implemented replicating the previous one used in 2018 in order to make the comparison significant [10]. In addition to this, it has been submitted only to companies that have answered in 2018 to be sure to obtain a snapshot of the situation of the same companies for both the periods. In this way, it is possible to study how companies evolved in the implementation level for Lean, Industry 4.0 and performance improvements. It includes different sections related to general information, Lean Practices, Industry 4.0 technologies and operational performance improvement indicators.

Following the characteristics of the sample defined in 2018, the selected companies must have one manufacturing plant located in Europe. With respect to 2018, few changes were made in the questionnaire of 2021 in order to make the questionnaire more streamlined for respondents. Changes have been only referring to the first part related to contextual factors and keeping essential information to conduct the longitu-dinal study.

Data analysis has been performed in different step. In the first step, Cronbach's alpha coefficient has been computed to check the internal consistency and the degree of reliability of the data collected [11]. The second step defined clusters of companies. In this clustering analysis, K-means clustering is used to assign each company to a specified cluster, after having defined the optimal number of clusters with the Elbow method. This two-step procedure has been applied for clustering the companies' answers (in 2018 and 2021) separately regarding their Lean implementation level, Industry 4.0 implementation level and Performance improvements, which are the three core sections of the questionnaire. Consequently, an Analysis Of Variance (ANOVA) one-way was performed to verify if the mean of a cluster is far enough from the mean of another one. In the third step, data normality has been checked for the means of each of the three aspects through a Shapiro-Wilk test. After that, the specific group assigned in the previous clusterization was considered as a categorical variable, thus allowing the application of the Chi-squared tests with contingency tables and adjusted residuals to provide a basic picture of the interrelation between variables.

The last step of the longitudinal analysis was the development of different t-tests (after checking the equality of variances) on the means of the different aspects. The first type of t-tests has been used to check if companies' level of Lean, I4.0 and Performance Improvements has changed significantly among the two years, using their means. Secondly, t-tests have been performed on the questions of Lean and I4.0. The idea was to check if a specific practice or technology had undergone a major development or backwardness because for example to specific investments or because it has become a key aspect in recent years.

3   Results

The survey resulted in 41 companies' answers, corresponding to a response rate of 41%. In order to check non-response bias, "late respondents" were used as an approximation of the companies which did not answer to the questionnaire, and after a statistical analysis there was no evidence of it. Cronbach alpha was calculated for each section of the questionnaire for both the years to guarantee a good level of the dataset reliability proving that the scales used were appropriate for successive analysis.

Then, clustering analysis resulted in optimal number of clusters obtained equal to two for each variable (Lean, I4.0 and performances), both in 2018 and 2021. For each variable and each year, clusters have been defined as Low or High performing for each of elements (Lean, I4.0, perfomances). Then, an ANOVA one-way analysis was performed affirming that for each aspect analysed in both the years the robustness of cluster division is guaranteed with the means of the two clusters significantly unequal.

Concerning the relationship between Lean Manufacturing and I4.0 technologies, a significant association was discovered both in 2018 and 2021. Figure 1 sums up the distribution of the answers for Lean adoption in 2018 and 2021, while Fig. 2 sums up the implementation level of i4.0 technologies.

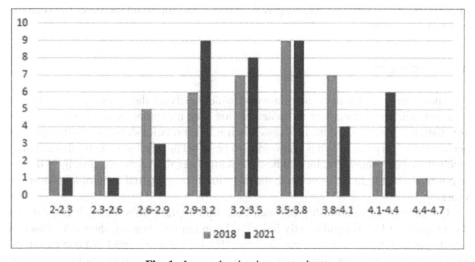

Fig. 1. Lean adoption by respondents.

Then, the association between I4.0 and Performance resulted to be significant in the two years.

Lastly, some t-tests were used to check if companies' level of Lean, I4.0 and Performance Improvements has changed significantly among the two years, using their means. There was no statistical evidence of a change in any of the aspects even if I4.0 undergoes a major improvement in its level of adoption (p-value 0.053). Going more in depth, some t-tests were performed also on specific Lean practices and I4.0 technologies. JIT adopted by suppliers, reduction of set-up time and suggestion programs by operators to

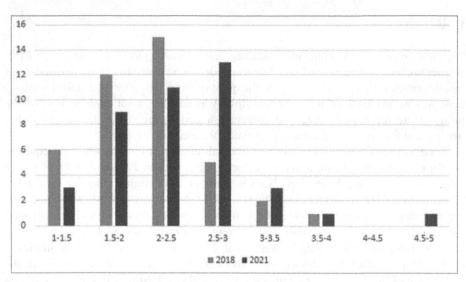

Fig. 2. I4.0 adoption by respondents.

improve processes were three Lean practices that faced important increases between the two years analysed.

4   Conclusions

This preliminary research is the first work, which analyses the evolution of Lean and I4.0 and their connection over the years. In this way, it explores how the two domains are changing, trying to find the root causes behind their relationships and their impact on performances. In particular, it is noteworthy to point out the level of Lean implementation reached by companies remained almost the same over the years. Regarding I4.0, it is important to highlight the increase in the adoption level of digital technologies over the years.

Concerning the relationship between Lean and digital technologies, it is clear that the adoption of I4.0 is significantly linked to Lean implementation: their association is significant and stable over the years showing that having a low level of Lean practices. implementation does not allow companies to strongly adopt I4.0 technologies. Future developments of this research must investigate whether Lean is actually significant in the development of I4.0 implementation, giving to management a more clear perspective on the benefits of introducing i4.0 technologies in Lean systems.

References

1. Rossini, M., Powell, D.J., Kundu, K.: Lean supply chain management and Industry 4.0: a systematic literature review. *Int. J. Lean Six Sigma* (2022)

2. Buer, S.V., Semini, M., Strandhagen, J.O., Sgarbossa, F.: The complementary effect of lean manufacturing and digitalisation on operational performance. Int. J. Prod. Res. **59**(7), 1976–1992 (2021)
3. Rossini, M., Cifone, F.D., Kassem, B., Costa, F., Portioli-Staudacher, A.: Being lean: how to shape digital transformation in the manufacturing sector. J. Manuf. Technol. Manage. **32**(9), 239–259 (2021)
4. Kolberg, D., Zühlke, D.: Lean automation enabled by industry 4.0 technologies. IFAC-PapersOnLine **48**(3), 1870–1875 (2015)
5. Powell, D., Morgan, R., Howe, G.: Lean first… then digitalize: a standard approach for industry 4.0 implementation in SMEs. In: Dolgui, A., Bernard, A., Lemoine, D., von Cieminski, G., Romero, D. (eds.) Advances in Production Management Systems. Artificial Intelligence for Sustainable and Resilient Production Systems. APMS 2021. IFIP Advances in Information and Communication Technology, vol 631, pp. 31-39. Springer, Cham (2021) https://doi.org/10.1007/978-3-030-85902-2_4
6. Rossini, M., Costa, F., Tortorella, G. L., Valvo, A., Portioli-Staudacher, A.: Lean production and industry 4.0 integration: how lean automation is emerging in manufacturing industry. *Int. J. Prod. Res.*, 1–21 (2021)
7. McDermott, O., Antony, J., Sony, M., Swarnaker, V.: Mapping the terrain for the lean supply chain 4.0. In: 26th International Symposium on Logistics (ISL 2022), pp 167–179. Cork University Business School, Ireland (2022)
8. Antony, J., McDermott, O., Powell, D., Sony, M.: The evolution and future of lean Six Sigma 4.0. TQM J. (2022). https://doi.org/10.1108/TQM-04-2022-0135
9. Tortorella, G., van Dun, D.H., de Almeida, A.G.: Leadership behaviors during lean healthcare implementation: a review and longitudinal study. *J. Manuf. Technol. Manage.* (2019)
10. Tortorella, G.L., Rossini, M., Costa, F., Portioli Staudacher, A., Sawhney, R.: A comparison on industry 4.0 and lean production between manufacturers from emerging and developed economies. Total Qual. Manage. Bus. Excellence **32**(11–12), 1249–1270 (2021)
11. Cronbach, L.J., Warrington, W.G.: Time-limit tests: estimating their reliability and degree of speeding. Psychometrika **16**(2), 167–188 (1951)

Lean in Manufacturing

Implementing a Forecast Methodology as a Precursor to Lean Management

Goda Zvikaite[1], Sean Moore[1], and Olivia McDermott[1,2(✉)]

[1] University of Limerick, Limerick, Ireland
olivia.mcdermott@nuigalway.ie
[2] National University of Ireland, Galway, Ireland

Abstract. The paper aims to develop a new forecast methodology to enable an automotive manufacturer to achieve required service level agreements. The research proposes to develop a forecasting model to predict production demand accurately and thus reduce inventory, lead time to customers, improve on-time delivery and save costs. A new forecast methodology facilitated >80% forecast accuracy on distributor shipments to end customers and thus improved the manufacturer's response to customers. The researcher shifted focus from a system driven to actual customer demand-based forecast by focusing on distributor shipments to customers rather than bookings placed with the manufacturer. It was discovered that any forecasting methodology would fail unless the underlying process were stable. Hence, the forecasting model is an enabler for applying Lean principles to enhance inventory reduction and customer lead time further. It is recommended for future research focus on how Lean tools can impact forecasting and lean manufacturing.

Keywords: Forecasting · Inventory · Lean

1 Introduction

The research organisation requires transforming its manufacturing environment from reactive to proactive, capable of meeting 98–99% on-time delivery targets in ≤ 7 days. Such challenging objectives require a two-step approach, firstly - the development of a forecasting model that can predict production demand with >80% accuracy and implementing of Lean principles. Gligor et al. [1] discuss that accurate forecasting is needed to reduce manufacturing costs. Furthermore, an accurate forecast is needed in the organisation because of its wide variety of parts. In order to establish if implementing a forecasting accuracy model prior to a further Lean deployment would be successful, a pilot area was selected in the manufacturing areas' Cold Forming department. Accurate predictive forecasting should also positively impact inventory levels and product flow. One of the aims of this research is to find a way to implement forecasting to deploy LM later. Implementing Lean without an accurate forecasting system can result in inventory waste, poor customer service level agreements (SLA) and defects. Thus, a forecasting

© IFIP International Federation for Information Processing 2023
Published by Springer Nature Switzerland AG 2023
O. McDermott et al. (Eds.): ELEC 2022, IFIP AICT 668, pp. 151–164, 2023.
https://doi.org/10.1007/978-3-031-25741-4_14

system should enable the manufacturing facility to meet required SLAs and achieve project objectives.

This research aims to validate an all-encompassing model that would enable the research organisation to reconcile its supply and demand process. With the help of LM and new forecasting techniques, such a process would improve flow, and organisational flexibility, increase the company's responsiveness and forecast correct parts. The accurate predictive forecast would also improve production capacity planning [2].

Several key performance indicators (KPIs) will be used to validate project success. These are Lead Time (LT), on-time delivery (OTD), internal inventory and forecast accuracy.

The research questions are:

1. What is the best method of forecasting?
2. What forecast accuracy, lead time and internal inventory level can be achieved?

2 Literature Review

Gligor et al. [1] discuss that accurate forecasting is needed to reduce manufacturing costs. An accurate and robust forecast methodology should help the company to forecast required parts into the buffer or the finished goods holding area in the warehouse. Both quantitative and qualitative forecasting techniques [3] will be used to evaluate forecast effectiveness. Danese and Kalchschmidt (2010) recommend supplementing statistical forecast methods with qualitative information, such as knowledge of subject matter experts, because >61% of executives do not trust statistical predictions (Wacker and Sprague 1995). A robust forecasting process must be implemented to improve the organisation's responsiveness to market demands. According to Danese and Kalchschmidt [4], a forecaster has to blend techniques with the "knowledge and experience of management". Fildes et al. [5] and the American Production & Inventory Control Society (APIC's) [3] both suggest that a small number of statistical forecasting models should be used to avoid confusion, which should later be supplemented with qualitative methods such as Delphi, end customer feedback, a panel of experts (could be management) or historical analogy.

It is understood from the literature that the selection of the right statistical model will be based on trial-and-error experimentation. Danese and Kalchschmidt [4] advise that companies should be very focused in their efforts to improve forecast accuracy and should use it to improve their decision- making. In addition, qualitative methodologies are used when "forecasted events" cannot be quantified accurately by statistical tools [6]. Quayle [7] recommend combining qualitative and quantitative models and advise starting the forecast at the end user level, then cascading it up to the supply chain partners, ensuring that all partners use the same forecast measure and models. Overall, the literature review identified that LM practices could help to create organisational flexibility, while robust forecasting methodologies can aid in achieving organisational responsiveness. Therefore it is necessary to understand and manage the relationship between both.

3   The Research Methodology for the Project

The research organisation requires transforming its manufacturing environment from reactive to proactive, capable of meeting 98–99% on-time delivery targets in ≤ 7 days. Such challenging objectives require a two-step approach, firstly - the development of a forecasting model that can predict production demand with $>80\%$ accuracy [8].

An accurate and robust forecast methodology should help the company to forecast required parts into the buffer or the finished goods holding area in the warehouse. Both quantitative and qualitative forecasting techniques [3, 7] will be used to evaluate the effectiveness of forecasting techniques. Danese and Kalchschmidt [4] recommend supplementing statistical forecast techniques with qualitative information, such as knowledge of subject matter experts because $>61\%$ of executives do not trust statistical forecasts [9]. An accurate forecast is needed in this case study organisation because of its wide variety of parts. In order to establish if a forecasting model would have the desired impact, a pilot area was selected in the Cold Forming department. This approach of the accurate predictive forecast should also have a positive impact on inventory levels and product flow. One of the aims of this research is to find a way for forecasting as a precursor for future projects on LM, e.g. Kanban, Total Preventative Maintenance (TPM), and Overall Equipment Effectiveness (OEE) can be subsequently implemented. Both should enable the manufacturing facility to meet required service level agreements (SLAs) and achieve project objectives.

In parallel, new forecasting methodologies will be developed, ensuring that the company manufactures correct buffer and non-buffer parts (also known as Finished Goods (FG) inventory). Not all products can go into an inventory buffer since some automotive parts are bespoke, governed by strict quality and engineering regulations and have unique configurations from the beginning.

Quality function deployment (QFD) tool will be adopted to identify business requirements (known as the voice of the business (VOB)) related to the development of new forecasting methodologies. Together with technical requirements, VOB should help define the forecast re-design plan. QFD tool has been selected as a quality improvement tool because of its systemic approach to assessing and prioritising improvements in existing processes [10]. This practical problem-solving tool will help to structure customer needs and assesses whether the new process can meet critical project requirements.

Based on the initial organisational assessment and literature review, the researcher identified that only 2 or 3 statistical forecast models should be selected to make the forecast re-design process more manageable [3, 7]. Therefore, the authors plan to experiment with 3 forecasting models, namely (3/6 month moving average, 3 months weighted moving average and exponential smoothing) using the Microsoft Excel platform. Once experiments are complete, the most accurate statistical forecast model will be selected. The research analysis for the forecast models is shown in Fig. 1.

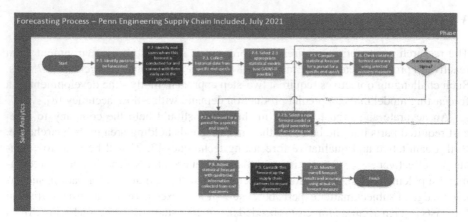

Fig. 1. Forecasting Process – Penn Engineering Supply Chain Included, Source: Quayle [7]

After completion of trials, data will be studied and analysed using SAS JMP statistical software tool. This forecasting methodology with practical problem-solving tools such as QFD should help evaluate forecast accuracy. Moreover, such an approach will ultimately aid in shifting production from push-to-pull systems, meaning that it will be more reactive and authorised by actual demand [11].

4   Results

Initial organisational current state analysis helped the researcher to understand the company's reliance on short-term customer bookings rather than forecasts. The existing Performance Optimisation platform used as a forecasting tool was abandoned due to its low accuracy levels (<60% accuracy). In addition, this tool used many different forecasting models that were too complex. The company wanted to design a long-term forecasting capability to predict market demand. Lead time (LT) in the cold forming (CF) department was, on average, 10 days, with a 12- day standard deviation (Fig. 2).

Some outliers were as high as 272 days. Meeting OTD targets were unattainable, and unreliable machines and bottleneck operations obstructed production flow. This process was not under control and was highly unpredictable. To overcome these organisational challenges, the researcher conducted an extensive literature review which identified a very broad and fragmented volume of literature on the topic.

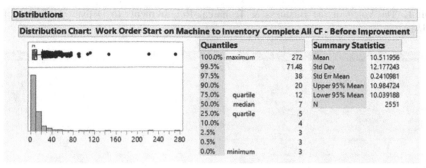

Fig. 2. Distribution diagram work order start on machine to inventory complete before improvement

The research organisation previously relied on customer bookings as a forecast, but the company president requested to develop of a forward-looking forecast to ensure that the right parts could be built into the Kanban buffer or the finished goods warehouse. The president also stated that the company's long-term forecast was based on short-term sales without a long-term horizon, i.e., the organisation relied on 3–6-month direct customer forecasts and distributor quarterly bookings. Operationally the business needed to build long-term forecasting capability that enabled the company to predict market demand trends by getting closer to end-customers.

The Quality Function Deployment tool set the foundation for the re-design forecasting process and helped define business requirements (an image of the completed VoB and technical requirements for deployment are shown in Table 1 below). Five senior company executives were interviewed to complete VOB and technical requirement sections. Forecast model technical elements that got the highest scores were not deployed in this project because the organisation could not implement them at this stage. The voice of the business was listed in the order of priority as gathered during the QFD process, while all 19 technical requirements identified during the 5 interviews were listed. It shows that only requirements: 11, 14, 17, 18 and 19 were selected for deployment in this phase. This implementation, with selected technical requirements, focuses on quantitative forecast supplemented by qualitative data; it also focuses on distributor sales, called point of sale (POS), which is explained later. The new forecast model re-design will lay the foundation for sales & operations planning (S&OP) process development and more LM systems integration in the future.

Table 1. The Voice of the Business & Technical Requirements to Deliver the Voice of the Business.

	Voice of Business	Tech. Req.
1.	Map out supply chain Ecosystem to develop an understanding of who our customers are (start at the end-user level).	17, 18, 19
2.	Develop relationships with customers in the supply chain to get demand depending our growth areas.	17, 18, 19
3.	Develop field sales strategies to collect long term needs and future trends for growth areas and capture that knowledge in a centralised way using technology.	17, 18, 19
4.	Fast development of new innovative product ideas to satisfy market wants/needs based on PESTEL and competitor analysis.	18, 19
5.	Create ability to react to customers faster than our competitors.	17, 18, 19
6.	React to other market supplier issues and capitalise on their weaknesses.	
7.	Identify all the data sources that could be used to forecast demand and connect them.	
8.	Regular, methodological competitor evaluation against our top market differentiators (quality, reactivity, tech. support, engineering, cust. service, OTD).	
9.	Regular, methodological competitor evaluation against our top market differentiators (quality, reactivity, tech. support, engineering, cust. service, OTD).	
10.	Improve on product design.	
11.	Capture End Customer long terms needs to achieve early booking predictions. Develop structure and methods.	
12.	Understand our own existing quantitative (GAINS) methodologies and accuracy.	11, 14, 17
13.	Create Lead Time variation depending on the industry, product and customer e.g., differentiated lead time. Feed back into supply chain map.	
14.	Profiling all aspects of our competitors' businesses e.g., R&D, financials, any new products.	
15.	Centralise sales-based forecast using available or new technology and standardised approach.	
16.	Include project ramp curve as a part of formal S&OP (it should be capacity planning) and forecast methodology by including all project life cycle phases : Year 1 - 10% Year 2 - 30%; Year 3 - 60%; End of life	
17.	Track relevant trends in European market in an official, centralised manner as opposed to leaving it to individual initiatives. Then capitalise on this intelligence through actionable plans on new trend development before they grow.	
18.	Develop structure and methods to analyse distributor targets and growth areas.	
19.	Analyse distributor forecast and question it.	
20.	Develop methodologies to collect voice of the customer for the lost projects in our pipeline (customer surveys, interviews, focus groups) and use the feedback to develop our product (pricing, lead times, product offering, tech. support, installation offering) based on customers' requirements.	
21.	Improve inventory turns.	19
22.	Improve on Price.	

	Technical Requirements to Deliver Voice of Business	Phase 1 of Implementation
1.	To map SCM ecosystem.	
2.	Review POS against market to identify the makeup of our customers, then rate and rank.	
3.	Develop Sales Force (SF) analytics to track wins, trends etc. Use SF as a central intelligence data collection system.	
4.	Link sales force to JDE via Qlik	
5.	Competitor analytics (using SF); regular info gathering about competitors: create a framework, study competitor parts, financial strength, history, profitability, build profiles, rate & rank. Action driven.	
6.	Customer analytics: gather info from end customers via customer focus groups, interviews etc. Use centralized database like Sales Force to store info , analyze, drive decisions.	
7.	Implement a new forecasting process 50% system based on statistics, 50% human based qualitative info.	
8.	Build reliable stock quantities during non-busy periods.	
9.	Economic index review, analysis and comparison to our strengths and weaknesses.	
10.	Allocate sufficient resources.	
11.	Reduce number of forecasting models used by GAINS and use only 2 or 3 models that are easily understood and make sense.	Y
12.	The same quantitative (statistical) forecasting models and forecast accuracy measure to be used by all SCM partners.	
13.	To start qualitative forecast at the end-user level, then cascade this forecast up to the supply chain partners (SCM).	
14.	To measure statistical forecast accuracy and if it is =<2 Sigma, then intervene using qualitative info gathered from the field sales from all SCM partners, starting with end-users.	Y
15.	Partner with academic institutions and research centers.	
16.	Segment Lead Time based on customer requirements.	
17.	Run continuous improvement programs to meet customer service level in terms of Lead Time.	Y
18.	Continue review of distributor quarterly reviews and annual plans (to measure, report back and apply metrics, performance reports and actions plans).	Y
19.	Expand S&OP Process.	Y

Following the agreement to reduce BOMs and start forecasting model testing. In addition, a kanban buffer was created for high-volume parts, which would also have to be pushed into the buffer using a new forecast and then pulled based on customer demand. Therefore, it was important to work on machine schedules, available capacity, and demand during the lead-time assessment and set up safety stock (SS) and Economic Order Quantities (EOQs). These parameters were simulated on Excel sheets; then, a pilot was launched on the S-M6 group of parts, which proved this project's viability; as a result, the roll-out commenced. Table 2 shows the calculated *Weekly Demand*, which was based on a historical 52-week production average. *Production Run Lengths* were set based on reduced changeover numbers. *LT Weeks'* value reflected the period between production runs. *Pieces Made* determined the number of pieces made during each run. Product bin sizes limited EOQs; SS was set up using supply chain standards from APICS Certified Planning & Inventory Management (CPIM) 2019 manual. *Re-order Point* reflected production pieces excluding weekly demand with Safety Stock (SS) and EOQ levels. The weight of the re-order point quantity then determined the minimum number of bins required to keep in the Kanban buffer.

Table 2. Pull system simulation parameters

SA #	LT Weeks	Production Run Length	# Shifts	EOQ	# of EOQ	Pieces Made	Re-order Point: SS+EOQ	# Bins for Re-order Point	Weekly Demand
S-M6-1SA	2	2 weeks (10 days)	3	350,000.00	6	2,100,000.00	819,870.04	3.06	737,163.32
S-M6-2SA	2	1.6 week (8 days)	3	350,000.00	5	1,750,000.00	899,752.81	3.72	437,864.04
S-M6-0SA	3	0.9 week (4.5 days)	3	350,000.00	2	700,000.00	550,131.24	1.98	83,343.60
						4,550,000.00	2,269,754.09	9 bins	

Inventory re-order point required significant amounts of stock to be built into the buffer; therefore, at the time of writing this project, the roll-out was partially completed for M6, M8 and M10 parts. The remaining M3, M4 and M5 parts were still outstanding; nevertheless, a 33% reduction in FG inventory was observed from this partial completion, with a further 25% to come from the full roll-out. WIP in the Kanban buffer increased accordingly, meaning that around 5 million pieces (worth around 100,000 USD) of inventory were no longer at risk of obsoletion in the warehouse. While the target was to reduce FG by 58%, these results proved that the objective to reduce inventory would be achieved after the full roll-out. Regarding the response to customer improvement, Fig. 3

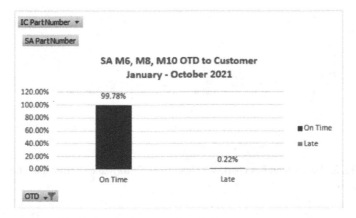

Fig. 3. Kanban part on-time delivery to customers

shows a 99.78% on-time delivery to customers for launched M6, M8 and M10 parts, while the overall OTD metric for the company is 92%, as shown in Fig. 4.

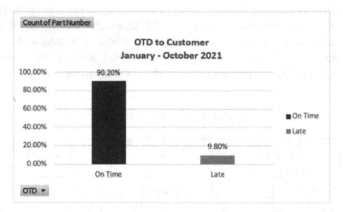

Fig. 4. All part on-time-delivery to customers

Aside from OTD improvements and reduced finished goods - significant lead-time improvements have also been noticed. Figures 5 and 6 show the Kanban buffer impact on lead-time reduction and compare the before and after stages. Such results show significant improvements compared with a 10-day lead-time average for all CF parts in the before sections of Fig. 5.

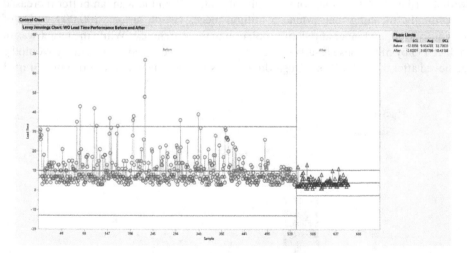

Fig. 5. Levey Jennings chart: WO lead-time performance before and after#

Regarding forecast, Quayle [7] recommends creating a process that supplements statistical results with qualitative information (Fig. 3, Appendix 5). As a result, senior company executives agreed to focus on one or two quantitative forecast models, supplemented with qualitative aspects such as management expertise and historical analogy [3]. The statistical forecasting tool based on the GAINS software had been switched off before writing this project because this system gave forecast accuracy that was <60%. This tool used multiple quantitative forecasting models and generated too many messages that had to be actioned on the Enterprise Requirements Planning (ERP) system. In order to re-design forecasting processes, the researcher selected 3 models as recommended by the APICS CPIM [3] and Quayle [7] and tested them using different levels. A design of experiments methodology did not appear viable because only one factor was at play.

Findings show that CF Kanban buffer parts could be forecasted with 88-100% accuracy. However, the researcher discovered that distributor bookings forecast for non-Kanban parts resulted in around 60% forecast accuracy. Therefore, senior executives during November 2021 meeting recommended forecasting distributor sales, known as POS, instead. They further advised comparing POS forecast findings against bookings that distributors placed. According to executives, it made more sense to forecast POS instead of bookings because the former reflected the real customer demand. As a result, POS forecast resulted in >80% forecast accuracy, mainly because there is less volatility in distributor shipments compared to the orders they place with the manufacturer.

In order to find out which model could give the best forecast accuracy, the following were tested: moving average, moving weighted average and exponential smoothing [3, 7]. The researcher used the Microsoft Excel platform to test each model at different levels. For example, moving average and weighted moving average models were tested using 3- and 6-month sample data, while the exponential smoothing model was tested using 0.1, 0.2, 0.3, 07, 0.8 and 0.9 alpha smoothing constants. Fig. 6 shows in - One-way Analysis of Predictive 2022 Q1 Forecast Accuracy by Experimental Setting that the *best* results were obtained from the exponential smoothing model, and the average forecast accuracy of >80% was achieved when POS was forecasted. APIC's CPIM [3] recommends using the following formula to calculate the exponential smoothing forecast:

New Forecast $= (\alpha * \text{Latest Demand}) + ((1 - \alpha) * (\text{Previous Forecast}))$

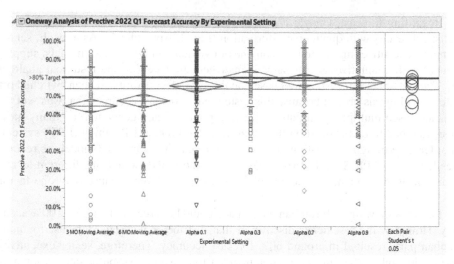

Fig. 6. One-way analysis of predictive 2022 Q1 forecast accuracy by setting

There was a small challenge related to these forecast models, which can predict the new forecast only when the latest demand data is available. Unfortunately, the latest demand data in the company is not available for *the previous* period until the middle of *the next* period for which the forecast is needed. To overcome this challenge, a qualitative technique called historical analogy was used [3], which looks at historical forecasts and accuracy. In this case, this technique uses the last available information to predict *the next* period. To illustrate this, Table 3 has been prepared, where the researcher recommends forecasting 2022 Q1 using the 2021 Q4 forecast and 2021 Q3 accuracy.

Table 3. Forecast and accuracy for catalogue POS 2019–2021

Catalogue POS Forecast Accuracy 2019-2021			
Experimental Setting	Part Number	2021 Q3 Accuracy 80%	2021 Q4 Forecast
Alpha 0.3	S-M3-1ZI	80%	4,479,425.33
Alpha 0.3	S-M4-1ZI	81%	3,589,284.22
Alpha 0.3	S-M4-2ZI	94%	3,192,926.37

The above information was presented to senior executives, who recommended comparing predictive exponential smoothing forecast for POS and actual bookings while considering distributor channel inventory. As the exponential smoothing forecast is based on distributor shipments, this analysis will allow the management team to ascertain whether distributors book orders with the company in line with their shipments, also known as POS. Table 4, *Bookings vs Exponential Smoothing Forecast on Distributor Shipments* column marks in red bookings that are under-booked compared to POS forecast; and overbooked bookings marked in black. The table shows that some distributors are over-booked by 71%, while others are underbooked by 58%. Distributor inventory should also be close to *Predicted Exponential Smoothing Forecast for Distributor Shipments 2022/Q1* value because the company has a legal agreement to keep 25–35% of annual distributor shipments in the distributor warehouse. However, as seen from *the Distributor Inventory* analysis, some distributor inventory is too low.

Table 4. Exponential smoothing forecast vs. actual bookings

Part Number	Distributor Name	Predicted Exponential Smoothing Forecast for Distributor Shipments 2022/Q1	Distributor Inventory December 2021	Distributor Bookings 2022/Q1	Bookings v.s. Exponential Smoothing Forecast in Pieces	Bookings v.s. Quarterly Average Distributor Shipments	Bookings v.s. Exponential Smoothing Forecast on Distributor Shipments
S-M3-1ZI	Distributor 1	230,604.99	15,720.00	200,000.00	- 30,604.99	8%	15%
S-M3-1ZI	Distributor 2	168,181.75	232,700.00	400,000.00	231,818.25	46%	58%
S-M3-1ZI	Distributor 3	146,170.27	228,500.00	#N/A	#N/A	#N/A	#N/A
S-M3-1ZI	Distributor 4	643,596.94	1,118,595.00	500,000.00	- 143,596.94	13%	29%
S-M3-1ZI	Distributor 5	2,629,440.39	2,865,200.00	3,000,000.00	370,559.61	18%	12%
S-M3-1ZI	Distributor 6	137,107.45	263,797.00	105,000.00	- 32,107.45	25%	31%
SS-M5-2ZI	Distributor 1	158,495.45	44,000.00	100,000.00	- 58,495.45	76%	58%
SS-M5-2ZI	Distributor 2	160,662.00	365,800.00	200,000.00	39,338.00	23%	20%
SS-M5-2ZI	Distributor 3	114,813.18	169,600.00	-	- 114,813.18	#DIV/0!	#DIV/0!
SS-M5-2ZI	Distributor 4	360,773.48	322,220.00	754,000.00	393,226.52	52%	52%
SS-M5-2ZI	Distributor 5	869,661.26	705,700.00	1,250,000.00	380,338.74	35%	30%
SS-M5-2ZI	Distributor 6	96,483.55	38,810.00	336,000.00	239,516.45	73%	71%

5   Discussion

The research findings indicate significant improvements in lead time, inventory, on-time delivery and forecast accuracy. Furthermore, accurate predictive forecasts can significantly improve operations and smooth demand to meet required customer service level agreements. Even though inventory improvements were achieved *only* in the CF department and predictive forecast methodology was newly developed, this project provided confidence that the same methodologies could be used for consecutive roll-outs. Therefore, this work proved that LM practices and robust forecasting methods must be in place to achieve the required customer SLAs in volatile environments to enable more Lean pull and JIT production. In summary, this work proved that robust forecasting could be a precursor for LM to improve JIT and OTD measures.

Despite several challenges faced throughout the implementation of this project, the research objectives were achieved as outlined in the results and findings section. The organisation also needed to reduce the risk of inventory obsoletion and FG levels. A historical 52-week average forecasting method was selected to predict buffer parts requirements. Such a simplistic method was chosen to forecast Kanban buffer parts because selected parts were in high demand, and not much volatility was present in bookings. However, non- Kanban/non-buffer parts required the implementation of more complex forecasting methodologies because of their demand volatility.

Most of the literature on forecasting discussed either qualitative or quantitative models, while some academics believe that forecasts are rarely accurate and that company executives do not trust them [9]. Industry research revealed that combining qualitative and quantitative methods would improve forecasts [3, 7]. However, the research findings suggest that the company was not in a position to consider more advanced qualitative forecasting techniques, such as the Delphi model [3] or end customer information collection because of time constraints. Only management expertise and historical analogy [3] could be used as qualitative methodologies at this stage. However, the Delphi model or end user feedback should provide a forward-looking forecast; therefore, the organisation must investigate these possibilities in the future.

Overall, >80% forecasting accuracy was achieved for POS forecasts. Senior executives confirmed that forecasting distributor bookings were not as important, as these did not reflect the real demand, while POS more accurately showed customer needs. Table 5 shows the company's POS and bookings forecast accuracy using exponential smoothing alpha constant 0.3 for 2019, 2020 and 2021. Bookings show lower forecast accuracy, which indicates higher volatility. POS results show higher accuracy, which indicates that distributor sales are less volatile than their bookings with the research company.

Table 5. Exponential smoothing forecast to forecast POS and distributor bookings

Average	2019	2020	2021 till September
Monthly POS Shipments Qty	68,647,760.00	63,103,992.17	80,699,824
POS Forecast Accuracy	84%	70%	88%
Channel Monthly Ending Inventory Qty	300,016,675.00	315,319,790	248,819,518
PEM Backlog	233,762,224.00	168,553,999	295,656,927
PEM Europe Monthly Bookings Qty	60,985,115.00	56,780,471	96,469,430
Bookings Forecast Accuracy	78%	59%	61%
PEM Europe Inventory	83,404,847.00	87,317,458	61,444,300

This paragraph discusses how > 80% of POS forecast findings should be used together with LM practices by the research organisation to meet required SLAs. When the researcher compared bookings versus forecast, it was noted that some distributors were over-booked, and some were under-booked (Table 6). This is because distributors use inaccurate forecast models, and price incentives drive their bookings. Such practices create difficulties at the manufacturing facility because they cause demand volatility. Overbooked Distributors compromise the organisation's manufacturing capability to produce parts to customers that are under-booked, e.g., *Distributor 1* is under-booked by 58% for the part number: SS-M5-2ZI. The research organisation will supply the same part to *Distributor 6*, which is over-booked by 71%, and at the same time will ensure that *Distributor 1* also gets all demand. This puts much pressure on production lines at the facility, even if the right LM systems are in place. Therefore, the company should communicate forecast and over-booked/under-booked values to distributors requesting deferrals in line with the forecast, which has high accuracy levels. Such actions should smooth out demand and reduce pressure on the manufacturing facility. In addition, distributor inventory is not aligned with the contractual manufacturer's requirement (i.e., 25–35% of annual POS). It is either too low or too high, meaning that distributors place orders to replenish their inventory when it is too low. At the time of writing this project, the customer service team was asked to reach out to distributors to smooth their bookings in line with the forecast, and due to time constraints, results were not available to report here.

By having high accurate POS forecast, the company overcomes volatility related to orders that distributors place with the factory. When writing this project, the researcher could not show smoothed demand based on POS forecast accuracy, but the recommendation to the organisation has been provided. In addition, significant inventory turnover improvements have been observed since the beginning of this project, as demonstrated in the *before* and *after* phases in Table 6. It is highly recommended that management continue to monitor these KPIs and identify building blocks that link LM to increased inventory turns.

Table 6. KPIs before and after improvements

High-Level Project KPIs	Before	After
Lead-time:	10 days	<5 days
Forecast Accuracy:	NA for POS*	70-88% for Point of Sale
Critical Impact KPIs	Before	After
Inventory Turnover:	4.9	8.98

6 Conclusion

The paper aims to develop a new forecast methodology to enable an automotive manufacturer to achieve its required service level agreements. The research developed a forecasting model to predict production demand accurately, thus reducing inventory and lead-time to customers, improving on-time delivery and saving on costs. The new forecast methodology facilitated >80% forecast accuracy on distributor shipments to end customers and thus improved the manufacturer's response to customers. The forecasting model is an enabler for the future stage of the research to apply Lean principles to enhance inventory reduction and customer lead time further. Lean tools will be applied to impact forecasting efficiencies and enable a leaner manufacturing process.

A limitation of this research was that Production planning process inefficiencies are not discussed in this research due to scope considerations, although this problem can be addressed by management. In summary, it is necessary to emphasise that while the company is trying to implement correct forecasting and LM practices using pull and JIT principles, it should also focus on other production aspects, such as the production planning process, because ignoring it may have a negative impact on the outcomes of this project.

References

1. Gligor, A., Vlasa, I., Dumitru, C.-D., Moldovan, C.E., Damian, C.: Power demand forecast for optimisation of the distribution costs. Procedia Manuf. **46**, 384–390 (2020). https://doi.org/10.1016/j.promfg.2020.03.056
2. Chien, C.-F., Hsu, C.-Y., Hsiao, C.-W.: Manufacturing intelligence to forecast and reduce semiconductor cycle time. J. Intell. Manuf. **23**, 2281–2294 (2012). https://doi.org/10.1007/s10845-011-0572-y
3. APICs: CPIM Part 1 : Basics of Supply Chain Management. ASCM, Chicago
4. Danese, P., Kalchschmidt, M.: The role of the forecasting process in improving forecast accuracy and operational performance. Int. J. Prod. Econ. **131**, 204–214 (2011). https://doi.org/10.1016/j.ijpe.2010.09.006
5. Fildes, R., Goodwin, P., Lawrence, M., Nikolopoulos, K.: Effective forecasting and judgmental adjustments: an empirical evaluation and strategies for improvement in supply-chain planning. Int. J. Forecast. **25**, 3–23 (2009). https://doi.org/10.1016/j.ijforecast.2008.11.010
6. Cornel, L., Mirela, L.: Delphi-the highest qualitative forecast method. Buletinul Universităţii Petrol–Gaze din Ploieşti Seria Ştiinţe Economice., 31–36 (2008)
7. Quayle, M.: Purchasing and Supply Chain Management: Strategies and Realities. Idea Group, Hershey (2006)
8. Kim, I., Tang, C.S.: Lead time and response time in a pull production control system. Eur. J. Oper. Res. **101**, 474–485 (1997). https://doi.org/10.1016/S0377-2217(96)00174-9
9. Wacker, J.G., Sprague, L.G.: The impact of institutional factors on forecast accuracy: manufacturing executives perspective. Int. J. Prod. Res. **33**, 2945–2958 (1995)
10. Erdil, N.O., Arani, O.M.: Quality function deployment: more than a design tool. Int. J. Qual. Serv. Sci. **11**, 142–166 (2019). https://doi.org/10.1108/IJQSS-02-2018-0008
11. Pyke, D.F., Cohen, M.A.: Push and pull in manufacturing and distribution systems. J. Oper. Manag. **9**, 24–43 (1990). https://doi.org/10.1016/0272-6963(90)90144-3

Sustaining the Effectiveness of Lean Six Sigma Implementation in a Medical Device Company

Aaron McHugh$^{(\boxtimes)}$ and Fionnuala Farrell

Department of Mechanical and Manufacturing Engineering, Atlantic Technical University-Sligo, Sligo, Ireland
arnmcu@gmail.com, Fionnuala.farrell@atu.ie

Abstract. Lean Six Sigma (LSS) is a common methodology adopted by organizations to improve operational and financial performance by removing waste and reducing variation. While literature agrees LSS is beneficial, it is unclear whether the initial improved performance is sustained over time. Research has identified several critical success (CSFs) and failure (CFF's) factors which determine the effectiveness of LSS implementation along with its sustainability. Integral in sustaining the initial positive impact is recognizing these success factors during LSS implementation in conjunction with identifying and preventing critical failure factors.

This study aims to investigate whether the implementation of LSS has sustained a positive impact on the operational and financial performance of a Medical Device Company based in the West of Ireland. Using a mixed method approach; a case-study within one Medical Device organization was conducted. Key performance indicators (KPI's) such as defects and non-conformances were analyzed and trended. Additionally, survey data of critical success and failure factors in the areas of management, training, and culture was collated. The quantity of unit rejects, which ultimately leads to increased costs was used as the financial indicator in this study. The influence of Quality 4.0 and the global pandemic were also considered. A comparison was then made with two other similar sized companies in the region using semi- structured interviews.

Results indicated LSS has a sustained positive impact on the organization's operational and financial performance. Findings suggest Quality 4.0 was a significant contributing factor for sustaining this positive performance. The pandemic was shown to magnify the failure factors albeit offset somewhat by Quality 4.0. The comparison with the other two medical device organizations suggested that LSS alone could not sustain a positive impact highlighting the need to conduct further research into self-sustaining LSS methodologies along with the value to consider the new 'LSS 4.0' approach.

Keywords: LSS implementation · LSS sustainability · Critical success factors · Critical failure factors · Medical device

© IFIP International Federation for Information Processing 2023
Published by Springer Nature Switzerland AG 2023
O. McDermott et al. (Eds.): ELEC 2022, IFIP AICT 668, pp. 165–183, 2023.
https://doi.org/10.1007/978-3-031-25741-4_15

1   Introduction

1.1   Introduction to Lean and Six Sigma Methodologies

Lean manufacturing, embedded in the Toyota Production System, is a technique which identifies opportunities to *eliminate waste* and non-value add activities [1–3]. Lean works as a cost-cutting strategy targeting an organization's competitiveness by improving process efficiency, optimizing human resources, and lowering costs by eliminating steps which provide no additional value [4, 5]. There are 5 core principles for lean manufacturing practices which comprise of defining the value, mapping the value stream, creating flow through the process, establishing pull, and seeking perfection [5, 6].

Six sigma is a technique used for process improvements aiming to maximize profits and uses statistical measures such as Statistical Process control (SPC); Design of Experiments (DOE) and Failure Mode and Effects Analysis (FMEA) to determine the efficiency/quality of a product/service [7]. Studies by Costa et al., [8], and Sim et al., [5], both suggest that six sigma focuses on business process improvements through *minimizing process variation* and conducting root cause analysis to reduce defects, therefore enhanced quality. The DMAIC process (Define, Measure, Analyze, Implement, Control) is Six Sigma's most utilized methodology aiming to improve existing business processes [7, 9, 10]. Six Sigma has progressed from solely using statistical tools and is currently used by organizations to improve their overall operational and financial performance, eliminate, or reduce defects, reduce process lead times and ultimately improve customer satisfaction [5, 11, 12].

1.2   Lean Six Sigma (LSS)

Combining both Lean and Six Sigma methodologies enhances an organization's ability to produce optimal results in terms of operational and financial efficiency, allowing for an overall greater performance than if each method was implemented separately [5, 6, 13, 14]. LSS has a two-pronged approach to minimizing waste and increasing value while also addressing quality issues that affect product and process performance and repeatability [7, 15, 16]. Alhuraish, et al., [17] theorized that an integrated LSS methodology improves a company's ability to achieve optimal results through waste reduction. LSS techniques are more efficient, resulting in a more prosperous manufacturing process with less waste and defects [18].

Despite the popularity of LSS, companies often revert to their old ways or let their standards falter after initially showing promising results, but which ultimately prove to be somewhat unsustainable due to various failure factors [19, 20]. While the research tends to agree that the implementation of LSS techniques is beneficial, the sustained impact that LSS has on operational and financial performances in the Medical Device Industry is not adequately measured [2, 8]. Prior research on LSS has tended to focus more on the key or critical success and failure factors of either lean, six sigma, or LSS but it is more focused on its implementation rather than sustaining LSS over time [19, 21, 22].

Many companies struggle to sustain LSS methodologies after implementation as they are unaware of the success or positive impact that these tools have [16]. The difficulty sustaining LSS initiatives may be due to failures in identifying new projects, a lack of support or focus from management or a failure to assign skilled personnel [14]. This research aims to bridge that gap for an Irish Medical Device company based in the West of Ireland through providing empirical evidence to prove if LSS can sustain a positive impact on the operational and financial performance. Specifically, the research questions considered in this study are two-fold:

1. *Does the implementation of lean six sigma techniques have a sustained positive impact on the operational and financial performance in a Medical Device Company based in the West of Ireland?*
2. *Is there any indication that this impact is shared by similar Medical Device Companies in the West of Ireland?*

Structured into five sections, this paper presents *Sect.* 1 covering an introduction of Lean, Six Sigma, LSS and Sustainability of LSS and outlining the study's aim. *Section* 2 covers a literature review, which includes a review of Lean Six Sigma in Industry, Operational and financial performance indicators, the critical success and failure factors, the influence of Quality4.0 and the global pandemic on LSS. *Section* 3 explains the research methodology, details of the survey and limitations. *Section* 4 covers results and analysis. *Section* 5 provides a discussion and concluding comments specifying the implications of this research and directions for future research.

2 Literature Review

2.1 Lean Six Sigma in Industry

Lean Six Sigma (LSS) continues to grow in popularity and is considered one of the most effective methodologies used in the manufacturing industry for continuous improvement with larger manufacturing organizations more likely having LSS implemented than smaller ones typically due to resource constraints [13, 23, 24]. In contrast with most of the literature reviewed, Singh and Rathi, [2] found that LSS is implemented in the manufacturing sector to a lesser extent, albeit rapidly growing, than in the service and automobile sector. A study by Iyede, et al., [12], found that the extent of LSS implementation by manufacturing companies based in the West of Ireland was low in comparison to countries such as the UK, Belgium and Australia. This may be due to resource scarcity and lacking implementation know-how. Within the medical device industry, where strict regulatory standards by the US Food and Drug Administration (FDA), International Standards Organization (ISO) 13485, which outlines the requirements for Quality Management Systems for Medical Devices, and European Union Medical Device Regulation (EU MDR) need to be met, LSS has been shown to help with compliance [25–27].

The reasons why LSS is implemented tends to vary by industry and organizational strategic objectives, however the top reason given, according to research by Patel and Desai [23], was process improvement at 29%, followed by defect reduction, rework, and scrap at 16%. Continuous improvement methodologies such as LSS are proving to be the key for organizations to achieve operational excellence. Interestingly, even despite being in a highly regulated industry, McDermott et al.'s study [28]; which assessed the readiness and maturity of continuous improvement (CI) deployment in the medical device industry; found there was an overall *'positive culture of acceptance and embracing of CI methods and initiatives'*. It was suggested by Nour and Laux [27] that the Define-Measure-Analyze- Improve and Control (DMAIC) methodology has shown potential to improve the Corrective and Preventive Action (CAPA) process within medical device organizations which can help them to meet FDA regulations.

Organizations tend to implement different LSS tools and there is no set standard or set structure for the LSS tools that should be implemented – see Fig. 1. Although not all companies possess the capabilities or resources to implement either LM or six sigma, Alhuraish, et al., [17] show that a sequential integration of both in the form of lean six sigma methodologies produce the optimal results for companies in terms of operational and financial performance.

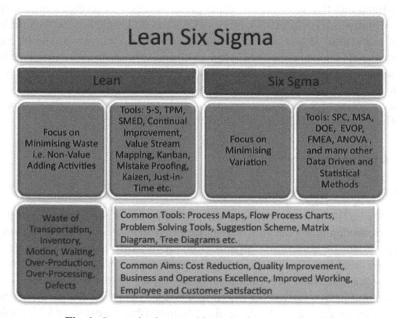

Fig. 1. Lean, six sigma and lean six sigma overview [3]

Notwithstanding this, however, Cortes et al., [30] highlight that it can be difficult to evaluate the success of lean six sigma due to the lack of relevant methods or indicators from which to evaluate them. Some of the most effective LSS tools used within organizations are 5S, Poka-Yoke, Kanban, Value Stream Mapping (VSM), Kaizen, DMAIC, and Plan-do-check-act (PDCA) [2, 29]. However, DMAIC is one of the least utilized tools with brainstorming, Standardized work and visual control most often deployed [16] as illustrated in Fig. 2.

Tools	Used %	Tools	Used %
Brainstorming	100	Poka-yoke	81.8
Standardized Work	97	VSM	81.8
Visual Control	97	Gemba	78.8
PDCA	97	Kanban	78.8
Cause and effect diagram	97	SMED	72.7
5S	93.9	Control chart	72.7
Pareto chart	93.9	Takt time	69.7
Flow chart	93.9	Design of Experiment	63.6
Check sheet	90.9	DPMO	60.6
TPM	84.8	Once piece Flow	57.6
VOC	84.8	DMAIC	57.6
FMEA	84.8	Cellular layout	48.5
Kaizen team	81.8	Regression analysis	39.4

Fig. 2. Status of lean manufacturing and six sigma tools within industry [16]

2.2 Operational and Financial Performance Indicators

Organizations are continuously looking for ways to achieve optimal financial and operational performance. Literature indicates that companies that implement both Lean and Six Sigma have an enhanced operational, financial; customer satisfaction and innovation performance since certain tools are more advantageous towards different metrics [5, 7, 8, 13, 16, 17, 31].

Most industries use annual savings or benefits as a performance measure after implementing LSS methodology, followed by the sigma index, defect reduction, and cost reduction but key performance indicators (KPIs) are more effective if they are tailored to the organization's own specific goals and values [23, 32]. KPI's tend do vary greatly between organizations or even internally in an organization and therefore it can be difficult to get a true sense of the success of LSS, but nevertheless they are invaluable if used in the right manner [23, 33]. Some of the most common operational KPI's include defects, lead time, down time, on-time delivery, and rework [13, 23, 34, 35, 36].

2.3 Critical Success and Critical Failure Factors

LSS implementation has not always been successful in the manufacturing and service industries and can be a result of various critical failure or success factors [37]. Summarized concisely, in a study by Yadav, et al., [3], were the factors responsible for the success of LSS implementation from multiple perspectives and the study focused primarily on the success factors for when LSS is implemented using Quality 4.0 technologies. Part of their literature review also identified the barriers of LSS implementation. These critical success factors were summarized by Jeyaraman, K. and Kee Teo, L. [38] and are presented in Fig. 3.

Management's commitment, resources, training, and organizational culture were identified as areas of criticality in relation to the implementation and sustained success of LSS [10, 21, 22]. Management must be actively involved and support LSS for it to be a success while ensuring that sufficient resources are in place and any obstacles which may arise are dealt with [22, 37, 38]. An organization's top management's vision and strategies must be clearly communicated and aligned with LSS goals which the employees will work towards [40, 41, 42]. Creating this communication channel allows for information to be passed through management which is critical for employees to understand the objectives of the organization [20, 22, 43, 44].

As the LSS methodology becomes established within an organization, the employees should be sufficiently trained on all aspects of the LSS implementation to ensure that there is the necessary knowledge base which empowers the employees to take action when needed [21, 43, 44]. Training employees is a critical success factor for organizations which allows the employees to understand the tools and philosophy around LSS [38, 44]. Additionally, continuous improvement must be embedded within an organization's culture for successful LSS and if absent needs to be developed [22, 43, 45]. Significant organizational change is required for LSS implementation which may be initially daunting for employees, but they must be encouraged to embrace the change as part of the cultural shift [6, 17].

LSS should be set up for sustained success during the Control phase of the DMAIC methodology [5, 11, 12]. However, many companies have difficulty sustaining LSS and identifying critical success factors is crucial in allowing the company to sustain the benefits [14, 24, 46]. Introducing LSS into an organization is relatively straight forward and well understood however, sustaining the improvements gained can be more of a challenge [14, 42]. Knowledge and the ability to ensure the presence of the critical success factors, as summarized in Fig. 3, is vital in attempting to sustain its positive influence on performance. Highlighted in this figure are the top three areas of Management commitment, organizational belief & culture, and effective training.

2.4   Influence of Industry 4.0 and Quality 4.0 on Lean Six Sigma

Lean Six Sigma can be integrated with Industry 4.0 to optimize process efficiency. A systematic literature review on the integration of Industry 4.0 and Lean Six Sigma, conducted by Antony *et al.*, [32] found that *"there are benefits, motivations, critical success factors, and challenges to integrating Lean Six Sigma and Industry 4.0"*. Specifically, their literature review found that lean practices have a positive association with Industry 4.0 technologies and implementing them simultaneously leads to greater performance improvements [32]. Interestingly, it was found that Industry 4.0 provides little/no support for waste reduction via the softer lean principles of people and teamwork, one which was highlighted as a critical success factor through management and culture [32].

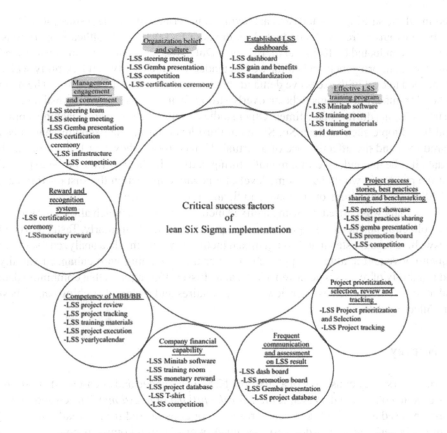

Fig. 3. Critical success factors of lean six sigma implementation [38]

Quality 4.0 is the application of Industry 4.0 technologies such as the Internet-of-Things (IoT), Machine Learning, Artificial Intelligence (AI), Big-Data and Robotics to ensure quality improvement. Fundamentally it is the digitalization of total quality management, and the core concept is to align the practice of quality management with the emerging capabilities of Industry 4.0 to help organizations towards operational excellence [47]. Quality 4.0 has a positive impact on LSS and the combination of the two optimizes the service supply process while also reducing the waste of both human and material resources [48, 49]. The introduction of quality 4.0 is beneficial in overcoming some of the common barriers for LSS implementation and can help organizations to sustain LSS [3, 48].

2.5 Impact of Global Pandemic on Lean Six Sigma

Covid-19 has had a significant impact on the manufacturing industry in terms of workforce reductions, worker health and safety, and other financial constraints resulting from production losses and site closures [50]. As a result, the importance of maintaining a competitive edge has expanded even more. LSS strategies can assist organizations' in meeting these shifting demands and achieving long-term, sustainable results [40]. There has been extensive research conducted on impact of COVID on healthcare operations. In a study conducted by Kuiper *et al.* [51] on a Dutch healthcare institution, it was found that process improvement in healthcare has tended to cut capacity and flexibility which are needed to deal with excessive demand shocks, such as during a pandemic. The main reason for this failure seems to be an overly strong focus on cost reduction instigated by Lean Six Sigma during stable times. Other studies around the impact on teaching a practical based topic such as Lean Six Sigma at third level during the pandemic have been shared [52] and the effective use of a virtual 'Kaizen room', however limited research to date has been conducted in a manufacturing setting. In theory, it would be expected that the pandemic would have some level of a negative impact on the sustained impact of LSS for organizations operational and financial performance.

This study was carried out using a mixed methods approach which allows for greater data collection and achieves a greater overall perspective [53]. Similarly, Tashakkori and Creswell, [54] suggested that through mixed methods, where the data analyzed uses both a quantitative and qualitative approach, a better understanding with enhanced validity and reliability of results is achieved. Collis and Hussey, [55] advises that combining data collection methods such as interviews, questionnaires and archive searching can be best for collecting data.

3 Survey

A structured survey consisting of a mixture of 27 closed-ended and open-ended questions was used to collect the data (see *Table 1 for the full list of questions*). The closed-ended questions used a 5- point Likert scale (response options ranged from 'greatly increased or much better' to 'greatly decreased or much worse') with comment boxes added to allow for feedback for each question and a non-applicable 'N/A' option– this aligned to previous research conducted [16]. The questions constructed for the survey were primarily informed by literature findings in terms of the main key performance indicators [35, 36, 44, 51, 56, 57].

The final questionnaire was administered to 108 participants across three different business units within the company. The questionnaire was distributed electronically to participants through Survey Monkey, via email, and in printed format, distributed in person where Covid restrictions allowed. 76 responses were received giving a 70% response rate. This is in line with Yun GW and Trumbo CW [58], who carried out a study on response rate using a multi-mode approach where a 72% response rate was achieved; an improvement from an earlier study carried out by Schaefer DR and Dillman DA [59] which ascertained that a multimode approach to email administration of a survey will enhance response rates and obtaining rates close to 60% could be expected.

3.1 Case Study

An archival study of available data within the researcher's own company was carried out which analyzed some of the key metrics such as non-conformances, yield and number of rejects. Data for the number of non-conformances, yield and the number of reject units for each of the three business units from the fiscal years of 2016 to 2022 were collected.

From the results of the survey questionnaire, summarized in Sect. 4 of this paper, a set of 8 general questions were developed *[as presented in Table 2]* which aimed to further develop the survey findings and to examine if these findings were common with two similar sized Medical Device companies based in the West of Ireland. The criteria to participate in this qualitative interview was that of being a Medical Device company based in the West of Ireland, have LSS techniques implemented and be of similar size in terms of employee numbers when compared to the researcher's company. The first company was represented by a Senior Quality Engineer while the second company was represented by a Process Improvement Program Manager. All semi-structured interviews were performed via individual Zoom calls and each interview was recorded through an electronic device after receiving the consent of the interviewee. The interview was replicated with a senior representative from the Lean department from the researcher's own company to validate the findings from the in-house survey.

Table 1. Survey questions

	Section
Question	1) Introduction
1	My role is:
2	How many years of experience do you have in the Medical Device sector?
3	What area or department do you work in?
4	Which of these most common Lean Six Sigma tools are in use in your area?
	2) Key Performance Indicators
5	Over the last 3 years, the average number of defects in your work area has:
6	Over the last 3 years, the average number of man or method related NCMR's has:
7	Over the last 3 years, the process or work-step lead time has:(i.e. the time between the initiation and completion of a process/step)
8	Over the last 3 years, the number of A3's (DMAIC) being actively worked on has:
9	Over the last 3 years, the use of LSS tools in my working area has:
10	Over the last 3 years, the downtime of the workflow or process has (e.g. machine out of action or components unavailable):
11	Over the last 3 years, the on-time delivery of results being met has: (e.g. daily manufacturing targets met or product released on time)
12	Over the last 3 years, the number of escapes has: (e.g. product released without complete worksteps)
13	Please leave any comments in relation to KPI's (Questions 5-12) and Lean Six Sigma below:
	3) Management
14	Over the last 3 years, encouragement from management to implement change or improvement ideas has:
15	Over the last 3 years, communication of successes or results from improvement projects has:
16	Over the last 3 years, resources allocated to continuous improvement initiatives has:(e.g. of resources are personnel, funding, time)
17	Please leave any comments that you may have in relation to management (questions 14-16) and Lean Six Sigma below.
	4) Training
18	Over the last 3 years, the amount of training received for the use of continuous improvement tools (e.g. A3's) has:
19	Over the last 3 years, my teams understanding of how to use LSS tools has:
20	Please leave any comments that you may have in relation to training (questions 18-19) and Lean Six Sigma below.
	5) Culture
21	Over the last 3 years, employee engagement in continuous improvement ideas or initiatives has:
22	Over the last 3 years, the company has maintained a strong emphasis on quality.
23	Over the last 3 years, I feel like I can voice my suggestions or improvement ideas:
24	When changes have been made to improve the work process, the improvement efforts are sustained over the long run
25	Please leave any comments in relation to culture (questions 21-24) and Lean Six Sigma below:
	6) Closing Questions
26	In your own opinion, what impact do you believe the pandemic has had on operations, if any?
27	Any further Comments in releation to LSS?

Table 2. List of semi-structured interview questions

	Question
1	What is your role, how long are you working in company X and how does your role relate to LSS?
2	What are the most common LSS tools used in your company?
3	What LSS tools have you found to be the most effective?
4	LSS has been shown to have a positive impact on operational performance. Have you found that this is the case in your company?
5	Have you found that LSS has been capable of sustaining the impact over the last 3 years?
6	Have you found that LSS has been capable of sustaining a positive financial impact over the last 3 years?
7	What impact has the pandemic had on sustaining LSS in operations?
8	Has your company any plans to digitalise any of your processes through industry 4.0 or quality 4.0 methods which could benefit LSS?

4   Results

From the eligible responses there was an even split across job roles albeit a somewhat higher number of operators [44%] as captured in Fig. 4. Three Business units within the organization were represented equally as seen in Fig. 5 with approximately one third from each business unit – Peripheral, Aortic and Coronary.

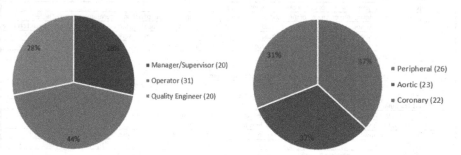

Fig. 4. Respondents job role   **Fig. 5.** Respondents operating unit

4.1   Analysis of Results

The results of the survey were analyzed using Minitab software at a 95% confidence level. The answers to the survey's closed ended questions were gathered using a Likert Scale with N/A at a score of 1 and the corresponding scoring classified as per Table 3 from very positive to very negative. One- tailed t-tests were carried out to test the statistical hypothesis and to show that the sample mean either accepts or rejects the null hypothesis [H0] which states that:

'the implementation of Lean Six Sigma techniques does not have a sustained positive impact on the operational and financial performance of a Medical Device Company based in the West of Ireland'.

Table 3. Likert scale classification

Very positive	Positive	Unchanged	Negative	Very negative
2.0–2.49	2.5–3.49	3.5–4.49	4.5–5.49	5.5–6.0

Additionally, ANOVA tests were performed to analyze the statistical significance of survey results from different job functions and different business units within the company. Since LSS is a methodology for continuous improvement, the performance measurements over time should improve or at least maintained at the initial positive performance results obtained once critical failure factors were mitigated [5, 11, 12, 62, 14]. Therefore, it was anticipated that the results for the key performance indicators should improve or maintain performance over the last 3 years. A result of ≤ 4.5 was a positive or neutral result based on the Likert scale while a result of > 4.5 was considered negative as per Table 3. The only result which proved to be negative was the critical success factor of training.

4.2 Key Performance Indicators and Critical Success Factors

The overall company results can be seen in Fig. 4 below. The Key Performance Indicators (KPIs) and Critical Success Factors (CSFs) were all less than 4.5 except for the CSF for training at 4.51 which marginally received a negative result. While the remaining CSF's and the KPI's did not improve over the last 3 years, they remained unchanged and therefore sustained their level of performance. 10 respondents claimed that the performance would have been lower over the last 3 years had it not been for 'SAP-ME' (SAP Manufacturing Execution) which is a Quality 4.0 enhancement tool which converted many manual or paper-based processes into automated and system-controlled processes. Absenteeism during the pandemic was shown to be the main obstacle for maintaining KPIs' performance. Not only was there a lack of resources in terms of personnel, but the survey responses (Fig. 5) showed that supply chain was greatly impacted by the unavailability of components resulting in significant downtime in operations. The pandemic led to several personnel working from home and there were restrictions on movement in the workplace. The responses showed that this led to a reduction in the quality and level of training received over the previous 3 years. This was reflected in the 'training' CSF result showing a marginally negative response; further analysis of the results highlights this specifically in one business unit [see Table 4] (Fig. 7).

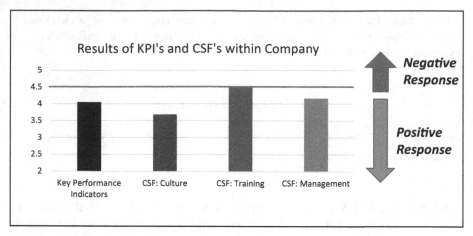

Fig. 6. Mean results of KPI's and the perception of existence of LSS critical success factors

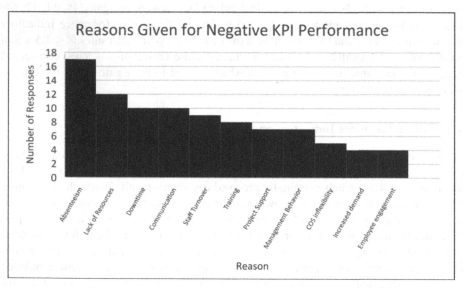

Fig. 7. Reasons for KPI/CSF being sustained at the same level of performance

4.3 Business Unit Comparison

The results shown in Table 4 below presents a comparison across the 3 business units - Peripheral, Aortic and Coronary. The difference in results found across the 3 business units were significant (p- value of 0.00 between each unit) with the Peripheral business unit returning the most negative results followed by Aortic and then the Coronary unit responses were most positive. Unlike the Aortic and Coronary units, the Peripheral unit did not implement Quality 4.0 enhancements, including the introduction of SAP-ME. Comments on the responses given highlighted that SAP-ME was accredited for maintaining several of the KPI's within the Aortic and Coronary units. The main LSS technique which was found to be in use within the company was the cell-operating-system (COS). The COS combines many of the LSS tools including standardized work, 5s, Heijunka, and Kaizen. During the pandemic, the Peripheral unit was unable to maintain its COS due to a lack of resources and knowledge of the COS technique. This stemmed from a lack of training, a high turnover of staff and a high absenteeism rate which all resulted in significantly worse results when compared to the Aortic and Coronary units. Through the COS disbanding and the lack of Quality 4.0 implementation, the Peripheral unit returned the most negative KPI and CSF results overall.

Table 4. Comparison of KPIs, tools and CSF's between business units.

Mean values			
Measurement:	Peripheral	Aortic	Coronary
Key performance indicators	4.47	4.00	3.73
Tools/DMAICs	4.65	3.63	3.42
CSF: Culture	4.01	3.46	3.27
CSF: Training	5.08	4.06	3.87
CSF: Management	4.74	3.75	3.49

4.4 Non-conformances, Yield and Rejects

The non-conformance data seen in Fig. 6 shows the 'man and method' related non-conformance data. The number of man or method Non-conformance Material Reports (NCMRs) generated within the Peripheral and Coronary units reduced by almost 50% after COS implementation which shows the benefits of this LSS technique. Quality 4.0 was introduced via SAP-ME in May 2019 to the Coronary and Aortic units. There was a slight reduction in the number of NCMR's after this introduction which further enhanced the COS LSS implementation. More crucially however, it shows that the number of NCMR's opened remained relatively consistent since its introduction. To the contrary, the Peripheral unit began to show an increase in the number of NCMR's since September 2020. The Peripheral unit did not implement SAP-ME, so it was solely relying on COS LSS. Additionally, the COS implemented was unable to sustain itself within the Peripheral group resulting in the COS disbanding. The effects can be seen in Fig. 6 where the number of NCMR's directly started to increase and have remained increased since the COS was removed. It must be noted that the production volumes vary between the 3 units, therefore each line in Fig. 6 is analyzed individually and they are not proportional to each another (Fig. 8).

Similar patterns were seen in the yield and reject data. Like the NCMR data, the implementation of COS had a positive impact and the manufacturing yield increased by as much as 20%. Quality 4.0 enhancements maintained the high yield and low reject rates which remained constant within the 2 units which implemented it. The major change over the last 3 years however was the reduction in yield and increase in rejects within

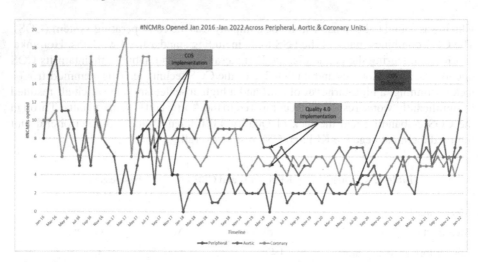

Fig. 8. Man and method quantity of non-conformances raised per business unit

the Peripheral group by almost 15% since one of its COS lines reverted to a non-cell manufacturing line. This shows that the loss of the COS in the manufacturing line has had a negative impact on the operational performance, leading to financial losses.

5   Discussion and Conclusion

As stated in the literature review section of this paper, organizations are continuously looking for ways to achieve optimal financial and operational performance. Those companies that implement both Lean and Six Sigma have an enhanced performance [5, 7, 8, 13, 16, 17, 31]. Introducing LSS into an organization is relatively straight forward and well understood however, sustaining the improvements gained can be more of a challenge [14, 42]. The primary research question of this study was to determine if the implementation of lean six sigma (LSS) techniques had a *sustained* positive impact on the operational and financial performance in a medical device company based in the West of Ireland. From an operational performance perspective the company's KPI's showed that the performance remained unchanged over the last 3 years and therefore indicating that LSS implemented was capable of sustaining the positive impact. This aligns with the literature which showed that LSS improves the overall efficiency, effectiveness and performance of an organisation in addition to sustaining the level of success over time through the use of the control phase in the DMAIC process [5, 11, 12, 60].

However, it must be stated that Quality 4.0 likely had a significant positive role in sustaining this impact over the last 3 years aligning with previous studies [3, 49]. This was particularly evident amongst the Peripheral Unit, who did not have Quality 4.0 implemented, whereby a borderline negative result was seen for the operational key performance indicators. Further study would need to be carried out to assess the sustained impact of LSS as a standalone methodology, however it is worth noting Arcidiacono and Pieroni's [48] work where they suggested a new methodology called lean six sigma 4.0 due to the success of the LSS and quality 4.0 working in tandem.

In line with Antony et al., [57]; who claimed that the key performance indicators can be more effective for determining financial performance if they are tailored to the organizations own specific goals and values rather than Lamine's [61] typical return on investment, return on equity or return on total assets; and consistent with Ikumapayi et al., [7]; Lal Bhaskar, [6]; Sim et al., [5]; this study analyzed the financial performance based on the number of unit rejects, which are essentially due to defects, and non-conformances leading to increased inventory, transport and waiting resulting in increased costs to the company. Findings for this study show the number of units rejected has remained consistent over the last 3 years within the Coronary and Aortic business units thus indicating a positive sustained performance whilst the Peripheral business unit did see an increase in reject units after the disbanding of the COS even though some LSS techniques were still in place.

The semi-structured interviews conducted with two other medical device industries highlighted many of the critical failure factors within management, culture and training consistent with literature [38] and from the output of this data it was found these CFF's were likely to be a contributor to the negative trends in operational performance within these companies. Factoring in that they did not have any Quality 4.0 enhancements, it could further suggest that the main researched company may have experienced similar results had it not been for some Quality 4.0 techniques being implemented. The other companies aligned more with the findings of the Peripheral business unit's performance.

While we cannot conclude if LSS was the only factor for sustaining operational and financial performance, we can certainly conclude that together with quality 4.0 there are signs that both methodologies work symbiotically for improved performance. Therefore, it should be considered by companies to introduce quality 4.0 along with LSS, as per the LSS 4.0 methodology suggested by Arcidiacono and Pieroni [48] to make their processes more robust, particularly in times of adversity. Similar to the findings of Kumar et al.; [50] the pandemic had presented unprecedented challenges to the company from a resource and training perspective which greatly changed the landscape and the day-to-day operations.

Overall the results indicated LSS has a sustained positive impact on the organization's operational and financial performance. Findings suggest Quality 4.0 was a significant contributing factor for sustaining this positive performance. The pandemic was shown to magnify the failure factors albeit offset somewhat by Quality 4.0. The comparison with the other two medical device organizations suggested that LSS alone could not sustain a positive impact highlighting the need to conduct further research into self-sustaining LSS methodologies and value of considering the new Lean Six Sigma 4.0 methodology discussed by Arcidiacono and Pieroni [48].

References

1. Alkhoraif, A., Rashid, H., McLaughlin, P.: Lean implementation in small and medium enterprises: literature review. Oper. Res. Perspect. **6**, 100089 (2019). https://doi.org/10.1016/j.orp.2018.100089
2. Singh, M. and Rathi, R.: A structured review of lean six sigma in various industrial sectors. Int. J. Lean Six Sigmahttps://doi.org/10.1108/IJLSS-03-2018-0018

3. Yadav, N., Shankar, R., Singh, S.P.: Critical success factors for lean six sigma in quality 4.0. Int. J. Qual. Serv. Sci. **13**(1), 123–156 (2021). https://doi.org/10.1108/IJQSS-06-2020-0099

4. Yadav, N., Shankar, R., Singh, S.P.: Impact of Industry4.0/ICTs, Lean Six Sigma and quality management systems on organisational performance. TQM J. **32**, 815–835 (2020). https://doi.org/10.1108/TQM-10-2019-0251

5. Sim, C. L., Li, Z., Chuah, F., Lim, Y.J., Sin, K.Y.: An empirical investigation of the role of lean six sigma practices on quality performance in medical device manufacturing industry. Int. J. Lean Six Sigma (2021). https://doi.org/10.1108/IJLSS-06-2020-0089

6. Lal Bhaskar, H.: Lean six sigma in manufacturing: a comprehensive review. Lean Manuf. Six Sigma - Behind Mask (2020). https://doi.org/10.5772/intechopen.89859

7. Ikumapayi, O.M., Akinlabi, E.T., Mwema, F.M., Ogbonna, O.S.: Six sigma versus lean manufacturing - An overview. Mater. Today: Proc. **26**, 3275–3281 (2019). https://doi.org/10.1016/j.matpr.2020.02.986

8. Costa, L.B.M., Godinho Filho, M., Fredendall, L.D., Gómez Paredes, F.J.: Lean, six sigma and lean six sigma in the food industry: a systematic literature review. Trends Food Sci. Technol. **82**, 122–133 (2018). https://doi.org/10.1016/j.tifs.2018.10.002

9. Muraliraj, J., Zailani, S., Kuppusamy, S., Santha, C.: Annotated methodological review of lean six sigma. Int. J. Lean Six Sigma (2018). https://doi.org/10.1108/IJLSS-04-2017-0028

10. Ahmed, S.: Integrating DMAIC approach of lean six sigma and theory of constraints toward quality improvement in healthcare (2019). https://doi.org/10.1515/reveh-2019-0003/html

11. Beemaraj, R.K., Theni, T.: Six sigma concept and DMAIC implementation. Int. J. Bus. Manag. Res. (2018)

12. Iyede, R., Fallon, E.F., Donnellan, P.: An exploration of the extent of lean six sigma implementation in the West of Ireland. Int. J. Lean Six Sigma (2018). https://doi.org/10.1108/IJLSS-02-2017-0018

13. Albliwi, S.A., Antony, J., Lim, S.A.H.: A systematic review of lean six sigma for the manufacturing industry. Bus. Process Manag. J. (2015). https://doi.org/10.1108/BPMJ-03-2014-0019

14. Antony, J., Snee, R., Hoerl, R.: Lean six sigma: yesterday, today and tomorrow. Int. J. Qual. Reliab. Manag. (2017). https://doi.org/10.1108/IJQRM-03-2016-0035

15. Mousa, A.: Lean, six sigma and lean six sigma overview. Int. J. Sci. Eng. Res. **4**, 1137–1153 (2013)

16. Alhuraish, I., Robledo, C., Kobi, A.: Impacts of lean manufacturing and six sigma. In: Proceedings - 22nd ISSAT International Conference on Reliability and Quality in Design (2016)

17. Alhuraish, I., Robledo, C., Kobi, A.: A comparative exploration of lean manufacturing and six sigma in terms of their critical success factors. J. Cleaner Prod. **164**, 325–337 (2017). https://doi.org/10.1016/j.jclepro.2017.06.146

18. Raja Sreedharan, V., Raju, R.: A systematic literature review of lean six sigma in different industries. Int. J. Lean Six Sigma (2016). https://doi.org/10.1108/IJLSS-12-2015-0050

19. Sreedharan, R.V., Sunder, V.M., Raju, R.: Critical success factors of TQM, six sigma, lean and lean six sigma: a literature review and key findings. *Benchmarking* (2018). https://doi.org/10.1108/BIJ-08-2017-0223

20. Sony, M., Naik, S., Therisa, K.K.: Why do organizations discontinue lean six sigma initiatives? Int. J.Qual. Reliab. Manag. (2019). https://doi.org/10.1108/IJQRM-03-2018-0066

21. Albliwi, S., Antony, J., Lim, S.A.H., van der Wiele, T.: Critical failure factors of lean six sigma: a systematic literature review. Int. J. Qual. Reliab. Manag (2014). https://doi.org/10.1108/IJQRM-09-2013-0147

22. Swarnakar, V., Tiwari, A.K., Singh, A.R.: Evaluating critical failure factors for implementing sustainable lean six sigma framework in manufacturing organization: a case experience. Int. J. Lean Six Sigma **11**, 1069–1104 (2020). https://doi.org/10.1108/IJLSS-05-2019-0050

23. Patel, M., Desai, D.A.: Critical review and analysis of measuring the success of six sigma implementation in manufacturing sector. Int. J. Qual. Reliab. Manag. (2018). https://doi.org/10.1108/IJQRM-04-2017-0081

24. Laureani, A., Antony, J.: Leadership and lean six sigma: a systematic literature review. Total Qual. Manag. Bus. Excellence **30**, 53–81 (2019). https://doi.org/10.1080/14783363.2017.1288565

25. Aggarwal, S.: Lean six sigma for medical device excellence and regulation. Adv. Pharmacol. Clin. Trials (2016). https://doi.org/10.23880/apct-16000111

26. McDermott,O., Antony, J., Sony, M., Healy, T.: Critical failure factors for continuous improvement methodologies in the Irish MedTech industry (2021). https://doi.org/10.1108/TQM-10-2021-0289

27. Nour, R., Laux, C.: *APPLICATION OF LEAN SIX SIGMA TO REDUCE THE COST OF REGULATORYNONCOMPLIANCE* (2021). https://docs.lib.purdue.edu/cgi/viewcontent.cgi?article=1055&context=iclss

28. McDermott,O., Antony, J., Sony, M., Looby, E.: A critical evaluation and measurement of organizational readiness and adoption for continuous improvement within a medical device manufacturer. Int. J. Manag. Sci. Eng. Manag. (2022). https://doi.org/10.1080/17509653.2022.2073917

29. Nallusamy, S., Nivedha, R., Subash, E., Venkadesh, V., Vignesh, S., Vinoth Kumar, P.: Minimization of rejection rate using lean six sigma tool in medium scale manufacturing industry. Int. J. Mech. Eng. Technol. **9**, 1184–1194 (2018)

30. Cortes, H., Daaboul, J., Le Duigou, J., Eynard, B.: Strategic Lean Management: Integration of operational Performance Indicators for strategic Lean management. IFAC- PapersOnLine **49**, 65–70 (2016). https://doi.org/10.1016/j.ifacol.2016.07.551

31. Aichouni, A.B.E., Abdullah, H., Ramlie, F.: A scientific approach of using the DMAIC methodology to investigate the effect of cutting tool life on product quality and process economics a case study of a Saudi manufacturing plant. Eng. Technol. Appl. Sci. Res. **11**, 6799–6805 (2021). https://doi.org/10.48084/etasr.4008

32. Antony, J; McDermott, O; Powell, D.J, Sony, M.: Mapping the terrain for lean six sigma 4.0. In: 7th European Lean Educator Conference, ELEC 2021 Trondheim, Norway, 25–27 October 2021, pp. 193–204. https://doi.org/10.1007/978-3-030-92934-3_20

33. Hrgarek, N., Bowers, K.A.: Integrating six sigma into a quality management system in the medical device industry. J. Inf. Organ. Sci. **33**, 1–12 (2009)

34. Kumar, M., Antony, J.: Multiple case-study analysis of quality management practices within UK six sigma and non-six sigma manufacturing small- and medium-sized enterprises. Proc. Inst. Mech. Eng. Part B: J. Eng. Manuf. (2099). https://doi.org/10.1243/09544054JEM1288

35. Kumar Sharma, R., Gopal Sharma, R.: Integrating six sigma culture and TPM framework to improve manufacturing performance in SMEs. Qual. Reliab. Eng. Int. **30**, 745–765 (2014). https://doi.org/10.1002/qre.1525

36. Thomas, A.J., Francis, M., Fisher, R., Byard, P.: Implementing Lean Six Sigma to overcome the productionchallenges in an aerospace company. Prod. Plann. Control **27**, 591–603 (2016). https://doi.org/10.1080/09537287.2016.116530

37. Sreedharan, V.R., Gopikumar, G.V., Nair, S., Chakraborty, A., Antony, J.: Assessment of critical failure factors (CFFs) of lean six sigma in real life scenario: evidence from manufacturing and service industries. Benchmarking **25**, 3320–3336 (2018). https://doi.org/10.1108/BIJ-10-2017-0281

38. Jeyaraman, K., Kee Teo, L.: A conceptual framework for critical success factors of lean six sigma. Int. J. Lean Six Sigma **1**, 191–215 (2010). https://doi.org/10.1108/2040146101075008

39. O'Neill, P., Sohal, A., Teng, C.W.: Quality management approaches and their impact on firms× financial performance - An Australian study. Int. J. Prod. Econ. **171**, 381–393 (2016). https://doi.org/10.1016/j.ijpe.2015.07.015

40. Mundra, N., Mishra, R.P.: Business sustainability in post COVID-19 era by integrated LSS-AM model in manufacturing: a structural equation modeling. Procedia CIRP **98**, 535–540 (2021). https://doi.org/10.1016/j.procir.2021.01.147

41. Mustapha, M.R., Abu Hasan, F., Muda, M.S.: Lean six sigma implementation: multiple case studies in a developing country. Int. J. Lean Six Sigma (2019). https://doi.org/10.1108/IJLSS-08-2017-0096

42. Toledo, J.C., Gonzalez, R.V.D., Lizarelli, F.L., Pelegrino, R.A.: Lean production system development through leadership practices. Manag. Decis. (2019). https://doi.org/10.1108/MD-08-2017-0748

43. Sodhi, H.S., Singh, D., Singh, B.J.: A review of critical factors contributing towards failure of lean six sigma. Int. J. Manag. Technol. Eng. **9**, 1534 (2019)

44. Alnadi, M., McLaughlin, P.: Critical success factors of lean six sigma from leaders' perspective. Int. J. Lean Six Sigma (2021). https://doi.org/10.1108/IJLSS-06-2020-0079

45. Walter, O.M.F.C., Paladini, E.P.: Lean six sigma in Brazil: a literature review. Int. J. Lean Six Sigma (2019). https://doi.org/10.1108/IJLSS-09-2017-0103

46. Snee, R.D.: Lean six sigma – getting better all the time. Int. J. Lean Six Sigma (2010). https://doi.org/10.1108/20401461011033130

47. Carvalho, A.V., Enrique, D.V., Chouchene, A., Charrua-Santos, F.: Quality 4.0: An overview. Procedia Computer Science (2021). https://doi.org/10.1016/j.procs.2021.01.176

48. Arcidiacono, G., Pieroni, A.: The revolution Lean Six Sigma 4.0. Int. J. Adv. Sci. Eng. Inf. Technol. **8**, 141–149 (2018). https://doi.org/10.18517/ijaseit.8.1.4593

49. Park, S.H., Dhalgaard-Park, S.M., Kim, D.C.: New paradigm of lean six sigma in the 4th industrial revolution era. Qual. Innov. Prosperity **24**, 1–16 (2020). https://doi.org/10.12776/QIP.V24I1.1430

50. Kumar, A., Luthra, S., Mangla, S.K., Kazançoğlu, Y.: COVID-19 impact on sustainable production and operations management, sustainable operations and computers (2020). https://doi.org/10.1016/j.susoc.2020.06.001

51. Kuiper, A., Lee, R.H., Van Ham, V.J.J., Does. R.J.M.M.: A reconsideration of lean six sigma in healthcare after the COVID-19 crisis. Int. J. Lean Six Sigma **13**(1), 101–17 (2021)

52. McDermott, O.: The digitalisation and virtual delivery of lean six sigma teaching in an Irish university during COVID-19. In: Powell, D.J., Alfnes, E., Holmemo, M.D.Q., Reke, E. (eds.) Learning in the Digital Era. ELEC 2021. IFIP Advances in Information and Communication Technology, pp. 132–143, vol 610. Springer, Cham (2021). https://doi.org/10.1007/978-3-030-92934-3_14

53. Creswell, J.W., Clark, V.L.P.: Designing and conducting mixed methods research. Organ. Res. Methods (2018)

54. Tashakkori, A., Creswell, J.W.: Editorial: the new era of mixed methods. J. Mixed Methods Res. **1**, 3–7 (2007). https://doi.org/10.1177/2345678906293042

55. Collis, J., Hussey, R.: Business Research: A practical Guide for Undergraduate and Postgraduate Students, 4th edn. Palgrave Macmillan, London (2014)

56. Gomes, C.F., Lisboa, J.V., Yasin, M.M.: Performance measurement practices in manufacturing firms: an empirical investigation. J. Manuf. Technol. Manag. (2006). https://doi.org/10.1108/17410380610642241

57. Antony, J., Gijo, E.V., Kumar, V., Ghadge, A.. A multiple case study analysis of six sigma practices in Indian manufacturing companies. Int. J. Qual. Reliab. Manag. (2016). https://doi.org/10.1108/IJQRM-10-2014-0157

58. Yun, G.W., Trumbo, C.W.: Comparative response to a survey executed by post, e-mail, & web form. J. Comput. Mediated Commun. **6** (2000)

59. Schaefer, D.R., Dillman, D.A.: Development of a standard e-mail methodology. Publ. Opin. Q. (1998)
60. Kowang, T.O., Yew, L.K., Hee, O.C., Fei, G.C., Long, C.S.: Lean six sigma implementation: does success means sustainability? Int. J. Acad. Res. Bus. Soc. Sci. **9**, 907–914 (2019). https://doi.org/10.6007/ijarbss/v9-i6/6051
61. Lamine, K.: Lean six sigma and performance metrics. In: Lean Manufacturing and Six Sigma - Behind the Mask (2020). https://doi.org/10.5772/intechopen.85815
62. Laureani, A., Antony, J.: Critical success factors for the effective implementation of lean sigma. Int. J. Lean Six Sigma **3**, 274–283 (2012). https://doi.org/10.1108/204014612112 84743

The Impact of Lean on Occupational Safety in Organisations

José Carlos Sá[1]([✉]), José Dinis-Carvalho[2], Helena Fraga[3], Vanda Lima[4], Francisco J. G. Silva[1], and João Bastos[5]

[1] INEGI, ISEP, Instituto Politécnico do Porto, Rua Dr. António Bernardino de Almeida, 4249-015 Porto, Portugal
{cvs,fgs}@isep.ipp.pt

[2] Production and Systems Department, School of Engineering, University of Minho, Campus de Azurém, 4800-058 Guimarães, Portugal
dinis@dps.uminho.pt

[3] ISEP, Instituto Politécnico do Porto, Rua Dr. António Bernardino de Almeida, 4249-015 Porto, Portugal
1170056@isep.ipp.pt

[4] CIICESI, ESTG, Instituto Politécnico do Porto, Rua do Curral, 4610-156 Felgueiras, Portugal
vlima@estg.ipp.pt

[5] INESC TEC, ISEP, Instituto Politécnico do Porto, Rua Dr. António Bernardino de Almeida, 4249-015 Porto, Portugal
jab@isep.ipp.pt

Abstract. Occupational safety is a major concern these days because it is an important social issue promoting financial implications for organisations, employees, and society. But while occupational safety is an important concern, the top management of organizations usually prioritize waste and cost reduction. Therefore, there is a need for a technique that reduces waste and simultaneously improves occupational safety. Lean has been effective in reducing waste and costs. Some researchers have shown that Lean can also improve occupational safety. The objective of this work was to determine wether, in organizations where Lean tools were implemented, if there was an improvement in occupational safety conditions, namely in the reduction of accident rates, and to verify which Lean tools contributed the most to that improvement. A survey was conducted by sending a questionnaire to Portuguese organizations, from north to south and islands, who had potentially Lean tools implemented. In total, 189 answers have been obtained from organizations, 59 of which had Lean tools implemented, being considered valid answers for the study. Through statistical analysis of the data obtained, it was found that no organisations had worsened their safety indicators, some had maintained the same level and a reasonable number stated that their indicators had improved. Of these, the vast majority said that their accident rates had decreased by 20%, this being the figure that statistically showed the best results in terms of change.

Keywords: Safety · Lean philosophy · Lean tools · Lean safety · Occupational safety

© IFIP International Federation for Information Processing 2023
Published by Springer Nature Switzerland AG 2023
O. McDermott et al. (Eds.): ELEC 2022, IFIP AICT 668, pp. 184–192, 2023.
https://doi.org/10.1007/978-3-031-25741-4_16

1 Introduction

Fatal accidents at work in Portugal, after a decrease for some years, had a substantial increase in 2018. Thus, the area of safety assumes a relevant importance in organizations. Although safety at work is a major source of concern, top management generally prioritizes reducing waste and cutting costs. Therefore, there is a need to adopt measures that reduce waste and costs while improving safety. The Lean approach has been effective in reducing waste and costs while at the same time it can improve safety at work [1, 2]. Accidents at work and occupational diseases most often happen because organisations do not comply with safety standards and do not act preventively [3]. This study aims to see how Lean tools can help organisations to identify potential occupational risk situations, and the impact they have on reducing accidents. Money and time spent on accidents and workers' compensation is classified as a waste, which is something that should be avoided based on the Lean philosophy. Lean aims to reduce the 3 M's (Muda, Mura, and Muri), and safety aims to reduce accidents at work and occupational diseases, looking at these two goals they end up intersecting. This is because occupational diseases and accidents generate waste, and Lean tools have an impact on the aspects related to occupational safety. For several authors, Lean has been frequently associated with safer, high quality, and high-commitment work environments, by sustainable human performance. For example, many Lean operating practices increase the level of workplace "transparency" (clear visibility of hazards, cleaner work environment, etc.) so that workers can identify, evaluate and suggest controls. And this helps reducing health and safety risks in the workplace. In particular, visual boards and other display artefacts are devices that make human/technology interactions easier and more effective. This means that effective and safe standards and procedures can be maintained, and continuous improvement processes can be facilitated. In this way, systems can provide information, signal deviations, control and ensure the correctness of processes, and, in turn, improve safety in the workplace [4]. This work aims to verify wether, in the Portuguese organizations where Lean tools were implemented, if there was a positive impact on the reduction of the accident rates, Incidence Rate (Ii), Frequency Rate (If), and Severity Rate (Ig).

2 Literature Review

2.1 Lean Approach

Lean designates a concept that is known to increase manufacturing effectiveness [5, 6]. Toyota has been successful in Lean deployment, and this has inspired many organisations around the world to start a 'Lean journey'. The Lean concept is now discussed as relevant not only in manufacturing, but also in services and healthcare delivery [7, 8]. Lean focuses on reducing the 3M's, maximizing value-adding activities from the customer's perspective. Moreover, from the customer's perspective, value is equivalent to whatever the customer is willing to pay for a provided product or service. Thus, the elimination of waste (*Muda*) is one of the basic concepts linked to Lean production [9]. An essential aspect of Lean philosophy is continuously striving for perfection in products that can be delivered customer-specific, on-demand, without waste of material, labor hours, and other resources (energy) in a safe working environment (physical, emotional and professional) [10]. The application of Lean principles depends on an organisation's commitment to continuously improving the value delivered to a customer [11].

Womack and Jones [12] proposed a set of principles to achieve a Lean enterprise. Companies should adopt these principles and incorporate them into their operations, sequentially. Thus, the Lean approach can be summarized in six principles: value specification, value chain identification, value stream, pull system, perfection, and respect for people [13].

2.2 Occupational Safety

Safety is defined as a state in which hazards and conditions leading to physical, psychological, or material harm are controlled to preserve the health and well-being of individuals and the community [14, 15]. This state is not only related to the absence of intentional or unintentional injuries. It should also lead to a perception of being pro- tected from danger [16]. Therefore, it includes two dimensions: one is objective and is assessed by measuring the number of injuries or factual behavioural and environmental parameters (e.g., traffic-related deaths recorded in a community, number of collisions at a dangerous intersection) [17]. The other is subjective and assessed according to the feeling of being out of danger. Both dimensions can sometimes influence each other positively or negatively [18]. Safety results from a complex process in which humans interact with their physical, social, cultural, technological, political, economic, and organisational environments [19]. Safety in companies plays a major role in motivating workers [20]. Any business knows that employee attrition and absenteeism can be major obstacles [16]. When a healthy and safe workplace is created, these problems are reduced in several ways. By budgeting for safety improvements and making safety part of the operating plan, trust is built. Involving employees in safety decisions - through reports, committees, guidelines, and meetings - demonstrates that their opinion matters to the employer. If top management pays attention to employees' opinions and improve their safety, this can tangibly prove that comapny care about their welfare [21].

2.3 Integration of Lean and Safety

Lean can be an opportunity to avoid professional risks as long as it is possible to approach it without changing the steps and without distorting the spirit. Today, the implementation of the Lean model is done with much more care. The implementation of a Lean approach can, and should, be accompanied by reflections in favor of health and safety at work [22–24]. The results will depend on how the Lean tools relate to the policy of prevention of risks at work. They will vary greatly from one company to another [20]. But taking this approach can also be an opportunity for prevention. Some situations allow addressing occupational health and safety issues either as part of standard performance improvement objectives or as a site-specific objective [16]. The two biggest challenges in the construction industry are low productivity and high injury rates, and they can be addressed simultaneously by combining Lean production strategies and traditional safety analysis tools. A study was conducted that integrated safety and a Lean tool, Kaizen, into the construction of modular housing [22]. The research team analysed the current process, determined, and implemented process improvements, and analysed the improved process. The changes made resulted in a 16% increase in the value added to the activities and by making these low-cost changes, safety risks were reduced or eliminated in some situations. These results support the hypothesis that productivity and safety can be improved simultaneously through combined safety and Lean tools [22]. In 2002, the largest Danish construction company conducted an experiment on the impact of implementing Lean tools on profit (level and predictability), safety, customer satisfaction, and administrative costs. This implementation was carried out in about 30 projects that the company had in progress. To confirm the impact of the Lean tools, projects that used Lean tools were compared with projects not using Lean tools.

With only a limited number of projects with Lean tools implemented, they found that customer satisfaction increased by two decimal points on a scale of 1 to 5. It had a positive impact on profit; the average profit of three projects with Lean tools implemented is approximately 25 percent higher than the average profit of projects that did not have Lean tools implemented. It was also proved that the accident rate is lower for projects with Lean implemented [25].

3 Methodology

The type of approach was qualitative research of basic nature, involving a biblio- graphic survey on the topic under study. Subsequently, as a data collection technique, the option fell on the elaboration of a questionnaire, whose questions were carefully thought out to provide an answer to the proposed problem. The questionnaire includes 13 questions with the following content (Table 1):

Table 1. Questionnaire sent to companies

Questions
1. Name of the Organization
2. In which department does the person responsible for completing the questionnaire work
3. Location of the Organization
4. Sector of Activity
5. No. of Workers in the Organization
6. If the Organization is safety certified
7. How many years ago the certification occurred (ranges: less than 1 year | between 1 and 3 | between 3 and 5 | between 5 and 10 | more than 10),
8. If company knows Lean tools,
9. Identify the Lean tools that company knows,
10. It the organization have any Lean tools implemented,
11. Identify the Lean tools implemented in the organization and how many years ago they were implemented (ranges: less than 1 year | between 1 and 3 | between 3 and 5 | between 5 and 10 | more than 10),
12. After the implementation of Lean tools there was an improvement in the Accident Rates (options: Worsened | No change | -20% | -40% | -60% | -80% | -100%)
13. Indicate up to 5 tools, which in the company's opinion contributed to the improvement of safety. Number, considering value 5 for the one that had more impact and value 1 for the one that had less impact.

4 Development and Results

A set of 1600 Portuguese organisations was selected, from north to south and islands, potentially with Lean tools implemented, to which the questionnaire was sent via email. Only those that had Lean tools implemented were analysed. A total of 189 organisations have responded, 59 of which had Lean tools implemented (Fig. 1), which were considered valid responses for the study.

The data collection process took place from 7 August 2019 to 06 October 2019. All responses to the questionnaires were recorded and automatically transferred to an MS Excel® file, functions provided by the Google Forms® platform. This also helped to make the research more reliable as it provided easy traceability of the data obtained. These data were subsequently worked/coded in MS Excel® and then transferred to the SPSS® (Statistical Package for the Social Sciences) application. The organisations that make up the sample are located essentially in the northern region and with special incidence in the metalworking sector. Concerning their size, the vast majority are medium and large sized. The sample includes 27 organisations with safety certification, 14 of which have been certified for over 10 years .

According to the data obtained in Table 2, it was observed that there are no organizations that have worsened their rates, some have maintained the rates and a reasonable

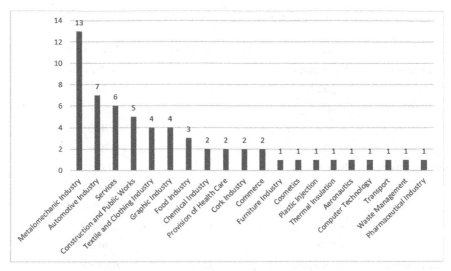

Fig. 1. Characterization of the sample of companies that responded to the survey

number attested that the rates suffered improvement alterations, of these, their great majority, said that the accident rates decreased 20%, making this the value that statistically presented the best results in terms of improvement. A correlation test was conducted between the Lean tools implemented and the three accident rates, which confirmed that there are statistically significant correlations between the Lean tools. But they are not correlated with the accident rates. The accident rates have a strong correlation between them, most probably, the higher the accident rate, the higher the probability of having serious accidents. It was found that there is no correlation between accident rates and the variables of activity sector, organisation size, safety certification, and years of certification. From the descriptive statistical analysis, it was found that the implementation of Lean tools has an impact on accident rates. Most of the companies that managed to improve their accident rates were within the 20% threshold. The thresholds of improvement of accident rates between 20% and 60% has been chosen and analysed for the three rates to ascertain if there was a difference between the groups for four variables: activity sector, number of workers, safety certification, and years of certification.

The test chosen, based on the type of variables available was the Kruskal Wallis (KW). According to Pestana and Gageiro [26], the KW test is an extension of the Wil- coxon-Mann-Whitney test, which is a non-parametric test used to compare three or more populations. It is used to test the null hypothesis that all populations have equal distribution functions against the alternative hypothesis that at least two of the populations have different distribution functions. From the KW test for the incidence index, differences were found between the groups for the variable safety certification, ($p = 0.04$) and years of certification ($p = 0.014$). No significant differences were found between the groups for the variable sector of activity ($p = 0.7$) and the number of workers ($p = 0.472$). Based on these results, it was tried to confirm which group was causing the difference. Applied the KW test for the Frequency Index, it was found that there are no significant differences between the groups for the variables, activity sector

Table 2. General table of impact by index

	Percentage of answers	Organisations	Marginal percentage
Incidence index	No changes	36	61,00%
	− 20%	16	27,10%
	− 40%	5	8,50%
	− 60%	1	1,70%
	− 100%	1	1,70%
Frequency index	No changes	34	57,60%
	− 20%	15	25,40%
	− 40%	8	13,60%
	− 60%	1	1,70%
	− 100%	1	1,70%
Severity index	No changes	37	62,70%
	− 20%	12	20,30%
	− 40%	7	11,90%
	− 60%	2	3,40%
	− 100%	1	1,70%
Total valid		59	100%

($p = 0.793$), the number of workers ($p = 0.126$), safety certification, ($p = 0.551$) and years of certification ($p = 0.051$). The KW test was applied to the Severity index, and it was verified that there is no difference between the groups for the variables: sector of activity ($p = 0.947$), number of workers ($p = 0.223$), safety certification ($p = 0.153$) and years of certification ($p = 0.430$). With the KW test for the grouping variable Index of Incidence, it was possible to verify that there are differences between groups for the variable's certification and years of certification. However, with this test, it was not possible to affirm if these differences had a certain linear pattern. Thus, it was opted for a comparison of means. For the certification variable, the average of the incidence index was calculated separately for non-certified and certified organisations, and it was found that the average value increased, which leads to the conclusion that in certified companies the impact of the implementation of Lean tools on the incidence index is statistically more significant.

Next, it was analysed whether, within the group of organisations certified in safety, the variable years of certification influenced the incidence rate. This analysis was again based on the comparison of averages, in this case, the average Ii was calculated for each date interval. For the interval of less than one year of certification, no case was registered.

The mean comparison analysis showed that there is an upward trend in Ii from the interval 1 to 3 years to the interval 5 to 10 years of certification. In the interval of more than 10 years, the average drops significantly. It cannot be said that the average value of Ii increases as the years of safety certification also increase. What can be said is that for the organisations that participated in the study, there was more impact of Lean tools in improving the incidence index in the certified organisations whose certification occurred in the interval between 5 and 10 years. Statistical analysis showed that it was possible to prove that Lean tools have positive impact on safety by reducing accident rates.

5 Conclusion

Safety has historically been treated as a separate function or issue which could be improved in isolation away from production. However, safety is an integral part of every production process, not an afterthought or an add-on, because safety depends on all actions, materials and people used. Work processes are inherently safe or hazardous according to the safety risks present at each step required to complete a process. Safety performance depends on the nature of the work and must be maintained and continuously improved as part of these processes [14, 16]. Based on the data collected from the organisations that participated in this study and through statistical analysis, some support was obtained for the prediction that the acci dent rates will be improved with the implementation of Lean tools.

It was found that no organisations had worsened their rates, some had maintained their rates and a reasonable number stated that their rates had improved. Of these, the vast majority said that their accident rates had decreased by 20%, which was the value that statistically presented the best results in terms of change. The KW test was applied to the three accident rates and it was found that there were differences between groups for the variables certification (in safety) and years of certification in relation to the Incidence Index. With this test, it was not possible to affirm if these differences had a certain linear pattern. Thus, it was opted to make a comparison of means. It could not be affirmed that the Ii increases as the years of certification in safety also increase. What could be affirmed is that for the organisations that participated in the study, there is more impact of the Lean tools in the improvement of the incidence index in those that are certified and whose certification took place between 5 and 10 years. It was possible to demonstrate that Lean tools have a positive impact on the occupational safety of organisations, through the reduction of accident rates.

The analysis and discussion presented in this paper provide a theoretical and empir ical rationale for the link between Lean tool implementation and improved occupational safety outcomes.

Research Funding. The work of the author Vanda Lima is supported by national funds, through the FCT— Portuguese Foundation for Science and Technology under the project UIDB/04728/2020.

References

1. Cordeiro, P., Sá, J.C., Pata, A., Gonçalves, M., Santos, G., Silva, F.J.G.: The impact of lean tools on safety—case study. In: Arezes, P.M., et al. (eds.) Occupational and Environmental Safety and Health II. SSDC, vol. 277, pp. 151–159. Springer, Cham (2020). https://doi.org/10.1007/978-3-030-41486-3_17

2. Sá, J.C., et al.: Lean safety-assessment of the impact of 5S and visual management on safety. In: IOP Conference Series: Materials Science and Engineering, vol. 1193(1), p. 012049 (2021)
3. Bastos, A., Sá, J., Silva, O., Fernandes, M.C.: A study on the reality of Portuguese companies about work health and safety. Occup. Saf. Hyg. II **1**, 687–691 (2014)
4. Camuffo, A., De Stefano, F., Paolino, C.: Safety reloaded: lean operations and high involvement work practices for sustainable workplaces. J. Bus. Ethics **143**(2), 245-259. (2017). https://doi.org/10.1007/s10551-015-2590-8
5. Kim, C.S., Spahlinger, D.A., Kin, J.M., Coffey, R.J., Billi, J.E.: Implementation of lean thinking: one health system's journey. Jt. Comm. J. Qual. Patient Saf. **35**(8), 406–413 (2009)
6. Womack, J.P., Jones, D.T.: Lean thinking—banish waste and create wealth in your corporation. J. Oper. Res. Soc. **48**(11), 1148–1148 (1997)
7. Pettersen, J.: Defining lean production: some conceptual and practical issues. The TQM Journal **21**(2), 127–142 (2009)
8. Antas Aguiar, J., Telhada, J., Sameiro Carvalho, M., Sá, J.C.: Value measurement in health care delivery process for a paediatric hospital in guinea- bissau. In: International Conference Innovation in Engineering, pp. 186–196. Springer, Cham (2023). https://doi.org/10.1007/978-3-031-09360-9_16
9. Arlbjorn, J., Freytag, P.: Evidence of lean: a review of international peer- reviewed journal articles. Eur. Bus. Rev. **25**(2), 174–203 (2013)
10. Fullerton, R., Wempe, W.: Lean manufacturing. Int. J. Oper. Prod. Manag. **29**, 214–240 (2009)
11. Bartels, N.: Lean in the most generic sense. Manuf. Bus. Technol. **23**, 32–36 (2005)
12. Womack, J., Jones, D.T.: Lean Thinking. Simon and Schuster, New York (1996)
13. Shah, R., Ward, P.T.: Defining and developing measures of Lean production. J. Oper. Manag. **25**, 785–805 (2007)
14. Koskela, L.: Application of the New Production Philosophy to Construction, vol. 72. Stanford university, Stanford, CA (1992)
15. Maurice, P., Lavoie, M., Chapdelaine, A., Bélanger-Bonneau, H.: Safety and safety promotion: conceptual and operational aspects. Chronic Dis Canada **18**(4), 179–186 (1997)
16. Morgado, L., Silva, F.J.G., Fonseca, L.M.: Mapping occupational health and safety management systems in portugal: outlook for ISO 45001:2018 adoption. Procedia Manuf. **38**, 755–764 (2019)
17. Cooper, M.D.: Towards a model of safety culture. Saf. Sci. **36**, 111–136 (2000)
18. Baram, M., Schoebel, M.: Safety culture and behavioral change at the workplace. Saf. Sci. **45**, 631–636 (2007)
19. Hudson, P.: Implementing a safety culture in a major multi-national. Saf. Sci. **45**, 697–722 (2007)
20. Brito, M., Vale, M., Leão, J., Ferreira, L.P., Silva, F.J.G., Gonçalves, M.A.: Lean and Ergonomics decision support tool assessment in a plastic packaging company. Procedia Manuf. **51**, 613–619 (2020)
21. Reason, J.: Managing the Risks of Organizational Accidents. Ashgate, Aldershot (1998)
22. Ikuma, L.H., Nahmens, I., James, J.: Use of safety and lean integrated kaizen to improve performance in modular homebuilding. J. Constr. Eng. Manag. **137**(7), 551–560 (2010)
23. Arezes, P.M., Dinis-Carvalho, J., Alves, A.C.: Workplace ergonomics in Lean production environments: a literature review. Work **52**(1), 57–70 (2015)
24. Carter, B., Danford, A., Howcroft, D., Richardson, H., Smith, A., Taylor, P.: 'Stressed out of my box': employee experience of Lean working and occupational ill- health in clerical work in the UK public sector. Work Employ. Soc. **27**(5), 747–767 (2013)
25. Thomassen, M.A., Sander, D., Barnes, K. A., Nielsen, A.: Experience and results from implementing lean construction in a large Danish contracting firm. In: Proceedings of 11th Annual Conference on Lean Construction, pp. 644–655, July 2003
26. Pestana, M.H., Gageiro, J.N.: Análise de dados para ciências sociais: a complementaridade do SPSS (2008)

Critical Success Factors for Operational Excellence in the Pharmaceutical Industry: Insights from a Qualitative Study

Elizabeth O'Callaghan[1,3]([⊠]), Olivia McDermott[2], Gavin Walker[3], and Mark Southern[1,3]

[1] School of Engineering, University of Limerick, Limerick, Ireland
elizabeth.ocallaghan@ul.ie
[2] College of Science and Engineering, University of Galway, Galway, Ireland
[3] School of Chemical Sciences, Bernal Institute, University of Limerick, Limerick, Ireland

Abstract. The paper aims to investigate the Critical Success Factors that exist for Operational Excellence methodology deployment in the Pharmaceutical industry. The research will seek to establish the levels of current Operational Excellence awareness and integration in the Pharmaceutical industry in terms of the deployment of Continuous Improvement methodology. The study involves the analysis of the pros, cons, strengths, weaknesses, and limitations of management commitment for the application to the deployment of Continuous Improvement methodologies in the Pharmaceutical industry. A qualitative methodology was utilised by interviewing a cohort of 28 Pharmaceutical manufacturing Operational Excellence and Continuous Improvement practitioners. The study found that while participants advocated and supported the requirement and importance of Operational Excellence, a key Critical Success Factor identified was senior management support in fostering Operational Excellence culture. A top challenge highlighted for Operational Excellence and Continuous Improvement success, particularly in regulated industries, was a regulatory compliance culture and regulatory bureaucracy. The paper provides a valuable resource for organisations to obtain insight into Critical Success Factors for Continuous Improvement and Operational Excellence and in particular, in a regulated Pharmaceutical manufacturing industry.

Keywords: Operational Excellence · Manufacturing · Continuous Improvement · Pharmaceutical industry · Lean

1 Introduction

Operational Excellence (OpEx) attainment is a journey of Continuous Improvement (CI). CI is defined as "*a learned and stable pattern of collective activity through which the organisation systematically generates and modifies its operating routines in pursuit of improved effectiveness*" [1, 2]. OpEx is defined as the continuous pursuit of improvement of a production plant in all dimensions [3]. In Ireland, the Pharmaceutical sector

O. McDermott et al. (Eds.): ELEC 2022, IFIP AICT 668, pp. 193–203, 2023.
https://doi.org/10.1007/978-3-031-25741-4_17

employs more than 30,000 people, with as many more in spin-off jobs and has grown from a mere 5,200 people in nineteen eighty-eight [4]. The sector has seen continued capital investment averaging €1 billion per annum since 2011 attributed to manufacturing success [4, 5]. Ireland hosts 75 Pharmaceutical companies, comprised of 9 of the world's top 10 Pharmaceuticals, and is currently the largest net exporter (over 50% of Pharmaceuticals in the European Union (EU)) [4].

Integrating OpEx into all policies and procedures gives a company the ability to develop and supply superior products to the customer [6]. Having created an OpEx culture, companies achieve a competitive advantage that they can capitalise on in the market without current or potential competitors [7, 8]. The Food and Drug Administration (FDA) has reported that OpEx still has a long way to go in the Pharmaceutical industry because Quality is still kept separate from OpEx both organisationally and culturally [9, 10]. Lean as an enabler for OpEx has been largely studied [11–13]. Studies on CI in the Pharmaceutical and Medtech sector have acknowledged that the regulated industry can stifle CI [5, 14]. Thus, sustaining CI activities for OpEx has been challenging [2, 15]. Therefore, there is a need for a study analysis of the applicability of CI activities in a regulated industry. This research contributes to a gap in published literature by investigating CSFs for OpEx in the highly regulated Pharmaceutical industry [16, 17].

This research will explore the relationship between workers' perceptions of their manager's commitment to OpEx and CI and the organisation's OpEx culture. The research questions as follows were set by the researchers for this empirical study:

1. What is the current level of awareness and benefits for OpEx and CI within the Pharmaceutical Industry?
2. What are the CSFs and challenges of OpEx and CI deployment?

2   Literature Review – Background and Context

Within the Pharmaceutical industry, OpEx has a long way to go because Quality and Compliance are kept separate from OpEx organisationally and culturally [9]. A survey on CI groups found that, according to 71% of participants, the major issues are around people's engagement in CI methods, e.g. Lean at the shop floor and middle to senior management levels [18]. Other major issues worth noting related to the sustainability of CI and OpEx efforts. One way of looking at OpEx is as an "umbrella concept" [19]. OpEx challenges can be accommodated by values, a shared vision, commitment, and dedication from everyone. Opportunities exist to embrace OpEx culture and CI methodologies which play a key role for OpEx from the manufacturing floor to the customer or patient (as in the case of Pharmaceutical applications). Moreover, culture and CI are paramount for manufacturing the innovative pipeline of complex products to meet unmet medical and Pharmaceutical needs [4].

Evidence-based body of knowledge reveals that OpEx philosophy is based on 'research [11, 18, 20–23] and based on 'learning by doing" [20]. This demonstrates that the winners of tomorrow's *'Big Pharma'* landscape will emphasise an integrated approach from an overall system perspective for enhanced overall OpEx performance. According to Antony et al. [24], many OpEx initiatives fail to sustain in organisations for

7 key reasons including; lack of awareness and importance of a structured CI program; no belief in OpEx; lack of leadership for OpEx, not sure of the benefits of OpEx; implementing OpEx without a strategy in place; senior management not convinced of OpEx benefits; and a perception that OpEx is time-consuming and costly. The implementation of CI and culture is driven directly by business strategy and led by management [8, 25].

Research shows that successful OpEx implementation is closely related to organisational and culture change [26]. CI practices help to install organisational habits and mindsets that favour systematic process improvements [27]. Trust and openness with praise for all workers is an integral part of the management process while shaping the vision for a sustainable healthy OpEx workplace environment [9, 17, 27].

Studies have investigated the transformation of OpEx across multiple industries, including the Pharmaceutical industry, about CI [11, 33]. Sustainability is an important factor in OpEx CI and culture. The CSFs of engaging people in Lean efforts at the shop floor including middle to senior management levels were identified as 'mindset', 'language', 'confidence', and 'passion for excellence'. Moreover, it is not about people using the tools, systems, or indeed what people see [18].

Case studies by OpEx experts [20, 22, 23] discuss the key learnings and CSFs of the CI journey using Lean and Six Sigma as well as Agile [28, 29]. Benefits of OpEx CI include: increasing levels of overall equipment efficiency; increasing positive OpEx culture across all teams; increasing productivity; zero accidents; zero complaints; zero recalls; zero stoppages; zero downtime; reduced inventory; and reduced operational costs [20].

However, to implement sustainable Lean manufacturing, the top three most crucial CSFs are 'top-management commitment', 'internal expertise' and 'employee involvement. Top management's involvement directly impacted the working culture [30].

Lastly, studies have discussed how OpEx and CI projects do not thrive in regulated environments, with various studies highlighting heavily regulated environments as difficult to maintain a CI culture [31]. The Pharmaceutical industry is one of the most regulated industries in the world, and thus, any improvements or changes that may affect the product's compliance with regulations or perhaps have a patient safety impact requires regulatory submissions [14, 32, 33]. This regulatory submission takes time to submit to regulatory authorities. It can require a lot of data, justification, and resources to follow through to gain, for example, FDA approval, thus deterring many CI solutions from being implemented or even submitted for approval in the first place [14]. The requirement for revalidation and requalification of processes after an improvement action or change is suggested also takes a lot of time, paperwork and resources [31].

3 Research Methodology

The primary instrument chosen was semi-structured, in-depth and face-to-face interviews, utilising purposive sampling [34–37]. The interview questions were outlined in Table 1 and consisted of two sections: the first aimed to obtain respondents' general information and the second aimed at their organisational knowledge.

Table 1. Interview questions and themes

SECTION A
Department
Q1 Role in your Company
Q2 What is your belt qualification -yellow/green/black?
Q3 No of years experience in your present company
Q4 No of employees in your company globally
SECTION B
Q1 What is your opinion/awareness of OpEx?
Q2 Which departments in your company is OpEx implemented in?
Q3 What OpEx tools do you use daily at work?
Q4 What are the challenges of the pursuit of OpEx and CI implementation in your organisation?
Q5 What are the CSFs for OpEx implementation in Pharmaceutical organisations?

Twenty-eight purposively selected Pharmaceutical professionals were interviewed over eight weeks from seven Pharmaceutical companies, and all wished to remain anonymous while the researchers assured confidentiality [38]. Participant details were obtained using LinkedIn as a professional networking site [39]. Each interview was carried out on the MS Teams platform and audio-taped, lasted 25 minutes and covered all open-ended questions in one sitting for speed of data collection from participants expediently [40]. For consistency, the same questions were asked to all respondents. The interviews and quotes are verbatim and indicate participant number (P number), as pseudo names are given for anonymity. Qualitative studies help to investigate participants' opinions regarding issues, events, or incidents [45]. The authors adopted a qualitative phenomenological approach using a method by Colaizzi [41]. This research approach aims to acquire knowledge by considering the world from other viewpoints [42]. This allows the behaviour and reactions of others to be anticipated, as our perceptions may be largely influenced by social observations and interactions [43]. Finally, it enabled the researcher to listen to employees 'hidden voices' about management commitment and OpEx culture and these impacts within a manufacturing context [44]. Significant statements were highlighted, clustered into dimensions [45] and sorted into several thematic areas, which helped answer the research questions.

4 Results

The authors interviewed professionals from functions such as Production, Quality and R&D. The interviewees had experience in various OpEx and CI methodologies such as Lean and Six Sigma and were selected from several Pharmaceutical companies.

In terms of the interviewees, they represented the following functions: Production Operator (53%), Line Manager (32%); Global OpEx Lead (7%); Supervisor (4%); and Site Lead (4%) positions. In addition, 15 out of 28 interviewees (i.e., nearly 54%) had an OpEx/CI training or belt qualification, with 13 interviewees (i.e., nearly 46%) stating they were trained but had no belt qualification. All interviewees had over 2 years of experience within their Pharmaceutical organisations and were from large Pharmaceutical companies based in Ireland with over 1500 employees.

4.1 Opinion and Awareness of OpEx and CI

In section B, the first question was: *"What is your opinion/awareness of OpEx?"*. This question relates to participants' beliefs and feelings on the culture of OpEx in their work environment and whether they use CI tools daily. The selected quotes from the interviews are outlined in Table 2. Generally, there was a positive consensus around having an OpEx and CI program with employee involvement and training in CI projects. Concerning OpEx organisations, typical benefits of having Lean tools implemented can include a "more innovative and embedded culture at work", "a CI mindset", and "driving efficiencies for improvements on the shop floor with buy-in from management". Some respondents spoke about the pros of having management styles that demonstrated leadership in driving OpEx. They also reiterated the need for "transparency" and "consistency" around OpEx integration and alignment of OpEx and CI with strategy. Lean tools, in particular, were highlighted as a good foundation to enable a smooth integration of OpEx as part of the company culture.

Table 2. The opinions and awareness of OpEx and CI

"I have done much internal training here on the job over the years... people can do green and black belt through projects... the consultants said you will need to give autonomy to the people on the floor... you will need to become leaders, not managers. I use all Lean tools". P4
"I like the concept of CI and reducing the standard deviations and putting ownership and responsibilities to the people at the front line. I do not use Lean tools". P6
"For three years now, we have been rolling out OpEx across our global functions... So when they have questions on OpEx, we can help them.". P1
"It has been a good experience (with OpEx) because when I started with the company, they had already started the Lean journey for two years previously... so there was a good foundation... I tried to bring my experience to improve what they had done, and this is my focus and trying to move onto the next step ..people were friendly and open... so I had a good opening for new ideas and new proposals ... I led the governance, but my main responsibility is to integrate OpEx as part of the culture of the company. I use mainly Lean tools". P19
"So, I have a multi-site position, so I see some with a variety of OpEx systems... some very mature and embedded into their organisations... while others have very little OpEx. It is a broad range of integration. I use all Lean tools". P3
"12 months into my job from starting here... the OpEx department was known as CI department...I did a six-sigma course which was the start of my OpEx experience here. I use all Lean tools". P4
"In my view, OpEx is an extremely important sector in process improvement... process times are reviewed and analysed, improvement is continuous.". P27
"They give us training and let us attend conferences and webinars and internal training assisting us... so these activities help us know about OpEx... if they notice any problems, we are facing... everyone discusses issue together and give suggestions too". P21
"I have support from my team and my boss, who is senior management, but I need to go to him always... in all areas, we have an escalation system where they fill in a card on maintenance, CI and engineering, and it is put up on the system and dealt with". P4
"Good support... CI has much focus now". P7
"Full support from management... each person gets trained equally... no one is left out". P1"

4.2 Integration of OpEx and Tools Utilised

A question related to *"Which departments is OpEx implemented in?"* was asked to understand the levels of integration throughout the participant's organisations. The quotes are outlined in Table 3. The next question asked was *"What OpEx tools do you use daily?"*. Again, there was an emphasis on all types of Lean tools used. Almost all interviewees cited Lean as the CI methodology of choice within their Pharmaceutical organisations. Only 3 interviewees stated they *"did not know"* or *"we are not sure"*. A theme amongst the questions as to where OpEx was integrated led to comments about the lack of integration due to the *"regulatory standards"*, *"bureaucratic"* processes and *"time"* consuming processes.

Table 3. The Integration of OpEx by function/department

"We do not have OpEx specifically in each department, but in this fiscal year we have OpEx team projects in quality, supply chain, and production areas guided by our KPIs... the directors set the targets". P18
"Focused on Manufacturing, Product Supply including Quality only... not in Human Resources, Finance, Commercial... in my current Pharma company. "But in my last pharma company, OpEx was in every department because they planned to train people in OpEx from every department...". P6
"The mindset of our people working on the shop floor, I say if you do this, your department will receive this or that... it is a motivating factor honestly, very hard to keep people motivated to keep going". P15
"With much demand for production and with reduced staff... it has been very difficult to maintain OpEx integration across the company and be able to participate in CI implementations and actions". P24
"What usually makes progress in an improvement project difficult is the Pharma regulatory standards... so when improvement is proposed... it often comes up against Regulatory standards and getting Regulatory approvals...". P27

A common theme around the integration of OpEx was the difficulty of people's behaviours and engagement. To effectively implement changes at work, an organisation must be aware of strategically aligning the business model with the organisational system. The focus is on creating the best environment to get its people to work together to carry out the business [8] to improve the process by degrees every day [18, 46].

4.3 Challenges of the Pursuit of OpEx and CI in Your Pharmaceutical Organisation

There was an emphasis that management commitment was a challenge in deploying CI in all Pharmaceutical organisational functions, not just in Production and Engineering. A high level of openness and trust was needed for a truly effective relationship between management and non-management at work. One respondent stated that *"Over 10 years of using our original OpEx model...it had done well...I noticed over the next three years that it started to plateau...it was hard to keep people motivated...when the new Director came...we rebranded a new OpEx model and redesigned it" P2*. OpEx can be seen by some corporate management as just "a passing management fad" [47] which is due to poor leadership and lack of commitment.

A comprehensive list of responses is outlined in Table 4. Several respondents commented on the difficulties in implementing and closing out the CI cycle. Many interviewees mentioned that while there are plenty of resources, there were incomplete OpEx open actions as *"management do not latch on to the fact that OpEx also applies to other departments apart from Manufacturing"*. One respondent maintained that *"the Regulatory authorities do not reward the continuous improvement side of Pharmaceutical processing and that the FDA think and act differently to their FDA field inspectors"*. A respondent questioned, *"how do you energise the organisation to take on OpEx CI cycles when there is such a focus on Regulatory compliance and not rocking the boat with regulatory submissions?"*

Table 4. Challenges to OpEx and CI

"For the implementation of OpEx projects... there are plenty of resources but not so many to complete actions or improvement". P9
"Poor support". P10
"There is a difficulty in the dynamics to resolve or implement improvements such as budget, approvals and implementations". P24
"They praise me for achieving the financial performance, but they do not realise that I am doing fundamental OpEx... they do not latch on to the source that OpEx also applies in Engineering. They only see it as in manufacturing". P6
"If people are not following the OpEx tools procedures, then this is a management and cultural issue". P3
"Certainly, no one from senior management ever appears". P4
"I often wanted to visit other sites to learn about OpEx which the local Skillnet used to email us about. Unfortunately, we never visited any, which I felt we could have brought back good ideas for our company... also, the OpEx team on site never got us trained on 5S or yellow belt". P12
"Over 10 years of using our original OpEx model... it had done well... I noticed over the next three years that it started to plateau... it was hard to keep people motivated... when the new Director came... we rebranded a new OpEx model and redesigned it". P2
"The Regulatory authorities do not reward the continuous improvement side of Pharmaceutical processing and that the FDA think and act differently to their FDA field inspectors". P6.
"How do you energise the organisation to take on OpEx CI cycles when there is such a focus on Regulatory compliance and not rocking the boat with regulatory submissions?" P5.

The "*lack of senior management visibility*" and "*interaction with people on the shop floor*" was referenced by many interviewees as outlined in the following Table 5.

Table 5. CSFs for OpEx and CI

"The biggest barrier to OpEx is people not buying into it and not understanding that the reason for the change has a long-term benefit. Sometimes the barriers presented are short-term in nature, e.g., resources... all different departments do not want to see OpEx coming in because they are too busy doing their work their way and they do not want to change the way they are doing their work, and they cannot see the benefit as a result because OpEx will change their systems". P3
"The difficulty is motivating them. It comes down to the type of management to push it actively forward over several years. People need to be encouraged with good clear examples ...our focus now is working on our third OpEx programme called 'health check', where an audit is done daily on team tasks,.. but it is such hard work for our department at the senior level where management is pushing it so that we improve the topics and it shows you can change the mindset of people. It starts with many baby steps for this great outcome: it is a long continuous journey". P1

4.4   CSFs for OpEx and CI in Pharmaceutical industries

The interviewee's opinions on the CSFs were broad. However, most interviewees suggested a key CSF to implement OpEx as a phased approach across all departments.

Management's support and buy-in were highlighted as a critical CSF and an opportunity to foster a positive OpEx culture. Emphasis needs to be on changing and moving the industry from being primarily '*compliance and bureaucratic centric*' to '*people and process and purpose centric*' by engaging all people from the shop floor to senior management levels and deploying behaviour for CI "*through involvement and learning*". The participants suggested that change is challenging, but clear commitment from management is essential. This is very much in line with the body of literature [20], [48–50] regarding the success of OpEx initiatives. A shared vision of the importance of OpEx is created with management's leadership - "*This has 2 different perspectives...one is it has to be implemented as routine because people will say we do not have the time to do each tool, I am being overloaded and we do not have the training, there is more room to apply OpEx intensively. OpEx is the responsibility of every line manager...it must be in their DNA"* P5.

Companies that enjoy enduring success have core values and a fixed purpose while their strategies and practices continuously adapt to changes in the ecosystem [51]. Core ideology is the main component of a company's envisioned future, where ideology is understood as culture.

To improve engagement between management and employees, the line managers bring human resources to life at the Gemba [34]. *"Yes, management talked about doing a weekly Gemba walk which was announced, and we took different employees... we got their ideas and their information and what they would like to change...it was great to hear the shop floor employees' impressions because they are with the hands-on process 100% of the time...this is great, this is fantastic to gather information from shopfloor"* P17. The literature agrees that employees are the company's most underutilised resource [22, 48, 49, 52]. Change in an organisation can be met with resistance and grinds to a halt if it does not have the support of corporate management [26].

A final CSF theme highlighted was to try and counteract the "regulatory culture" and "fear of regulatory burden" at the site level. Many CI initiatives that were seen as larger process changes did not go ahead according to the interviewees as they required complicated, bureaucratic time consuming regulatory submissions, revalidation and requalification of processes as highlighted in similar studies [5, 31, 33, 52].

5   Conclusion, Limitations, and Future Research Direction

OpEx is gaining momentum globally and has room for improvement, as evidenced by the limited studies related to its applicability, level of integration and deployment within the Pharmaceutical industry. According to this research study, there is a lack of buy-in from senior and middle management and a lack of visibility supporting and utilising all people on the shop floor. As there is a lack of real case examples demonstrating OpEx and CI deployment within the Pharmaceutical industry, this gap can motivate researchers to carry out further research in the Pharmaceutical industry. Future research could look at how some OpEx and Lean models, such as implementing the Shingo Model, will facilitate OpEx deployment further.

The main limitation of this research study is that all the Pharmaceutical companies were from large Pharmaceutical enterprises and did not include Pharmaceutical enterprises of a small and medium size. However, building on previous research, this study provides a more concrete understanding of OpEx and CI within regulated Pharmaceutical industries. The authors would like to conduct a more longitudinal case study on one Pharmaceutical organisation starting with an OpEx journey and study its deployment over time while measuring its impact on organisational performance. The findings from this research are a valuable source for Lean and OpEx practitioners currently deploying these CI methodologies and for anyone considering undertaking training in Lean settings. In summary, in this article, an attempt has been made to provide a general overview of CSFs for OpEx in the Pharmaceutical industry.

Conflict of Interest.   The authors declare no conflict of interest.

References

1. Dale, B.G.: Sustaining a process of continuous improvement: definition and key factors. TQM Mag. **8**(2), 49–51 (1996)
2. Zollo, M., Winter, S.G.: Deliberate learning and the evolution of dynamic capabilities. Organ. Sci. **13**(3), 339–351 (2002)
3. Friedli,T., Bellm, D.: OPEX: a definition. In: Friedli, T., Basu, P., Bellm, D., Werani, J. (eds.) Leading Pharmaceutical Operational Excellence. Springer, Berlin, pp. 7–26 (2013). https://doi.org/10.1007/978-3-642-35161-7_2
4. Irish Pharmaceutical Healthcare Association (IPHA), Code of Practice for the Pharmaceutical Industry, V8.5 (2021)
5. McDermott, O., Antony, J., Sony, M., Daly, S.: Barriers and enablers for continuous improvement methodologies within the Irish pharmaceutical industry. Processes **10**(1), 73 (2022)
6. Bunn, G.P.: Good Manufacturing Practices for Pharmaceuticals. CRC Press, Boca Raton (2019)
7. Barney, J.: Firm resources and sustained competitive advantage. J. Manag. **17**(1), 99–120 (1991)
8. Wit, B.D.: Strategy: an international perspective (2017)
9. Friedli, T., Kohler, S., Buess, P., Eichs, P.: FDA quality metrics research. University of St. Gallen Report #1, 1 November 2018
10. Friedli, T., Kohler, S., Buess, P., Eichs, P.: FDA Quality Metrics Research, (2) (2018a)
11. Antony, J., Kumar, A., Banuelas, R.: World Class Applications of Six Sigma, 1st edn. Butterworth-Heinemann, Oxford Burlington MA (2006)
12. Chatterjee, B.: Applying Lean Six Sigma in the Pharmaceutical Industry. Routledge, Milton Park (2016)
13. Witcher, M.F.: Integrating development tools into the process validation lifecyce to achieve six sigma pharmaceutical quality. BioProcess. J. **17** (2018)
14. McDermott, O., Antony, J., Sony, M., Healy, T.: Critical failure factors for continuous improvement methodologies in the Irish MedTech industry. TQM J. **34**(7), 18–38 (2022). https://doi.org/10.1108/TQM-10-2021-0289
15. Mauri, F., Garetti, M., Gandelli, A.: A structured approach to process improvement in manufacturing systems. Prod. Plan. Control **21**(7), 695–717 (2010)
16. Brown, A., Eatock, J., Dixon, D., Meenan, B.J., Anderson, J.: Quality and continuous improvement in medical device manufacturing. TQM J. **20**, 541–555 (2008)
17. Moore, S.: Next generation medical device manufacture: a strategic assessment. J. Enterp. Excell1 (2016)
18. Hines, P., Butterworth, C.: The Essence of Excellence: Creating a Culture of Continuous Improvement, 1st edn. SA Partners, Caerphilly (2019)
19. Åhlström, P., et al.: Is lean a theory? Viewpoints and outlook. Int. J. Oper. Prod. Manag. (2021)
20. Willmott, P., Quirke, J., Brunskill, A.: TPM: A Foundation of Operational Excellence.1st ed. Caerphilly (2019)
21. Bajaj, V., Reffell, B.: Research Report 2019/2020: The Global State of Operational Excellence. An Exclusive Business Transformation and Operational Excellence World Sumit (BTOES): Critical Challenges and Future Trends, (2020)
22. Bernhard, G.: Lean manufacturing in a high containment environment. Innovations in Pharmaceutical Technology, pp. 74–76 (2010)
23. Falco, L.: Deploying standard work in the lab. American Pharmaceutical Review, pp. 1–9 (2015)

24. Antony, J., et al.: An empirical study into the reasons for failure of sustaining operational excellence initiatives in organizations. TQM J., January 2022. https://doi.org/10.1108/TQM-05-2022-0176.
25. Chandrasekaran, A., Toussaint, J.: Creating a culture of continuous improvement. Harvard Bus. Rev. 5(24), 2–5 (2019)
26. Huang, S.-J., Wu, M.-S., Chen, L.-W.: Critical success factors in aligning IT and business objectives: a Delphi study. Total Qual. Manage. Bus. Excellence 24(9–10), 1219–1240 (2013)
27. Shahin, M., Babar, M.A., Zhu, L.: Continuous integration, delivery and deployment: a systematic review on approaches, tools, challenges and practices. IEEE Access 5, 3909–3943 (2017)
28. McDermott, O., Antony, J., Douglas, J.: Exploring the use of operational excellence methodologies in the era of COVID-19: perspectives from leading academics and practitioners. TQM J. 33(8), 1647–1665 (2021). https://doi.org/10.1108/TQM-01-2021-0016
29. McDermott, O., Antony, J.: Lean six sigma as an enabler for healthcare operational excellence in COVID-19. In: Six Sigma for Healthcare & Leadership, Purdue University, Indiana, 26–27 June. https://docs.lib.purdue.edu/iclss/2021/hl/3.
30. Mathiyazhagan, K., Gnanavelbabu, A., Agarwal, V.: A framework for implementing sustainable lean manufacturing in the electrical and electronics component manufacturing industry: an emerging economies country perspective. J. Cleaner Prod. 334, 130169 (2022)
31. McGrane, V., McDermott, O., Trubetskaya, A., Rosa, A., Sony, M.: The effect of medical device regulations on deploying a lean six sigma project. Processes 10(11), 2303 (2022)
32. Trubetskaya, A., Manto, D., McDermott, O.: A review of lean adoption in the Irish MedTech Industry. Processes 10(2), February 2022. Art. no. 2. https://doi.org/10.3390/pr10020391.
33. Byrne, B., McDermott, O., Noonan, J.: Applying lean six sigma methodology to a pharmaceutical manufacturing facility: a case study. Processes 9(3), 550 (2021). https://doi.org/10.3390/pr9030550
34. Forza, C.: Survey research in operations management: a process-based perspective. Int. J. Oper. Prod. Manag. (2002)
35. Charmaz, K., Belgrave, L.: Qualitative interviewing and grounded theory analysis. SAGE Handb. Interview Res. Complex. Craft 2, 347–365 (2012)
36. Denzin, N.K., Lincoln, Y.S.: Introduction: the discipline and practice of qualitative research (2008)
37. Punch, K.F.: Introduction to Social Research: Quantitative and Qualitative Approaches. Sage, Newcastle upon Tyne (2013)
38. Kanyesigye, S.T., Uwamahoro, J., Kemeza, I.: Data collected to measure the impact of problem-based learning and document physics classroom practices among Ugandan secondary schools. Data Brief 44, 108534 (2022)
39. Unkelos-Shpigel, N., Sherman, S., Hadar, I.: Finding the missing link to industry: LinkedIn professional groups as facilitators of empirical research. In: Presented at the 2015 IEEE/ACM 3rd International Workshop on Conducting Empirical Studies in Industry, pp. 43–46 (2015)
40. Polit, D.F., Beck, C.T.: Nursing Research: Generating and Assessing Evidence for Nursing Practice. Lippincott Williams & Wilkins, Philadelphia (2008)
41. Morrow, R., Rodriguez, A., King, N.: Colaizzi's descriptive phenomenological method. Psychologist 28(8), 643–644 (2015)
42. McMullen, J.S.: Perspective taking and the heterogeneity of the entrepreneurial imagination. In: What is so Austrian about Austrian economics? Emerald Group Publishing Limited (2010)
43. Davis, M.H.: Measuring individual differences in empathy: evidence for a multidimensional approach. J. Pers. Soc. Psychol. 44(1), 113 (1983)
44. Khan, S.N.: Qualitative research method-phenomenology. Asian Soc. Sci. 10(21), 298 (2014)
45. Clarke, V., Braun, V.: Thematic analysis. J. Positive Psychol. 30(5), 385–399 (2016)

46. Muazu, M.H., Tasmin, R.: Operational excellence in manufacturing, service and the oil & gas: the sectorial definitional constructs and risk management implication. Traektoriâ Nauki= Path of Sci. **3**(9) 3001–3008 (2017)
47. Raghunath, A., Jayathirtha, R.: Critical success factors for six sigma implementation by SMEs. Int. J. Sci. Eng. Res. **4**(2), 1–7 (2013)
48. Edgeman, R.: Excellence models as complex management systems: an examination of the Shingo operational excellence model. Bus. Process Manag. J. **24**(6), 1321–1338 (2018)
49. Kelly, S., Hines, P.: Discreetly embedding the Shingo principles of enterprise excellence at Abbott diagnostics manufacturing facility in Longford Ireland. Total Q. Manage. Bus. Excellence **30**(11–12), 1235–1256 (2019)
50. Carvalho, M., Sá, J.C., Marques, P.A., Santos, G., Pereira, A.M.: Development of a conceptual model integrating management systems and the Shingo model towards operational excellence. Total Q. Manage. Bus. Excellence, 1–24 (2022)
51. Collins, J.C., Porras, J.I.: Building your company's vision. Harvard Bus. Rev. **74**(5), 65 (1996)
52. McDermott, O., Antony, J., Sony, M., Looby, E.: A critical evaluation and measurement of organisational readiness and adoption for continuous improvement within a medical device manufacturer, 1–11, May 2022. https://doi.org/10.1080/17509653.2022.2073917

Challenges Facing Medical Device Companies in Ireland and Why Operational Excellence is not Enough

David McKernan[✉] and Olivia McDermott

College of Science and Engineering, National University of Ireland, Galway, Ireland
D.McKernan3@nuigalway.ie

Abstract. Ireland has developed a highly successful medical device cluster. The cluster experience accelerated growth during the 1990s when many USA multinationals established manufacturing sites. Manufacturing is the driving force that created the cluster with linkages between, universities, venture capital, entrepreneurs, suppliers, and supporting industry. Using Lean tools and principles the sites have established a reputation for excellence. A generation since the sites have been established changes outside of the cluster are impacting its competitiveness. Lean tools and systems may no longer be enough to sustain the cluster. This paper examines the key changes affecting the cluster and highlights the reasons lean principles may not be enough for the cluster to continue to thrive for another generation. The paper provides valuable insights into a strategy for individual firms, and the medical device cluster in Ireland and has lessons for any other industrial cluster.

Keywords: Cluster · Medical devices · Ireland · Lean · Operational excellence

1 Introduction

Ireland's Medtech cluster is seen as a significant success triggered initially by foreign direct investment from USA multinationals [1]. The Med Tech sector in Ireland is dominated by several US multinational companies [2]. The manufacturing sites have matured and developed and reputation for operational excellence and execution [3]. The use of lean tools and principles is engrained in the operations of the sites [4]. In the 1990s medical device regulations enabled Irish sites to commercialise new products faster than USA sites [5, 6]. This significantly improved the competitiveness of an industry where time to market is critical [6]. Also, since the 1990sthe Irish government could offer significant tax incentives to companies. Today because of the OECD/G20 inclusive framework on Base Erosion and Profit Shifting (BEPS) large groups must pay a minimum of 15% in every jurisdiction they operate [7].

The selling price for undifferentiated medical devices declines year on year [8]. Lean tools and systems can help the manufacturing site respond but typically this will not be enough by itself [9]. The sites have a risk of having production relocated to lower-cost

O. McDermott et al. (Eds.): ELEC 2022, IFIP AICT 668, pp. 204–217, 2023.
https://doi.org/10.1007/978-3-031-25741-4_18

locations as has happened in the computer and electronic industries in Ireland [10, 11]. The medical device industry has developed a cluster that can provide a difficult-to-copy competitive advantage [12–14]. The clustering effect can improve competitiveness and make the manufacturing site more "sticky" [15]. The site must employ a strategy of product differentiation for long-term success [16]. Just using lean tools to improve efficiency may delay the closure of a highly efficient site but it will not enable the manufacturing site to thrive [17].

The research objectives for this paper are to review the Irish Medtech cluster and how Lean has helped operational excellence in this sector. The study proposes areas where the cluster is weak and why Lean may not be enough if not expanded into the wider cluster network.

2 Research Methodology

A literature review was completed to assess the nature of the global medical device industry. Academic databases, and other relevant sites such as the World Health Organisation, World Trade Organisation, and European Patent Office, MedTech companies in Ireland and regulatory legislation all provided insights into the medical device sector. These sources gave insight into the global scale of the industry, the growth trends, product categories, and key the nations and clusters that dominate the industry. Based on the data the researchers looked at how the global forces affect the competitiveness of Irish medical device cluster. We used recently published literature and global databases for enterprise excellence awards to assess the maturity of continuous improvement within the Irish cluster. The global changes affecting Ireland and the maturity level of the cluster was distilled into a strategic model describing the cluster.

3 Review and Results-Medical Device Industry in Ireland

Medical devices are products, services, or solutions that prevent, diagnose, monitor, treat, and care for human beings by physical means [18]. The medical device industry has become an important part of the Irish economy and is recognized as a global MedTech cluster.

Medical Device companies based in Ireland are estimated to have exported €12.2B in 2018 [19]. There are 42,000 people directly employed by the MedTech industry in Ireland, 1.5% of national employment [19, 20]. Ireland has the highest percentage of people employed in MedTech of any European country, (3 times the rate of Germany and 5.5 times the UK rate) [20]. Ireland is the second-largest European exporter of medical devices. Ireland's exports make an impact globally some key exports include [21].

25% of the world's diabetics are treated with products made in Ireland. 1/3 of global contact lenses are made in Ireland and accounted for exports worth up to €1B in 2020. Ireland is the world's largest exporter of cardiology stents, it exported €2B worth of product in 2020. Artificial joints accounted for €1.3B in 2020, making Ireland the World's fourth-largest exporter of these devices. The country is also the 3rd largest exporter of diagnostic reagents for patient administration. Approximately 50% of ventilators worldwide in acute hospitals are Irish-made.

There are 450 Medical device companies in Ireland [2]. A review of the 450 companies reveals that 90% of medical device employees work in multinational companies that were first established in Ireland before 2000. The 43 largest Medical Technology companies were identified [22]. These 43 companies have 71 sites in Ireland. 75% of these are US-based multinationals, 10% are Irish and 4% are German. The USA is the world's largest producer and market for medical devices [23].

The Irish MedTech cluster is highly dependent on USA multinationals that first invested in Ireland in the 1990s. The data show many of the major global companies have had a presence in Ireland for over 30 years. The sites have matured to become global centres of excellence supporting business units and have developed R&D centres [3] (Fig. 1).

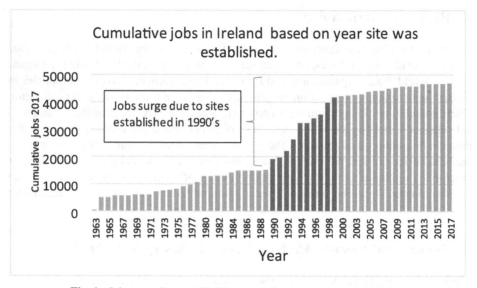

Fig. 1. Jobs growth up to 2017 based on the year site was established.

The Irish MedTech cluster is highly dependent on USA-headquartered multinational companies that first invested in Ireland in the 1990s. These data show, many of the major companies have had a presence in Ireland for over 30 years. The sites have matured to become global centres of excellence supporting business units and have developed R&D centres [3].

3.1   Drivers of Growth in Medical Devices

Global spending on healthcare has doubled from 2000 to 2020 [24]. An aging population is the most significant factor that causes increased spending on healthcare [25]. There has been a six-fold increase in healthcare spending between those aged over 85 and those aged between 55 and 59 years [26]. Globally, in 2020, there are 728 million people aged 65 or over. This number is projected to double to 1.5 billion in 2050 [27] (Fig. 2).

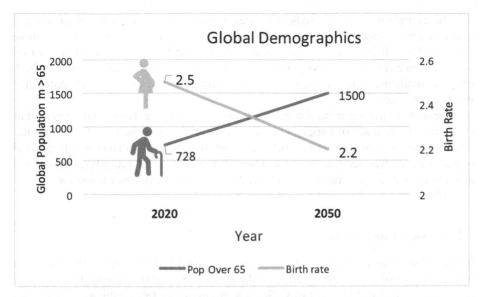

Fig. 2. Global population over 65 [27] and births per female [28].

Economic development and increasing urbanisation are leading to more sedentary lifestyles and greater consumption of unhealthy foods linked with obesity. This is driving a rise in chronic conditions such as type II diabetes [29]. Early detection and improved treatments mean people are living longer with chronic conditions [29] (Fig. 3).

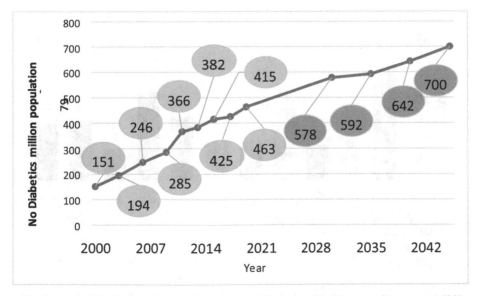

Fig. 3. Actual/Prediction of the global number of diabetics (20–79 years of age group) [29]

The availability of novel medical devices to treat unmet clinical needs has created new markets for medical devices. An example of new demand is Endovascular Stroke Therapy (EST). Saber et al showed a continuous increase in EST over the 10-year period from 2006 to 2016. The number of ESTs went from less than 50 in 2006 to 1000 in 2016 [30]. A significant jump in demand occurred when multiple clinical trials confirmed positive outcomes.

There is a growing trend towards minimally invasive interventional surgery. For example, a USA study of Peripheral Arterial Disease showed the use of endovascular interventions grew by a factor of 3 between 1996 and 2006. Simultaneously traditional bypass surgery was reduced by 43%. Overall, the number of procedures completed almost doubled in the decade. Patients benefited as the rate of amputation reduced by 29% [31].

3.2 Impact of Regulations

In the 1990s, typically,medical devices could be approved for sale on the European market in 9 months. In January 2022 guidance for approval of medical devices under the Medical Device Regulations (MDR) is a minimum of 18 months with significant uncertainty in the time for approval [5].

The average approval for a medical device in the USA through a 510 (k) pathway (2016 to 2020) is 150 days [32]. The regulatory regime for the medical device industry can slow continuous improvement project implementation [33]. The data from the afore-mentioned studies show that, in the 1990s, medical device companies could get their products to market in Ireland 21 months faster than in the USA. Today Ireland has lost that advantage and it now takes longer to gain approval to sell in the EU. In 2022 most

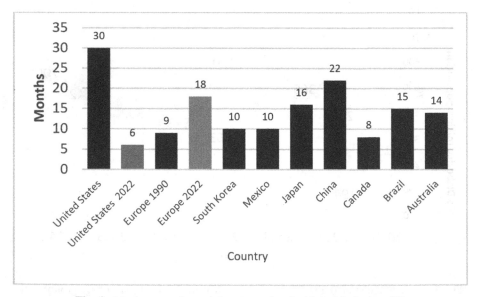

Fig. 4. Maximum estimated time to market for high-risk devices [5].

Medical Device manufacturers regard the product registration process under MDR as "cumbersomeand uncertain" [6]. 52% of medical device executives said their company would deprioritise entering the European market as a result of MDR [6] (Fig. 4).

3.3 Price Erosion

The overall medical device market is growing [34]. The price obtained for undifferentiated products is reducing for the following reasons: In the USA, groups of hospitals are pooling their purchasing power to reduce costs. Between 72 and 80 percent of non-labour purchases are completed through a Group Purchasing Organisation (GPOs) or Integrated Delivery Networks (IDNs) [8]. Centralised purchasing results in the standardisation of medical devices and downward price pressure. Increasingly. Purchasing decisions and medical device selection are being made by purchasing departments with physicians in an advisory role. Commodity products are particularly affected by downward pricing pressure. For example the Average Selling Price (ASP) for a carotid balloon catheter is expected to drop in value by 26 % from US$240 to US$178.90 over the 10 years from 2017 to 2027 [35]. Office-based labs (OBLs) are increasingly used for outpatient procedures. Almost all endovascular procedures are suitable for an OBL setting. OBL is gaining an increasing share of the USA market. Currently, 25% of peripheral vascular procedures are carried out in OBL settings [35]. OBLs are physician-owned and tend to be more cost-conscious than hospitals. OBLs often receive price discounts of 50% [35]. OBLs and GPOs are driving down the ASP of medical devices in the USA. China had introduced a centralised public procurement policy for medical devices in 2019. When the coronary stents were put to tender, 20 companies participated, 8 were chosen, and of these, six were Chinese. Only one company, which was Chinese, was given a guaranteed volume based on its price [36]. Reducing selling prices in the Chinese market will make it increasingly difficult for Irish-based MedTech companies to compete in the market (Table 1).

Table 1. Medical device price reductions resulting from centralised state procurement in China [36]

Average price reductions by-product arising from China's Centralised state procurement rounds	
Coronary stents	95%
Orthopaedics	55%
Intraocular lens	41%
Pacemakers	50%
Nursing consumables	~80–90%

3.4 Response to Reducing the Sales Price

Medical device manufacturers in Ireland attempt to maintain cost-effectiveness through enterprise excellence programs. The use of lean tools in the Irish MedTech cluster is widespread and is used to improve competitiveness [4]. All 19 MedTech companies in the Trubetskaya et al study were actively using lean tools and systems. The widespread use and effectiveness of lean tools can be demonstrated through global recognition of operational excellence. In the years 2011 to 2021 medical device companies in Ireland have won more Shingo Prizes per head of population than any other country in the world [37] (Table 2).

Table 2. Shingo prizes awarded to medical device companies per country 2011–2021 [37].

	Shingo prizes won (Medical companies)	Population M	Prizes per million population
Ireland	6	5	1.20
Costa Rica	3	5.094	0.59
Lithuania	1	2.79	0.36
Denmark	1	5.831	0.17
Israel	1	9.2	0.11
Mexico	9	128.9	0.07
USA	14	329	0.04
Canada	1	38	0.03
Germany	1	83.24	0.01

Continuous improvement as part of an enterprise excellence programme can improve profitability, but it is not normally sufficient [9]. Porter gives two reasons for this: 1. The rapid diffusion of best practices and that competitors can quickly copy best practices and 2. Competitive convergence -rivals imitate one another's improvements by often using the same suppliers and outsourcing to the same third parties. Medical device multinationals have manufacturing sites globally, with some in low-cost locations. Medtronic, Boston Scientific, Baxter, Abbott and Zimmer all have manufacturing sites in Costa Rica [38]. Ireland's labour costs are average for the euro area but are almost 5 times those of a low-cost location like Bulgaria [39] (Table 3).

Multinationals can move manufacturing to countries with lower labour costs. Advances in transport and information have reduced the impact of distance. Regions face a more difficult time in anchoring multinational investments [15]. The "stickiness" of a region is its ability to attract and keep industry [15]. Operational excellence can be copied by other regions and so does not, by itself, self-provide a competitive advantage that increases the "Stickiness" of the Irish MedTech sector.

Table 3. Hourly labour costs (2020 employee compensation plus taxes minus subsidies) [39]

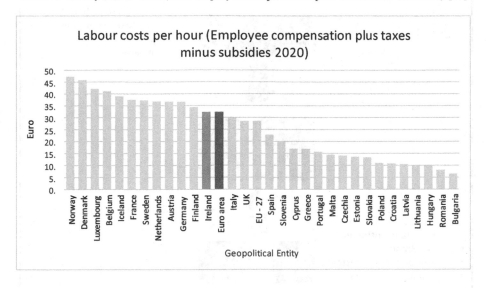

3.5 Strategy to Deal with Falling Prices

Medical Device manufacturers based in Ireland have a choice of two strategies [16]. The first is a low- cost strategy by focusing on reducing costs or to differentiate their site and product. This strategy requires choices to be made on the manufacturing site. If the site is to gain a competitive advantage through a low-cost strategy, then it is at risk from lower-cost locations within a multinational's list of sites. The cost reduction must stay ahead of price erosion in the product category so as to compete. This necessitates low overheads, careful management of headcount, and minimising spending (Fig. 5).

A low-cost strategy effectively prevents the site from moving up the value chain and attracting additional responsibilities to the site. To increase the remit of the site and expand its responsibilities it's recommended to "Over hire" and have capacity available [3]. In a low-cost strategy, there will always be a lower-cost region that multinationals can move to. Costa Rica has successfully attracted many of the same multinational companies to their shores [40]. The computer industry is an example of an industry that failed to stick as it largely left Ireland and moved to Asian countries in the 1990s [10, 11].

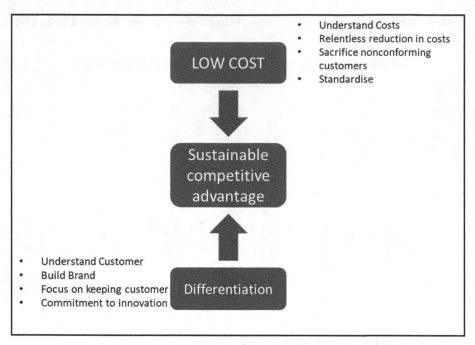

Fig. 5. Focus for low-cost v differentiated strategy [16]

The second is a differentiated strategy. In a differentiated strategy, the focus is on the site developing new products for unmet clinical needs. Differentiated products enable the creation of new markets with little competition [30, 31]. Multinational companies find it difficult to capitalise on disruptive innovation [41]. In effect, multinationals have outsourced much of their R&D to start-ups [42]. Small and medium firms are twice as likely to launch a disruptive innovation in the market [40]. In effect, multinational sites in Ireland face a dilemma. They must reduce costs to ensure their site remains competitive as the sales price of today's products inevitably reduces. At the same time, the site must introduce new differentiated products that will provide long-term commercial success (Fig. 6).

3.6 Medical Device Cluster

"Clusters are geographic concentrations of industries related by knowledge, skills, inputs, demand, and/ or other linkages" [12]. Clusters have a positive impact on regions' industrial performance including job creation [12]. These clusters should be considered a regional ecosystem. The clustering effect matters, as 39% of European jobs and 55% of European wages are located in clusters [43]. According to Porter, clusters are a source of strategic competitive advantage [44]. An example of a medical device cluster is Tuttlingen in Germany. This town has a population of 34,000 people but is recognized as a world leader in surgical instruments. In 1995, 90% of all surgical instruments firms in Germany were based in Tuttlingen [14]. Hill and Brennan states that industrial clusters

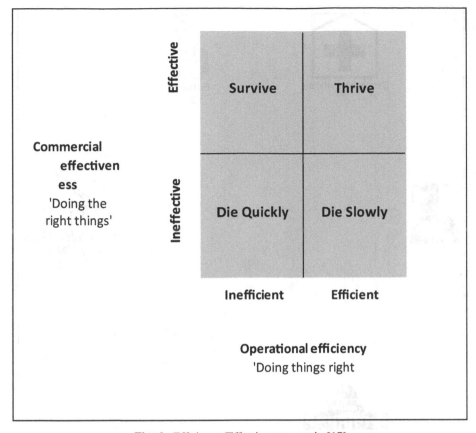

Fig. 6. Efficiency/Effectiveness matrix [17]

require driver industries at the centre [45]. Multinational companies are the driver of the medical device cluster in Ireland.

3.6.1 Elements of the Medical Device Cluster

Multinationals, start-ups, support companies and for example companies that will design and manufacture products to meet the start-up's needs are all part of the cluster. Other elements include universities who provide skilled labour, generate ideas and host incubators. Funding is essential for start-ups, particularly innovation driven enterprises (IDEs). Sources of funding start-ups include Enterprise Ireland's high potentials funds, venture capital and angel investors. These elements are interrelated and support each other. For example, it is important that medical practitioners can identify unmet clinical needs and provide knowledge to medical companies on how to improve medical devices. Reducing the effectiveness of this link has been shown to directly reduce innovation in both the volumes of innovations and the inventiveness of them [46] (Fig. 7).

Start-ups are a key part of the ecosystem. They are well-positioned to develop disruptive technologies that open new opportunities for products and can create completly

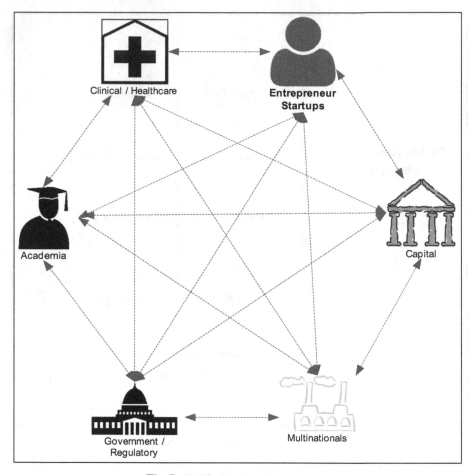

Fig. 7. Medical device cluster Ireland

new markets. For multinationals in Ireland, partnering with start-ups could be a key part of the site strategy. It will help the multinational's site to gain access to disruptive technologies while still having a focus on maintaining costs. It will enable the site to have a differentiated strategy, create new business opportunities and reduce the impact of price erosion. To execute a strategy of differentiation that is integrated within this ecosystem, the site needs to ensure it has competencies, for example, in integrating new companies, quickly scaling, and regulatory skills to launch the product in new markets. This is a different focus for the enterprise excellence program that must focus more on growing capabilities than cost savings. A wider focus on the ecosystem is required for long-term success.

4 Discussion and Conclusion

Ireland has developed a highly successful medical device industry that has proven to be resilient. Global spending on healthcare has doubled in the past 20 years. This is largely driven by an increasingly aging population. New innovations also create completely new market opportunities and benefit society through improved healthcare outcomes. During a rapid expansion of the Irish medical device industry, the time to market for the Irish subsidiary was significantly faster than the USA-based headquarters. This competitive advantage is now lost due to changes in European medical device regulations. The ASP of undifferentiated medical devices is falling year on year. This makes the cluster highly vulnerable to USA multinationals that could move manufacturing to lower-cost locations. Lean tools are widely deployed, with the Irish subsidiaries recognized for their application of operational excellence. However, Lean tools are unlikely to be enough to sustain the cluster. To obtain a long-term competitive advantage the Irish sites must have a strategy of differentiation. The sites must focus not just on internal metrics but on how the individual site integrates with the wider medical device cluster. The site must be prepared to spend money today in order to grow capabilities to innovate and differentiate itself from low-cost locations.

References

1. Brazys, S., Regan, A.: Small states in global markets. In: The Oxford Handbook of Irish Politics (2021). https://doi.org/10.1093/oxfordhb/9780198823834.013.24
2. Irish Medtech Association Strategy 2022–2025. Dublin (2022)
3. Walsh, P.: Achieving your R&D Ambition. Galway (2021)
4. Trubetskaya, A., Manto, D., McDermott, O.: A review of lean adoption in the irish MedTech industry (2022). https://doi.org/10.3390/pr10020391
5. Daigle, B., Torsekar, M.: United States International Trade Commission Journal of International Commerce and Economics The EU Medical Device Regulation and the U.S. Medical Device Industry (2019)
6. Johnson, C., et al.: Interstates and Autobahns Global Medtech Innovation and Regulation in the Digital Age (2022)
7. European Commission: Minimum corporate taxation: Questions and Answers, https://ec.eur opa.eu/commission/presscorner/detail/en/qanda_21_6967. Accessed 24 Jan 2022
8. Wilson, B.: GPO & IDN Sales Process: Unraveling Affiliations and Identifying Decision Makers - Carevoyance, https://www.carevoyance.com/blog/gpo-and-idn-sales-process. Accessed 20 Jan 2022
9. Porter, M.E.: What Is Strategy? Harv. Bus. Rev. **74**, 61–78 (1996)
10. Barry, F., van Egeraatt, C.: The decline of the computer hardware sector: how Ireland adjusted, pp. 38–57 (2008)
11. van Egeraat, C., Jacobson, D.: The rise and demise of the Irish and Scottish computer hardware industry. Eur. Plan. Stud. **12**, 809–834 (2004). https://doi.org/10.1080/0965431042000251873
12. Delgado, M., et al.: Defining Clusters of Related Industries. Cambridge (2014)
13. Hobbs, J., Moloney, R., Walsh, M.: Cluster or satellite platform: a comparative study. In: Business Clusters, pp. 1–22 (2020). https://doi.org/10.4324/9780367817954-1
14. Halder, G.: The Surgical Instrument Cluster of Tuttlingen, Germany, Duisburg (2002)
15. Markusen, A.: Sticky places in slippery space: a typology of industrial districts (1996)

16. Lafley, A.G., Martin, R.L.: Playing to Win, How Real Strategy Works. Harvard Business Review Press, Boston (2019)
17. Hines, P., Found, P., Griffiths, G., Harrison, R.: Staying Lean, Thriving, Not Just Surviving. Lean Enterprise Research Center, Cardiff (2008)
18. Med Tech Europe: What is Medical Technology? (2021)
19. Department of Business, E. and I.: Focus on Medical Technologies (2020)
20. Med Tech Europe: The European Medical Technology Industry in figures 2020 (2020)
21. Industrial Development Authority (IDA): Medical Technology in Ireland | IDA Ireland, https://www.idaireland.com/doing-business-here/industry-sectors/medical-technology. Accessed 11 Feb 2022
22. Irish Times: The Irish Times Top 1000 Companies, https://www.top1000.ie/. Accessed 05 Dec 2021
23. Maresova, P., Penhaker, M., Selamat, A., Kuca, K.: The potential of medical device industry in technological and economical context (2015). https://doi.org/10.2147/TCRM.S88574
24. World Health Organisation: Global expenditure on health: Public spending on the rise? 2021. Geneva (2021)
25. Gregersen, F.A.: The impact of ageing on health care expenditures: a study of steepening. Eur. J. Health Econ. **15**(9), 979–989 (2013). https://doi.org/10.1007/s10198-013-0541-9
26. Murakami, Y., Morgan, D.: Focus on health spending (2016)
27. Krys, C., Born, D.: Megatrend 1 People & Society (2021)
28. Worldometer: World Demographics 2020 (Population, Age, Sex, Trends) -, https://www.worldometers.info/demographics/world-demographics/. Accessed 22 Jan 2022
29. Williams, R.: IDF Diabetes Atlas 9th (edn.) (2019)
30. Saber, H., et al.: Real-world treatment trends in endovascular stroke therapy. Stroke **50**, 683–689 (2019). https://doi.org/10.1161/STROKEAHA.118.023967
31. Goodney, P.P., Beck, A.W., Nagle, J., Welch, H.G., Zwolak, R.M.: National trends in lower extremity bypass surgery, endovascular interventions, and major amputations. J. Vasc. Surg. **50**, 54–60 (2009). https://doi.org/10.1016/J.JVS.2009.01.035
32. Darrow, J.J., Avorn, J., Kesselheim, A.S.: FDA Regulation and approval of medical devices: 19762020. JAMA – J. Am. Med. Assoc. **326**, 420–432 (2021). https://doi.org/10.1001/jama.2021.11171
33. McDermott, O., Antony, J., Sony, M., Healy, T.: Critical failure factors for continuous improvement methodologies in the Irish MedTech industry. TQM J. **34** (2022). https://doi.org/10.1108/TQM10-2021-0289
34. World Health Organisation: Global Health Expenditure Database. https://apps.who.int/nha/database/ViewData/Indicators/en. Accessed 26 Dec 2021
35. Amador, F.: Peripheral Vascular Devices Market Analysis. USA, Toronto (2018)
36. Erixon, F., Guildea, A., Guinea, O., Lamprecht, P.: China's Public Procurement Protectionism and Europe's Response: The Case of Medical Technology (2021)
37. Shingo Institute: Shingo Prize - Awa rds - Shingo Institute. https://shingo.org/awards/. Accessed 17 March 2022
38. Lo, C.: Inside Costa Rica's super-sized medical device sector. https://www.medicaldevicenetwork.com/features/inside-costa-ricas-super-sized-medical-device-sector/. Accessed 18 March 2022
39. Eurostat: Statistics | Eurostat. https://ec.europa.eu/eurostat/databrowser/view/LC_LCI_LEV__custom_1956891/default/table?lang=en. Accessed 23 Jan 2022
40. Bamber, P., Gereffi, G.: Costa rica in the medical devices global value chain: opportunities for upgrading (2013)
41. Chatterji, A.K.: Spawned with a silver spoon? Entrepreneurial performance and innovation in the medical device industry. Strateg. Manag. J. **30**, 185–206 (2009). https://doi.org/10.1002/smj.729

42. Lynn, S., O'Malley, P., Tanner, D., Moore, S.: Refining early stage interventional composite catheter design. Procedia Manuf. **38**, 282–290 (2019). https://doi.org/10.1016/J.PROMFG. 2020.01.037
43. European Union: Smart Guide to Cluster Policy (2016). https://doi.org/10.2873/48105
44. Porter, M.E.: The competitive advantage of nations porter (1990)
45. Hill, E.W., Brennan, J.F.: A methodology for identifying the drivers of industrial clusters: the foundation of regional competitive advantage. Econ. Dev. Q. **14**, 65-96 (2000). https://doi. org/10.1177/089124240001400109
46. Chatterji, A.K., Fabrizio, K.R.: Does the market for ideas influence the rate and direction of innovative activity? Evidence from the medical device industry. Strateg. Manag. J. **37**, 447–465 (2016). https://doi.org/10.1002/smj.2340

Lean Learning in the Digital Era

Effective Learning Method Using Extended Reality: Digital TWI

Serkan Eren(✉) ⓘ, Eivind Reke, and Daryl John Powell ⓘ

SINTEF Manufacturing AS, Raufoss, Norway
{serkan.eren,eivind.reke,daryl.powell}@sintef.no

Abstract. Training within Industry was created under World War II by the U.S. Department of War, within the War Manpower Commission, to assist defense industries meet the high production output demand from less or inexperienced labor. It ran from 1940 to 1945, made its way to Japan after the war and became a foundational component of the Toyota Production System (TPS). TWI is a well-proven lean education methodology consists of four main modules: Job Instructions (JI), Job Relations (JR), Job Methods (JM) and Program Development. This paper aims to explore combining TWI Job Instructions (JI) module with extended reality (XR) smart glasses and technologies that may create an effective and innovative lean education program.

Keywords: Lean · Training Within Industry (TWI) · Education · Digitalization · Industry 4.0

1 Introduction

Training within Industry, a well-proven lean education methodology, consists of four main modules and was developed during World War II by the U.S. Department of War to assist defense industries meet the high production output demand from less or inexperienced labor. A recent study of the impact on the organizations exposed to the TWI program revealed that companies who had received training had experienced a substantial gain in both productivity and sales year on year [1]. COVID-19 pandemic made difficult to meet in-person for many. Since March 2020, there has been a surge quest for remote access technologies [2]. This paper aims to explore combining TWI Job Instructions (JI) module with extended reality (XR) smart glasses and technologies that may create an effective and innovative lean education program. Even though TWI was designed as an in-person teaching method, a digital version of TWI method may remove the need of travelling to meet in-person and provide some further advantages related to re-training and onboarding. Conceptual research is exploited as framework and literature review is used as methodology. The paper is divided into 7 sections. The next section provides a theoretical background. Section 3 explains the research method used in this paper. Section 4 gives an overview over existing possibilities and examples of the combination of AR technologies and TWI, while a framework how combination of

© IFIP International Federation for Information Processing 2023
Published by Springer Nature Switzerland AG 2023
O. McDermott et al. (Eds.): ELEC 2022, IFIP AICT 668, pp. 221–232, 2023.
https://doi.org/10.1007/978-3-031-25741-4_19

TWI and AR may contribute to the new industry era, industry 5.0 and the four concepts within this framework is suggested in Sect. 5. Discussions, conclusion, and suggestions for future work are presented in Sect. 6 and Sect. 7.

2 Background

2.1 Training Within Industry (TWI)

"If the worker hasn't learned, the instructor hasn't taught." A key tenet to the Job Instruction method of Training Within Industry (TWI) emphasizes the importance of instructor's responsibility [3]. The TWI Service developed and established in August 1940 by the National Defense Advisory Commission and was eventually placed under the Federal Security agency as a part of War Manpower Commission During World War II. Allied forces needed significant war supplies and TWI Service assisted war production industries to meet their manpower needs through a "train-the-trainer" program aimed at the supervisor level. Thereby enabling production to keep pace with war demands [4]. Foundation of the TWI were already laid at the beginning of World War I in US by Charles R. Allen, a vocational instructor from Massachusetts, when he developed his four-point method of Preparation, Presentation, Application, and Testing. The Emergency Fleet Corporation of the United States Shipping Board initiated a training program to increase the number of shipyard workers to 10 times the current number and Charles R. Allen's method was used to train 500,000 people at the shipyards successfully [5]. The 4-step method formed the basis for the TWI programs developed over 20 years later.

Developing standardized programs that could meet the unique needs of various businesses, to neutralize the standard rejoinder that "our business is different", was a challenge. To tackle this challenge, TWI explained first the purpose of the different modules, so-called the "J" programs by describing the five basic needs of supervisors: [6].

Knowledge of the work, Knowledge of responsibilities. Skill in instructing, Skill in improving methods, Skill in leading. TWI directly addressed the need for skills mentioned above through the three J courses: [7] Job Instruction (JI) Training on how to instruct employees, Job Methods (JM) Training on how to improve job methods, and Job Relations (JR) Training on how to lead people.

TWI service monitored six hundred companies during the service to measure the impact. The following percentage of plants reported at least 25% improvement in each of the following areas: [3] (Table 1).

Table 1. TWI results in september 1945 [3]

Increased production	86%
Reduced training time	100%
Reduced labor-hours	88%
Reduced scrap	55%
Reduced grievances	100%

Although the Service was disbanded in 1945, millions of people in the USA, Canada, Great Britain, and Australia had already benefited from the programs and saw opportunity to share their knowledge with the rest of the world. Many of them formed consulting companies and continued to spread the TWI programs around the world, including, Japan, Italy, France, Spain, Belgium, Turkey, Indonesia, New Zealand, Ireland, Nepal, India, The Netherlands [8, 9]. Among all countries, TWI has indeed had a strong influence in Japan. Until 1992, TWI usage dropped off in Unites States, while it was used heavily in Japanese companies. Toyota started to use TWI programs in 1951 and became the backbone of Toyota's standardization philosophy [7, 10].

Four Steps of Job Instruction
According to Graupp and Wrona [11], showing alone or telling alone to instruct employees is not effective, even though they are important elements of instructing. Job Instruction is a method to get a person quickly remember how to do a job, correctly, safely and conscientiously. [9] Graupp and Wrona [11] claims that the JI 4-Step Method, when applied properly, can assure a successful training experience every time. The JI 4-Step Method is illustrated in Fig. 1.

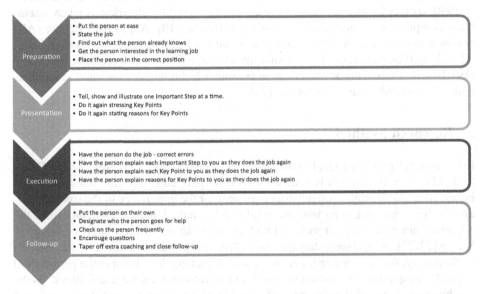

Fig. 1. Four steps of job instruction [11]

The first step is about preparing the employee for training. At this step, it is crucial to make the trainee comfortable, understand the knowledge state of the trainee and create an interest in the learning job. The second step is where the job is introduced and explained in detail. This step is where instructor tell, show, and illustrate each important step at a time and repeat with underlining the Key Points and the reasons for Key Points again. Third step is the execution step for the trainee. Trainee performs the job and repeat with explaining Key Points, and then repeat again with the reasons for Key Points, as the instructor did on the previous step. Finally, on the fourth step, the main duty of the instructor is auditing the trainee at fixed interval.

2.2 Extended Reality (XR)

The term extended reality (XR) is an umbrella term that often used as a generic expression covering both augmented reality (AR) and virtual reality (VR). Milgram's Reality Virtuality Continuum, spans between the real environment and the virtual environment comprise Augmented Reality and Augmented Virtuality (AV) in between, locates AR closer to the real world [12].

Augmented Reality (AR) refers to a live view of physical real-world environment whose elements are merged with augmented computer-generated images creating a mixed reality [13]. It is a combination of digital information with the real world that is presented in real-time [12, 14, 15]. According to Azuma [14], AR as systems combine real and virtual, are registered in 3-D and interactive in real time. The concept of augmenting the view of the world has mentioned already in 1901 by L. Frank Baum in his novel "The Master Key" [16]. Even though the concept of AR dates back to the 1950s [17], AR phrase is considered to have been coined by Tom Caudell and David Mizell in 1990 to describe how the head-mounted displays used by electricians when assembling complicated wiring harnesses worked at Boeing [18]. Augmented Reality (AR) was perceived as science fiction for decades until it had its mainstream breakthrough when 21 million gamers used an AR smartphone game within one week after the release [19]. In recent years, the advancement of computer technologies motivated researchers to develop new ideas and uses for AR [20].

3 Research Method

In this research paper, we adopt a conceptual research framework, as presented by Crawford [21], wherein research is conducted by observing and analyzing already present information. We attempt to establish an argument for the importance of the study, underline the relationships among who and what will be studied and finally demonstrate the alignment among concept, trends, and findings with our framework that is presented in Sect. 5 [22, 23]. We use secondary qualitative data and literature review as main research methodology. We developed a literature review in the Google Scholar in the period 1990 to 2022. The question and sub-questions that guided this review were as follows: "Is the combination of extended reality and TWI used as a learning/instructional method?" and from this question: "What type of products/factories mostly benefit from this combined learning method?", "What are the advantages of the method based on gained experiences?", "What are the disadvantages and/or obstacles based on experiences?", "What are the trends for TWI and combination of TWI and XR?".

The string used was "training within industry" AND "augmented reality". These were searched in title, abstract, and keywords for the period from 1990 to the present.

The outcome of this conceptual paper is planned to be tested on a case study after this paper is published.

4 Findings

Our literature search on Google Scholar gave 51 related results related to "training within industry" and "augmented reality" while a search on Google with the same phrases resulted in about 3160 results where most of the results were not related to the concept of combining them since results were containing two phrases independently. Date of the articles on the internet indicates a rising trend on virtual training solutions (not necessarily combined with TWI) in the recent years. This trend may be related strongly to the COVID-19 pandemic and subsequent workforce disruptions which have created and/or strengthen challenges in employee recruitment/retention and training without local presence areas in the industry worldwide. Based on a Manufacturing Institute and Deloitte study, the National Association of Manufacturers estimates that manufacturers will need to fill 4.6 million jobs by 2028 [24]. Out of this 4.6 million jobs, the operators are the most flexible part of the production system and they have to be prepared for increasing complexity [25]. Thus, an effective learning method assisted with AR technology may contribute to face these challenges.

4.1 Examples from the Literature

In our research, we have found many examples of virtual reality (VR) applications combined with TWI for training purposes in the industry. It is tested and evaluated in companies in automotive and aerospace industry mainly. Scania in Södertälje, Sweden tested and evaluated virtual training based on TWI Job Instruction methods and found the method promising even though the study did not result in any greater improvements [26]. Bernhartz and Malis's [25] study on workflow for virtual training for assembly of the bogie cross member at Volvo GTO in Tuve Plant in Göteborg, Sweden reveals that virtual training cannot fully replace the current training practices, but can act as a support to ease the cognitive load. Numerous use cases, applications indicates that VR training within industry have been tested out and used widely in the industry. The next leap in innovative training is incorporating augmented reality where a user can see the real-world environment around them with an overlay of instruction through an AR device, including checklist items for a first time student performing a task or allow a senior technician to provide remote assistance to a less experienced technician [27]. Even though there are challenges in application, pioneering organizations, such as Amazon, Facebook, General Electric, Mayo Clinic, and the U.S. Navy, are already implementing AR and seeing a major impact on quality and productivity [28].

The BMW Group (2019) was the first major company to implement AR into their assembly employee training. Through AR in assembly training, one tutor becomes capable of training three trainees with the same outcome quality, instead of one-to-one teaching. Thus, personnel need for assembly training can get reduced [29].

At Boeing, AR was used to guide trainees through the 50 steps required to assemble an air-craft wing section involving 30 parts, resulted in 35% reduced time in completion of work compared to traditional 2-D drawings and documentation. In addition, the number of trainees with little or no experience who could perform the operation correctly the first time increased by 90%. Thus, AR training has had a dramatic impact on the productivity and quality of complex aircraft manufacturing procedures [30].

Newport News Shipbuilding (NNS) was an early adopter of the TWI programs during WWII and is now enhancing its effectiveness by coupling TWI principles with augmented reality application coined "Augmented TWI". Since 2007, they have explored Augmented Reality as a means to shift away from paper-based documentation in the work environment [31]. With AR, they can now see the final design superimposed on the ship, which reduces inspection time by 96%—from 36 h to just 90 min. Overall, time savings of 25% or more are typical for manufacturing tasks using AR [28].

Implementation of augmented reality to train unskilled operators on a busbar bending process resulted in easier achievement of the task [32]. General Electric (GE) achieved an increase in productivity and efficiency by applying AR [33]. Honeywell also improved its operator training by implementing AR [32]. DHL's need for traditional instructors is reduced while the onboarding speed for new employees is increased by providing AR real-time training [28]. The TWI Institute announced a partnership with Dozuki, an industry leader in standard job instruction software. Companies aim to provide personalized, one-on-one instructions with strong visual guides. Expected outcome is that learners can use Dozuki guides as references and "memory joggers", since they can mirror the Job Instruction Breakdowns used in TWI training [34]. An empirical analysis from Loch [35] compared video instruction with a screen-based augmented reality assistance for a LEGO assembly task with 27 steps. Results of the study indicate a lower completion time, significantly less number of errors and a lower mental workload for the students trained by means of the augmented reality application. Finally, Chen [36] suggests a framework for the application of artificial intelligence (AI) technology to training and managerial challenges, which can be applied to the training process, including knowledge management (KM), needs analysis, training organization, and results feedback.

5 Framework for Digital TWI

Use cases and examples from the industry on implementing AR technologies for training purposes given in Sect. 3 shows that skill improvement, onboarding processes may benefit from this technology in many ways. In this section, we suggest a frame work for applications of augmented reality assisted TWI, so called "Digital TWI". The framework consists of four concepts are described later in this section: 1) AR-enhanced Job Instruction augmented TWI (ATWI), 2) Remote Job Instruction remote augmented TWI (RTWI), 3) Retraining Job Instruction assisted with instructor on demand (RJI), and 4) Self-training Job Instruction assisted with instructor (SJI) .

These suggested concepts differ from each other with their area of usage and the presence of instructor as shown in Table 2. As mentioned in 1.1, instructor's responsibility is crucial for a successful training according to TWI. Therefore, each concept suggested in this framework does include local or remote presence of the instructor, either all the time, partially or on demand.

Table 2. Digital TWI concepts

Concept	Area of usage	Instructor presence
AR-enhanced JI	Onboarding, Internal Training, Retraining	Local Presence
Remote JI	Onboarding, Internal Training, Retraining	Remote Presence
Retraining JI	Retraining	Local and/or Remote on Demand
Self-training JI	Onboarding, Internal Training, Retraining	Local and/or Remote Partially

5.1 AR-Enhanced Job Instruction

This concept is the closest method to the traditional TWI, where instructor and trainee are physically in the same place. Trainee is equipped with AR/XR smart glasses. Ideally, instructor can control the flow of the content on trainee's smart glasses. If this is not possible, it is also sufficient that instructor can see the progress of the trainee on another screen, or maybe on his own AR glasses. In this way, instructor still controls the flow of the training while trainee gets visual aids and feedbacks through the AR smart glasses. Finally, the training session may be recorded. Thus, recorded session may be used to review the session by going through together with the trainee.

This concept combines the advantages of both TWI method and AR capabilities. The local presence and guidance of the instructor all the time maintain the most important element of the training, namely the teacher. The drawback of this concept is that it requires a presence of an instructor all the time. To overcome this disadvantage, an instructor may teach more than one trainee simultaneously. However, the efficiency of training groups should be studied. AR-enhanced JI may be used in any kind of training at any phase of an employee, from onboarding to retraining.

5.2 Remote JI

This concept is similar to the AR-enhanced JI, with one big difference; the instructor is not locally present. Ideally, instructor has his/her own AR and can control the flow of the training remotely. It is advantageous that instructor can also see what the trainee does and/or see simultaneously. This will give a better picture of the situation of the trainee to the instructor. Thus, instructor can give better feedback through the training. Again, group training may be possible, but it is anticipated that it will be even less efficient than previous method, due to the fact it will be more difficult to have an over view of many people at the same time for the instructor remotely.

The most important advantage of this concept is undoubtedly that the instructor and the trainee does not have to be in the same place. Especially COVID-19 pandemic showed us recently that industry requires such remote solutions. In some areas it is also approved that using AR may improve the productivity by decreasing operators' error [32]. Like AR-enhanced JI, remote JI may be suitable for any kind of training in a company at any phase of an employee, including onboarding, internal training, and retraining.

5.3 Retraining JI

This concept is ideal for an employee that has already been taught by using AR enhanced JI or Remote JI as explained above. It requires that the training session is recorded earlier. If an employee needs to refresh his/her skills, it may be possible to use this recorded material to retrain the employee. Even though this method may sound like a traditional video on demand training, there is a still big difference compared that the training material that was recorded earlier is unique to the employee. Thus, it will be easier to remember for the employee the training session. As mentioned earlier in this section, we always chose to include the instructor on any training method suggested in this framework. For this concept, we suggest that the instructor may be available on demand and/or for the final review. Thus, there will be minimal resource need of the instructor which is the biggest advantage of this concept. As the name implies, this concept is meant to be used at retraining and refreshing skills cases in the company.

5.4 Self-training JI

This concept is an attempt to generate a more generic (but not full) training material and method for the employees. Even though TWI underlines that every trainee is unique, and training should be applied individually, some (or maybe even most) of the training steps may be common. By generating a generic digital training material which can be followed with AR glasses, it may be possible to train employees. Partially presence (either local or remote) of the instructor may ensure personal and unique training. Finally, it may be also suggested to prepare variations of the training programs so that the instructor may choose to offer different variations of the training to the trainees. Similar to Blended Learning [37], self-training JI may also represent some combination of face-to-face and online (remote) learning. This concept may be suitable for any kind of training at any phase of an employee and may have an advantage of reducing the instructor resourced need for training tremendously. However, it requires resource and investment for generating/supporting training materials.

6 Discussion and Conclusion

Section 4 reveals that there many possibilities available by combining TWI method with AR technologies. In this section, we discuss why JI is only chosen among all TWI methods, and the maturity and ease-of-use of the method and technology. Finally, we conclude our paper by summarizing some of the generic advantages and the challenges, mainly based on literature.

As described in 1.1, TWI service consists of three J courses, namely Job Instruction (JI), Job Methods (JM) and Job Relations (JR). In this paper, we choose to combine only Job Instruction with AR, due to the following arguments: JI is often the first TWI method that is used in companies and is the most used method of TWI Service. JI is a method for effective training and AR solutions are tested/evaluated heavily for training purposes. Preparation for visual aids/instructions may be very complex for Job Methods since it may involve heavy technical discussions, etc. and finally, there is minimal need of visualization for Job Relations.

By looking at JI method and AR technology separately, we can conclude that JI is an old and well-proven method that was used worldwide. The method is not much in development. In most companies that use JI, the original documents from World War II are still used. Mostly, the method is adapted, rather than further developed. AR technologies have been in development and still under development heavily. The technology is in use in many companies worldwide. Thus, we may conclude that the technology is mature enough to be used on the market. Authors of this paper predict that this development will continue rapidly and will create new possibilities and features.

It is very crucial that a method and/or technology is easy enough to be accepted by users. We summarize our conclusions on ease-of use of JI and AR in this section. JI is based on four simple steps, explained in 1.1.1. The four-step method makes the JI easy to remember and easy to implement. As an instructor that wants to learn JI, it takes only 10 h session and some practice. JI pocket card eases even more the process, since they can be carried all the time in case steps are forgotten. AR may be challenging to use for some at the beginning. As like all other technologies gadget, using AR solutions may be difficult for some individuals more than others. Thus, training of the technology use in advance may be required. Updates/changes in hardware/software may create new challenges, which may require retraining for the technology.

The study also found some advantages of combining TWI and AR, mainly based on literature and state-of-the-art in the industry. Augmented reality type visualization levelling out performance difference by giving more support to inexperienced workers than experienced [38]. Despite of advancements in intelligent automation, humans/operators still have an essential role in manufacturing operations [32]. JI can be a resource intensive process since it requires one person responsible to teach each operator during learning [39]. Combining it with AR and using the concepts that are suggested in Sect. 4, resource need may be minimalized. Learning the skills to carry out a set of tasks can only be obtained through learning-by-doing and this learning action should be at the "Gemba" the real place instead of in the classroom [40]. AR can provide the information right at the workplace [34]. Furthermore, they can be trained step-by-step to a work process without causing serious damage [41]. Further training or retraining is useful in order to bring employees back to less frequent process steps as needed [42, 43]. AR training allows location-independent training attuned to the individual learning curve [37]. Particular errors that are repeated by operator may be eliminated by providing tailored instructions and repeat the training [28]. Due to the fact that our brain matter is mostly dedicated to vision (30 to 50% opposed to 10% to touch, and only 3% to hearing), any visual information is processed seamlessly and unconsciously [44]. Using AR-enhanced training may provide an effective job instruction method, since it is mainly driven by visual aids. According to Powell and Reke, lean Production can be reframed as a learning system and lean thinking is not possible without learning [45, 46]. Therefore, it is crucial to establish and implement an effective learning method based on a well-proven lean learning method JI, especially for the companies want to cultivate a lean culture within their organizations.

There are also some disadvantages and challenges associated with JI and AR. In vestment costs of AR technologies can be high. Continuous development of AR digital materials may be needed. This will add another cost for the training. Support for the technology may be needed, which adds another cost. AR technology may not be accepted by some of the users. According to Syberfeldt, Danielsson, Holm, and Wang [47], key factors to improve the acceptability of AR systems are as follow: 1) Identify tasks of high enough complex so that the user to feel that it is worth using the AR system. 2) Ensure improved efficiency so that the user see meaning in using it. 3) Aim for a perfect system so that imperfections do not create skepticism. 4) Emphasize the advantages so that the new users of the technology will "buy" it easily. Finally, JI method may be perceived as outdated, old method, which may decrease the user acceptance.

Implementing new technologies and methods in an organization may be challenging. Bernhartz and Malis [25], summarized challenges in virtual training as follow: 1) Usability – training system should be adapted to the users and be intuitive since users may have various experience and backgrounds with technology. 2) User acceptance – users should be engaged already in the development phase to minimize skepticisms. High acceptance is a key factor for AR technology [47]. 3) Cybersickness – a complex issue that is hard to prevent, resulting in nausea and headache, especially for VR system. IT should be evaluated whether this can be a challenge for AR or not.

These challenges may be present for AR-enhances solutions as well. Therefore, it is beneficial to think about possible countermeasures to overcome these challenges, especially in designing phase of the training program.

7   Conclusion and Suggestions for Further Research

This paper presents a framework with four main concepts that attempts to combine TWI Job Instruction method with extended reality technologies. We conclude that it is worth to empirically validate the concepts in real-world use cases since it can provide an efficient learning method that increases productivity and operator's flexibility while it decreases the cost of training and the operator's error. For future research, we suggest an empirical research based on a real-world case. The framework and the concepts that are introduced in Sect. 5 may be tested on real use case studies and the results may be evaluated. Critical success factors for the concepts should also be evaluated.

References

1. Bianchi, N., Giorcelli, M.: The dynamics and spillovers of management interventions: evidence from the training within industry program. J. Polit. Econ. **130**, 1630–1675 (2022)
2. Netland, T., Hines, P.: Teaching in virtual reality: experiences from a lean masterclass. In: Powell, D.J., Alfnes, E., Holmemo, M.D.Q., Reke, E. (eds.) Learning in the Digital Era: 7th European Lean Educator Conference, ELEC 2021, Trondheim, Norway, 25–27 October 2021, Proceedings, pp. 155–162. Springer International Publishing, Cham (2021). https://doi.org/10.1007/978-3-030-92934-3_16
3. Service, U.S.T.W.I., Training, U.S.W.M.C.B. of training, Kirkpatrick, F.: The training within industry report, 1940–1945: A record of the development of management techniques for improvement of supervision, their use and the results. war manpower commission, bureau of training, training within industry service (1945)
4. Huntzinger, J.: The roots of lean
5. Roser, C.: All about lean. https://www.allaboutlean.com/training-within-industry/

6. Graupp, P., Wrona, R.J.: Implementing TWI: Creating and Managing a Skills-Based Culture. Productivity Press, New York (2018)
7. Robinson, A.G., Schroeder, D.M.: Training, continuous improvement, and human relations: the US TWI programs and the Japanese management style. Calif. Manage. Rev. **35**, 35–57 (1993)
8. Dinero, D.A.: Training within industry: The foundation of lean. Productivity Press, New York (2005)
9. Dinero, D.A.: The TWI Facilitator's Guide: How to Use the TWI Programs Successfully. Productivity Press, New York (2016)
10. Liker, J.K.: Toyota way: 14 Management Principles from the World's Greatest Manufacturer. McGraw-Hill Education, Columbus (2004)
11. Graupp, P., Wrona, R.J.: The TWI Workbook: Essential Skills for Supervisors. CRC Press, Boca Raton (2017)
12. Furht, B. (ed.): Handbook of Augmented Reality. Springer New York, New York (2011)
13. Milgram, P., Takemura, H., Utsumi, A., Kishino, F.: Augmented reality: a class of displays on the reality-virtuality continuum. In: Presented at the Proceedings of the SPIE December 21 (1995).https://doi.org/10.1117/12.197321
14. Azuma, R.T.: A survey of augmented reality. Presence Teleoperators Virtual Environ. **6**, 355–385 (1997). https://doi.org/10.1162/pres.1997.6.4.355
15. Feiner, S., MacIntyre, B., Haupt, M., Solomon, E.: Windows on the world: 2D windows for 3D augmented reality. In: Proceedings of the 6th Annual ACM Symposium on User Interface Software and Technology, pp. 145–155 (1993)
16. Baum, L.F.: The Master Key An Electrical Fairy Tale. Bottom of the Hill Publishing, San Francisco (2014)
17. Carmigniani, J., Furht, B., Anisetti, M., Ceravolo, P., Damiani, E., Ivkovic, M.: Augmented reality technologies, systems and applications. Multimedia Tools Appl. **51**, 341–377 (2011). https://doi.org/10.1007/s11042-010-0660-6
18. Berryman, D.R.: Augmented reality: a review. Med. Ref. Serv. Q. **31**, 212–218 (2012)
19. Serino, M., Cordrey, K., McLaughlin, L., Milanaik, R.L.: Pokémon Go and augmented virtual reality games: a cautionary commentary for parents and pediatricians. Curr. Opin. Pediatr. **28**, 673–677 (2016)
20. Heidler, N.: Intelligent Augmented Reality Assembly Training
21. Burkholder, G.J., Cox, K.A., Crawford, L.M., Hitchcock, J.H.: Research Design and Methods: An Applied Guide for the Scholar-Practitioner. Sage Publications, Los Angeles (2019)
22. Jozkowski, A.C.: Reason & Rigor: How Conceptual Frameworks Guide Research, 2nd (edn.) (2017). Occupational Therapy in Health Care, vol. 31, pp. 378–379 (2017). https://doi.org/10.1080/07380577.2017.1360538
23. Miles, M.B., Huberman, A.M., Saldaña, J.: Qualitative Data Analysis: A Methods Sourcebook. Sage Publications, Los Angele (2018)
24. The Manufacturers' Guide to Finding and Retaining Talent. https://www.nist.gov/system/files/documents/2022/05/26/Manufacturers_Guide_to_Finding_and_Retaining_Talent_WEB.pdf (2022)
25. Bernhartz, H., Malis, L.: Workflow for training in virtual reality (2019)
26. Augustsson, N., Löfström, H.: Evaluation of the virtual training softwares SeQualia and Vizendo (2017)
27. Bringing technology to today's Air Force. https://www.travis.af.mil/News/Com-mentaries/Display/Article/1859305/bringing-technology-to-todays-air-force/. Accessed 07 July 2022
28. Porter, M. E.: Why Every organization needs an augmented reality strategy. https://hbr.org/2017/11/why-every-organization-needs-an-augmented-reality-strategy

29. Group, B.M.W.: Absolutely real: virtual and augmented reality open new avenues inthe BMW group production system. https://www.press.bmw-group.com/global/article/detail/T0294345EN/absolutely-real:-virtual-and-augmented-reality-open-new-avenues-in-the-bmw-group-production-system?lan-guage=en (2019)

30. Porter, M.E., Heppelmann, J.E.: Why every organization needs an augmented reality strategy. HBR'S 10 MUST. 85 (2017)

31. Next generation skilled workers using augmented reality I Association for Manufacturing Excellence. https://www.ame.org/target/articles/2016/next-generation-skilled-workers-using-augmented-reality. Accessed 09 July 2022

32. Na'amnh, S., Miklós Daróczi, I.H.: Implementing the augmented reality as an industry 4.0 application to simplify the busbar bending process during the Covid-19 pandemic. Transactions of FAMENA, **45**(3), 115–125 (2021). https://doi.org/10.21278/TOF.453026921

33. Smart Specs: OK Glass, Fix This Jet Engine I GE News. https://www.ge.com/news/reports/smart-specs-ok-glass-fix-jet-engine. Accessed 09 July 2022

34. Graupp, P.: New Partnership: TWI Institute & Dozuki. https://www.twi-insti-tute.com/twi-dozuki/. Accessed 11 July 2022

35. Loch, F., Quint, F., Brishtel, I.: Comparing video and augmented reality assistance in manual assembly. In: 2016 12th International Conference on Intelligent Environments (IE), pp. 147–150. IEEE (2016)

36. Chen, Z.: Artificial intelligence-virtual trainer: innovative didactics aimed at personalized training needs. J. Knowl. Econ. 1–19 (2022). https://doi.org/10.1007/s13132-022-00985-0

37. Powell, D.J., de Vries, M., van Roij, M., Slomp, J.: Blended network action learning – a digital lean approach to solving complex organizational problems across space and time. In: Powell, D.J., Alfnes, E., Holmemo, M.D.Q., Reke, E. (eds.) Learning in the Digital Era: 7th European Lean Educator Conference, ELEC 2021, Trondheim, Norway, October 25–27, 2021, Proceedings, pp. 213–224. Springer International Publishing, Cham (2021). https://doi.org/10.1007/978-3-030-92934-3_22

38. Kurdve, M.: Digital assembly instruction system design with green lean perspective-Case study from building module industry. Procedia CIRP **72**, 762–767 (2018). https://doi.org/10.1016/j.procir.2018.03.118

39. Liker, J.K., Meier, D.: Toyota Way Fieldbook. McGraw-Hill Education, New York (2006)

40. Reke, E., Powell, D.: Rethinking value–a means to end the whispering game. Procedia CIRP **104**, 1041–1045 (2021)

41. Makris, S., Karagiannis, P., Koukas, S., Matthaiakis, A.-S.: Augmented reality system for operator support in human–robot collaborative assembly. CIRP Ann. **65**, 61–64 (2016)

42. Kroeker, K.L.: Mainstreaming augmented reality. Commun. ACM **53**, 19–21 (2010)

43. Peddie, J.: Augmented Reality. Springer International Publishing, Cham (2017). https://doi.org/10.1007/978-3-319-54502-8

44. Ballé, M., Chartier, N., Coignet, P., Olivencia, S., Powell, D., Reke, E.: The Lean Sensei. The Lean Enterprise Institute Inc., Boston (2019)

45. Powell, D., Reke, E.: No Lean without learning: rethinking lean production as a learning system. In: Ameri, F., Stecke, K.E., von Cieminski, G., Kiritsis, D. (eds.) APMS 2019. IAICT, vol. 566, pp. 62–68. Springer, Cham (2019). https://doi.org/10.1007/978-3-030-30000-5_8

46. Netland, T.H., Powell, D.J.: The Routledge Companion to Lean Management. Routledge, Milton Park (2016)

47. Syberfeldt, A., Danielsson, O., Holm, M., Wang, L.: Visual assembling guidance using augmented reality. Procedia Manuf. **1**, 98–109 (2015)

Learning to Teach Lean in the Age of Digitalization: A Review of Recent ELEC Literature

Eivind Arne Fauskanger[1]([✉]), Seyedehemehrsa Fatemi[1], Sara Tavassoli[1],
Traian Ionut Luca[2], George-Silviu Cordos[2], and Daryl John Powell[1]

[1] University of Southeastern Norway, Kongsberg, Norway
eivind.fauskanger@usn.no
[2] Babes-Bolyai University, Cluj, Romania

Abstract. Digitalization presents us with new and novel means of teaching Lean which enhances the effectiveness of Lean education programs. Despite the increased trending role of digitalization in Lean research publications over the past few years, there is still a lack of clear understanding of how to incorporate digitalization into Lean thinking and practice, and indeed which pedagogical tools facilitate the digital Lean transition. In this paper, we present a review of recent European Lean Educator Conference literature on the theme of teaching and learning Lean in the digital era. We address the need to develop effective training content in relation to Industry 4.0 and the importance of selecting the appropriate training strategy to maximize the transfer of knowledge. Following this, we discuss the appropriateness of different teaching platforms and compare the benefits and challenges of each. Based on our review of virtual and physical learning factories, we encourage organizations to pursue a hybrid learning approach that combines the physical and virtual environment and lets remote and on-site users benefit from both advantages.

Keywords: Lean · Digitalization · Learning · Teaching

1 Introduction

Lean manufacturing has been one of the distinguished methodologies for optimizing and improving the operational performance in manufacturing enterprises in the last two decades, and it consists of different philosophies from eliminating waste to enhancing quality [1]. Recently, the concept of Industry 4.0 has caused a paradigm shift in the manufacturing sector and its associated technologies such as the Internet of Things (IoT), big data and data analytics, additive manufacturing, 3D printing, advanced robotics, augmented and virtual reality, cloud computing, simulation, machine learning, and artificial intelligence have brought along significant changes with respect to manufacturing processes and supply chains. The integration of Industry 4.0 technologies and Lean practices has yielded extensive opportunities for industries to target operational excellence

O. McDermott et al. (Eds.): ELEC 2022, IFIP AICT 668, pp. 233–245, 2023.
https://doi.org/10.1007/978-3-031-25741-4_20

and allow manufacturers to maintain their competitive edge by improving productivity, efficiency, quality, and flexibility [2].

In the wake of digital transformation, many firms are inclined to jump into this trending topic of digitalization, especially those manufacturing companies that act dynamically and competitively in the market. However, there is still a lack of adequate understanding of the meaning, relevance, and application. Despite the increasing trend of incorporating theoretically Industry 4.0 and digital transformation concepts in recent research, organizations face challenges when implementing such concepts in practice. Firstly, Industry 4.0 is more a concept than a ready-to-implement solution since it is implemented in various companies based on pilot projects that ignore key aspects within the organization such as its structure and culture [3]. Additionally, the complexity of Industry 4.0 causes delays to the successful implementation of Industry 4.0 systems or even failure despite revenue growth potential [4]. Industry 4.0 revolutionizes all organizational aspects and levels and is touching not just processes but also people [3]. Adapting to this transition requires the development of skill sets of employees for industrial application, and training, learning, and competencies have a significant role in the accomplishment of success.

Workforces currently working in the industry did not receive training in technologies such as AI, big data analytics, and virtual reality, which are the drivers of change. Therefore, there is a great need to prepare the workforce with the required skill set and the mindset of continuous improvement and learning, enabling them to exploit Lean manufacturing methodologies and Industry 4.0 in enterprises. Training operators and other company actors are essential for achieving a Lean structure in the combination of industry 4.0. The main aim of this project is to investigate which pedagogical tools, including visual, interactive, and physical, have the most significant effect on preparing the workforce for this digital transition.

2 Research Design

This paper provides a synopsis of a review that will summarize the recent ELEC literature on the theme of teaching and learning Lean and Industry 4.0. We selected the latest ELEC book of proceedings, which is dedicated to the 'learning in the digital era' theme and includes recent peer-reviewed publications in the domain.

Out of 42 papers presented at ELEC 2021, we selected 13 papers that specifically addressed learning and teaching Lean in the digital era. Furthermore, the so-called snowball method was used, in which other relevant publications were identified by using the reference lists or citations to achieve more realistic results [5]. As such, this review paper aims to extend the current understanding of the critical role of organizational learning and training in business transformation (Lean and/or digital) and distinguishes between different learning tools that have been applied in practice.

3 Findings

3.1 Training Approaches

Training and development can have a significant impact on organizations' bottom line. Moreover, it has also been demonstrated to reduce threatening errors in high-risk environments [6]. Based on reviewed articles, there are different training approaches applied by the practitioners and scholars. Yet, no attempt has been made to elucidate explicitly which training content in relation to Industry 4.0 is most effective. Depending on the training's situational process, selecting the appropriate strategy is a crucial step to maximizing the transfer of training.

Most training programs that struggle to build skills and enhance learning should have these four components: information, demonstration, practice, and feedback [6]. The most suitable training approaches should give confidence to users to place their acquired skills in adopting Lean tools and techniques and the concept of industry 4.0 [7]. Training approaches are commonly categorized into passive learning, active learning, and cooperative learning [8].

A passive learning environment is the traditional lecture format where students are the receivers of information. In contrast, active learning is defined as any instructional method that requires students to do meaningful learning activities, reflect upon ideas and think about what they are doing and how they are using those ideas [8]. Cooperative or group learning, a subset of active learning, is defined as a structural form of group where students pursue common goals while being assessed individually to improve individual learning rather than social interaction and teamwork. Experiment based learning approach is the approach based on student-centered instructions and can be selfpaced (active learning) or in a group (cooperative learning). That is, the learner is placed in the centre of the learning process, and the instructor provides students with opportunities to learn both independently and from one another by involving students in simulation and coaching them in the skills they need to do so effectively [9].

Bonwell and Eison provided a review of the literature on active learning and concluded that properly implemented student-centred instruction could lead to increased learning motivation, more excellent retention of knowledge, deeper understanding, and more positive attitudes towards the subject being taught [10]. In another study, Riely and Ward examined the differential effect of active (both individual and cooperative) and passive learning methods on student outcomes. In this study, students reported positive feedback on satisfaction and perceived learning in both individual and cooperative active environments, while students who worked individually in an active environment significantly improved their outcomes [11].

The importance of experiment-based learning approaches within university environments in order to become the student as an active participant in the learning procedure has been recently discussed in academia. Active learning setups are particularly beneficial in engineering education considering the need for multidisciplinary technologies curricula required by Industry 4.0 [12] and have proven to improve classical teaching approaches significantly. The lack of efficiency in teaching Lean by using traditional expositive lectures (passive learning) caused the active learning methodologies used for Lean education by academics and practitioners.

In another classification, Roser et al. have introduced five classes of training approaches for Lean practices: Theoretical training, Interactive training, Learning by doing, Being coached, and Coaching, which are explained in detail [13].

Theoretical Training: Theoretical training refers to teacher-centred education as traditional expositive lectures in a classroom. It is frequently adopted as a face-to-face instructional method, but it may also involve a self-taught course using videos, written texts, and other materials. The majority of Lean training approaches in the industry are classroom-based, with simulation games are included occasionally [13].

Traditional teaching methods show limited effects on the development of skill sets for industrial applications. Due to the absence of practical use, applying for Lean courses in a classroom setting is challenging. Joksimovic et al. argued that classical teacher-centred pedagogical methods cause learners to be passive and bored in the class, which results in misunderstanding or missing material, losing interest in the subject, and slower progress overall [14].

The majority of classes turned to online during the covid pandemic, and it has been shown that online teaching can be a successful approach to learning despite certain obstacles. Surprisingly, only minor differences are reported between face-to-face and online classes from the lecturer's perspective [15]. However, while the virtual online delivery does not significantly affect student learning, the students are less satisfied with this format than with face-to-face classes [16]. To sum up, there have been some challenges and drawbacks with e-learning approaches, such as lack of human contact, technological ambiguity, and unreliability of broadband. However, organizations are increasingly encouraged to switch to online training delivery as it offers convenience and flexibility, in addition to being a cost-effective method. Training accessibility (no requirement for travel) and consistency of content and training delivery facilitate knowledge management [17].

Interactive Training: Interactive or experiential training aims to boost learners' motivation and engagement, and it includes Problem Based Learning (PBL), active learning, blended learning, flipped learning, and simulation and gaming [17]. Due to the active nature of these learning methods, students are more involved than just theoretical training [18]. Previous research has illustrated that the implementation of flipped classroom pedagogical approaches significantly improves students' success rate and their average marks on the following criteria: student involvement, task orientation, and promoting collaborative learning [19].

Moreover, gamification as a personalized learning approach is recognized as effective training approach for Lean learning due to developing problem-solving and decision-making skills. Incorporating aspects of play elements into a formal environment, such as the workplace, may significantly boost employees' engagement and interest [20]. According to Bloom's Revised Taxonomy, a tool for gamification evaluation, it is suitable for Lean learning to reach the highest level of Bloom's Taxonomy, which is expected to achieve critical thinking results and a reduction in the learning cycle time. Gamification may also help professionals be ready for demanding multidisciplinary work environments [21].

Another interactive learning method is Vestibule training, in which employees perform their jobs in a setting that stimulates their actual workplace [7]. Simulation of the industrial environment is the most frequently mentioned learning strategy for online Lean virtual teaching [22]. A virtual training simulation is an immersive and interactive training method that engages learners in virtual activities using virtual reality (VR), typically demonstrated through in-person demos. VR-based simulations offer learners an opportunity to practice their knowledge and abilities before using them in real-world settings [23]. The VR environment can be 'offline' —without real-time interaction with other users—or 'online' with real-time interaction. In a study conducted by Bariuad, also a real-time immersive VR was used to teach how Lean concepts evolved with the advent of the fourth industrial revolution and led to transformational change [24]. They concluded that VR could be an appropriate platform for teaching Lean, but it is insufficient since the essence of learning Lean is tied to actual observation and interventions in real-life processes. Real-time immersive VR is the best tools as part of a blended teaching approach and is a viable and available alternative to classroom and online teaching [24].

Learning by Doing and Being Coached: The primary goal of learning by doing is to foster skill development and the learning of factual information in the context of how its intended application. On-the-job training, which emphasizes the learning-by-doing approach, refers to the training imparted at the actual job location involving hands-on training. Employees are directly trained on a one-to-one basis while carrying out their tasks or can also be transferred to different jobs or rotated among various workstations to acquire wider knowledge and increase motivation [7]. Even though participation in theoretical training courses tends to be higher than participation in on-the-job training, in some countries, particularly in small and medium enterprises, firms are only slightly more likely to organize training courses than to rely on employee on-the-job training [25]. The combination of theoretical lectures and practical hands-on sessions seems to be very effective in knowledge transfer and improvement regardless of people's profession [26]. This is in consistent with another work conducted by Fauskanger and Hellberg. They created a course focused on quality improvement based on PDCA (Plan, Do, Act, Check) methodology in which students were asked to detect the problems existing at their workplace to take steps to find a solution during their training sessions, and finally check the effects of these solutions in practice, during the hand-on sessions. At the end of the course, students were expected to have developed their problem-solving and self-driven learning skills [27].

Toyota uses the Training Within Industry (TWI) program to support effective staff training. TWI is a technique that teaches individuals how to think analytically and approach their works. Instead of offering a ready solution to a problem, TWI's goal is to teach individuals how to frame a situation in order to come up with workable alternatives [28]. To improve the bottom line, TWI trains employees to think independently, take responsibility for their choices, and collaborate with others. TWI consists of three programs: 1) Job Instruction training (JI), 2) Job Relation training (JR), and 3) Job Methods training (JM). JI is concerned with how to instruct a person to perform a job correctly and safely. JR deals with how to solve personnel problems using an analytical, nonemotional method. Finally, JM relates to how to improve the way jobs are performed [28]. A recent study found that the companies who had received TWI training, especially JI, had experienced a positive effect on firm performance, and those leaders who were prepared by Gemba-based training can improve the job with frontline workers [29]. They suggested that real learning can only happen on Gemba, not through classroom training and simulations.

Coaching: Coaching is another training approach where a person with advanced experience, called a mentor or sensei, personally follows the development of a worker with very little experience, named mentee [7]. The learning process is straightforward; mentors will share their knowledge and expertise with their mentees and closely supervise them until they are able to function well on their own. Nevertheless, it's not just the mentees who will benefit. Coaching is a win-win solution since mentors will also develop their leadership and communication skills along with mentoring. The varied fresh viewpoints of the mentee may expand the sensei's horizon and further the understanding of the coach. Reke and Böhlmann have pointed out that middle managers can shift the organization towards continuous learning by taking the trainer role [29]. On one hand, they develop leadership skills through Gemba-based training and Hansei, a deep self-reflection, while digesting and discussing what they have learned on the Gemba regarding theory of Lean. On the other hand, they have the responsibility as mentors to help their own staff grow by coaching them and providing a greater understanding of the changes required with Lean and digital transformation [29].

3.1.1 Remarks

Organizational learning which includes all the learning processes within an organization with the aim of maintenance or improvement in performance based on experience, contributes to the organization's success. Organizational learning is characterized by a tension between assimilating new knowledge (exploration) and applying what has been learned (exploitation) and being multi-level (individual and group) [30]. Powell and Coughlan developed different learning interventions based on the distinction between exploration and exploitation and learning at home and away. Based on this distinction, simulation is considered as exploration away while exploitation at home. Meanwhile, on-the-job training and coaching are categorized as exploration and exploitation at home [31].

The thorough examination conducted by Zanchi et al. concluded that various training approaches are not alternatives but rather complementary to each other. In other words, while theoretical and interactive training are fundamental for learning the basic knowledge in terms of availability of resources, learning by doing and coaching are deemed to be essential as well, since they place mentees in front of real challenges on the shopfloor - where they can apply their knowledge and adjust its usage [7].

3.2 Learning Factory

With the emergence of the fourth industrial revolution, industrial companies have faced new requirements and challenges, necessitating a need for modification and change of the content of training which has been shaped to prepare employees with new and required competencies [2].

As discussed earlier, the combination of theoretical training with experimental learning has great outcomes, enabling firms to get the advantages of both. More and more firms are embracing experimental learning. Learning spaces for industries shifted from traditional ones such as classrooms to sophisticated spaces that leverage emerging technologies to facilitate and enhance active, social, and experiential learning. Information technology has brought unique capabilities to learning spaces, whether stimulating more significant interaction through the use of collaborative tools or opening virtual worlds for exploration [32]. A variety of learning spaces such as Learning factories, Fab Labs, Hackerspaces, and Makerspaces which are equipped with modern technology, enable hands-on experiential learning for employees and students. Callupe and Rossi compared these different learning spaces and asserted that learning factories offer an optimal setting for the teaching of Lean manufacturing. They addressed Lean thinking as a core component of their research and educational agenda, utilizing their production lines to showcase the implementation of Lean tools and practices [33].

As the fourth industrial revolution goes forward, the concept of learning factories has received more interest. Learning Factories are complex learning environments for the manufacturing context that contain authentic replicas of real production systems and value chains, allowing participants to learn experientially and practically with an emphasis on active learning. They often have a variety of machines and equipment that can be used to enable a changeable setting for the problem and action-oriented learning.

Learning factories can be seen as a promising environment for education, training, and research, especially in manufacturing-related areas [34]. The learning factory concept focuses on the development of the qualification and competencies of employees, which are required for Industry 4.0 implementation, and incorporates Lean principles in conjunction with information technology, digitalization, and automation. Implementing Lean methods on a manufacturing line and then demonstrating the performance enhancements by industry 4.0 is a most cited strategy seen in various learning factories [33]. They give the opportunity of solving real-world problems through experiential learning as well as self-organized group learning in both physical and virtual settings.

Learning factories have become widespread in recent years, particularly in Europe. They come in a variety of scopes and sizes and serve a variety of functions and complexities, with the aim to enhance the learning experience of students and industrial trainees in one or more areas of manufacturing engineering knowledge and allow students to be trained by addressing appropriate real-life engineering problems [35]. Moreover, the learning factory allows exploring many aspects related to the teaching-learning process through interactive and collaborative methods, which yields to the company's knowledge expansion. Powell and Coughlan have described the Lean lab factory as an eye-opener that introduces participants to fundamental Lean knowledge and devises a clear understanding of the misunderstood concepts, and also creates a common language for participants to speak about confusing terminologies used in Lean [31].

Witeck and Alves provided a comprehensive review of how learning factories have utilized different learning strategies and concluded that the simulations of the industrial environment are the most frequently used not only for Lean learning but also for the concepts related to industry 4.0 [36]. Some universities strongly emphasise Lean 4.0, where students are taught how Industry 4.0 technologies can be integrated with Lean practices and concepts. The competencies required are technical ad social competencies. These learning factories aim to teach the fundamentals of concepts related to Industry 4.0 and promote the student's development of Lean competencies and skills [36]. Any training content for learning the concept of industry 4.0 is deemed essential if it tackles the technological knowledge and complements the knowledge about how to drive digital transformation and change within an organization.

3.2.1   Digital Lean Lab

The learning processes in the learning factory are inspired by problem-based and experiential learning to develop competencies in digitalization. Various digital learning tools can be used to adapt the learning factory concept to Lean and Industry 4.0 issues. New technologies such as virtual reality (VR) have opened a new horizon for training and learning in learning factories. Due to the trend of the digitization of production and processes, virtual and digital learning factories have gained increased attention in this context. Virtual environments are considered as important strategic means to enable education in the manufacturing domain and are utilized with the aim of incrementing the quality of teaching.

Peron et al. have developed a digital lab called Logistics 4.0 Lab, where a conventional production and logistics system have been integrated with a wide range of cutting-edge technologies, including indoor positioning systems, motion capture systems, augmented and virtual reality, visual interactive boards, real-time control and advanced simulation tools, 3D mapping, mobile robots, and other tools for smart operators and managers to create new knowledge [37]. They developed teaching materials relevant to the Lean 4.0 concept, which show how the integration of Lean and industry 4.0 positively affects the design and the operational level. The aims were mainly to minimize waste such as loss of resources and time by increasing efficiency at the design level and lower the probability that operators would make mistakes at the level of operation [37].

A hybrid learning factory refers to the integration of physical and virtual components [38]. It combines the benefits of the digital and virtual environment and a physical learning environment in order to design or analyse industrial manufacturing/production systems with the focus on the Lean concept and learning the Industry 4.0 concept. By enabling students to apply newly acquired knowledge to real-world tasks actively, the Digital Lean Lab facilitates developing competencies to get prepared for this new digital era and workplace. The principles to capture the required competencies can be categorized by five features [39]:

- **Holism and complexity:** The Learning factory should reflect the real production system that has multidimensional aspects of processes and technologies and address more than one real industrial problem.
- **Self-activity or self-organized learning:** The Learning factory should allow students to do the activities by themselves and experience hands-on learning.
- **Practical and learning orientation**: The Learning factory should be able to run repeatedly with economic cost in order to enable effective learning.

- **Social and cooperative action:** The Learning factory should be able to be played in a group so that social interaction and cooperative teamwork can be fostered among the students. This is an important feature because digitalization requires innovative and highly complex human to machine or human to human communication.
- **Target orientation and critical reflection:** The Learning factory should be able to be evaluated based on the learning activities carried out corresponding to the learning objectives.

Virtual learning factories enable the visualization of digital models by providing visual software tools and infrastructure [34]. Different scenarios and environments can be simulated through VR as a technology for digital simulation. Additionally, the virtual learning scenarios can be personalized to the learner since the virtual environment is adaptable. As such, the acquired knowledge is tested in the virtual environment without generating economic damage, and the level of difficulty of the exercises can be varied to suit the participants' needs [38]. The prerequisite for competency development in a virtual environment is the use of the interaction possibilities and the link to a learning outcome. Riemann et al. have developed virtual learning scenarios that aim to develop the intended competencies while being adaptive and individualizable by implementing the advantages of VR technology. Following a training course in the physical learning factory, participants conduct a personalized exercise in the virtual environment [38].

However, it should be borne in mind that the advantages of virtual learning factories should act as a supplement for the physical learning experience so that virtual learning factories should accurately replicate the real learning factory's procedures, activities, and resources. Thiede et al. attempted to bridge the gap between purely virtual and dominantly physical learning factories by proposing a multi-user hybrid learning environment. It pairs physical and virtual learning factory elements and enables remote participants to experience a shared learning experience together with other remote and onsite participants [40].

It can be concluded that the concept of a hybrid learning factory combines the advantages of the physical and the virtual environment, and training can be conducted in a real or a virtual environment, depending on the purpose and the context.

4   Conclusion and Implications

With the emergence of Industry 4.0, many organizations are inclined to embrace digitalization in addition to Lean manufacturing methodologies. However, very few have been able to fully exploit Lean thinking since it is more a concept than ready to implement the solution. The development of competencies and skill sets of employees for industrial application by continuous learning and improvement facilitate the digital Lean transformation. We investigated the effectiveness of different pedagogic approaches by mainly reviewing some studies published at the ELEC 2021 conference which had the theme of *"Learning Lean in the digital era"*. We examined different learning approaches proposed by previous scholars and investigated how they successfully prepare workforces with the required skill set and the mindset of continuous improvement and learning. Findings reveal that the combination of different training approaches with new technologies such as virtual reality has opened a new horizon to academia and industries on how to learn and teach Lean tools in the age of digitalization. Following this, recent studies on learning factories have been reviewed, which demonstrates how effective it is in expanding learners' knowledge with active learning. Most significantly, the Digital Lean lab has been recognized as the most promising learning environment which enables learners to apply and test their newly acquired knowledge to real-world tasks without generating financial damage and risks. In terms of limitations, we realize that restricting our literature review to only the ELEC 2021 proceedings may confine our results. However, as a research paper on learning to teach lean in the age of digitalization - specifically for the ELEC community – we suggest that this limitation can be resolved with future research. We also suggest that future research on this exciting theme should adopt action-based research approaches – to truly understand this important challenge, in practice.

Acknowledgments. The authors would like to acknowledge the support of EEA for the research project POI4.0 (21-COP-0044) and Business Development and Innovation in Viken 2021 for the project Digital Lean Demonstrators for Transforming to Industry 4.0 (2021-0983).

References

1. Womack, J., Jones, D.T., Roos, D.: The machine that changed the world : the story of lean production -- Toyota's secret weapon in the global car wars that is revolutionizing world industry (1991). https://www.semanticscholar.org/paper/The-machine-that-changed-the-world-%3A-the-story-of-Womack-Jones/4cac51c7ab0b49824feab0b5645b22eb22b378e5. Accessed 11 July 2022
2. Calabrese, A., Levialdi Ghiron, N., Tiburzi, L.: 'Evolutions' and 'revolutions' in manufacturers implementation of industry 4.0: a literature review, a multiple case study, and a conceptual framework. Prod. Plan. Control. **32**(3), 213–227 (2021). https://doi.org/10.1080/09537287.2020.1719715
3. Issa, A., Hatiboglu, B., Bildstein, A., Bauernhansl, T.: Industrie 4.0 roadmap: framework for digital transformation based on the concepts of capability maturity and alignment. Procedia CIRP **72**, 973–978 (2018). https://doi.org/10.1016/j.procir.2018.03.151
4. Björkdahl, J.: Strategies for digitalization in manufacturing firms. Calif. Manage. Rev. **62**(4), 17–36 (2020). https://doi.org/10.1177/0008125620920349
5. Mundher, R., et al.: Aesthetic quality assessment of landscapes as a model for urban forest areas: a systematic literature review. Forests **13**(7), 7 (2022). https://doi.org/10.3390/f13070991
6. Salas, E., Tannenbaum, S., Kraiger, K., Smith-Jentsch, K.: The science of training and development in organizations: what matters in practice. Psychol. Sci. Public Interest **13**, 74–101 (2012). https://doi.org/10.2307/23484697
7. Zanchi, M., Gaiardelli, P., Powell, D.J.: The impact of different training approaches on learning lean: a comparative study on value stream mapping. In: Powell, D.J., Alfnes, E., Holmemo, M.D.Q., Reke, E. (eds.) Learning in the Digital Era. ELEC 2021. IFIP Advances in Information and Communication Technology, vol. 610, pp. 109–117. Springer, Cham (2021). https://doi.org/10.1007/978-3-030-92934-3_12
8. Prince, M.: Does active learning work? A review of the research. J. Eng. Educ. **93**(3), 223–231 (2004)

9. Joel, M.: Where's the evidence that active learning works?. Adv. Physiol. Educ. **30**, 159–167 (2006). https://journals.physiology.org/doi/full/10.1152/advan.00053.2006?. Accessed 31 July (2022)
10. Bonwell, C.C., Eison, J.A.: Active learning: creating excitement in the classroom. ASHE-ERIC Higher Education Reports. ERIC Clearinghouse on Higher Education, The George Washington University, One Dupont Circle, Suite 630, Washington, DC 20036–21183 (1991). https://eric.ed.gov/?id=ED336049. Accessed 01 Nov 2022
11. Riley, J., Ward, K.: Active learning, cooperative active learning, and passive learning methods in an accounting information systems course. Issues Account. Educ. **32**(2), 1–16 (2015). https://doi.org/10.2308/iace-51366
12. Prieto, M.D., Sobrino, A.F., Soto, L.R., Romero, D., Biosca, P.F., Martinez, L.R.: Active learning based laboratory towards engineering education 4.0. In: 2019 24th IEEE International Conference on Emerging Technologies and Factory Automation (ETFA), pp. 776–783. Zaragoza, Spain (2019). https://doi.org/10.1109/ETFA.2019.8869509
13. Roser, C., Langer, B., Wuttke, C.C.: A framework and qualitative comparison on different approaches to improve the lean skillset. In: Powell, D.J., Alfnes, E., Holmemo, M.D.Q., Reke, E. (eds.) Learning in the Digital Era. ELEC 2021. IFIP Advances in Information and Communication Technology, vol. 610, pp. 333–338. Springer, Cham (2021). https://doi.org/10.1007/978-3-030-92934-3_34
14. Joksimović, A., Veg, E., Vojislav, S., Regodić, M., Sinikovic, G., Gubeljak, N.: Implementation of inverted classroom methodology in 3D modelling course. FME Trans. **47**, 310–315 (2019). https://doi.org/10.5937/fmet1902310J
15. Martinez, F.: Proposing VSM as a tool to compare synchronic online teaching and face-to-face teaching. In: Powell, D.J., Alfnes, E., Holmemo, M.D.Q., Reke, E. (eds.) Learning in the Digital Era. ELEC 2021. IFIP Advances in Information and Communication Technology, vol. 610, pp. 50–59. Springer, Cham (2021). https://doi.org/10.1007/978-3-030-92934-3_6
16. Summers, J., Waigandt, A., Whittaker, T.: A comparison of student achievement and satisfaction in an online versus a traditional face-to-face statistics class. Innov. High. Educ. **29**, 233–250 (2005). https://doi.org/10.1007/s10755-005-1938-x
17. McDermott, O., Walsh, P., Halpin, L.: A lean six sigma training providers transition to a 100% online delivery model.In: Powell, D.J., Alfnes, E., Holmemo, M.D.Q., Reke, E. (eds.) Learning in the Digital Era. ELEC 2021. IFIP Advances in Information and Communication Technology, vol. 610, pp. 144–154. Springer, Cham (2021). https://doi.org/10.1007/978-3-030-92934-3_15
18. Tortorella, G., Cauchick-Miguel, P.: Combining traditional teaching methods and PBL for teaching and learning of lean manufacturing. IFAC-Pap. **51**(11), 915–920 (2018). https://doi.org/10.1016/j.ifacol.2018.08.465
19. Prashar, A.: Assessing the flipped classroom in operations management: a pilot study. J. Educ. Bus. **90**(3), 126–138 (2015). https://doi.org/10.1080/08832323.2015.1007904
20. Dichev, C., Dicheva, D.: Gamifying education: what is known, what is believed and what remains uncertain: a critical review. Int. J. Educ. Technol. High. Educ. **14**(1), 1–36 (2017). https://doi.org/10.1186/s41239-017-0042-5
21. Witeck, G.R., Alves, A.C., Bernardo, M.H.S.: Bloom taxonomy, serious games and lean learning: what do these topics have in common?. In: Powell, D.J., Alfnes, E., Holmemo, M.D.Q., Reke, E. (eds.) Learning in the Digital Era. ELEC 2021. IFIP Advances in Information and Communication Technology, vol. 610, pp. 308–316. Springer, Cham (2021). https://doi.org/10.1007/978-3-030-92934-3_31
22. McDermott, O.: The digitalisation and virtual delivery of lean six sigma teaching in an Irish university during COVID-19. In: Powell, D.J., Alfnes, E., Holmemo, M.D.Q., Reke, E. (eds.) Learning in the Digital Era. ELEC 2021. IFIP Advances in Information and Communication

Technology, vol. 610, pp. 132–143. Springer, Cham (2021). https://doi.org/10.1007/978-3-030-92934-3_14

23. Bariuad, S.: 10 Interactive Training Ideas. EdApp Microlearning Blog (2021). https://www.edapp.com/blog/10-interactive-training-ideas/. Accessed 23 Jul 2022

24. Netland, T., Hines, P.: Teaching in virtual reality: experiences from a lean masterclass. In: Powell, D.J., Alfnes, E., Holmemo, M.D.Q., Reke, E. (eds.) Learning in the Digital Era. ELEC 2021. IFIP Advances in Information and Communication Technology, vol. 610, pp. 155–162. Springer, Cham (2021). https://doi.org/10.1007/978-3-030-92934-3_16

25. Cedefop. Learning by doing: the importance of on-the-job training. CEDEFOP (2010). https://www.cedefop.europa.eu/en/data-insights/learning-doing-importance-job-training. Accessed 23 Jul 2022

26. Franz, S., Heutehaus, L., Weinand, S., Weidner, N., Rupp, R., Schuld, C.: Theoretical and practical training improves knowledge of the examination guidelines of the international standards for neurological classification of spinal cord injury. Spinal Cord **60**(1), 1 (2022). https://doi.org/10.1038/s41393-020-00578-1

27. Fauskanger, E.A., Hellberg, R.: Lean courses in process form - do as we learn, success or not?. In: Powell, D.J., Alfnes, E., Holmemo, M.D.Q., Reke, E. (eds.) Learning in the Digital Era. ELEC 2021. IFIP Advances in Information and Communication Technology, vol. 610, pp. 121–131. Springer, Cham (2021). https://doi.org/10.1007/978-3-030-92934-3_13

28. Dinero, D.: Training Within Industry: The Foundation of Lean. CRC Press, Boca Raton (2005)

29. Reke, E., Böhlmann, N.: Developing Middle Managers with Gemba Training.In: Powell, D.J., Alfnes, E., Holmemo, M.D.Q., Reke, E. (eds.) Learning in the Digital Era. ELEC 2021. IFIP Advances in Information and Communication Technology, vol. 610, pp. 271–277. Springer, Cham (2021). https://doi.org/10.1007/978-3-030-92934-3_27

30. Crossan, M., White, R., Ivey, R.: An organization learning framework: from intuition to institution. Acad. Manage. Rev. **24**, 522–537 (1999). https://doi.org/10.2307/259140

31. Powell, D.J., Coughlan, P.: Rethinking lean supplier development as a learning system. Int. J. Oper. Prod. Manag. **40**(7/8), 921–943 (2020). https://doi.org/10.1108/IJOPM-06-2019-0486

32. Oblinger, D.: Learning Spaces (2006). https://www.educause.edu/research-and-publications/books/learning-spaces. Accessed 26 Jul 2022

33. Callupe, M., Rossi, M.: Learning spaces for engineering education: an exploratory research about the role of lean thinking. In: Powell, D.J., Alfnes, E., Holmemo, M.D.Q., Reke, E. (eds.) Learning in the Digital Era. ELEC 2021. IFIP Advances in Information and Communication Technology, vol. 610, pp. 13–20. Springer, Cham (2021). https://doi.org/10.1007/978-3-030-92934-3_2

34. Abele, E., et al.: Learning factories for future oriented research and education in manufacturing. CIRP Ann. **66**(2), 803–826 (2017). https://doi.org/10.1016/j.cirp.2017.05.005

35. PwC, Skills for industry curriculum guidelines 4.0: future proof education and training for manufacturing in Europe : final report. LU: Publications Office of the European Union (2020). https://data.europa.eu/doi/10.2826/097323 Accessed 26 July (2022)

36. Witeck, G., Alves, A.: Lean learning factories: concepts from the past updated to the future. In: Powell, D.J., Alfnes, E., Holmemo, M.D.Q., Reke, E. (eds.) Learning in the Digital Era. ELEC 2021. IFIP Advances in Information and Communication Technology, vol. 610, pp. 100–108 (2021). https://doi.org/10.1007/978-3-030-92934-3_11

37. Peron, M., Alfnes, E., Sgarbossa, F.: Learning through action: on the use of logistics 4.0 lab as learning developer. In: Powell, D.J., Alfnes, E., Holmemo, M.D.Q., Reke, E. (eds.) Learning in the Digital Era. ELEC 2021. IFIP Advances in Information and Communication Technology, vol. 610, pp. 205–212. Springer, Cham (2021). https://doi.org/10.1007/978-3-030-92934-3_21

38. Riemann, T., Kreß, A., Klassen, L., Metternich, J.: Hybrid learning factories for lean education: approach and morphology for competency-oriented design of suitable virtual reality learning environments. In: Powell, D.J., Alfnes, E., Holmemo, M.D.Q., Reke, E. (eds.) Learning in the Digital Era. ELEC 2021. IFIP Advances in Information and Communication Technology, vol. 610, pp. 60–67. Springer, Cham (2021). https://doi.org/10.1007/978-3-030-92934-3_7
39. Tan Ivander, H.S., Oktarina, R., Reynaldo, V., Sharina, C.: Conceptual development of learning factory for industrial engineering education in Indonesia context as an enabler of students' competencies in industry 4.0 era. IOP Conf. Ser. Earth Environ. Sci. **426**(1), 012123 (2020). https://doi.org/10.1088/1755-1315/426/1/012123
40. Thiede, B., Mindt, N., Mennenga, M., Herrmann, C.: Creating a hybrid multi-user learning experience by enhancing learning factories using interactive 3D environments. Rochester, NY (2022). https://doi.org/10.2139/ssrn.4074712

Sustaining Continuous Improvement of a Higher Health Education Service Through Analytical Methodologies for Determining Customer Satisfaction

Alfonso Maria Ponsiglione[1], Angelo Rosa[2], Teresa Angela Trunfio[3]([✉]),
Eliana Raiola[4], Giuseppe Longo[4], Maria Triassi[5,6], and Francesco Amato[1]

[1] Department of Electrical Engineering and Information Technology, University of Study of Naples "Federico II", Naples, Italy
[2] Department of Management, Finance and Technology, University LUM "Giuseppe Degennaro" of Casamassima, Puglia, Italy
[3] Department of Advanced Biomedical Sciences, University of Naples "Federico II", Naples, Italy
teresa.trunfio@gmail.com
[4] A.O.R.N. "A. Cardarelli", Naples, Italy
[5] Department of Public Health, University of Naples "Federico II", Naples, Italy
[6] Interdepartmental Center for Research in Healthcare Management and Innovation in Healthcare (CIRMIS), University of Naples "Federico II", Naples, Italy

Abstract. The transformation of hospitals into companies has made the concept of quality even more important. The hospital to compete must be able not only to provide good service, but also to put in place a whole series of actions that lead the user throughout the service delivery process. To do this, it requires skills and training programs that can verify and evaluate the services offered to the citizen/patient. In this study, the aim is to evaluate the level of quality achieved in the delivery of a High Health Education service provided at the Biotechnology Center of the A.O.R.N. "A. Cardarelli" in Naples. The main method adopted for collecting the desired information was a questionnaire, identified as the tool for excellence for quantitative measurement. The questionnaires were submitted to 341 learners who attended the following Higher Education courses. Then, analysis was carried out using two different methodologies: the constant sum scale and pairwise comparison. The decomposition of the problem into criteria and sub-criteria of interest made it possible to identify the degree of importance of each requirement. In general, learners preferred attributes such as the duration, preparation and interpersonal skills of the teacher and fewer elements of logistics. A training program, of whatever nature, cannot ignore an evaluation aimed at determining its effectiveness and efficiency. In this study, we intend to propose analysis strategies based on simple collection tools, such as questionnaires, that help to understand learners' needs. In this way, changes in these needs over time can be monitored in order to activate a process of continuous service improvement.

Keywords: Healthcare · Quality · High health education service · Constant sum scale · Pairwise comparison

© IFIP International Federation for Information Processing 2023
Published by Springer Nature Switzerland AG 2023
O. McDermott et al. (Eds.): ELEC 2022, IFIP AICT 668, pp. 246–257, 2023.
https://doi.org/10.1007/978-3-031-25741-4_21

1   Introduction

Healthcare is a very complex area and quality improvement can be a common paradigm to address needs [1]. However, the definition and measurement of quality in this field is extremely complicated. Different healthcare characteristics such as intangibility, heterogeneity and simultaneity combined with the intricate nature of healthcare and its many participants with own interests are just a few examples that define its complexity [2]. In addition, quality standards are more difficult to establish when delivering a service. The service is delivered differently by different operators, elements such as experience, individual skills and personality are affected [3]. Moreover, they are produced and consumed at the same time and the customer can only judge the quality at the end [4].

According to Mosadeghrad [2], the definition of quality is also linked to the standardisation of processes. Various management strategies can be deployed to search for inefficiencies and optimise processes. One example is Lean Six Sigma, which from industry has been applied in various areas of healthcare, such as the management of hospital infections [5, 6] or the optimisation of care pathways [7, 8]. To support these strategies, data-driven techniques, e.g. regression [9, 10], classification [11, 12] and analysis models, which have already been validated in other applications, such as the study of biomedical data [13, 14], support for diagnosis and therapy processes [15, 16] or hospital resource management [17, 18], are indispensable. These same techniques can be successfully applied to the quality assessment process.

Another key element is the training of healthcare personnel. The education system in health care needs continuous development and improvement because of the important role played by practitioners. Any deficiency or omission in education will result in operators who are unable to adapt to the rapid and competitive changes typical of this sector [19]. To ensure this development, it is crucial to know the opinion and needs of customers. The voice and opinion of customers influence quality improvement and provide an opportunity for organisational learning [20]. Furthermore, it is the provision of quality services that creates loyal consumers. Borishade et al. [21] demonstrated a significant association between service quality and student loyalty. However, this relationship is mediated by their satisfaction. Collecting information on learner satisfaction is therefore indispensable both for the optimisation of the service and to ensure continuity.

In this study, the opinions of 241 learners of a Higher Health Education service provided at the Biotechnology Center of the A.O.R.N. 'A. Cardarelli' in Naples (Italy) were collected. In particular, the learners were given questionnaires written in different ways according to the methodology under investigation. In this paper, 166 questionnaires will be analysed with two different methodologies; the Constant Sum Scale and the Classic Pairwise Comparison. The aim is to detect learners' opinions and determine the most suitable methodology to gather information and support improvements.

2   Methodology

In this study, data on satisfaction with a Higher Health Education service provided at the Biotechnology Center of the A.O.R.N. 'A. Cardarelli' in Naples were processed. Using questionnaires, the opinions of 166 learners who attended the Higher Education courses were collected. In this paper, in accordance with what was proposed by Y. M. Wang and K. S. Ching [22], different questionnaire formats were used without the use of conversions, and the processing of the data, as obtained from each questionnaire, was conducted according to two methodologies: the constant sum scale and pairwise comparison. The sub-dimensions, or sub-criteria, represent the Customer Requirements (CRs). In particular, structure, teacher and organisation were chosen as the main dimensions (criteria).

The following sub-dimensions (sub-criteria) were associated with the structure dimension:

- Location: meaning the location of the building both within the hospital, and in the vicinity of car parks, subways and other means of transport that can enable it to be reached;
- Equipment: meaning the presence and suitability of the equipment provided for the purposes of achieving the objectives of the training courses;
- Comfort of the environments: meaning those aesthetic characteristics that make the available spaces pleasant and comfortable.

The following sub-dimensions were associated with the teacher dimension:

- Preparation: meaning the adequacy of the teacher's level of training and preparation for teaching purposes;
- Interpersonal skills: meaning the teacher's ability to relate to learners by interpreting their requests and providing clear and comprehensive answers;
- Effectiveness: meaning the teacher's ability to deal with topics aimed at achieving the course objectives.

Finally, organisation is the criterion that includes the general aspects that characterise the entire training process that can be better defined through the following sub-criteria:

- Cost: this means the cost incurred for the course under consideration;
- Duration: means the duration of the course under examination;
- Content: means the correspondence of the topics covered in the course under examination to the user's expectations.

The user preferences are only an estimate of the importance weights $WW = (ww1, \dots, wwww)^T$ relative to the CRs. Below is the detail of the adopted methodologies.

2.1 Constant Sum Scale

In this type of questionnaire the learner is asked to allocate 100 points, in proportion to the degree of importance, from 0 not at all important to 100 only important, within each of the identified levels. The weights can be linked by three types of relationships:

- $ww_{jj}^{(1)} > ww_{kk}^{(1)}$ close order of preference;

- $ww_{jj}^{(1)} \geq ww_{kk}^{(1)}$ weak preferential order;
- $ww_{jj}^{(1)} = ww_{kk}^{(1)}$ indifferent preferential order.

2.2 Pairwise Comparison

This technique involves comparing a set of alternatives $WW = (ww1, \ldots, wwww)$, two at a time. For each comparison, learners were asked to determine which of the two compared parameters had, in their experience, greater importance in determining service quality. Specifically, learners express their judgement within the semantic scale shown in the Table (Table 1).

Table 1. Saaty's Fundamental Scale

Intensity of importance	Definition	Explanation
1	Equal importance	The two elements contribute equally to the goal
3	Moderate importance	The judgment is slightly in favour of one element over the other
5	Strong importance	The judgment is decidedly in favour of one element over the other
7	Very Strong importance	The predominance of the element is amply demonstrated
9	Extreme importance	The evidence in favour of an element is of the highest order
2, 4, 6, 8	Intermediate value between adjacent judgments	When a compromise is needed
Reciprocal	If activity i takes on a certain value when it is compared with activity j, when j is compared with i it will take on the corresponding reciprocal value	

The results of these comparisons are placed within a pairwise comparison matrix $AA = (aa_{iijj})$, such that $AA \subset WWWWWW$. The element $aaiijj$, called the dominance coefficient, represents the preference ratio of alternative $wwii$ over alternative $wwjj$. The dominance coefficients of the matrix $AA = (aa_{iijj})$, must respect the following properties:

- $\forall aa_{iijj} > 0 \; \forall ii, jj \in \{1, \ldots, ww\}$
- $aa^{iiii} = 1 \; \forall ii \in \{1, \ldots, ww\}$
- $aa_{iijj} * aa_{jjii} = 1 \; \forall ii, jj \in \{1, \ldots, ww\}$
- $aa_{iijj} * aa_{jjkk} = aa_{iikk} \; \forall ii, jj, kk \in \{1, \ldots, ww\}$

The pairwise comparison matrix provided by the learners in the group is shown below:

$$AA^{(2)} = \begin{bmatrix} aa_{11}^{(2)} & aa_{12}^{(2)} & \cdots & aa_{1nn}^{(2)} \\ aa_{21}^{(2)} & aa_{22}^{(2)} & \cdots & aa_{2nn}^{(2)} \\ \vdots & \vdots & \ddots & \vdots \\ aa_{nn1}^{(2)} & aa_{nn2}^{(2)} & \cdots & aa_{nnnn}^{(2)} \end{bmatrix}$$

This matrix must fulfil the following conditions:

$$aa_{iiii}^{(2)} = 1 \; \forall ii \in \{1, \ldots, ww\}$$

$$aa_{iiii}^{(2)} = 1 \; aa_{iiii}^{(2)} > 0 \; \forall ii, jj \in \{1, \ldots, ww\}$$

$$aa_{iiii}^{(2)} \, aa_{iijj}^{(2)} = aa_{iijj}^{(2)} \; \forall ii, jj, kk \in \{1, \ldots, ww\}$$

The logarithmic geometric mean will be used to construct the matrix.

3 Results

A portion of the questionnaires was eliminated from the final analysis as it was assumed to be subject to the response effect phenomenon. The166 questionnaires were analysed as follows:

- 100 with the Constant Sum Scale method;
- 66 with the Classic Pairwise Comparison.

As far as the Constant Sum Scale (CSS) is concerned, Fig. 1 shows the results obtained.

The average scores obtained for Methodology 1, $ww_1^{(1)} = 30$, $ww_2^{(1)} = 40$ e $ww_3^{(1)} = 30$, show how learners give more weight to the Organisation and less to teachers and structure. Figures 2, 3 and 4 show the results obtained for each dimension.

With regard to the average values for each area, learners attributed a higher weight to the teacher's interpersonal skills, the course content and the classroom equipment. The least weight was attributed to the cost of the course followed by the location of the classroom. As far as the Classic Pairwise Comparison (CPC) is concerned, the overall result is shown in Fig. 5.

Using the logarithmic geometric mean for the calculation of the elements aij, in the case of the Teacher/Structure comparison we obtained $aa13 = 3.25$ ($aa31 = 0.31$), for Organisation/Structure we obtained $aa23 = 2.39$ ($aa32 = 0.42$) and finally between Organisation/Teacher $aa21 = 1.08$ (a12=0.93). From a general point of view, therefore, learners gave more weight to the teacher and the organisation rather than the structure while between organisation and teacher the former is given more weight. Figures 6, 7 and 8 show the intermediate results for each CRs.

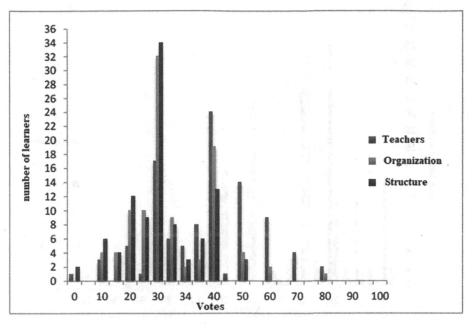

Fig. 1. Summary of data collected with CSS.

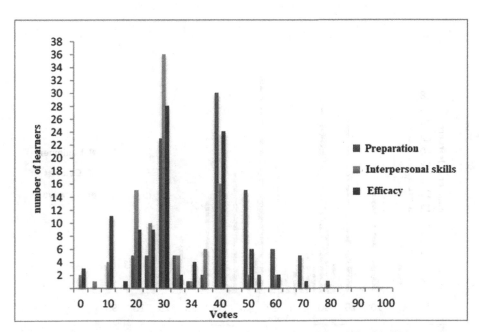

Fig. 2. Data collected for the CRs of the Teacher dimension with CSS.

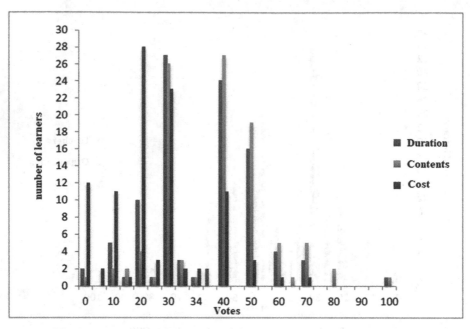

Fig. 3. Data collected for the CRs of the Organisation dimension with CSS.

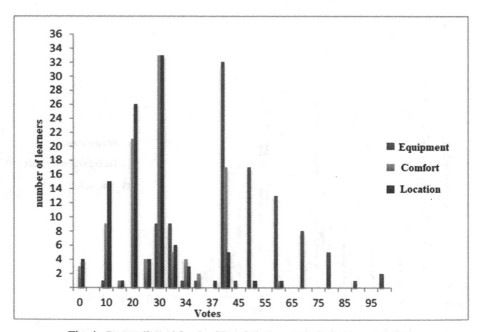

Fig. 4. Data collected for the CRs of the Structure dimension with CSS.

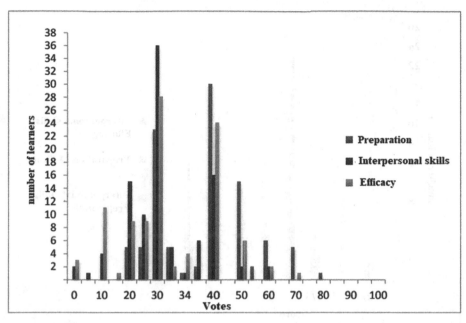

Fig. 5. Data collected for the CRs of the Teacher dimension with CSS.

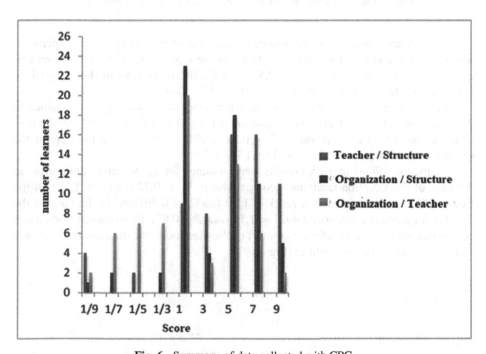

Fig. 6. Summary of data collected with CPC.

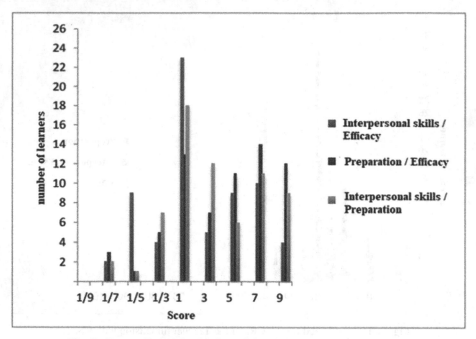

Fig. 7. Data collected for the CRs of the Teacher dimension with CPC.

For the teacher dimension, we obtained in the case of the comparison Interpersonal Skills/Efficacy $aa13 = 1.47$ ($aa31 = 0.68$), in the case of the comparison Preparation/Efficacy $aa23 = 2.72$ ($aa32 = 0.37$) and finally in the case of the comparison Preparation/Interpersonal Skills $aa21 = 2.16$ ($aa12 = 0.46$).

For the organisation dimension, on the other hand, the following were obtained in the case of the Duration/Contents comparison $aa12 = 1.68$ ($aa21 = 0.59$), in the case of the Cost/Content comparison $aa32 = 0.84$ ($aa23 = 1.19$) and in the case of the Cost/Duration comparison $a31 = 0.81$ ($aa13 = 1.23$).

Finally, the following partial results were obtained for the Structure dimension: in the case of the Location/Equipment comparison $aa31 = 0.72$ ($aa13 = 1.39$), in the Comfort/Equipment comparison $aa23 = 1.70$ ($aa32 = 0.59$) and in the case of the Comfort/Equipment comparison $aa21 = 1.15$ ($aa12 = 0.87$). From these results it can be deduced that learners prefer the comfort of the classroom, the duration of the course and the preparation of the lecturer (Fig. 9).

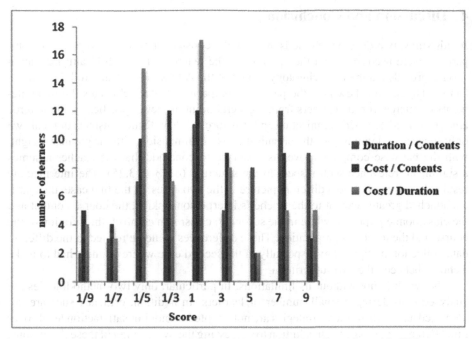

Fig. 8. Data collected for the CRs of the Organisation dimension with CPC.

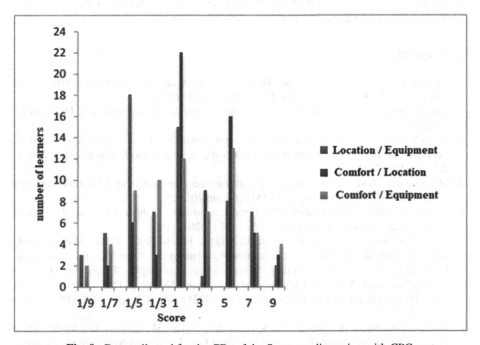

Fig. 9. Data collected for the CRs of the Structure dimension with CPC.

4 Discussion and Conclusion

In this study, two different methods, namely the constant sum scale and pairwise comparison, were used to collect the opinions of the learners of a High Health Education service provided at the Biotechnology Center of the A.O.R.N. "A. Cardarelli" in Naples (Italy). The results show how the pairwise comparison better delineates the main elements of interest for the learners from a general point of view. Specifically, in the three areas identified, teacher, organisation and structure, while with the constant sum scale we only succeed in defining how the organisation is the dimension with the greatest weight, with the pairwise comparison we also manage to conclude that the teacher assumes a significant relevance with respect to the structure ($aa13 = 3.25$). The intermediate results, however, showed a different picture in the two cases. In the first case, the learners attached greater weight to the teacher's interpersonal skills, the course content and the classroom equipment, while in the second to classroom comfort, the duration of the course and the teacher's preparation. These differences could be related to the different data collection methodology, especially in the second case where learners had to make a choice between the two sub-criteria.

This work is not without its limitations. In particular, only two methodologies are analysed considering a small number of learners. In addition, critical issues are not identified and improvement strategies are not adopted to monitor satisfaction levels over time. Future developments, in addition to addressing the overcoming of these limitations, will also involve the use of synthesis techniques, such as the Linear Goal Programming technique, to recompose the hierarchy realised based on the Analytic Hierarchy Process [23] in order to derive the final synthesis result of the survey.

References

1. Aggarwal, A., Aeran, H., Rathee, M.: Quality management in healthcare: The pivotal desideratum. J. Oral Bio. Craniofac. Res. 9(2), 180–182 (2019)
2. Mosadeghrad, A.M.: Healthcare service quality: towards a broad definition. Int. J. Health Care Qual. Assur. (2013)
3. Mosadeghrad, A.M.: Towards a theory of quality management: an integration of strategic management, quality management and project management. Int. J. Model. Oper. Manag. 2(1), 89–118 (2012)
4. Mosadeghrad, A.M.: Factors influencing healthcare service quality. Int. J. Health Pol. Manag. 3(2), 77–89 (2014). https://doi.org/10.15171/ijhpm.2014.65
5. Ferraro, A., et al.: Implementation of lean practices to reduce healthcare associated infections. Int. J. Healthc. Technol. Manag. 18(1–2), 51–72 (2020)
6. Cesarelli, Giuseppe, Montella, Emma, Scala, Arianna, Raiola, Eliana, Triassi, Maria, Improta, Giovanni: DMAIC Approach for the Reduction of Healthcare-Associated Infections in the Neonatal Intensive Care Unit of the University Hospital of Naples 'Federico II.' In: Jarm, Tomaz, Cvetkoska, Aleksandra, Mahnič-Kalamiza, Samo, Miklavcic, Damijan (eds.) EMBEC 2020. IP, vol. 80, pp. 414–423. Springer, Cham (2021). https://doi.org/10.1007/978-3-030-64610-3_48
7. Trunfio, T.A., Scala, A., Borrelli, A., Sparano, M., Triassi, M., Improta, G.: Application of the Lean Six Sigma approach to the study of the LOS of patients who undergo laparoscopic cholecystectomy at the San Giovanni di Dio and Ruggi d'Aragona University Hospital. In: 2021 5th International Conference on Medical and Health Informatics, pp. 50–54 (2021)

8. Improta, G., Borrelli, A., Triassi, M.: Machine learning and lean six sigma to assess how COVID-19 has changed the patient management of the complex operative unit of neurology and stroke unit: a single center study. Int. J. Environ. Res. Public Health **19**(9), 5215 (2022)

9. Trunfio, T.A., et al.: Multiple regression model to analyze the total LOS for patients undergoing laparoscopic appendectomy. BMC Med. Inform. Decis. Mak. **22**(1), 1–8 (2022)

10. Scala, A., et al.: Regression models to study the total LOS related to valvuloplasty. Int. J. Environ. Res. Public Health **19**(5), 3117 (2022)

11. Montella, E., Ferraro, A., Sperlì, G., Triassi, M., Santini, S., Improta, G.: Predictive analysis of healthcare-associated blood stream infections in the neonatal intensive care unit using artificial intelligence: a single center study. Int. J. Environ. Res. Public Health **19**(5), 2498 (2022)

12. Trunfio, T.A., Borrelli, A., Improta, G.: Is it possible to predict the length of stay of patients undergoing hip-replacement surgery? Int. J. Environ. Res. Public Health **19**(10), 6219 (2022)

13. Ponsiglione, A.M., Cosentino, C., Cesarelli, G., Amato, F., Romano, M.: A comprehensive review of techniques for processing and analyzing fetal heart rate signals. Sensors **21**(18), 6136 (2021)

14. Ponsiglione, A.M., Amato, F., Romano, M.: Multiparametric investigation of dynamics in fetal heart rate signals. Bioengineering **9**(1), 8 (2021)

15. Improta, G., Mazzella, V., Vecchione, D., Santini, S., Triassi, M.: Fuzzy logic–based clinical decision support system for the evaluation of renal function in post-transplant patients. J. Eval. Clin. Pract. **26**(4), 1224–1234 (2020)

16. Santini, S., et al.: Using fuzzy logic for improving clinical daily-care of β-thalassemia patients. In: 2017 IEEE International Conference on Fuzzy Systems (FUZZ-IEEE), pp. 1–6. IEEE (2017)

17. Improta, G., Converso, G., Murino, T., Gallo, M., Perrone, A., Romano, M.: Analytic hierarchy process (AHP) in dynamic configuration as a tool for health technology assessment (HTA): the case of biosensing optoelectronics in oncology. Int. J. Inf. Technol. Decis. Mak. **18**(05), 1533–1550 (2019)

18. Improta, G., et al.: An innovative contribution to health technology assessment. In: Ding, W., Jiang, H., Ali, M., Li, M. (eds.) Modern advances in intelligent systems and tools. Studies in Computational Intelligence, vol. 431, pp. 127–131. Springer, Berlin, Heidelberg (2012). https://doi.org/10.1007/978-3-642-30732-4_16

19. Saif, N.I.: The effect of service quality on student satisfaction: a field study for health services administration students. Int. J. Humanit. Soc. Sci. **4**(8), 172–181 (2014)

20. Carlucci, D., Renna, P., Schiuma, G.: Evaluating service quality dimensions as antecedents to outpatient satisfaction using back propagation neural network. Health Care Manag. Sci. **16**(1), 37–44 (2013)

21. Borishade, T.T., Ogunnaike, O.O., Salau, O., Motilewa, B.D., Dirisu, J.I.: Assessing the relationship among service quality, student satisfaction and loyalty: the NIGERIAN higher education experience. Heliyon **7**(7), e07590 (2021)

22. Wang, Y.M., Chin, K.S.: A linear goal programming approach to determining the relative importance weights of customer requirements in quality function deployment. Inf. Sci. **181**(24), 5523–5533 (2011)

23. Ponsiglione, A.M., Amato, F., Cozzolino, S., Russo, G., Romano, M., Improta, G.: A hybrid analytic hierarchy process and Likert scale approach for the quality assessment of medical education programs. Mathematics **10**(9), 1426 (2022)

Lean, Green and Sustainability

Lean for Social Enterprises: Doing the Right Things

Alinda Kokkinou[1,2(✉)] ⓘ and Ton van Kollenburg[1] ⓘ

[1] AVANS University of Applied Sciences, Breda, The Netherlands
{a.kokkinou,ajc.vankollenburg}@avans.nl
[2] Breda University of Applied Sciences, Breda, The Netherlands

Abstract. Social enterprises need to meet their 'profit' goals in order to achieve their 'people' and/or 'planet' goals. Currently, many social enterprises seem to have a more expensive business model than their competitors, and thus rely either on charging price premiums or receiving (governmental) subsidies to remain in business. By applying the principles of Lean, and more generally continuous improvement, social enterprises should be able to improve their efficiency and productivity, enabling them to achieve their objectives. The aim of this study is to explore how social enterprises can use Lean or other continuous improvement methods in order to meet the profit goals needed to fulfil their social mission.

Keywords: Lean · Continuous improvement · Social enterprises

1 Introduction

Social enterprises (SEs) are businesses whose primary objective is to generate social and/or ecological impact, as opposed to financial gain for their owners. SEs have been recognized for the role they can play towards a more inclusive society [1]. In their pursuit of societal value creation, SEs contribute to social issues such as well-being (e.g. by lifting people out of poverty and working on social integration of the disadvantaged), social wealth and cohesion (e.g. by encouraging people to care for each other and for the environment and by creating community), and ecology (e.g. by tackling issues such as global warming, smart mobility, sustainable agriculture and preservation of the environment) [2–4].

Even though SEs operate on the same principles as the private sector and thus need to be financially self-sustaining, they differ from traditional businesses in that their financial goals are merely the means to achieve social impact [2, 5, 6]. They are also unlike traditional businesses pursuing a corporate social responsibility agenda as, in a bind, for-profit business will still prioritize financial objectives over social impact [2]. SEs therefore differ from traditional businesses in that they need to balance the dual objectives of economic and societal value creation [3].

The barriers that SEs encounter in the startup and growth phase and how to overcome them have received extensive attention from academia [3, 5], governmental organizations

O. McDermott et al. (Eds.): ELEC 2022, IFIP AICT 668, pp. 261–272, 2023.
https://doi.org/10.1007/978-3-031-25741-4_22

[1], and professional organizations [7, 8]. Despite these efforts to promote and support SEs, an often overlooked issue impacting the growth and longevity of SEs has been their profitability. Of the 175 Dutch SEs surveyed by McKinsey in 2016, 45% reported being loss-making. In a similar study conducted by Social Enterprise NL [7], 36% of SEs reported being loss-making in 2019. This lack of profitability has been attributed to SEs being in the start-up or scale-up phase [7–9]. This was partially supported by a report by ABN AMRO [9], that showed that the older an SE, the more likely it was to be profitable. Nevertheless, after five years, a vast group of SEs was still loss-making (37%) or merely breaking even (30%), limiting their impact potential. While SEs aim for social impact, they still need to achieve financial objectives in order to realize the intended impact [8].

Some anecdotal evidence suggests that the production processes of SEs are more time consuming and costly, in part due to handmade and/or artisanal production processes and ethically sourced raw materials [10]. A social entrepreneur quoted in a UK newspaper summarized it succinctly by saying: *"my commitment to ethics makes everything more expensive and much more time-consuming"* [11]. The delicate balance that SEs need to achieve between economic and societal value creation seems to be a barrier to financial sustainability and, by extension, impact.

The need for SEs to improve the competitiveness of their operating model, and thus make greater impact, could in theory be aided by the implementation of Lean [12]. The initial seeds of Lean manufacturing were planted by Henry Ford in the early 1900s as part of his pursuit of mass production [13]. In the 1950s, the Toyota Production System was pioneered by Taiichi Ohno as an efficient production system, creating the basis for Lean. The book "the Machine that Changed the World" by Womack et al. [14] subsequently introduced Lean to the rest of the world. Lean thinking, an organizational paradigm promoting efficiency by delivering better value to customers and removing non-value adding activities, is now successfully used in industries as diverse as agriculture [15], logistics [16], hospitality [17], financial services [18], education [19] and healthcare [20].

In the context of for-profit companies pursuing sustainability initiatives, programs have been developed combining Lean and "Green" [21]. Both Lean and Green manufacturing aim to reduce waste and make efficient use of resources [22]. Programs combining both paradigms have been found to be successful either through synergies between them, or by implementing green manufacturing practices as an extension of an existing Lean program [21, 23].

To this date, literature addressing the implementation of Lean by SEs is scarce. The similarly very limited literature addressing Lean implementation by non-profit organizations seems to support the notion that these organizations could also increase their efficiency by implementing Lean [24]. Yet, in the context of SEs, the pursuit of efficiency has a negative connotation [5] as it is perceived to jeopardize their dual mission pursuit and put them at risk of "mission drift" [25].

Therefore, the purpose of this conceptual paper is to examine how Lean or other continuous improvement methods can be adapted to fit the multiple objectives of SEs. Given the multiple forms that SEs can take [26], we narrow our scope to match

Davies *et al.*'s definition of SEs, namely "market oriented social enterprises that seek to generate revenue from the sale of products and services" [3].

2 Review of the Literature

2.1 Social Enterprises

SEs exist on a continuum between traditional purely commercial for-profit companies and non-profit purely philanthropic organizations [27, 28]. Traditional for-profit businesses are those that primarily pursue financial goals by selling products or services to customers. Increasingly, due to either societal or other external pressures, for-profit businesses are embracing CSR agendas and social goals, and engaging in sustainable business practices. Yet, what characterizes these as for-profit businesses is that, if needed, they will still prioritize their financial goals over their societal ones [2].

Non-profit organizations are those that primarily pursue societal objectives by catering to beneficiaries [27]. They are typically reliant on subsidies and other donations. Non-profit organizations also have specific legal forms linked to tax benefits for the organization and its funders and donors [27]. Hybridization trends have led non-profit organizations to attempt to generate their own revenue streams through sales. These attempts were relatively unsuccessful as they created tension between the core non-profit activities and the commercial activities [27].

SEs, positioned in the middle of the continuum between traditional for-profit companies and non-profit organizations, were conceived in response to a need to find innovative market-based solutions to social problems [28, 29]. SEs can take on different legal forms, also depending on the country in which their located [27]. While numerous definitions of SEs exist, they share the common aspect that SEs' hybrid model combines for- and non-profit aspects to produce social value and commercial revenue through a single comprehensive strategy [27]. Spear *et al.*'s [29] typology of SEs distinguished between mutuals (e.g. cooperatives), trading charities (e.g. businesses providing education), public sector spin-offs (e.g. WISE), and new-start SEs (e.g. green and fair trade SEs). SEs are related to, yet distinct from the concept of social entrepreneurship [26] which is more concerned with the process of creating SEs [30] and the characteristics, motivations, and mission of the individual social entrepreneurs [31, 32]. Social entrepreneurship is thus outside the scope of this paper.

2.2 Challenges and Barriers of Social Enterprises

SEs encounter several challenges due to the hybrid nature of their business model [3] and to the lack of awareness of their business model by their various stakeholders [1]. In the start-up phase, these challenges include the selection of a legal structure [29] and the pursuit of appropriate start up financing [27]. Financial institutions and more generally lenders might have difficulties identifying the value-creating potential of SEs beyond traditional financial measures [3] and balk at the requirement that SEs reinvest their profits in their social mission instead of distributing them to shareholders. More recent research suggests that funds for financing SE creation seem to become increasingly available, as more conservative lenders and financial institutions have been supplemented with other sources such as impact financers. Nevertheless, funds for financing SE growth remain less available [3].

SEs may have to deal with a more expensive business model [10]. Davies *et al.* [3] explain that SEs absorb "social costs into the financial architecture of the social enterprise, leading to higher prices and thus lower perceived customer value compared to similar products" [3]. Customers and retailers might not be aware of the SEs social mission and thus not value it accordingly in their purchase decision-making. This makes it difficult for SEs to find customers [7, 8]. SEs also encounter the issue that they may not be as competitive as traditional businesses [6, 33], which may put them at a disadvantage in the market.

The European Union, recognizing some of these challenges, formulated a research agenda consisting of three themes to support SEs. These themes included (a) making it easier for social enterprises to obtain funding, (b) removing legal barriers, and (c) increasing visibility of social enterprises [1]. SEs also have access to an extensive support infrastructure consisting of international networks such as Ashoka, B-Corp, and Skoll Foundation, and national and regional networks [34]. These organizations advocate on behalf of SEs, conduct research, and provide knowledge and professionalization services to social entrepreneurs.

As they grow, SEs might have difficulties maintaining the required trade-off between financial and social value creation [5, 35, 36]. SEs can encounter the challenge of reconciling the needs of their beneficiaries with those of their customers and other stakeholders [27, 29]. This issue extends to finding the right board members [29] and/or employees to grow their unique organizational culture [3]. If new employees are unable to navigate the complex decision-making characterizing SEs, they put it at risk for "mission drift" [5]. 'Mission drift,' defined as an organization's deviation from its goals, can happen to SEs either when they focus too much on their social mission at the expense of their business organization, or conversely when they sacrifice their social goals in pursuit of financial gain [25, 36], the latter scenario being perceived as more common [5], especially in situations where the survival of the SE is in jeopardy. This dread of being accused of "mission drift" makes social entrepreneurs averse to the concept of efficiency common to for-profit commercial enterprises and less interested in Lean.

2.3 Continuous Improvement and Lean

Continuous improvement is defined as "a company-wide process of focused and continuous incremental innovation" [37]. Continuous improvement helps organizations to come to "sustained improvements regarding effectiveness and efficiency" and more specifically quality, speed, flexibility, cost, and sustainability [38].

Lean management stems from the Toyota Production System (TPS), developed in the 1950s by Taiichi Ohno [13] as an alternative to the US-style mass production that seemed ill-suited to the Japanese automotive industry characteristics [14]. TPS is frequently represented as a house standing on two pillars, continuous improvement and respect for people. From this perspective of "respect for people," a Lean organization is described as one "that recognizes that its people are the most important resource and is one which adopts high performance work practices" and that "such an environment requires a culture of mutual respect and trust, open and honest communication, and synergistic and cooperating relationships of stakeholders" [39]. Actions that an organizations can take to promote "respect for people" include implementing teamwork, developing and challenging people, motivating people, developing people as problem solvers, assessing people's safety, displaying people's capabilities and removing waste [40]. The Toyota company was described by Womack et al. [14] as a community, where employees were guaranteed lifetime employment in return for being flexible and proactive in their work and in responding to problems.

More recently, in a conceptual paper, Ljungblom and Lennerfors refined the definition of "respect for people", by linking it to the concept of craftmanship, derived from the Japanese *takumi*. They state *"the notion of craftsmanship situates the employee in the middle of relationships to people and objects that demand his or her care. The good should not be understood in a merely technical sense but also in an ethical sense"* [41]. According to Ljungblom and Lennerfors [41], the concept of craftsmanship could be the missing piece to better understand Lean, by understanding its underlying values. From this perspective, the values of respect for craftsmanship, mutual respect and trust, open and honest communication, and synergistic and cooperating relationships of stakeholders [39, 41], seem consistent with those of SEs, making Lean, and more generally continuous improvement, an interesting methodology for SEs to use to improve their operating model.

2.4 Success Factors for Lean Implementation

For Lean implementation to be successful, a certain number of conditions need to be met. These are industry and context dependent [19], and have been called critical success factors [42] or alternatively readiness factors [43]. In general, the consensus has been that for for-profit companies implementing Lean, leadership and management involvement and commitment, linking Lean to the business strategy, and customer orientation are important critical success factors [44, 45]. Training employees is seen as an important mechanism to establish the link between Lean and business strategy and involving employees in the implementation [46].

In the context of SMEs, Achanga et al. [42] found leadership and management, and in particular strong project management skills to be an important critical success factor. Furthermore, financial resources are needed to acquire the skills and expertise, either through the hiring of consultant and/ or the training of employees. Finally, the creation of a supportive organizational culture is seen as necessary. In the context of non-profits, and in higher education in particular, the most important readiness factors have included (i) leadership and vision, (ii) management involvement, commitment and resources, (iii) link between Lean Six Sigma and strategy, and (iv) customer focus [43].

2.5 Lean and Sustainable Business Practices

While there is limited research on how SEs can benefit from Lean, a more extensive body of research exists about for-profit businesses embracing sustainable business practices in pursuit of sustainability goals. The potential of Lean to contribute to more sustainable business practices has so far been examined from the relatively narrow context of "Lean and Green", namely for-profit businesses pursuing environmental sustainability [47]. The focus has been on the synergy potential of Lean and Green practices with several models being developed and validated [12]. According to this stream of research, Lean and Green have been shown to have a synergetic impact on environmental sustainability through cost reduction, waste reduction, and pollution prevention [22, 23]. Nevertheless, Lean and Green remain distinct in terms of their primary focus, definitions of waste and techniques used and consequently in their impact on business performance [22].

Benefits of Lean and Green implementation extend beyond "profit" and "planet". From a "people" perspective, Lean and Green implementation can lead to improved worker empowerment, engagement, and safety; improved relationships with suppliers, unions, and other stakeholders; and increased transparency in the supply chain [47], values important to SEs. Taken together, these findings suggest that SEs could benefit from Lean.

3   Lean Implementation in SEs

This section sketches a preliminary framework for how Lean can be adapted for and implemented by SEs (Fig. 1). We consider existing models and tools and bring them together in a single framework, considering strategic, tactical and operational levels, and relationships with external stakeholders. We propose a four step approach to implementation that deviates from traditional top-down or bottom-up approaches [19, 48] to enable SEs to take maximum advantage Lean's benefits while respecting SEs capabilities, limited resources and dual objectives of economic and societal value creation.

3.1   Step 1: Translate Mission and Strategy to Actionable Impact Measures

An important first step for SEs is to translate their social mission and strategy to an actionable set of performance measures that they can use to monitor their progress towards their dual objectives, communicate with stakeholders, and guide operational decision-making.

Alignment with strategy is a critical success factor [42] for Lean. Implementing Lean can help SEs refocus on their strategic objectives, both financial and social, by translating them into measurable Key Performance Indicators (KPIs). While financial KPIs are common, social KPIs are less so. For the implementation of Lean by SEs to be successful, objectives and KPIs need to be set that incorporate a broader stake- holder perspective, including customers, beneficiaries, suppliers, and other relevant stakeholders. Models such as Social Impact for Local Economies (SIMPLEs) [49] can be used to translate SEs social missions into relevant and measurable social KPIs, that in turn can guide strategic, tactical, and operational decisions. The development of the impact measures needs to be done in a transparent way, to ensure the SE is not perceived to engage in 'mission drift'.

SEs, especially in the start-up phase, tend to be led top-down, with the sustainable entrepreneur taking on the leadership role. This synergizes well with an important success factor of Lean, namely commitment from senior leadership [42]. Furthermore, when the core values and ideologies of workers align with those of the organization, meaning is provided to workers who become more engaged [5]. SEs, with their explicit social mission, are thus better positioned to provide meaning to workers. This creates another potential synergy with Lean's emphasis on respect for people, and attention to worker engagement through empowerment.

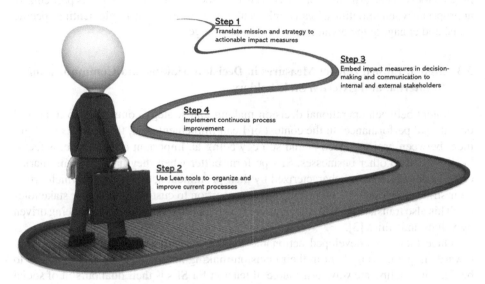

Fig. 1. Framework for Lean implementation by SEs.

3.2 Step 2: Apply Lean Tools to Improve Operational Processes

Like other businesses, SEs need to manage their growth as they evolve from small entrepreneurial firms to mid-sized or larger firms. This requires them to formalize their organizational structure, communication flows, roles and responsibilities, and processes. According to Bull *et al.* [50], setting organizational standards can also contribute to improved process quality, measurement and efficiency. In the context of resource-constrained SEs, implementing Lean tools will enable them to slowly build expertise in process improvement and concurrently achieve benefits of Lean without a costly upfront implementation. Nevertheless, social enterprises seem reluctant to invest in accredited quality standards such as ISO due to a lack of resources [50].

In the context of quality models used for self-assessment such as the Practical Quality Assurance System for Small Organizations (PQASSO) and Excellence Model (EM) by the British Quality Foundations, Paton et al. [51] found that the they required a greater time commitment than the non-profits applying them expected. The same study by Paton et al. [51] found that non-profits had difficulties applying the quality models due to unclear and unsuitable language. These models were originally proposed in the manufacturing sector and subsequently reworked to fit the context of small businesses.

Given the lack of process improvement knowledge and resources such as time and money, implementation in this second step should focus on the application of specific tools that fit issues encountered by the organization, without incurring unnecessary overhead costs. For example, outside expertise in the form of consultants should be brought in to scope the problem and identify the appropriate tools. A team of employees involved in the primary process should then receive the necessary training and coaching in Lean tools to perform the project. This customized form of training [46] is particularly appropriate when initiating a Lean implementation bottom-up, by implementing specific tools, and engaging the organization in visible change.

3.3   Step 3: Embed Impact Measures in Decision-Making and Communication to Internal and External Stakeholders

Alignment between operational decision-making and strategy contributes to improved operational performance. In the context of Lean implementation, this extends to alignment between project selection and strategy being an important critical success factor [42]. Similar to other businesses, SEs perform better when they have a strong market orientation [52]. SEs are characterized by their prominent social mission, which drives their strategy, operating model, and value proposition to customer and other stakeholders. This also translates into their operational decisions and business models being driven by values and ethics [3].

Once they have developed actionable impact measures in step 1, SEs can work towards implementing them in their decision-making and daily control. This needs to be done in a deliberate way, as a source of tension for SEs is their dual pursuit of social and financial goals, and the wariness towards 'mission drift' [5]. Senior leadership has an important role to play in the introduction of the new impact measures by ensuring that these measures are embraced as legitimate to the SEs mission.

Conversely, the implementation of a comprehensive set of KPIs also bring opportunities to SEs. By reporting on these KPIs, SEs enable their external stakeholders to incorporate non-financial aspects in their decision-making [1, 3]. For example, a customer that wants to engage in sustainable purchasing will now be able to assess the SEs value proposition more comprehensively.

3.4   Step 4: Implement Continuous Process Improvement

SEs' business models tend to be more expensive, amongst other factors, due to their artisanal production processes and ethical sourcing [10]. This places SEs at a disadvantage compared to traditional for-profit businesses [3]. While the implementation of social KPIs in communication (step 3) will help customers value SEs social impact more objectively, reducing the cost of the operating model will further improve the value proposition. Reducing costs means that SEs can either reduce prices and thus increase their market share, or maintain prices and generate more impact.

Implementing continuous improvement will enable SEs to identify non-value adding activities and improve their processes accordingly [13, 14]. However, this can only be achieved if the mission has been appropriately translated to social objectives and corresponding KPIs. For SEs, value is defined through a multi-stakeholder perspective. Implementing continuous improvement without having executed step 1 and step 3, (developing a comprehensive performance measure measurement system and implementing it) puts the SE at risk for mission drift [5]. The optimalization of a process could be at the expense of the SE's mission.

To successfully implement continuous improvement, SEs need to also concurrently harness their natural affinity with "respect for people" elements [40]. SEs should build on the technical expertise introduced in step 2 by further developing people as problem solvers and using teamwork. Particularly appropriate for SEs is the use of "quality circles" as a way to further develop, motivate, and challenge people. Many SEs also embrace artisanal and handmade product processes, stereotypical of craftsmanship [41].

4 Conclusions and Future Research

The reputation of Lean as a cost-cutting measure is a double-edge sword for SEs. To many SEs, Lean is seen as a primarily cost cutting measure [5], inconsistent with their values and ethics and thus making them reluctant to consider it. This is a consequences of the "respect for people" aspect of Lean receiving less attention than the tools and techniques [40, 53]. Conversely, Lean has the advantage of name recognition by the broader business community. For SEs pursuing commercial financing, employing Lean could help overcome a particular barrier to growth, namely low investor awareness of SEs and conservative investment policies [3]. However, for Lean to be successfully applied to SEs, it needs to be adapted to fit their unique organizational culture, capabilities, and resources. Therefore, we propose a framework to implement Lean in SEs harnessing the synergies between the values of Lean and those of SEs. This framework focusses on using a broader stakeholder perspective to set KPIs that support SEs' dual objectives of social and financial value creation.

This framework is based on conceptual work, and needs to be tested using empirical evidence. Action methodology should be used to confirm this framework and further develop it in cooperation with SEs. Action methodology can "integrate social sciences with organizational knowledge to generate actionable scientific knowledge" [54] and is thus particularly appropriate for the further development and validation of a theoretical framework in cooperation with SEs.

References

1. European Commission: The Social Business Initiative of the European Commission. (2015)
2. Verloop, W., Hillen, M.: Social Enterprise Unraveled: Best Practices from the Netherlands. Warden Press, Amsterdam (2014)
3. Davies, I.A., Haugh, H., Chambers, L.: Barriers to social enterprise growth. J. Small Bus. Manage. **57**, 1616–1636 (2019)
4. Defourny, J., Nyssens, M.: Social enterprise in Europe: recent trends and developments. Soc. Enterp. J. **4**, 202–228 (2008)
5. Battilana, J.: Cracking the organizational challenge of pursuing joint social and financial goals: Social enterprise as a laboratory to understand hybrid organizing. M@n@gement **21**, 1278–1305 (2018)

6. Kay, A., Roy, M.J., Donaldson, C.: Re-imagining social enterprise. SEJ. **12**, 217–234 (2016)
7. Social Enterprise NL: Social Enterprise Monitor (2019)
8. Dupain, W., et al.: European social enterprise monitor: the state of social enterprise in Europe 2020–2021. Euclid Network (2021)
9. ABN AMRO: De noodzaak van marktontwikkeling voor sociale ondernemingen (2017)
10. Bandyopadhyay, C., Ray, S.: Social enterprise marketing: review of literature and future research agenda. MIP. **38**, 121–135 (2019)
11. Sheppard, E.: "Social enterprises go bust all the time" - how the sector is tackling its image problem (2018). https://www.theguardian.com/small-business-network/2018/mar/12/social-enterprises-go-bust-all-the-time-how-the-sector-istackling-its-image-problem
12. Caldera, H.T.S., Desha, C., Dawes, L.: Exploring the role of lean thinking in sustainable business practice: a systematic literature review. J. Clean. Prod. **167**, 1546–1565 (2017)
13. Bhuiyan, N., Baghel, A.: An overview of continuous improvement: from the past to the present. Manag. Decis. **43**, 761–771 (2005)
14. Womack, J.P., Jones, D.T., Roos, D.: The Machine that Changed the World. Simon and Schuster, New York (2007)
15. Melin, M., Barth, H.: Lean in Swedish agriculture: strategic and operational per- spectives. Production Planning & Control. **29**, 845–855 (2018)
16. Jones, D.T., Hines, P., Rich, N.: Lean logistics. Int. J. Phys. Distrib. Logist. Manag. **27**, 153–173 (1997)
17. Perdomo-Verdecia, V., Sacristán-Díaz, M., Garrido-Vega, P.: Lean management in hotels: where we are and where we might go. Int. J. Hospitality Manag. **104**, 103250 (2022)
18. Koning, H.D., Does, R.J.M.M., Bisgaard, S.: Lean Six Sigma in financial services. IJSSCA **4**(1), 1–17 (2008)
19. Kokkinou, A., van Kollenburg, T.: Top down or bottom up: perspectives on critical success factors of lean in institutes of higher education. In: Powell, D.J., Alfnes, E., Holmemo, M.D.Q., Reke, E. (eds.) Learning in the Digital Era, pp. 32–41. Springer International Publishing, Cham (2021)
20. D'Andreamatteo, A., Ianni, L., Lega, F., Sargiacomo, M.: Lean in healthcare: a comprehensive review. Health Policy **119**, 1197–1209 (2015)
21. Bhattacharya, A., Nand, A., Castka, P.: Lean-green integration and its impact on sustainability performance: a critical review. J. Clean. Prod. **236**, 117697 (2019)
22. Garza-Reyes, J.A.: Green lean and the need for Six Sigma. Int. J. Lean Six Sigma. **6**, 226–248 (2015)
23. Dües, C.M., Tan, K.H., Lim, M.: Green as the new Lean: how to use Lean practices as a catalyst to greening your supply chain. J. Clean. Prod. **40**, 93–100 (2013)
24. Cheng, C.-Y., Chang, P.-Y.: Implementation of the Lean Six Sigma framework in non-profit organisations: a case study. Total Qual. Manag. Bus. Excell. **23**, 431–447 (2012). https://doi.org/10.1080/14783363.2012.663880
25. Cornforth, C.: Understanding and combating mission drift in social enterprises. Soc. Enterp. J. **10**, 3–20 (2014)
26. Defourny, J., Nyssens, M., Brolis, O.: Testing social enterprise models across the world: evidence from the "international comparative social enterprise models (ICSEM) project." Nonprofit Volunt. Sect. Q. **50**, 420–440 (2021)
27. Battilana, J., Lee, M., Walker, J., Dorsey, C.: In search of the hybrid ideal. Stanf. Soc. Innov. Rev. **10**, 49–55 (2012)
28. Dees, G.: The Social Enterprises Spectrum: Philanthropy to Commerce. Harvard Business Review, Brighton (1996)
29. Spear, R., Cornforth, C., Aiken, M.: The governance challenges of social enterprises: evidence from a UK empirical study. Ann. Pub. Coop. Econ. **80**, 247–273 (2009)

30. Haugh, H.: A research agenda for social entrepreneurship. Soc. Enterp. J. **1**, 1–12 (2005)
31. Dacin, M.T., Dacin, P.A., Tracey, P.: Social entrepreneurship: a critique and future directions. Organ. Sci. **22**, 1203–1213 (2011)
32. Alegre, I., Kislenko, S., Berbegal-Mirabent, J.: Organized chaos: mapping the definitions of social entrepreneurship. J. Soc. Entrepreneurship **8**, 248–264 (2017)
33. Ryan, P.W., Lyne, I.: Social enterprise and the measurement of social value: methodological issues with the calculation and application of the social return on investment. Educ. Knowl. Econ. **2**, 223–237 (2008)
34. McKinsey & Company: Scaling the impact of the social enterprise sector. McKinsey & Company (2016)
35. Costanzo, L.A., Vurro, C., Foster, D., Servato, F., Perrini, F.: Dual-mission management in social entrepreneurship: qualitative evidence from social firms in the united kingdom. J. Small Bus. Manage. **52**, 655–677 (2014)
36. Young, D.R.: The state of theory and research on social enterprises. In: Gidron, Benjamin, Hasenfeld, Yeheskel (eds.) social enterprises, pp. 19–46. Palgrave Macmillan UK, London (2012). https://doi.org/10.1057/9781137035301_2
37. Bessant, J., Caffyn, S., Gilbert, J., Harding, R., Webb, S.: Rediscovering continuous improvement. Technovation **14**, 17–29 (1994)
38. van Kollenburg, T., Kokkinou, A.: What comes after the transformation?: characteristics of continuous improvement organizations. In: Powell, D.J., Alfnes, E., Holmemo, M.D.Q., Reke, E. (eds.) Learning in the Digital Era, pp. 259–268. Springer International Publishing, Cham (2021)
39. Oppenheim, B.W., Murman, E.M., Secor, D.A.: Lean enablers for systems engineering. Syst. Engin. **14**, 29–55 (2011). https://doi.org/10.1002/sys.20161
40. Coetzee, R., van Dyk, L., van der Merwe, K.R.: Towards addressing respect for people during lean implementation. IJLSS. **10**, 830–854 (2019)
41. Ljungblom, M., Lennerfors, T.T.: The lean principle respect for people as respect for craftsmanship. IJLSS. **12**, 1209–1230 (2021)
42. Achanga, P., Shehab, E., Roy, R., Nelder, G.: Critical success factors for lean implementation within SMEs. J. Manu. Tech. Mnagmnt. **17**, 460–471 (2006)
43. Antony, J.: Readiness factors for the Lean Six Sigma journey in the higher education sector. Int. J. Prod. Perform. Manag. **63**, 257–264 (2014)
44. Antony, J.: Six Sigma in the UK service organisations: results from a pilot survey. Manag. Audit. J. **19**, 1006–1013 (2004)
45. Antony, J., Desai, D.A.: Assessing the status of six sigma implementation in the Indian industry: results from an exploratory empirical study. Manag. Res. News **32**, 413–423 (2009)
46. Kokkinou, A., van Kollenburg, T., Touw, P.: The role of training in the implementation of lean Six Sigma. In: EurOMA Proceedings Berlin (2021)
47. Piercy, N., Rich, N.: The relationship between lean operations and sustainable operations. Int. J. Oper. Prod. Manag. **35**, 282–315 (2015)
48. Kokkinou, A., van Kollenburg, T., Touw, P.: The road to operational excellence is scenic: tales of continuous improvement journeys. In: EurOMA Proceedings, Berlin (2022)
49. McLoughlin, J., et al.: A strategic approach to social impact measurement of social enterprises: the SIMPLE methodology. Soc. Enterp. J. **5**, 154–178 (2009)
50. Bull, M., Ridley-Duff, R., Whittam, G., Baines, S.: Challenging tensions and contradictions: critical, theoretical and empirical perspectives on social enterprise. IJEBR. **24**, 582–586 (2018). https://doi.org/10.1108/IJEBR-05-2018-526
51. Paton, R., Foot, J., Payne, G.: What happens when non-profits use quality models for self-assessment? Nonprofit Manag. Leadersh. **11**, 21–34 (2000)

52. Bhattarai, C.R., Kwong, C.C.Y., Tasavori, M.: Market orientation, market disruptiveness capability and social enterprise performance: an empirical study from the united kingdom. J. Bus. Res. **96**, 47–60 (2019)
53. Bhasin, S.: Prominent obstacles to lean. Int. J. Prod. Perf. Mgmt. **61**, 403–425 (2012)
54. Cronemyr, P., Eriksson, M., Jakolini, S.: Six Sigma diplomacy – the impact of Six Sigma on national patterns of corporate culture. Total Qual. Manag. Bus. Excell. **25**, 827–841 (2014)

Lean-Green 4.0: A Starting Point for an Assessment Model

Susana Duarte[1,2(✉)]

[1] UNIDEMI, Department of Mechanical and Industrial Engineering, NOVA School of Science and Technology, Universidade NOVA de Lisboa, 2829-516 Caparica, Portugal
scd@fct.unl.pt

[2] LASI, Laboratório Associado de Sistemas Inteligentes, 4800-058 Guimarães, Portugal

Abstract. Industry 4.0 offered the application of the advancing business operations with innovative digital technologies. With this new industrial era, management systems for example Lean and green management should incorporate the progress in digital technology. Lean and green management is deployed in all organizational areas and all types of industrial sectors, but it isn't yet understood how Lean and green practices will progress in this digitalization era. Companies must have a tool to evaluate the existing transformation level of Lean and green management. Therefore, this paper proposes a baseline framework to design an assessment model as regards to the implementation of Lean and green management in an Industry 4.0 environment. Different dimensions were identified namely: "leadership and strategy", "people", "process", "product", "customer", "supplier", "governance", and "technology". Several measurement items which are grouped into the dimensions are proposed to illustrate what can be measured in the current state within the industrial companies. Managers can adapt their businesses by knowing how to execute a Lean and green system in the new digitalization era. This research aims to contribute to the discussion of the relationships between these two subjects.

Keywords: Industry 4.0 · Lean · Green · Digitalization · Lean-green

1 Introduction

The well-known concepts of Lean and green management are based on continuous improvement, to eliminate all kinds of waste and use all kinds of resources in a more efficient way [1]. This approach allows organizations to pursue environmental efficiency alongside operational efficiency, making decisions that have a positive impact on the environment [2].

However, the recent evolution of the production and industrial process called Industry 4.0, and its related digital technologies have come to set a new course of new ways of creating customer value, and how organizations make products and deliver services today [3]. Through the integration and application of information and communication technologies, the business processes and engineering processes can be deeply integrated making

© IFIP International Federation for Information Processing 2023
Published by Springer Nature Switzerland AG 2023
O. McDermott et al. (Eds.): ELEC 2022, IFIP AICT 668, pp. 273–284, 2023.
https://doi.org/10.1007/978-3-031-25741-4_23

an environment intelligent [4]. Full automation and digitalization of systems allow an individual customer-oriented adaptation of products or services that will increase value-add for companies and customers. Both, the Lean and green management system, and Industry 4.0 are transversal themes crossing all parts of the industrial process. Several research works conduct analysis comparing Lean, green management, and Industry 4.0. Mayr et al. [5] stated that the Lean management system and I4.0 can coexist and support each other, stating Lean processes are regarded as a basis for the efficient and economic implementation of Industry 4.0. An opposite example is given by Enke et al. [6] who mentioned that digitization cannot replace the value-oriented approach of Lean production in processes, for example, the approach of continuous improvement through systematic problem-solving, the progress of employees' skills through defined goals, and on-site leadership. Although Bonilla et al. [7] point out several I4.0 characteristics that impact positively and negatively the environmental performance, the authors Enke et al. [6] mentioned that environmental/green management is still little explored in the I4.0 context.

Therefore, trade-offs can occur in the transition of Lean and green management to an I4.0 environment. To overcome these kinds of obstacles, new guidance and support are needed.

It is recognized that the assessment of Lean and green characteristics implementation will assist companies to become more efficient and competitive [8]. Also, the transition of the Lean and green management system to the new industrial era is something that is not well defined yet [1, 3].

To be developed from an analysis point of view of the company's business-level, new guidance and support are needed. Therefore, the purpose of this study is to bridge the gap in the current research in the Lean-green management system and the I4.0 environment, proposing a baseline model to evaluate that transition. This proposed framework is a starting point for the design of an assessment model.

This paper is organized as follows: in Sect. 2, a characterization of Lean and green management is presented and a brief review of literature on Industry 4.0 is illustrated in Sect. 3. In Sect. 4, a Lean and green 4.0 assessment framework is proposed considering the dimensions and several items to be assigned. Finally, some concluding remarks are drawn.

2 Lean-Green Management

Lean-green management is a system to help companies to improve their business performance [1]. Through the recent works [2, 9] it is possible to conclude that the importance given to Lean and green integrated management approaches is rising. The integrated approach is confirmed by several works [8–11]. The Lean and green approach are adopted alongside each other due to their synergetic characteristics and the resulting positive results and effects of their deployment in all organizational areas [9. 10, 11, 12]. In addition, John et al. [13] reinforce that the scope of this management approach includes multiple organizational areas, involving different processes, and revealing its adaptation to various sectors and business topics.

There are several frameworks where their integration is notorious. Duarte and Cruz-Machado [12] present a Lean and green framework to evaluate the organization through six different criteria: i) people, ii) leadership, iii) stakeholders, iv) strategic planning, v) processes and iv) results. According to the authors, these six criteria are interconnected and through continuous improvement it is possible to achieve better results in the way the organizations can reach a best-in-class structure [12]. Verrier et al. [10] developed, based on the "Lean house", a "Lean and green house" with three pillars: Lean, green, and human. For them, environmental and social factors are more evoked which proves the interest in the Lean and green approach at both, at the organizational and operational levels [10]. Salvador et al. [9] indicate an approach to the connection between Lean and green in five different organizational areas: i) product planning and design, ii) supply chain management, iii) quality management and performance, iv) organizational culture, and v) logistics. In their structured literature review, Farias et al. [2] considered Lean and green practices as enablers of performance outcomes and they could be the performance drivers of the Lean and green system. Another important point for this integration is mentioned by Munoz-Villamizar et al. [14] indicating that the success of Lean and green practices depends on employee participation, proper training, and the commitment of top management. Munoz-Villamizar et al. [14] adapted the classic "Lean house" proposing an extended Lean-green model adding several tools such as serious games, value stream mapping, overall equipment effectiveness, multi-objective optimization, and issues such as keeping the commitment from all members of the company, and production and environmental training programs. Ramos et al. [11] propose a method centered on a benchmarking methodology to evaluate the management aspects of people, information, products, suppliers, customers, and processes combining Lean management practices and cleaner production to achieve a more eco-efficient production.

The implementation of a Lean-green management system is important to put in action the right characteristics with the right principles giving more attention to their business and the value given to the customer. Table 1 presents several characteristics of the integration of Lean-green. The integration between Lean management and green management is indispensable, and it is expected that it will be evolved and adapt to the new trends that the new industrial era will require [8].

Table 1. Lean-green characteristics

References							
Lean-green characteristics	Verrier et al. [10]	Cabrita et al. [15]	Mittal et al. [16]	Duarte and Cruz-Machado [12]	Ramos et al. [11]	Rodrigues and Kumar [17]	Bhattacharya et al. [18]
Leadership participative and communication				X			X

(continued)

Table 1. (*continued*)

Lean-green characteristics	Verrier et al. [10]	Cabrita et al. [15]	Mittal et al. [16]	Duarte and Cruz-Machado [12]	Ramos et al. [11]	Rodrigues and Kumar [17]	Bhattacharya et al. [18]
References							
Management commitment and support							X
Employee involvement	X			X			X
Employee training and development				X	X		X
Problem-solving skills	X			X	X		X
Flexible workforce			X	X			
Organizational objectives and scope	X				X		
Customer value		X	X	X			
Cost reduction for all stakeholders		X					X
Customer satisfaction and loyalty	X			X		X	X
Supplier collaboration and involvement	X		X	X		X	X
Knowledge and information sharing				X	X	X	
Continuous improvement	X			X			X
Elimination/Tracking of Waste	X					X	X
Process technology		X				X	

3 Industry 4.0

I4.0 encompasses a variety of principles, methods, and technologies, to make production systems more autonomous, dynamic, flexible, and precise [4, 5]. The new business world with a new focus on digitalization is breaking down the traditional barriers of the industry [19]. By connecting systems, people, and objects, cyber-physical systems are created and allow higher flexibility and increased-on productivity [20]. Therefore, I4.0 and the related technological change, result in modifications that have impacts on organizations [20]. In fact, the dominating focus on I4.0 is on technological capabilities and digital transformation [21]. For Dillinger et al. [22] "I4.0 is a technological-oriented approach". However, the success of I4.0 technologies depends on several factors including selective supply of information, usability, approval of users, consideration of ethical, social, and legal impacts, and profitability [5].

For now, there is still a panoply of new opportunities and challenges allowing a new characterization of the assessment model. Muller et al. [23] considered the opportunities relevant for the I4.0 implementation and clustered them into categories like strategy, operations, environment, and people, competitiveness and future viability, organizational and production fit, and employee qualification and acceptance. Stock and Seliger [24] analysed the macro and micro perspectives of I4.0. To them, opportunities from a macro perspective are related to the business models and value creation networks. From a micro perspective, the opportunities are defined as equipment, human, organization, process, and product. Doh et al. [25] presented a model that assists in the implementation of the I4.0 concepts in an organization. The authors clustered the data by technology and, benefits and applications (this last considered the human-machine interaction, networking, and value-added). Schumacher et al. [21] proposed a maturity assessment model for I4.0 and extended the technology focus by including the organizational aspects. Their model has considered as basic dimensions of, i) products, ii) customers, iii) operations, and iv) technology, and as organizational dimensions of, v) strategy, vi) leadership, governance, viii) culture, and ix) people. Schumacher et al. [26] developed a maturity assessment model with 65 different items, which are grouped in eight dimensions: i) technology; ii) products; iv) customer and partners; iv) value creation processes; v) data and information; vi) corporate standards; vii) employees; and strategy and leadership. More recently, Wagire et al. [27] proposed in their Industry 4.0 maturity model seven different dimensions defined as i) organizational strategy; ii) people and culture; iii) industry 4.0 awareness; iv) industry 4.0 based technology; v) value chain and processes; vi) smart manufacturing technology; vi) product and services-oriented technology.

According to Ibarra et al. [19], the main requirements to face digitalization are: i) work organization, ii) standardization, iii) availability of products, iv) new business models, v) availability of skilled employees, vi) know-how protection, vii) research investment, viii) professional development and ix) legal frameworks.

Therefore, a digital cultural change is visible, and the management leadership plays a crucial role to achieve a successful change in industrial processes [20]. Digitalization not only involves technological progress and empowerment, but also the management prepared for such challenges [20]. In this environment, objects, machines, devices, people, and products communicate with each other. Therefore, many challenges are faced in an industry 4.0 implementation including technological challenges, economic challenges, scientific challenges, social problems, and political issues [28]. A representative sample of the several characteristics is compiled in Table 2.

Table 2. I4.0 Characteristics

References

Industry 4.0 characteristics	Schumacher et al. [21]	Muller et al. [23]	Ibarra et al. [19]	Mayr et al.[5]	Helming et al.[20]	Sony and Naik [29]	Wagire et al. [27]
Management support					X	X	X
Management competencies and methods	X					X	
Management transparency				X	X	X	
Employee training in new technology	X		X			X	X
Autonomy of employees	X			X			
ICT competencies of employees	X					X	X
New business models	X	X	X			X	
New value offers		X		X		X	
Decentralization of decision making			X			X	
Service orientation			X				
Customer orientation			X			X	X
Environmental impact reduction		X				X	
Resource allocation	X					X	
Avoiding waste				X	X	X	
Developing integral customer experiences			X			X	X
Cost reduction			X			X	X

(*continued*)

Table 2. (*continued*)

References							
Industry 4.0 characteristics	Schumacher et al. [21]	Muller et al. [23]	Ibarra et al. [19]	Mayr et al.[5]	Helming et al.[20]	Sony and Naik [29]	Wagire et al. [27]
Customer data	X		X			X	X
Process and products complexity			X	X		X	X
Real-time information			X			X	X
Individualization of products	X						
Digitalization of products	X					X	X
Standardized and transparent processes				X		X	X

In their work, Sony and Naik [29] mentioned that I4.0 includes every aspect of the organization, sector, or society. Indeed, they identify 10 critical success factors around the I4.0: i) organizational strategy; ii) top management support; iii) employees: iv) make your products or services smart; v) make efforts to digitize the supply chain; vi) digitize the organization; vii) change management; viii) project management; ix) sustainability [29]. Subsequently, these challenges create uncertainty about organizational capabilities and adequate management systems.

4   Lean-Green 4.0 Proposal Framework

The Lean-green management system can be a starting point for the I4.0 implementation [3]. There isn't a unique way to implement Lean and green practices [30], and to implement the requirements of I4.0 [19]. Mayr et al. [5] give an overview of the literature that supports the perception of the integration between Lean manufacturing and Industry 4.0: Lean manufacturing as an enabler for introducing I4.0 tools, or I4.0 tools as promoters of Lean manufacturing, or the positive synergies between them. This is strengthened by Pereira and Sachinanda [31] who mentioned that Lean and I4.0 are not synergetic, but they complement each other when applied in conjunction. Also, they indicate as an example that Lean manufacturing can impact I4.0 by automation. Undeniably, several works relative to the combination between lean manufacturing and I4.0 are encountered in literature [4, 5, 31]. Green in I4.0 is better considered because the allocation of resources such as products, materials, energy, and water can be realized in a more efficient way [24]. The latest technology developments and smart tools such as additive manufacturing, internet of things and services, cloud computing, cloud-based services, big data analytics, artificial intelligence, collaborative robots, additive manufacturing, artificial vision or augmented reality, and the human-machine interface allow a better understanding of customers' needs, improve the influence of Lean-green on processes and reinforces the entire network relationships [3, 19].

The integration of Lean and green management with the I4.0 approach was studied by many authors [1, 3, 8, 13, 14, 32]. The linkages between Lean and green characteristics and the I4.0 concepts were studied by Duarte and Cruz-Machado [3] through the subjects: manufacturing, logistics and supply, product and process design, product, customer, supplier, employee, information sharing, and energy. Also, John et al. [13] developed a conceptual model representing the integrated approach to Lean and green 4.0 which put in evidence the relation of drivers and design principles of Lean-green with I4.0 technologies and processes. Leong et al. [32] developed a model for the implementation of the Lean and green approach to solving dynamic industry problems associated with Industry 4.0. In their model, a Lean-green checklist was defined as the guideline to identify the performance indicators.

Based on the research background was consolidated and proposed the dimensions for the framework to evaluate the Lean and green implementation in I4.0 transformation (Fig. 1). These assessment models are examples of how organizations can be evaluated and indicates where improvement actions are needed.

Lean-green management		Industry 4.0	
Dimensions			
Duarte and Cruz-Machado [12]	Ramos et al. [11]	Schumacher et al. [21]	Schumacher et al. [26]
-Leadership -Strategic planning -People -Processes -Stakeholders -Results	-Management/ Responsibility -People -Information -Supplier/ Organization/Customer -Product Development -Production Process	-Products -Customers -Operations -Technology -Strategy -Leadership -Governance -Culture -People	-Technology -Products -Customer and partners -Value creation processes -Data and information -Corporate standards -Employees -Strategy and leadership

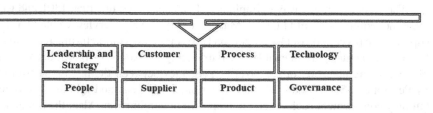

Fig. 1. The proposed dimensions to assign to the conceptual framework

For the proposed model, eight different dimensions were consolidated, namely: "leadership and strategy", "people", "process", "product", "customer", "supplier", "governance", and "technology". Such consolidation will serve as the basis for establishing the linkages between Lean and green management and the I4.0 approach. Each dimension will result in several items to evaluate the current state of the organization. Table 3 provides examples of items that can measure the state of organizations in terms of Lean and green 4.0.

Table 3. Dimensions and Measurement items for Lean-green 4.0

Lean-green 4.0 dimension	Measurement item	Ref.
Leadership and strategy	-Leadership with transparency in the communication -Virtual leadership only when it is possible -Management competencies -Company´s digital transformation vision and roadmap -Company with a flat hierarchy	Helming et al. [20]; Schumacher et al. [21]; Leong et al. [32]
People	-Employees' skills and qualifications -Employee training -Employee openness to digital transformation -Systematic problem-solving to improve digital transformation	Verrier et al. [10]; Ramos et al. [11]; Ibarra et al. [19]; Duarte and Cruz-Machado [12]
Product	-Product individualization considering eco-design -Innovation focus -Control of resource usage -Digitalization of products to integrate with other systems	Duarte and Cruz-Machado [3]; Mayr et al. [5]; Ramos et al. [11]; Ibarra et al. [19]; Helming et al. [20]; Duarte and Cruz-Machado [30]
Process	-Waste elimination and control -Environmental conscious design -Flexible workforce -Real-time monitoring and control -Digital information process -Process Technology	Duarte and Cruz-Machado [8]; Ramos et al. [11]; Helming et al.[20]; Schumacher et al. [21]; Schumacher et al. [26]; Duarte and Cruz-Machado [30]
Customer	-Digital channels -Customer focus/needs -Long-term relationship	Duarte et al. [1]; Duarte and Cruz-Machado [3]; Ibarra et al. [19]

(*continued*)

Table 3. (*continued*)

Lean-green 4.0 dimension	Measurement item	Ref.
Supplier	-Digital channels -Cross company collaboration -Sharing uncertainty -Knowledge sharing	Duarte et al. [1]; Duarte and Cruz-Machado [12]; Ibarra et al. [19]; Schumacher et al. [21]
Technology	-Information technology resources -Information technology integration -More transparent information sharing -Digital tools	Ibarra et al. [19]; Leong et al. [32]
Governance	-Legal requirements -Technological standards -Management Standards -Perception regarding the usefulness of I4.0 -Environmental impact	Duarte and Cruz-Machado [3]; Duarte and Cruz-Machado [8]; Duarte and Cruz-Machado [12]; Schumacher et al. [21]; Muller et al. [23]; Schumacher et al. [26]; Leong et al. [32]

5 Conclusion

The proposed framework is a starting point for the design of an assessment model, to guide the deployment of Lean and green management characteristics within the new industrial era. A model structure with dimensions and measurement items is identified. The model proposes eight different dimensions, namely: "leadership and strategy", "people", "process", "customer", "supplier", "governance", "product", and "technology". These dimensions will serve as the basis for establishing the linkages between Lean and green management and the I4.0 approach. In the line with the studies of Duarte and Cruz-Machado [12], Schumacher et al. [21], and Wagire et al. [27], this model should consider the weighting criteria for each dimension and related measurement items. This will go to help to evaluate the transition/implementation, reflecting what strategies, action plans, and improvements will have to be applied. So, it is intended that this model allows rigor in the transition process.

Thus, the main contribution of this study is to provide the research proposition, which can be developed and tested in future empirical studies. The model should present the new guidelines and weighting criteria to evaluate the level of transition. This model should be developed to systematically assess the industrial companies' state of development. Therefore, future research is needed. First, more measurement items can be introduced. After, it should be determined the importance of weights of dimensions and measurement items through a multi-criteria decision-making technique, for example, Analytic Hierarchy Process. Finally, the model should be empirically validated through qualitative multi-case study, in different industrial sectors.

Acknowledgment. Author acknowledge Fundação para a Ciência e a Tecnologia (FCT - MCTES) for its financial support via the project UIDB/00667/2020 (UNIDEMI).

References

1. Duarte, S., Cabrita, M.D.R., Cruz-Machado, V.: Business model, lean and green management and industry 4.0: a conceptual relationship. In: Xu, J., Ahmed, S. E., Cooke, F. L., Duca, G. (eds.) ICMSEM 2019. AISC, vol. 1001, pp. 359–372. Springer, Cham (2020). https://doi.org/10.1007/978-3-030-21248-3_27
2. Farias, L.M.S., Santos, L.C., Gohr, C.F., Oliveira, L.C., Amorim, M.H.S.: Criteria and practices for lean and green performance assessment: systematic review and conceptual framework. J. Clean. Prod. **218**, 746–762 (2019)
3. Duarte, S., Cruz-Machado, V.: Exploring linkages between lean and green supply chain and the industry 4.0. In: Xu, J., Gen, M., Hajiyev, A., Cooke, F. L. (eds.) ICMSEM 2017. LNMIE, pp. 1242–1252. Springer, Cham (2018). https://doi.org/10.1007/978-3-319-59280-0_103
4. Sanders, A., Elangeswaran, C., Wulfsberg, J.: Industry 4.0 implies lean manufacturing: research activities in industry 4.0 function as enablers for lean manufacturing. J. Ind. Eng. Manag. **9**(3), 811–833 (2016)
5. Mayr, A., et al.: Lean 4.0 - a conceptual conjunction of lean management and Industry 4.0. Procedia CIRP **72**, 622–628 (2018)
6. Enke, J., Glass, R., Kreb, A., Hambach, J., Tisch, M., Metternich, J.: Industry 40 – competencies for a modern production system. Procedia Manufact. **23**, 267–272 (2018)
7. Bonilla, S.H., Silva, H.R.O., Silva, M.T., Gonçalves, R.F., Sacomano, J.B.: Industry 4.0 and sustainability implications: a scenario-based analysis of the impacts and challenges. Sustainability **10**, 3740 (2018)
8. Duarte, S., Cruz-Machado, V.: An investigation of lean and green supply chain in the industry 4.0. In: Proceedings of the 2017 International Symposium on Industrial Engineering and Operations Management (IEOM), Bristol, UK, 24–25 July (2017)
9. Salvador, R., Piekarski, C.M., de Francisco, A.C.: Approach of the two-way influence between lean and green manufacturing and its connection to related organisational areas. Int. J. Prod. Manag. Eng. **5**(2), 73–83 (2017)
10. Verrier, B., Rose, B., Caillaud, E.: Lean and green strategy: the lean and green house and maturity deployment model. J. Clean. Prod. **116**, 150–156 (2016)
11. Ramos, A.R., Ferreira, J.C.E., Kumar, V., Garza-Reyes, J.A., Cherrafi, A.: A lean and cleaner production benchmarking method for sustainability assessment: a study of manufacturing companies in Brazil. J. Clean. Prod. **177**, 218–231 (2018)
12. Duarte, S., Cruz-Machado, V.: Green and lean implementation: an assessment in the automotive industry. Int. J. Lean Six Sigma **8**(1), 65–88 (2017)
13. John, L., Sampaio, M., Peças, P.: Lean & green on industry 4.0 context – contribution to understand L&G drivers and design principles. Int. J. Math. Eng. Manag. Sci. **6**(5), 1214–1229 (2021)
14. Munoz-Villamizar, A., Santos, J., Grau, P., Viles, E.: Toolkit for simultaneously improving production and environmental efficiencies. Cent. Eur. J. Oper. Res. **29**, 1219–1230(2020)
15. Cabrita, M.R., Duarte, S., Carvalho, H., Cruz-Machado, V.: Integration of lean, agile, resilient and green paradigms in a business model perspective: theoretical foundations. In: Proceedings of IFAC Conference on Manufacturing Modelling, Management and Control, pp. 1306–1311Troyes, France, IFAC- PapersOnLine (2016)

16. Mittal, V.K., Sindhwania, R., Kalsariyaa, V., Salrooa, F., Sangwanb, K.S., Singh, P.L.: Adoption of integrated lean-green-agile strategies for modern manufacturing systems. Procedia CIRP **61**, 463–468 (2017)

17. Rodrigues, V.S., Kumar, M.: Synergies and misalignments in lean and green practices: a logistics industry perspective. Prod. Plan. Control **30**(5–6), 369–384 (2019)

18. Bhattacharya, A., Nand, A., Castka, P.: Lean-green integration and its impact on sustainability performance: a critical review. J. Clean. Prod. **236**, 117697 (2019)

19. Ibarra, D., Ganzaraina, J., Igartuaa, J.I.: Business model innovation through Industry 4.0: a review. Procedia Manuf. **22**, 4–10 (2018)

20. Helming, S., Ungermann, F., Hierath, N., Stricker, N., Lanza, G.: Development of a training concept for leadership 4.0 in production environments. Procedia Manuf. **31**, 38–44 (2019)

21. Schumacher, A., Erol, S., Sihn, W.: A maturity model for assessing Industry 4.0 readiness and maturity of manufacturing enterprises. Procedia CIRP **52**, 161–166 (2016)

22. Dillinger, F., Bernhard, O., Reinhart, G.: Competence requirements in manufacturing companies in the context of lean 4.0. Procedia Cirp **106**, 58–63 (2022)

23. Müller, J.M., Kiel, D., Voigt, K.: What drives the implementation of industry 4.0? The role of opportunities and challenges in the context of sustainability. Sustainability **10**, 247 (2018)

24. Stock, T., Seliger, G.: Opportunities of sustainable manufacturing in industry 4.0. Procedia CIRP **40**, 536–541 (2016)

25. Doh, S.W., Deschamps, F., de Lima, E.P.: Systems integration in the lean manufacturing systems value chain to meet industry 4.0 requirements. In: Transdisciplinary Engineering: Crossing Boundaries, Borsato, M. et al. (Eds.), p. 4 (2016)

26. Schumacher, A., Nemeth, T., Sihn, W.: Roadmapping towards industrial digitalization based on an Industry 4.0 maturity model for manufacturing enterprises. Procedia CIRP **79**, 409–414 (2019)

27. Wagire, A.A., Joshi, R., Rathore, A.P.S., Jain, R.: Development of maturity model for assessing the implementation of Industry 4.0: learning from theory and practice. Prod. Plan. Control **32**(8), 603–622 (2021)

28. Zhou, K., Liu, T., and Zhou, L.: Industry 4.0: towards future industrial opportunities and challenge, In: Proceedings of 12th International Conference on Fuzzy Systems and Knowledge Discovery (2015)

29. Sony, M., Naik, S.: Critical factors for the successful implementation of Industry 4.0: a review and future research direction. Prod. Plan. Control **31**(10), 799–815 (2020)

30. Duarte, S., Cruz-Machado, V.: Green and lean supply-chain transformation: a roadmap. Prod. Plan. Control **30**(14), 1170–1183 (2019)

31. Pereira, C., Sachinanda, H.K.: Impact of Industry 4.0 technologies on lean manufacturing and organizational performance in an organization. Int. J. Interact. Design Manuf. **16**, 25–36 (2022)

32. Leong, W.D., et al.: Enhancing the adaptability: lean and green strategy towards the Industry revolution 4.0. J. Cleaner Prod. **273**, 122870 (2020)

Influence of the Lean Approach on Corporate Environmental Sustainability: A Case Study

Matteo Ferrazzi$^{(\boxtimes)}$ (ID), Stefano Frecassetti (ID), and Alberto Portioli Staudacher (ID)

Department of Management, Economics and Industrial Engineering, Politecnico Di Milano, via Lambruschini 4,b, Milan, Italy
`matteo.ferrazzi@polimi.it`

Abstract. The past few decades have witnessed relentless economic growth and increased human welfare due to extreme competition from companies globally and increasingly demanding users. This has led to extreme exploitation of natural resources, with dramatic consequences for the environment. In the coming years, the transition to more environmentally sustainable models must be central for companies. One possible solution for manufacturing companies, is to address environmental sustainability needs by developing a Lean approach. In recent years, the Lean approach to environmental sustainability has gained increasing attention, both from academia and companies. Nevertheless, there are still several aspects to investigate on the influence of the lean approach on environmental sustainability. This paper through the analysis of a case study of an Italian manufacturing company shows how the use of the lean approach, through the A3 problem solving framework, enabled the company to improve its sustainability performance. Specifically, the company was able to identify and eliminate non-value-added handling in its warehouse, decreasing forklift kilometrage and consequently limiting fuel consumption and CO_2 release.

Keywords: Lean approach · Lean management · A3 problem solving · Sustainability · Environmental sustainability · CO_2

1 Introduction

In recent decades, economic growth and increased human well-being around the world have come at the cost of rapidly increasing natural resource use. The debate has increasingly focused on how to reduce the use of raw materials and energy globally while keeping pace with a changing world [1, 2]. Today, the transition to more sustainable management solutions is a central topic for companies in all sectors. The concept of environmental sustainability must now be a priority for managers everywhere. Companies have been forced to rethink their management and operational strategies, seeking to remain competitive in the marketplace while at the same time reducing their impact on the environment [3, 4]. Among various solutions, one possible for manufacturing industries is to address environmental sustainability needs by developing a Lean approach [5, 6]. In recent years, the interaction between the Lean approach and environmental sustainability

O. McDermott et al. (Eds.): ELEC 2022, IFIP AICT 668, pp. 285–294, 2023.
https://doi.org/10.1007/978-3-031-25741-4_24

has gained more and more attention. Because of its rationale, which aims for production that optimizes resources and reduces waste, adopting a Lean approach is a solution that could push organizations to take advantage of a more sustainable rationale [7]. It is therefore interesting to investigate how lean methodology can be a tool for companies to improve their sustainable performance. The lean approach has among its fundamental pillars the reduction of waste, seeking to apply the vision of "doing more with less" [8]. The Lean Green approach is a current headline topic for both companies and academics. By its logic, the Lean approach is a solution that could prompt organizations to rethink their operations with the goal of embracing sustainability [9, 10]. Nevertheless, according to some authors, there is a need to better understand the compatibility and impact of lean initiatives on sustainability [11–13]. The literature review was crucial in trying to identify some still unclear aspects of the influence of the lean approach on environmental sustainability. The papers analyzed for the literature review clearly express that, the lean methodology has helped organizations achieve operational excellence and, in this way, achieve organizational goals such as profitability, efficiency, responsiveness, quality, and customer satisfaction [14, 15]. However, the effect of this approach on environmental performance is still unclear, as little empirical research has been conducted in this area. The literature review has shown that there is a positive influence of the lean approach, on environmental sustainability [16–18]. This influence, however, is not always manifested in the same way. In most of the cases studied, the influence of lean management is positive and brings benefits in terms of increased sustainable performance. For example, through the work of Garza-Reyes et al., 2018 [19], it is explained how five of the most important lean techniques (JIT, autonomy, kaizen/continuous improvement, total productive maintenance (TPM), and value stream mapping (VSM)), can influence four different environmental performances (material use, energy consumption, non-produced output, and pollutant release). This study shows that companies with the lean approach have seen most environmental performance improve. However, in some contexts the lean approach did not lead to the desired results, in terms of environmental sustainability. An analysis of another study by Dieste et al. 2019 [20], through a review of existing literature, shows that the impacts of lean practices do not always have a positive effect on sustainable performance. In fact, a portion of the analyzed studies claimed that the use of some lean techniques has a negative impact on the sustainability of companies. In addition, the identification and resolution of problems related to environmental sustainability is a topic that has yet to be studied. The lean methodology over the years has developed a framework capable, through sequential steps, of targeting and solving specific problems in even very complex environments [21, 22]. The framework is known as the "A3 model."

It is clear from the literature review that there is a lack of empirical studies that confirm the positive impact of the Lean approach on sustainable performance. The main objective of this research is, through the analysis a case study, to investigate the influence of lean on environmental sustainability and how this influence manifests itself. Specifically to fill the gap in today's literature, this paper seeks to answer the question, "If and how Lean approach is able to positively impact sustainable performance?." Specifically, this paper seeks to understand how the effect of the lean approach, using the A3 problem-solving framework, affects a company's sustainable environmental performance. As anticipated, this research is based on the analysis of a single case study of an Italian manufacturing company that, thanks to the A3 model, managed to optimize its internal logistics movements, reducing fuel consumption and consequently CO_2 emissions. The following paragraphs will present the case study, how the company tackled the problem by following the steps of the A3 model, and finally showing the results obtained.

2 Methodology

The case study proposed in this paper, considers an Italian manufacturing company, a leader in the production of tapes for the automotive sector, professional craftsmen, and industry, as well as for end users. The core business focuses on packaging and wrapping solutions, and in industrial production, on products for wrapping and fixing wiring harnesses and surface protection in the automotive industry, as well as for splicing, sealing, and repairing. The first warehouse is the largest and is mainly dedicated to raw materials used by all types of machines, while semi-finished products, packaging materials and resins are stored in the second. The case study analysis focused on material flows in the plant to increase logistical efficiency, optimize space, reduce transfer times, and increase operator safety. The company also has environmental sustainability as its first goal and consequently pushes everyone to work toward building green and lean operations. The main objective of the analysis in this case study is to understand how the 'use of a lean approach can help increase sustainable environmental performance for the company. Specifically, the company wants to reduce fuel consumption related to nonvalue-added movements made by forklifts.

2.1 Application of the Lean Approach through the A3 Model

The problem analyzed in the case study was addressed using the lean approach of the A3 problem solving framework. The A3 methodology is a structured approach to problem solving and continuous improvement, first used at Toyota and typically used by lean manufacturing professionals. It has been used by various cases in the literature [19, 20]. The following will explore how the company addressed the issue of environmental sustainability by going through the PDCA (plan, do, check, act) steps of the A3 model (see Fig. 1).

2.2 Problem Statement and Problem Background

Movements within the warehouses were the focus of the analysis because forklift movements are more frequent than in other areas of the plant. Based on the analysis of material receiving data, layouts, infrastructure, and warehouse strategies, the area where to go for change was identified. There is a lack of standardization in the raw materials warehouse, as positions for each product are not assigned in an optimized manner. Therefore, because of this problem, forklifts must travel a greater distance than required to locate/pick up products from their assigned positions. Due to the unavailability of storage racks, forklifts must make many extra movements. The company is aware that standardized material handling procedures and new warehouse strategies can generate

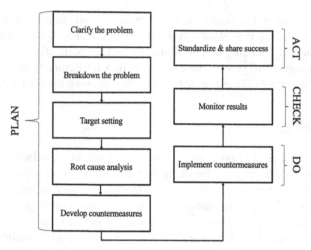

Fig. 1. A3 problem solving framework: PDCA steps

benefits if well utilized, so it has become a priority to find a way for all operators to execute the change with a unified approach, which is reflected in a decrease in forklift miles traveled and consequently a reduction in CO_2. Movements in the raw materials warehouse are more complex and have more room for improvement in terms of forklift operations, so the company decided to take the first corrective actions for environmental sustainability in this specific area. Next, to identify in greater detail the problem to be attacked, an ABC analysis was carried out on the inventory in the warehouse. ABC analysis is an inventory management technique that determines the value of items in inventory based on their importance to the business. ABC analysis ranks items based on demand, cost, and risk, and inventory managers group items into classes based on these criteria. This helps business managers understand which items are most critical to their organization's financial success. The company conducted the ABC analysis in terms of the number of movements in inventory considering the total movements made from January 2021 to March 2022. The analysis showed that 3.37% of the material was responsible for 70.16% of the number of movements. This analysis shows that there are very few categories of materials that contribute to most movements in the plant, but the strategy is the same for almost all materials. Once the company identified which materials have the greatest impact on the total warehouse movement, it mapped the non-value-added movements by dividing them into the five different categories, estimating for each the average number of kilometers traveled by forklifts (see Fig. 2).

- Extra movements in inbound logistics: In receiving goods into the warehouse, raw materials are temporarily stored in unsuitable locations due to limited warehouse space. Total Non-value-adding distance travelled = 1793 km/Year
- Extra movements to place goods on shelves: due to poor selectivity in the warehouse, forklifts make extra movements to select the desired material. Total Non-value-adding distance traveled = 433.47 km per year

- Extra movements to place goods for next shift: given the limited space available in both production departments and the warehouse, materials needed for the next shift are left in the aisles, causing extra movements. Total Non- value-added distance = 1802 km per year
- Incorrect/missing placement of identification labels on materials: mishandling of material labeling leads to avoidable handling. Total non-value-added distance = 624.5 km per year
- Non-optimized warehousing strategy: Material is randomly assigned to locations based on available free space. A partial strategy exists, but it is not formulated in an optimized manner. No ABC analysis is performed to define the material strategy. Total non-value-added distance = 4000 km per year

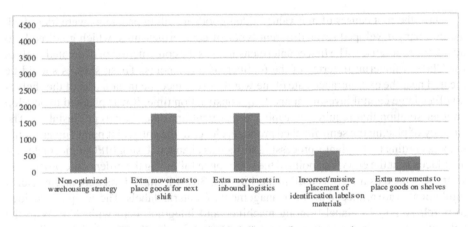

Fig. 2. Non value added distance (kms per year)

2.3 Targets

Once the problems related to material handling in the raw materials warehouse and the associated miles to the year of nonvalue-added handling were identified, the company decided to set targets for improvement. The quantitative targets defined by the company were essential both to have objective feedback on the improvement project and to always have a trail to follow when implementing countermeasures. The company estimated, for the five categories of moves explained above, a reduction in km per year ranging from 60% to 80% for must-have targets, up to 95% for nice-to- have targets. The company estimates to decrease the number of kilometers traveled in a year from 5770 to 7129, going to significantly impact the decrease of CO_2 emitted by the forklifts.

2.4 Devolving Countermeasures, Implementing, and Monitoring

The company after identifying the targets for improvement focused on analyzing the root causes related to the problems identified. The causes identified below are related to the reduction of non-value-added movement.

The causes are:

- Goods for the next shift are stored in the main aisles of the warehouse.
- Forklifts move around materials due to mislabeling.
- There is no interconnection in the forklifts.
- The efficiency of forklifts depends on the skill level of the operators.
- Material is not taken directly to the shelves after unloading.
- There are no assigned spaces for products.

Once the root causes of non-value-added goods handling problems were identified, the company developed seven different types of countermeasures, which go directly to attack the root causes. The first countermeasure was the construction of dedicated shelves for Class A material in terms of the number of movements. These shelves should be located near the exit/entrance gate of the warehouse. Since the installation of the shelves involves large capital investment and long construction time, it was planned to develop another solution that requires no capital investment until the shelves are installed. The strategy of placing the semi-finished products closer to the entry/exit point and grouping them according to the plant's processing shifts was changed. Using FIFO logic, materials are placed near the entry/exit point of the warehouse following the order of the processing shifts (Grouped as materials used in the 1st, 2nd, 3rd, 4th shift). Other countermeasures implemented are related to the mismanagement of material labels. The company decided to purchase portable label printing machines and integrate them with SAP. With the help of this machine, operators would be able to affix labels to materials while they are still inside the truck and take them directly to their assigned spaces. The second countermeasure is to sensitize suppliers to put the material in the trucks so that the labels are facing outward to facilitate unloading by the operators. In addition, the material is only labeled on one side, so when the forklift picks up a unit of material, there is a 50% chance that the label is on the other side, so the forklift must move to pick it up. As a countermeasure, affixing labels on both sides eliminates unwanted movement of the forklift around the material to handle it. To facilitate more complex unloading and placement of materials in the warehouse, forklifts should be equipped with GPS for better interconnection. If a forklift needs another forklift, the operator can send a request to the system, and it will be received by the nearest operator. If the latter rejects it, it will be passed on to the next nearest operator. In addition, the provision of single-ear headsets to the forklift operator would reduce the non-value-added time he or she spends answering calls with the forklift still on. Finally, as a last countermeasure, the company developed new warehouse strategies by optimizing handling. For the distance traveled to be minimized, materials with high handling must be kept closer to the point of entry/exit. Therefore, the company decided to place materials that move most with high frequency near the entry/exit point, ensuring that units of the same size remain grouped together.

Table 1. Relationship between problem, root cause and countermeasure

Problem	Root cause	Countermeasure
Non-optimized warehousing strategy	Goods for the next shift are stored in the main aisles of the warehouse	Changing warehouse strategy
Extra movements to place goods for next shift	Forklifts move around materials due to mislabeling	In-ear headphones
Extra movements in inbound logistics	There is no interconnection in the forklifts	Putting labels of both sides of the material
¢Incorrect/missing placementof identification labels on materials	The efficiency of forklifts depends on the skill level of the operators	Installing the labelling station near the unloading area
Extra movements to place goods on shelves	Material is not taken directly to the shelves after unloading	Changing the strategy of how to prepare the material for the shift
	There are no assigned spaces for products	Installing shelves
		InstallingGPSfor interconnectivity of the forklifts
		Efficient training modules for the forklift operators

As can be seen from the above table (see Table 1), there is a clear link between problem, root cause and countermeasure. Finally, the countermeasures to be implemented were classified according to two criteria, commitment, and impact. As a result, the seven countermeasures were clustered into four different groups. In this way, the company was able to define the priorities, resources to be invested, and the timeline for implementing the countermeasures (see Fig. 3).

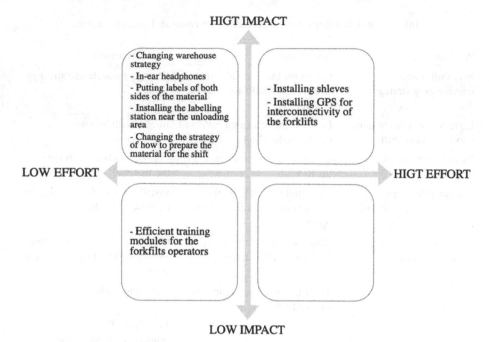

HIGT IMPACT

- Changing warehouse strategy
- In-ear headphones
- Putting labels of both sides of the material
- Installing the labelling station near the unloading area
- Changing the strategy of how to prepare the material for the shift

- Installing shleves
- Installing GPS for interconnectivity of the forklifts

LOW EFFORT ⟷ HIGT EFFORT

- Efficient training modules for the forkfilts operators

LOW IMPACT

Fig. 3. Countermeasure implementation matrix

3   Results

The company using the A3 framework was able to identify several countermeasures to limit non-value-added forklift movements. The company identified possible root causes and developed countermeasures to eliminate each of the identified problems. A total of seven countermeasures have been developed. The company estimates that through their implementation it aims to save about 17,000 to 21,000 euros per year and between 5700 and 7100 km per year, so perfectly in line with the targets shown above. In addition, two of the countermeasures include only changing the warehouse strategy and do not require any capital investment. About 40–50% of the total savings come from these solutions. While all other countermeasures require a capital investment, which the company will pay for because it is aware of the huge impact it will have on fuel savings and consequently on the company's sustainable performance. In fact, the company has been very pleased that it has met its goal of reducing CO_2 emissions through this lean problem-solving approach. The company estimates that the project will be able to reduce the carbon footprint created by the handling of the forklifts, aiming to reduce CO_2 emissions from 14 to 10 tons. Also, as a side effect, some of the countermeasures have also had an impact on increasing the safety of forklift operators. The effectiveness of these countermeasures is difficult to quantify, but the feedback received from operators and the logistics manager is very positive.

4 Conclusion

The lean approach proved essential in addressing and achieving the sustainability goals the company was aiming for. Through this satisfying project, the company gained awareness of the impact of its internal logistics processes with the goal of improving its environmental performance. Using the lean approach, through the adoption of the A3 methodology, the company managed to reduce the miles traveled by forklifts in its warehouse. Starting with the goal of improving sustainable environmental performance, the company using the A3 methodology was guided throughout the development of the project. The use of the A3 problem solving framework allowed, starting with a broad and ambitious goal of identifying and defining a concrete problem, to measure its AS- IS performance, identify the root causes of the problem, and develop tailor-made countermeasures. This approach had a direct effect on the reduction of nonvalue-added forklift movements, and consequently to a reduction in fuel consumption, reducing CO_2 emissions. In addition, as a result of this experience, the company has become more aware of environmental sustainability aspects. In fact, the results obtained allow workers to be more aware of the importance of their impact on the sustainable performance of the entire organization and the positive impact that can be achieved through lean thinking, generating greater motivation for their work. This article helps to show a real-life case in which lean thinking is applied with the goal of solving corporate issues related to the environment, and how the lean approach has affected the company's sustainable performance. The results obtained and the growing interest in environmental issues of both management and operators show that there is a positive influence of the lean approach on environmental sustainability issues. Through the spread of lean culture, the company in the future can continue to address issues related to environmental sustainability. The spread of lean culture is manifested in small, targeted continuous improvement projects with specific goals to measure performance and project success. Managers could benefit from this research to understand the simplicity and usefulness of using A3 methodology as a lean tool to address problems related to environmental sustainability. In conclusion through this paper important implications can be formulated for managers to develop a deeper and richer understanding of lean as a tool to achieve better environmentally sustainable performance, and to help them formulate more effective strategies for its use. The limitations of this paper's research are related to the use of a single case study; in fact, more empirical evidence studied in different contexts is needed to understand in depth the influence of lean approaches on environmental sustainability. Future research will seek to explore this issue further by outlining how the influence of the lean approach manifests itself on environmental sustainability, and how its benefit can be applied in other business contexts.

References

1. Garza-Reyes, J.A.: Lean and green – a systematic review of the state of the art literature. J. Clean. Prod. **102**, 18–29 (2015)
2. Kundu, K., Rossini, M., Portioli-Staudacher, A.: Analysing the impact of uncertainty reduction on WLC methods in MTO flow shops. Prod. Manuf. Res. **6**, 328–344 (2018)

3. Azadegan, A., Patel, P.C., Zangoueinezhad, A., Linderman, K.: The effect of environmental complexity and environmental dynamism on lean practices. J. Oper. Manag. **31**, 193–212 (2013)
4. Lindahl, P., Robèrt, K.H., Ny, H., Broman, G.: Strategic sustainability considerations in materials management. J. Clean. Prod. **64**, 98–103 (2014)
5. Sobek, D.K., II.: Understanding A3 Thinking 1(edn). Sobek (2022)
6. Shook, J., Womack, J.: Managing to Learn: Using the A3 Management Process to Solve Problems, Gain Agreement, Mentor and Lead (Pap/Chrt ed.). Lean Enterprises Inst Inc. (2008)
7. Gimenez, C., Sierra, V., Rodon, J.: Sustainable operations: their impact on the triple bottom line. Int. J. Prod. Econ. **140**(1), 149–159 (2012)
8. Womack, J.P, Johnes, D.T, Roos, D.: The Machine that changed the world (1990)
9. Abreu, M.F., Alves, A.C., Moreira, F.: Lean-green models for eco-efficient and sustainable production. Energy **137**, 846–853 (2017)
10. Silva, S., Sá, J. C., Silva, F. J. G., Ferreira, L. P., Santos, G.: Lean green—the importance of integrating environment into lean philosophy—a case study. In: Rossi, M., Rossini, M., Terzi, S. (eds.) ELEC 2019. LNNS, vol. 122, pp. 211–219. Springer, Cham (2020). https://doi.org/10.1007/978-3-030-41429-0_21
11. Sartal, A., Martinez-Senra, A.I., Cruz-Machado, V.: Are all lean principles equally eco-friendly? A panel data study. J. Clean. Prod. **177**, 362–370 (2018)
12. Bai, C., Satir, A., Sarkis, J.: Investing in lean manufacturing practices: an environmental and operational perspective. Int. J. Prod. Res. **57**(4), 1037–1051 (2018)
13. Govindan, K., Khodaverdi, R., Jafarian, A.: A fuzzy multi criteria approach for measuring sustainability performance of a supplier based on triple bottom line approach. J. Clean. Prod. **47**, 345–354 (2013)
14. Shah, R., Ward, P.T.: Lean manufacturing: context, practice bundles, and performance. J. Oper. Manag. **21**(2), 129–149 (2002)
15. Rossini, M., Cifone, F.D., Kassem, B., Costa, F., Portioli-Staudacher, A.: Being lean: how to shape digital transformation in the manufacturing sector. J. Manuf. Technol. Manag. **32**, 239–259 (2021)
16. EPA. Lean Manufacturing and the Environment 2003
17. EPA. The Lean and Environment Toolkit. Washington D.C 2007
18. Souza, J., Alves, J.: Lean integrated management system: a model for sustainability improvement. DEStech Trans. Eng. Technol. Res. icpr (2018)
19. Garza-Reyes, J.A., Kumar, V., Chaikittisilp, S., Tan, K.H.: The effect of lean methods and tools on the environmental performance of manufacturing organisations. Int. J. Prod. Econ. **200**, 170–180 (2018)
20. Dieste, M., Panizzolo, R., Garza-Reyes, J.A., Anosike, A.: The relationship between lean and environmental performance: Practices and measures. J. Clean. Prod. **224**, 120–131 (2019)
21. Rossini, M., Audino, F., Costa, F., Cifone, F.D., Kundu, K., Portioli-Staudacher, A.: Extending lean frontiers: a kaizen case study in an Italian MTO manufacturing company. Int. J. Adv. Manuf. Technol. **104**(5–8), 1869–1888 (2019). https://doi.org/10.1007/s00170-019-03990-x
22. Torri, M., Kundu, K., Frecassetti, S., Rossini, M.: Implementation of lean in IT SME company: an Italian case. Int. J. Lean Six Sigma **12**, 944–972 (2021)

Lean in Services

Enhancement of a Data Management System using Design for Lean Six Sigma

Roisin Eaton[1], John Noonan[1], and Olivia McDermott[2](✉)

[1] University of Limerick, Limerick, Ireland
{Roisin.Eaton,John.Noonan}@ul.ie
[2] University of Galway, Galway, Ireland
Olivia.McDermott@universityofgalway.ie

Abstract. The purpose of this study is to outline a transformation model that can help commercial enterprises to design, develop and launch a transformation programme of change for their data management system applying Design for Lean Six Sigma - Define-Measure-Analyse-Design-Verify methodology. Design for Lean Six Sigma methodology was chosen to develop/implement a five-year roadmap to enhance a data management system to effectively predict and react to customers' needs and competitors' actions and survive in a constantly changing financial services industry. Companies seek to enhance their level of data quality to comply with regulatory requirements, reduce uncertainty and improve the quality of decision-making with more accurate and timely data available. The model used conveys how the organisation will implement and sustain a standardised data management system to reduce the Cost of Poor-Quality data by 27.33%, decrease the electronic data retention cycle time to a maximum of 7 years, previously stored long-term, and achieve/sustain a 90% deletion target for emails older than seven years. Data deemed nonvalue added does not contribute to satisfying customer requirements, therefore Design for Six Sigma methodology was used as a vehicle to systematically identify, manage and delete same. This study is one of the first studies on Design for Lean Six Sigma application in a financial data management system.

Keywords: Data management system · Financial services · Design for Lean Six Sigma · DMADV · Continuous Improvement

1 Introduction

Financial service organisations operate in a heavily regulated industry and have fire fought continuously increasing their data storage capacities to accommodate storage of all data. However, in 2018, there was a strict requirement passed under Article 5(1) of the European General Data Protection Regulation (GDPR) for companies to only retain data for as long as necessary, regarding the purpose for which it was collected. Data should be

© IFIP International Federation for Information Processing 2023
Published by Springer Nature Switzerland AG 2023
O. McDermott et al. (Eds.): ELEC 2022, IFIP AICT 668, pp. 297–306, 2023.
https://doi.org/10.1007/978-3-031-25741-4_25

leveraged as an organisations strategic asset to reduce uncertainty, improve performance and profitability by learning or gaining insights from correct, comprehensive, consistent data to improve business processes and for analysing customer needs [1]. Organisations that increase the level of data quality improve the quality of decision-making, reducing uncertainty to provide more timely and accurate results [2–4], thus are better equipped to apply a reactive approach to both customer and competitors' actions more efficiently and effectively [5].

This research sets out to improve upon the current data management approach many companies adopt whereby only Value-add (VA) data is retained. The purpose of the study is to conceive and implement an data enhancement program with Lean Six Sigma tools and techniques using the Define for Lean Six Sigma (DFLSS) phases of Define-Measure-Analyse-Design-Verify (DMADV) methodology, which could potentially be used by other commercial businesses to decrease data cycle time, cost of poor quality (COPQ)data and enhance data integrity and control. For enhanced operational efficiency, the ultimate objective of any organisational Information Management Program is to have all data classified as Non- Value Add (NVA) and removed/deleted. Fulfilment of that vision successfully, entails the ongoing management of current, new and historic data over time to have automatic removal/deletion of unnecessary stored items. This research will combine Lean philosophy to determine the current state and eliminate waste and Six Sigma to achieve the future state and validate findings by focusing on improvement areas using statistical analysis. Additionally, De Koning, Does, and Bisgaard [5] argues financial service organisations need to manage culture to encourage process innovation/improvements. The researcher will seek to investigate the most suitable culture required for implementing a change program successfully.

2   Literature Review

Turban and Volonino [1] posit data management is one of the most difficult challenges facing organisations. With increasing global competition many companies are inspired to consider enhancing quality expectations, eliminate waste and prioritise customer satisfaction [6–13]. Heckl, Moormann and Rosemann [14] claims the catalyst for financial organisations seeking transparent processes with zero defects at lower costs was initiated by new regulatory requirements, to exploit unforeseen market opportunities and to increase customer satisfaction.

Many financial service organisations are focused on hard numbers i.e., profit margins, often losing sight of what is important to the customer. However, Turban and Volonino [1] argue that profitability increases when employees use data to increase revenues, reduce expenses or a combination of both. Nonetheless, Kumar [15] proposes data is increasing with the evolution of new technology requiring increased storage capacities and extra costs to facilitate same. Additionally, companies that move paperless need to manage the increase of data subsequently stored electronically in their cloud and servers. De Mast [16] suggests most organisations have no organisational infrastructure, plan or budget in place for managing incremental innovations. Lean Six Sigma (LSS) provides an infrastructure to 'improve operational efficiency and effectiveness' [17–19] combining the strengths of Lean and Six Sigma. De Koning, Does, and Bisgaard [5] claims Six Sigma facilitates the measurement of process performance while Lean enhances flow visibility. The main challenge facing financial service organisations attempting LSS implementations is the lack of research available which deters learning from and implementing same [14, 20–23]. Alblooshi, Shamsuzzaman, Khoo, Rahim, and Haridy [24] argue there is little or no evidence of the sustainability of LSS benefits in areas such as customer satisfaction, financial outcomes and process excellence. Francis, Bessant and Hobday [25] claims risks and challenges are inevitable for any organisation implementing radical change. According to Qiu, Gai, Zhao and Liu [26] with more data and more processing comes greater risk hence scrutinising information and demanding it meets certain criteria are paramount to achieving sustainable organisational performance. Financial service organisations need to focus on increasing productivity, increasing efficiency, reducing operational expenses and focusing on value adding activities to cope with change [18]. However Duarte Montgomery, Fowler, and Konopka [27] argues the success and failure of LSS is dependent on how and where it is applied. Many organisations fail to achieve the real benefits and anticipated results from LSS implementation [28, 29]. Many studies prove that poor, incomplete, delayed or lost information is the most serious quality problem [30–32]. A concerning statistic proposed by Redman [33] and Haug, Zachariassen, and Van Liempd [34] highlight the impacts of poor data quality in large companies can affect revenue by an average of 10 percent. On the contrary, English [30] estimated the costs of poor-quality data accounts to 10 to 25 percent of revenue. Redman [35] claims an estimated 5% of data found in companies are of poor quality and Malcolm [36] posits the average anticipated Cost of Poor Quality (COPQ) data in companies comprise of 10% of revenues. Low quality data may result in loss of revenue, waste of money, loss of opportunity and a tarnished image [37]. On the other hand, Keenan [38] claims financial service organisations are weak in information processing in comparison to other industries, when this should be considered a critical core competency requiring an integrated, centralised data infrastructure capable of storing far higher volumes of data than firms have held historically.

3 Methodology

A case study approach was used and within that a DFLSS methodology. As part of the DFSS methodology the DMADV approach was utilised. The problem in scope in this single case study was to identify and improve upon the current data management process and apply disciplined steps to identify and resolve the key factors/noise variables influencing the primary key performance indicator (KPI), data stored. To outline the problem the researcher gathered output (data) of the process retrieved from the organisation's Microsoft Azure portal and then input and analysed data using JMP software to understand process stability, explore patterns of variation and determine if the process was improving/deteriorating over time. Figure 1 visualises the primary problem/effect on the output of the process when the company migrated paperless in September 2020 which significantly increased electronic data stored by 60%. While the mean of data deleted remained stable at an average of 64,605 artefacts per month, the problem accelerated when the mean of data stored on the company cloud/servers increased from 115,002 emails/documents monthly to 176,712 in September 2021. With electronic data forecast to expand by 50% respectively over the next two years, the current data management system required a reactive approach to delete NVA data to meet the needs of a rapidly increasing data estate.

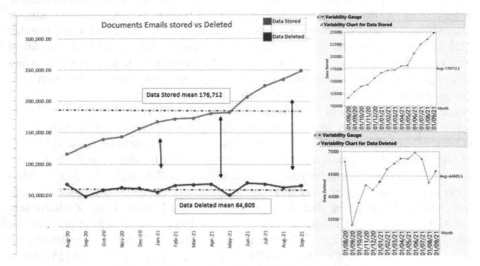

Fig. 1. Data stored vs data deleted in the business

Therefore, the leadership recognised the importance of implementing a systematic approach to begin downsizing the continuously increasing data infrastructure in the company, thus formulated a cross- functional core team required for the rollout of a five-year/tranche Data Enhancement Program.

The process improvement manager, as part of the core team, recommended the method proposed by Pepper and Spedding [40], integrating Lean and Six Sigma as a comprehensive approach for the process improvement. Moreover Pepper and Spedding [40] argue if Lean is implemented without Six Sigma, tools are underutilised to gain full potential to solve problems whereas Six Sigma provides a framework to implement tools systematically. A Lean approach focuses on the flow of a product through its value stream identifying NVA steps in processes with the objective to streamline the flow and eliminate waste [41]. Six Sigma then provides a systematic improvement methodology to achieve the future state by focusing on the improvement areas.

Ganesh and Marathe [42] posit that there is an abundance of research available on the successful applications of LSS in the manufacturing industry, however academic research and publications are lacking for LSS efforts in banking and financial service organisations. Furthermore, Heckl, Moormann and Rosemann [14] propose LSS has only been implemented in the financial services sector over the last decade. Heckl, Moormann and Rosemann [14] reported nine out of ten companies use Define-Measure-Analyse-Implement-Control (DMAIC) methodology for process improvements. Having synthesised the literature research and conducted interviews on previous transformation programs, DMADV was recommended by the researcher as the optimal methodology for the program, as this approach is most suitable when a process is not in existence, and one needs to be developed right first time. However, DMADV approach has been less frequently applied to financial services [43, 44], thus there is little, or no research documented on it. The main reason for applying DMADV methodology to process improvements is that it applies a systematic and proactive approach to foresee any potential issues to implement preventative measures and controls for the design and verification phases with LSS methodology and tools. DMADV involves understanding the customer requirements before deploying the improvement, which are mostly expressed qualitatively. Due to the intangible nature of services, service delivery and process performance are often difficult to measure, relying on the customer interaction and feedback to determine the quality of the service. Note the customer in the Information Management Program were the internal staff. The explicit and implicit wants and needs of the customer were identified throughout the program with staff engagement surveys, feedback and issues reported. Each phase of the program ended with a toll gate review approved by the project sponsor to facilitate review of progress of the previous phase and approve progression to the next phase. The DMADV phases, tools and their purposes used by the researcher to support the core team understand and achieve the program objectives systematically will be described below (Table 1).

Table 1. Methodology, tools and techniques applied to the Information Management Program

Phase of DMADV	Phase Deliverables	Tool/Technique applied	Reason for tool/technique
Define	To define project charter/resources before scope/objectives of the DMADV program.	Interviews and engagement survey with the core team	To determine acceptance for the transformation at the outset of the program.
		SIPOC	Identifies the key inputs/outputs, process and stakeholders to support scope.
		Pareto Diagram	Assists to identify the most significant opportunities to target/prioritise in the program.
		Project Charter	Outlines the objectives, scope, and deliverables of the program.
		House of Quality	Determines customer requirements/Critical to Quality (CTQ) attributes.
Measure	To understand business requirements/customer requirements.	Brainstorming	Techniques used to support the program.
		Histograms, Statistical Process Control Charts	Displays the program output investigating process stability/capability.
		Cause-and-effect diagram	Supports brainstorming outlining the potential process factors effecting the response.
Analyse	Analyse the options designing the concept and high-level design for the program	Process Maps	Provides a visual to outline the process.
		Histograms, Statistical Process Control Charts	Displays the program output investigating process stability/capability.
		Work Breakdown Structure	Breaks down the program into components that will be addressed in the verify phase.
Design	Develop a detailed design, control plan and roadmap for the program	Histograms, Statistical Process Control Charts	Displays the program output investigating process stability/capability.
		Gantt Chart	Establishes a sequenced timeline and anticipated roadmap for the program.
		Risk Assessment	To determine potential risks prior to rollout of the program.
		Roadmap Design	Lists the key transformation steps for the program.
		Program Communication Plan	Mediums of communication to inform all stakeholders of progress/actions.
Verify	Test, verify, design with pilot group rolling out company-wide when pilot groups proves successful.	Histograms, Statistical Process Control Charts	Displays the program output investigating process stability/capability.
		Staff engagement survey	To determine acceptance for the transformation at the end of the program.
		Lessons learned	Documentation from the core team and pilot group to improve other projects in the organisation.

For DMADV to be carried out effectively, extensive knowledge of JMP software assisted to measure progress by conducting statistical analysis in closing the gap between current/new data classified for automatic deletion (tranche 1) and historic data (tranche 2). Additionally, Brainstorming and Kaizen workshops were held with the core team and pilot users throughout the program.

4 Results

Data investigation, analysis and interpretation formed the basis for this study. The impact of the implementation process was to establish a design for a simplified, streamlined and stable practice to convert data into information indifferent to noise variables. According to Holsapple and Joshi [45] data is a collection of facts, measurements and statistics whereas information is organised or processed data that are timely and accurate.

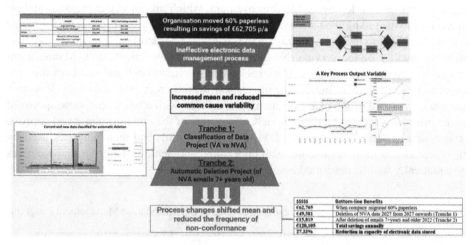

Fig. 2. Process improvement and impact to key process output variable

The bottom-line benefits of €128,105 savings per year, detailed in Fig. 2 targeted and achieved in the program to date consist of:

- €62,705 savings were achieved on direct and indirect print costs (paper, print and maintenance costs, lead time, staff costs for storage/retrieval/transport and Shred It) when the company migrated paperless.
- After completion of tranche 1 of the program, €49,581 are the anticipated cost savings through the classification of all new/future data processed in the company enabling automatic deletion of NVA data from 2027 onwards.

Despite this, there were also benefits achieved that were not originally targeted from the program. A standardised approach was implemented for data management companywide. The company can now apply a reactive approach to customers, competitors and market opportunities with VA data available when required for decision-making. A control plan was developed for managers of departments in scope, to monitor emails their staff stored/deleted aged 7 to 30 years, and flag when capacity of VA data exceeded 10% during the pilot phase to ensure optimal performance was maintained. Data analysis from the pilot phase conveyed only 6% of data was categorised as VA and archived for long- term retention (Fig. 3).

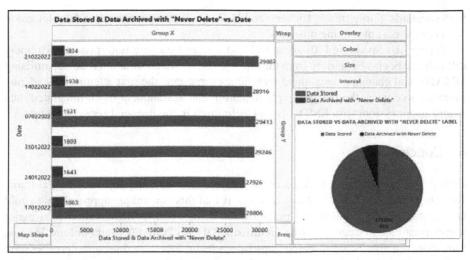

Fig. 3. Bar chart/Pie chart of data stored vs data labelled "Never Delete" for long-term retention

5 Discussion

This research conveys how to design and implement an integrated company-wide transformation program using DMADV methodology. It conveys the successful utilisation of LSS principles and methodologies to design and implement a five-year data transformation roadmap for a global company in the financial services sector. Fang and Zhang [47] argue traditional data management approaches distributes data across systems for specific functions, lacking a seamless holistic view, forcing companies to firefight installing custom cloud and archive solutions to accommodate same. DMADV was the chosen methodology, utilised for the first time for both the researcher and the company. The core team worked backwards from the customer, establishing that data security/management were CTQ's/unspoken needs in the service delivery, through the completion of the HOQ in the define phase. This approach ensured high quality information satisfied criteria specified by the user [30, 48, 49].

Redman [35] claims that organisations have 5% poor quality data. Results from the pilot phase conveyed that 94% of emails aged seven years and older were categorised as NVA for deletion. Surprisingly, results gathered from this research conveyed that only 6% of data was deemed as VA, requiring long-term retention. Strong propose the most appropriate measure for success is when staff intend to implement the solution. Tranche 1 of the program was successfully delivered in 2021 with staff trained to mandatorily classify new electronic data received or authored, to identify and begin automatic deletion of NVA data from 2027 onwards using DMAIC methodology. The results of this research project highlighted the importance of first rolling out to a pilot group to achieve Design for Reliability correcting any issues encountered before companywide rollout, equipping pilot users to become change champions. Selvi and Majumdar [46] say it proves beneficial to use a pilot group to set the standard within the company, to teach everyone the benefits of the project and then to be held responsible as leaders to these high standards. Furthermore, Bicheno and Holweg [39] propose the use of a pilot group 'reduces the cost of making mistakes'.

Pepper and Spedding [40] argue to build a Lean Learning Enterprise is extremely difficult and begins by starting from the top. The 5-year transformation roadmap utilising DMADV and change management techniques represents the first attempt in academic literature to convey the design, implementation and sustainment of an integrated data management system with LSS tools and techniques in the financial services sector.

6 Conclusion

Only 3% of organisations have successfully implemented company-wide digital transformations thus the novelty of this research is that this is a unique approach that could be adopted by any organisation pursuing the design and implementation of a major transformation/enhancement program utilising DFLSS DMADV methodology. Despite this, there are significant research gaps in academic literature due to the proliferation of Financial Technologies over the last 5 years, with little or no research completed on topics of identity, security, data privacy, cyber security and their regulation in financial services. This study will aid academics and financial services organisations in providing evidence of how DFLSS can be applied to data management. The next priority opportunity for the organisation to focus on, is the implementation of an email alerting system that will flag data that is breaching regulations/company policies to the IT Data Security team for review. This research provides a new comprehensive, structured paradigm to leverage the capabilities of LSS tools and techniques to support, complement or iterate any existing transformation methodologies or change programs.

References

1. Turban, E., Volonino, L.: Information Technology for Management, pp. 83–108. Wiley, Asia (2010)
2. Fuller, B., Redman, T.C.: Data quality lessons learned at telecom Australia. QUALCON 94, 379–386 (1994)
3. Ballou, D.P., Tayi, G.K.: Enhancing data quality in data warehouse environments. Commun. ACM 42, 73–78 (1999)
4. Alshikhi, O.A., Abdullah, B.M.: Information quality: definitions, measurement, dimensions, and relationship with decision making. Eur. J. Bus. Innov. Res. 6, 36–42 (2018)
5. De Koning, H., Does, R.J., Bisgaard, S.: Lean Six Sigma in financial services. Int. J. Six Sigma Compet. Advantage 4, 1–17 (2008)
6. Keisidou, E., Lazaros, S., Maditions, D.I., Thalassinos, E.I.: Customer satisfaction, loyalty and financial performance: a holistic approach of the Greek banking sector. Int. J. Bank Mark. 31, 259–288 (2013). https://doi.org/10.1108/IJBM-11-2012-0114
7. Fatima, J.K., Razzaque, M.A., Di Mascio, R.: Modelling satisfaction-commitment relationship in developing country context. Int. J. Qual. Reliabil. Manag. 33, 985–1001 (2016). https://doi.org/10.1108/IJQRM-01-2014-0013
8. Brun, I., Rajaobelina, L., Ricard, L.: Online relationship quality: scale development and initial testing. Int. J. Bank Mark. 32, 5–27 (2014)
9. Paul, J., Mittal, A., Srivastav, G.: Impact of service quality on customer satisfaction in private and public sector banks. Int. J. Bank Mark. 34, 606–622 (2016)

10. Jun, M., Cai, S.A, Kim, D.: The linkages of online banking service quality dimensions to customer satisfaction. In: Proceedings - Annual Meeting of the Decision Sciences Institute. Presented at the Decision Sciences Institute 2002 Proceedings, pp. 2125–2130 (2002)
11. Erginel, N.: Construction of a fuzzy QFD failure matrix using a fuzzy multiple-objective decision model. J. Eng. Des. **21**, 677–692 (2010). https://doi.org/10.1080/095448209028 10261
12. Paltayian, G.N., Georgiou, A.C., Gotzamani, K.D., Andronikidis, A.I.: An integrated framework to improve quality and competitive positioning within the financial services context. Int. J. Bank Mark. **30**, 527–547 (2012). https://doi.org/10.1108/02652321211274282
13. Adiandari, A., Winata, H., Fitriandari, M., Hariguna, T.: Improving the quality of Internet banking services: an implementation of the quality function deployment (QFD) concept. Manage. Sci. Lett. **10**, 1121–1128 (2020). https://doi.org/10.5267/j.msl.2019.10.029
14. Heckl, D., Moormann, J., Rosemann, M.: Uptake and success factors of Six Sigma in the financial services industry. Bus. Process. Manag. J. **16**, 436–472 (2010). https://doi.org/10.1108/14637151011049449
15. Kumar, R.B.M.: Enhancing data security by enabling tracking mechanism. Int. J. Innov. Sci. Res. Technol. **5**, 1328–1331 (2020)
16. De Mast, J.: Six Sigma and competitive advantage. Total Qual. Manag. Bus. Excell. **17**, 455–465 (2006)
17. George, M.: Lean Six Sigma for Service, The ROI of Lean Six Sigma for Services, pp. 1–19. McGraw Hill Professional, New York (2003)
18. Delgado, C., Ferreira, M., Castelo Branco, M.: The implementation of lean Six Sigma in financial services organizations. J. Manuf. Technol. Manage. **21**, 512–523 (2010). http://dx.doi.org/10.1108/17410381011046616
19. Snee, R.D., Hoerl, R.W.: Leading Six Sigma: a Step-by-Step Guide Based on Experience with GE and Other Six Sigma Companies. Ft Press, New York (2003)
20. Lokkerbol, J., Does, R., de Mast, J., Schoonhoven, M.: Improving processes in financial service organizations: where to begin? Int. J. Qual. Reliabil. Manage. **29**(9), 1047–1066 (2012)
21. Mahmutaj, L.R., Jusufi, G., Zylfijaj, K., Grubi, A.K.: The role of quality management practices in improving the efficiency and effectiveness of financial services. Mediterr. J. Soc. Sci. **6**, 218–225 (2015)
22. Snee, R.D., Hoerl, R.W.: Integrating lean and Six Sigma-a holistic approach. Six Sigma Forum Mag. **6**, 15–21 (2007)
23. Wang, L., Hussain, I.: Banking sector growth in China: can Six-Sigma be a solution? Int. J. Bus. Manage. **6**, 169–176 (2011)
24. Alblooshi, M., Shamsuzzaman, M., Khoo, M.B.C., Rahim, A., Haridy, S.: Requirements, challenges and impacts of Lean Six Sigma applications–a narrative synthesis of qualitative research. Int. J. Lean Six Sigma **12**, 318–367 (2020)
25. Francis, D., Bessant, J., Hobday, M.: Managing radical organisational transformation. Manag. Decis. **41**, 18–31 (2003)
26. Qiu, M., Gai, K., Zhao, H. and Liu, M.: Privacy-preserving smart data storage for financial industry in cloud computing. Concurr. Comput. **30** (2018). http://dx.doi.org/10.1002/cpe.4278
27. Duarte, B., Montgomery, D., Fowler, J., Konopka, J.: Deploying LSS in a global enterprise–project identification. Int. J. Lean Six Sigma **3**, 187–205 (2012)
28. Kumar, M., Antony, J., Madu, C.N., Montgomery, D.C., Park, S.H.: Common myths of Six Sigma demystified. Int. J. Qual. Reliabil. Manag. **25**, 878–895 (2008)
29. Moyano-Fuentes, J., Martínez-Jurado, P.J., Maqueira-Marín, J.M., Bruque-Cámara, S.: Impact of use of information technology on lean production adoption: evidence from the automotive industry. Int. J. Technol. Manage. **57**, 132–148 (2012)

30. English, L.: Improving Data Warehouse and Business Information Quality. Wiley, New York (1999)
31. Ferguson, B., Lim, J.N.W.: Incentives and clinical governance: money following quality? J. Manag. Med. **15**, 45 (2001)
32. Crump, N.: Managing professional integration in an acute hospital - a socio-political analysis. Int. J. Public Sect. Manag. **15**, 107–117 (2002)
33. Redman, T.C.: The Impact of poor data quality on the typical enterprise. Commun. ACM **41**, 191–204 (1998)
34. Haug, A., Zachariassen, F., Van Liempd, D.: The costs of poor data quality. J. Industr. Eng. Manag. **4**, 168–193 (2011). https://doi.org/10.3926/jiem.2011.v4n2
35. Redman, T.C.: Data Quality: The Field Guide. Digital press, Boston (2001)
36. Malcom, A.: Poor data quality costs 10% of revenues, survey reveals. Wellington: Computerworld (1998). http://computerworld.co.nz/news.nsf/UNID/CC256CED0016AD1ECC256 84C000E0278?OpenDocument&Highlight=2,Poor,data,quality,costs
37. Kim, W., Choi, B.J., Hong, E.K., Kim, S.K., Lee, D.: A taxonomy of dirty data. Data Min. Knowl. Disc. **7**, 81–99 (2003)
38. Keenan, S.C.: Financial Institution Advantage and the Optimization of Information Processing. Wiley, New Jersey (2015)
39. Bicheno, J., Holweg, M.: The Lean Toolbox, 5, pp. 2–144. PICSIE Books, Buckingham (2016)
40. Pepper, M.P., Spedding, T.A.: The evolution of lean Six Sigma. Int. J. Qual. Reliabil. Manag. **27**(2), 138–155 (2010)
41. Womack, J., Jones, D.T.: Lean Thinking: Banish Waste and Create Wealth in Your Corporation, pp. 1–7. Simon and Schuster, London (1996)
42. Ganesh, L.S., Marathe, R.R.: Lean Six Sigma in consumer banking–an empirical inquiry. Int. J. Qual. Reliab. Manag. **36**, 1345–1369 (2019)
43. Yang, K.: Design for Six Sigma for Service. McGraw-Hill Education, New York (2005)
44. Wilson, G.: Six Sigma and the Product Development Cycle. Elsevier Butterworth-Heinemann, London (2005). https://doi.org/10.4324/9780080493084
45. Holsapple, C.W., Joshi, K.D.: A formal knowledge management ontology. In: Holsapple, C.W. (ed.) Handbook on Knowledge Management 1, vol. 1, pp. 89–124. Springer, Verlag, New York (2003). https://doi.org/10.1002/asi.20007
46. Selvi, K., Majumdar, R.: Six sigma-overview of DMAIC and DMADV. Int. J. Innov. Sci. Mod. Eng. **2**, 16–19 (2014)
47. Fang, B., Zhang, P.: Big data in finance. In: Yu, S., Guo, S. (eds.) Big Data Concepts, Theories, and Applications, pp. 391–412. Springer, Cham (2016). https://doi.org/10.1007/978-3-319-27763-9_11
48. Salaun, Y., Flores, K.: Information quality: meeting the needs of the consumer. Int. J. Inf. Manage. **21**, 21–37 (2001)
49. Strong, D.M.: IT process designs for improving information quality and reducing exception handling: a simulation experiment. Inf. Manag. **31**, 251–263 (1997)

Cost of Quality in Construction

Cora O'Connor[1] and Olivia McDermott[2](✉)

[1] University of Limerick, Limerick, Ireland
Cora.OConnor@ul.ie
[2] University of Galway, Galway, Ireland
Olivia.McDermott@universityofgalway.ie

Abstract. The cost of quality while a well-established measure in the manufacturing and other industries, has shown to have limited data available within the construction industry. This case study research article seeks to establish within the construction industry the cost of quality throughout the project lifecycle. The Lean Six Sigma methodology of Design, Measure, Analyse, Improve and Control was used to develop a framework to raise awareness and track the cost of quality both good and bad. The Prevention Appraisal Failure model was used to determine the cost of quality across a portfolio of construction projects completed. The research found that cost of failure was in excess of the cost of appraisal and prevention and thus was leading to non- value add effects waste. During the internal audit process a lack of adherence to documented processes within the quality system was identified as directly contributing to the cost of poor quality in a number of projects. An improvement in the tracking of costs was delivered due to the implementation of a structured framework for data capture and a training presentation to raise awareness. The framework is to be a robust structure and framework that could be adapted in other construction companies and possibly other industries.

Keywords: Cost of quality · DMAIC (Define, Measure, Analyse, Improve, Control) · Lean six sigma systems · PAF (Prevention, Appraisal, Failure)

1 Introduction

Mahmood, et al, [1] describe a construction project as a onetime activity completed within a defined scope, schedule, and budget. Project completion within these constraints and maintaining quality can be difficult to achieve. Research has shown that the costs associated with implementing and maintaining quality can outweigh the tangible benefits [2]. The arrival of the Covid Pandemic in 2020 and the Russian invasion of Ukraine in 2022 has had a significant impact on the construction industry. A recent survey by Construction Industry Federation noted increased prices on steel and difficulties in obtaining it as with lumber and other imperative aggregate materials. Construction Europe (2022) report that the Russian invasion of Ukraine could reduce economic growth in 2022 by 2% which will have a significant impact on the construction industry growth [3]. Evidence gathered through the internal function audits in the case study organisation

© IFIP International Federation for Information Processing 2023
Published by Springer Nature Switzerland AG 2023
O. McDermott et al. (Eds.): ELEC 2022, IFIP AICT 668, pp. 307–317, 2023.
https://doi.org/10.1007/978-3-031-25741-4_26

has noted estimators experiencing as much as 30% rises in the cost of project materials and services. This information further emphasises the need to ensure that cost of defects and rework are managed within the controls of a quality management system. The construction industry does not have a realistic idea of the actual cost of quality on projects in relation to how much profit is lost to attain a sufficient level of quality [4]. Only two studies [4, 5] have offered a framework for analysis of cost of quality in construction. These studies fail to provide any insight either within conformance or nonconformance costs [6].

Total Quality Management (TQM) and Lean practices such as just in time, engineering and reengineering are being adapted by the construction industry to some extent [7]. Most recently, due to the case study organisations exponential growth, the development of a Lean Framework for Offsite Manufacturing is in development. Projects are becoming more complex and onerous which is exposing the company to greater risk which must be managed. The high cost of quality is one of these risks. Off Site Manufacture (OSM) encompasses the design, construction, validation, verification and transportation of building elements. The Construction industry has been referred to as a unique industry that faces challenges that other industries such as Manufacturing, and Healthcare do not.

Construction projects are capital intensive and characterized by long, complex and interconnected processes of planning, design and execution [8]. There are limited publications on the Cost of Quality in construction projects in particular according to Rosenfeld [8] but some studies within construction industries have set out ot study or quantify the costs of quality [9] and the costs of reworks [10]. However despite Irish Construction companies striving to remain competitive in the market; most of the research on the costs of quality in construction has been outside of Ireland [8–10]. The case study organisation in this study is an example of one Irish company that is expanding geographically over the last number of years. This growth creates great risk for the company and it is imperative that there is awareness on where costs are being lost. The lack of research literature around the cost of quality in construction is indicative of the need for further research for construction companies to leverage from.

Thus the research questions for this study is:

1. Establish the cost of quality in the construction industry utilising Lean Six Sigma methods
2. Create a robust framework for projects costs to include process updates, training programmes and a COQ tracking mechanism.

By meeting RQ's 1 and 2 the expected results were to build a base for lessons learned, an ability to develop data driven decisions, an ability to attract future efficiencies through prevention initiatives and right first time. Finally by tracking costs establish a potential for data driven predictive project decision making.

Section 2 outlines the Literature Review, Sect. 3 the methodology followed by the results and discussion in Sects. 4 and 5. Finally the conclusion is outlined in Sect. 6.

2   Literature Review

Quality standards can increase the cost of production of products and services which may translate into higher prices. This is a point of concern especially in the construction industry where competition is fierce, and margins are tight [11]. In order to maintain quality, companies must allow for the associated costs of achieving quality as improvement is not only about customer satisfaction, but also about sustainability and delivering projects on time and within budget [12]. Joseph Juran developed the concept of the cost of poor quality in 1951 and sought to recognize the economic impact of poor quality as the total costs that could be saved if there were no quality issues [13]. It was Juran's belief that it was imperative to link the cost of quality to the bottom line. He believed that creating this measure was the only way to change the mindset and drive change [14]. English estimated the costs of poor-quality data accounts to 10 to 25% of revenue.

According to Escobar et al. [15] traditionally quality control was about looking for defects and fixing them to prevent reoccurrence. In today's market, it is about customer requirements and starting upstream to build quality at the design concept stage. In-order to comply with the project scope, schedule and quality, right first time must be achievable. Haupt and Whitman [16] report that the construction industry has been unaccepting of the concept of TQM and unlearn the traditional practices. Change is notably difficult in the competitive environment in which construction operates and where making margin is the primary motivation. One of the main factors to be considered by construction companies in such a competitive environment is to endeavour to find a balance between the product or service quality and concomitant expenses [5]. Waste in the construction industry is due to process variation and non-value adding activities [17]. According to Aziz and Hafez [18] up to 30% of construction work is rework and at least 10% of materials are wasted. Waste in the construction industry has contributed to the low performance over a number of decades [7].

The key to success of any improvement initiative is leadership and management commitment. Leaders should lead by example and adapt a situational style of leadership that inspires employees to deliver value for the company [19]. Very little research has been done in the construction industry alone in relation to the cost of waste and rework [3]. The statistics for waste are much lower in the manufacturing industry which has seen the construction industry look to the practices of the manufacturing industry as suggested by [7].

3   Methodology

The objective of this research is to determine the cost of quality and the level of knowledge and awareness relative to the cost of quality in construction projects. The approach used for this research was inductive [20] with data collection from literature and empirical data was gathered through the internal audit process carried out with Project and Operations Managers [21]. The objective is to determine the true cost of quality through analysis of good and bad quality.

There is significant amount of waste in the construction industry due to nonconformance or bad quality. Rework is a large part of that and is not being quantified in

relation to its impact on the overall project margins. The cost of good quality will also be looked at in terms of appraisal and preventative activities. It will be determined if there is more value in building quality into processes to reduce dependence on appraisal and preventative activities and therefore reduce the cost of good and bad quality.
Internal Function Audit
An internal function audit was conducted to examine the current cost of quality across projects completed in the year 2021. The criteria for the audit was based on the Prevention, Performance, and Appraisal (PAF) Model using the Internal Function Audit Checklist. For ease of understanding, the checklist was designed to ensure the audit criteria of the prevention appraisal and failure was aligned with the practical project delivery requirements. The audit was carried out over a number of weeks. Project Managers were notified of the audit as is a requirement of stage 1 audits in line with the requirements of ISO 9001:2015 and the associated audit guideline of ISO 19001 [22]. The concept of Six Sigma follows a defined structured approach to completing an improvement project namely, Define, Measure, Analyse, Improve, and Control, known as DMAIC [23]. DMAIC methodology together with Lean tools will be used to deliver this research objectives. De Mast et al., [24] suggest that a Lean Six Sigma (LSS) approach may be more appropriate to the construction industry as Lean encourages a decrease in process instability by reducing process waste (Muda) and Six Sigma supports a decrease in process variability (Mura).

4 Results

4.1 Define

The first step of the project was to define the cost of quality and measure it. Figure 1 demonstrates the breakdown of the types of COQ issues that may arise and from then the COQ could be measured.

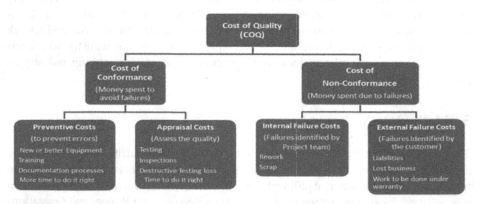

Fig. 1. Defining the costs of quality and types of costs and measures

The Cost of Quality for projects opened and closed over a 12 month was analysed based on the PAF model resulting in costs of €659,844. The approximate collective value of 33 projects over the 12 month period was €325m. This shows the cost of quality was operating at 0.20% of the gross value of the projects. There were limitations on the results as due to the confidential nature of the company finances, the net values were not made available. Recording of non-conformances increased from 3 in the year prior to the project to 13 in the year of the project aided by the development and roll out of a cost of quality training programme to create an awareness of the Cost of Quality.

Improved collection capability of operational data was realised due to the development of a database to facilitate the collection of key data in relation to impact, contributing factors and cost both estimated and actual.

4.2 Measure

The audit checklist was based on the methodology of establishing a consistent measuring system by asking the following questions:-

1. What is to be measured?
2. What are the criteria for measurement?
3. What is the scope of measurement?

For this audit preventative costs were measured in-terms of what were the critical to quality measures i.e., time taken by the Project Manager to review the contract and a % of salary was assigned over the 33 projects under review. The appraisal section considered the cost of time applied to checking key operational activities throughout the project life cycle through the quality assurance and quality control audits. Failure costs considered the cost of internal failure or non-conformance and external failure (Table 1). When analysed by project specific criteria it revealed that the majority of internal failures were due to subcontractor issues. This is not surprising as the case study organisation is highly reliant on outsourced activities for project delivery.

4.3 Analyse and Improve

A fishbone diagram and 5 Whys exercise were used to ascertain the root cause of the problem using the 6M methodology. During a brainstorming session with the quality team and operations the existing company culture, commitment and leadership were the top 3 issues identified that need to be considered.

A framework was developed in MS Excel to facilitate the logging and tracking of key data to allow for effective data analysis on which decision could be based and actions taken. A key principle of Total Quality Management is fact-based management. Decisions have to be based on fact and not precedent or opinion [5]. The case study organisation are striving towards operational excellence. According to Mahmood [1] it is fundamental that cost information is used in decision making. A Nonconformance Master Register database was developed to capture any non-conformances that lead to quality issues and cost issues.

The process for non-conformance and corrective action was revised to reflect the updated controls as and integrated into the QMS as part of a procedure - Control of Non-conforming Outputs & Corrective Action Process. Two new forms (Fig. 2) were

Table 1. Costs of quality derived from internal audit checklist (example)

Type of Cost	Item	Responsible	Cost	Total cost
Prevention	Contract review	PM	€ 22,000	€ 150,000
Prevention	CTQ Matrix	PM	€ 26,000	
Prevention	QA Plan	QC	€ 14,450	
Prevention	Internal Training Plan	QC	€ 7,300	
Prevention	Quality Management System	QA	€ 50,000	
Prevention	Internal Quality Training	QC/QA	€ 20,000	
Prevention	External Quality Training	External	€ 10,250	
Appraisal	Project Managers & Directors Inspections	PM/SS/Directors	€ 10,000	€ 127,776
Appraisal	Walk-downs/Snagging	PM/SS	€ 5,000	
Appraisal	Tests	QC	€ 10,000	
Appraisal	Internal Audits Projects	QC	€ 25,776	
Appraisal	Internal Audits Offices	QC/QA	€ 25,000	
Appraisal	External Audits	External	€ 32,000	
Appraisal	Internal Audits to Supplier	QC	€ 20,000	
Internal /External failure	Internal NCR	Projects	€ 382,068	€ 382,068

created to capture detailed operational data at project level. A summary of the details will feed into the Nonconformance Master Register to collate all internal and external failure costs. These forms were developed to ensure the impact of the issues were considered together with the contributing factors, remedial work, root cause analysis and associated costs.

4.4   Control

Roll out of the cost of quality training programme and knowledge commenced in December 2021 with invites from the inhouse training platform issued to relevant roles within site and management staff. Over 33% of staff were trained initially with a plan in place ot deploy to all employees. Due to the success on the uptake of the training, it will be rolled out to all site, engineers, and management before end of 2023. The implementation of the improvements will be monitored in line with the internal function audit

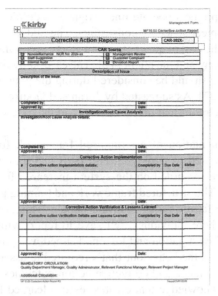

Fig. 2. Corrective action report template

process as illustrated in Table 1 on the Internal Audit Process. This process is written in accordance with the requirements of the international standard ISO9001:2015 [22] for Quality management systems requirements and ISO19011, Guidelines for auditing management systems [25].

5 Discussion

This research conveys how to design and implement an integrated company-wide transformation. This research demonstrates how the DMAIC methodology was used to develop a structured framework to raise awareness and track cost of quality on construction projects. It is evident through this research that the complete cost of quality is not considered on construction projects in the case study organisation. As reported by Abdelsalam and Gad [4] the construction industry does not have a realistic view of the actual cost of quality on projects and how much profits are lost to attain a sufficient level of quality. This was evident in this research as a knowledge gap was revealed in areas that previously may have not been considered as directly impacting the cost of quality such as prevention and appraisal or conformance costs. The cost of failure is considered due to the potential negative impact it could have on project profit margins but the cost of prevention and appraisal or conformance is not fully recognised as a tangible area that can be measured or has an obvious benefit [6]. Within construction projects there is always an emphasis on maintaining the project profit margin which leads to speeding up the rate of construction at the cost of quality to maintain the schedule and subsequently the budget. This is where rework becomes an issue therefore increasing the costs [26]. Utilising the cost of quality failure analysis shows that the majority of internal failures occurred during the installation phase by a supplier/subcontractor. The installation or construction phase of projects operate under tight schedule constraints where quality may be overlooked to meet schedule constraints. The budget and schedule have to be structured to allow for the cost of quality to ensure there is continuous improvements that adds value to the company and the client [12]. The case study organisation realised that the cost of conformance should be considered during the planning phase of the project in line with Sebastian [27]. As suggested by Juran and Godfrey [14] these costs should be directly linked to the profit margin of projects and the case study organisation found this approach effective.

Due to the implementation of a structured framework for measuring the COQ and recording NC's as well as deploying and the COQ training the number of non-conformances or failures recorded on the system increased from quarter one of 2021 to quarter one in 2022. The structured framework and training presentation emphasised the process behind the failure rather than the people. This created a more blameless method of reporting where individuals felt save to report with the view that process improvement through investigation and lessons learned was possible [28]. This is supported by management as the behaviour that's required to assert a culture change. The recording of non-conformance and corrective action outcomes needs to be recognised as vital organisational knowledge that creates lessons learned to prevent reoccurrence [29]. This thinking should be considered as an aspect of the case study organisation's overall strategic direction.

For the purposes of this research the total cost of quality was determined by gathering operational data from 33 projects initiated and completed in 2021, 19 of which recorded non-conformances. It is difficult to determine if the details are completely accurate as some of the costs were hidden or estimated either over or under. The nature of the business is to subcontract work and purchase manufactured items, this creates difficulty for project manages to accurately assess the true cost of failure. It is also often the case that suppliers and subcontractors do not fully realise the implications of not protecting the supply chain. This research shows the cost of quality as operating a 0.20% of gross project value prior to the project. This figure will increase further due to the implementation of the improvements outlined in this research - until the COQ is measured it cannot be managed.

Research tells us that traditionally within the construction industry quality control was about looking for defects, fixing them and putting plans in place to prevent reoccurrence in the future [29]. Having a COQ framework ensures the industry takes a more preventive, proactive approach as much as is practicable [26]. This research has highlighted the majority of issues recorded in the case study organisation are due to subcontractor or supplier performance which aligns with Abdul-Aziz's study on quality management in Japanese construction [30]. The area of subcontractor and supplier approval and evaluation may need to be reviewed to assess if the criteria currently in place is sufficient for the growing needs of the case study organisation.

The structured framework created for the gathering of operational data in relation to non- conformance and corrective can be digitised in future to further improve its capabilities in the future.

6 Conclusion

This research fulfilled its research objectives by creating a structured framework to which vital operational data could be gathered to determine the true cost of quality and the rollout of a training program to create awareness around and measure the total cost of quality.

This research resulted in creating an understanding of all the elements of cost of quality both good and bad. A structured RCCA process to understand and record the causes of failure and the importance of root cause analysis though the corrective action process. The development of a structured framework to act as a single source of truth to record issues and where future projects can look to for lessons learned is important.

While data gathering may have had limitations initially in terms of a reluctance to disclose the costs, the implementation of the structured framework for data collection and training presentations were instrumental in changing the mindset, behaviours and project management costing in a positive way. The improvements were rolled out during a 6 month period and their success can be verified by the increase in non-conformance reporting from the year after the changes were implemented.

The results of this research illustrate how efficient and effective the LSS DMAIC methodology is at providing a framework to drive continuous improvement. Using this methodology led to the provision of a transparency around the cost of quality that had not previously existed. The success of this project demonstrates the value adding capabilities of the DMAIC methodology and how it could greatly benefit other areas of the industry. Future research can delve more into the types of improvements that can be made by measuring the COQ in the construction industry.

References

1. Mahmood, S., Ahmed, S.M., Panthi, K., Ishaque Kureshi, N.: Determining the cost of poor quality and its impact on productivity and profitability. Built Environ. Proj. Asset Manag. **4**, 296–311 (2014). https://doi.org/10.1108/BEPAM-09-2013
2. Zimon, D., Zimon, G.: The impact of implementation of standardized quality management systems on management of liabilities in group purchasing organizations. Qual. Innov. Prosperity **23**, 60–73 (2019)
3. Construction Network Ireland: Ireland Construction Market Size, Trends and Forecasts by Sector - 2022–2026. Construction Network Ireland, Dublin (2022)
4. Abdelsalam, H.M.E., Gad, M.M.: Cost of quality in Dubai: an analytical case study of residential construction projects. Int. J. Project Manage. **27**, 501–511 (2009). https://doi.org/10.1016/j.ijproman.2008.07.006
5. Heravi, G., Jafari, A.: Cost of quality evaluation in mass-housing projects in developing countries. J. Constr. Eng. Manage.-asce. **140**, 04014004 (2014)
6. Garg, S., Misra, S.: Understanding the components and magnitude of the cost of quality in building construction. Eng. Constr. Archit. Manag. **29**, 26–48 (2022). https://doi.org/10.1108/ECAM-08-2020-0642
7. Hoonakker, P.L.T., Carayon, P., Loushine, T.W.: Barriers and benefits of quality management in the construction industry: an empirical study. Total Qual. Manag. Bus. Excell. **21**, 953–969 (2010)

8. Rosenfeld, Y.: Cost of quality versus cost of non-quality in construction: the crucial balance. Constr. Manag. Econ. **27**, 107–117 (2009). https://doi.org/10.1080/01446190802651744

9. Hall, M., Tomkins, C.: A cost of quality analysis of a building project: towards a complete methodology for design and build. Constr. Manag. Econ. **19**, 727–740 (2001). https://doi.org/10.1080/01446190110066146

10. Love, P.E.D., Li, H.: Quantifying the causes and costs of rework in construction. Constr. Manag. Econ. **18**, 479–490 (2000). https://doi.org/10.1080/01446190050024897

11. Lyons, T.: How resilience and values helped Kirby create a €300 m business (2021). https://www.kirbygroup.com/how-resilience-and-values-helped-kirby-create-a-e300m-business-mark-flanagan-speaks-to-the-currency/

12. Vaxevanidis, N.M., Petropoulos, G., Avakumovic, J., Mourlas, A.: Cost of quality models and their implementation in manufacturing firms. Int. J. Qual. Res. **3**, 27–36 (2009)

13. Bisgaard, S.: Quality management and Juran's legacy. Qual. Reliab. Eng. Int. **23**, 665–677 (2007). https://doi.org/10.1002/qre.860

14. Juran, J.M., Godfrey, A.B., Hoogstoel, R.E., Schilling, E.G.: The Quality Improvement Process. Juran's Quality Handbook. McGraw-Hill, New York (1999)

15. Escobar, C.A., Morales-Menendez, R.: Machine learning techniques for quality control in high conformance manufacturing environment. Adv. Mech. Eng. **10**, 1687814018755519 (2018)

16. Haupt, T.C., Whiteman, D.E.: Inhibiting factors of implementing total quality management on construction sites. TQM Mag. **16**, 166–173 (2004). https://doi.org/10.1108/09544780410532891

17. Alwi, S., Hampson, K., Mohamed, S.: Non value-adding activities: a comparative study of Indonesian and Australian construction projects. Presented at the (2002)

18. Aziz, R.F., Hafez, S.M.: Applying lean thinking in construction and performance improvement. Alex. Eng. J. **52**, 679–695 (2013)

19. McDermott, O., Nelson, S.: Readiness for Industry 4.0 in west of Ireland small and medium and micro enterprises. College of Science and Engineering, University of Galway (2022). https://doi.org/10.13025/8sqs-as24

20. Sauce, B., Matzel, L.D.: Inductive Reasoning. In: Vonk, J. and Shackelford, T. (eds.) Encyclopedia of Animal Cognition and Behavior, pp. 1–8. Springer International Publishing, Cham (2017). https://doi.org/10.1007/978-3-319-47829-6_1045-1

21. Robsen, C.: Real World Research: A Resource for Social Scientists and Practitioner-Researchers. Blackwell Publishers, Oxford (2002)

22. International Organisation for Standardisation: ISO 9001:2015. https://www.iso.org/obp/ui/#iso:std:iso:9001:ed-5:v1:en. Accessed 15 Feb 2021

23. Arnheiter, E.D., Maleyeff, J.: The integration of lean management and six sigma. TQM Mag. **17**, 5–18 (2005). https://doi.org/10.1108/09544780510573020

24. de Mast, J., Lokkerbol, J.: An analysis of the six sigma DMAIC method from the perspective of problem solving. Int. J. Prod. Econ. **139**, 604–614 (2012). https://doi.org/10.1016/j.ijpe.2012.05.035

25. ISO 19001:2018. https://www.iso.org/cms/render/live/en/sites/isoorg/contents/data/standard/07/00/70017.html. Accessed 17 Nov 2022

26. Xiao, H., Proverbs, D.: The performance of contractors in Japan, the UK and the USA: a comparative evaluation of construction cost. Constr. Manag. Econ. **20**, 425–435 (2002). https://doi.org/10.1080/01446190210145859

27. Sebastian, B., Jan, G., Monika, P., Wojciech, S.: The most economically advantageous tender in the public procurement system in the European union. In: Bilgin, M.H., Danis, H., Karabulut, G., Gözgor, G. (eds.) Eurasian Economic Perspectives. ESBE, vol. 12/1, pp. 403–420. Springer, Cham (2020). https://doi.org/10.1007/978-3-030-35040-6_26

28. Rother, M., Shook, J.: Learning to See: Value Stream Mapping to Add Value and Eliminate Muda. Lean Enterprise Institute, Cambridge (2003)
29. Chiarini, A.: Japanese total quality control, TQM, deming's system of profound knowledge, BPR, Lean and six sigma: comparison and discussion. Int. J. Lean Six Sigma. **2**, 332–355 (2011). https://doi.org/10.1108/20401461111189425
30. Abdul-Aziz, A.: The realities of applying total quality management in the construction industry. Struct. Surv. **20**, 88–96 (2002). https://doi.org/10.1108/02630800210433864

Design for Lean Six Sigma Application in a Family Run Multi-generational Micro Enterprise – A Case Study

John O'Shanahan[1(✉)], Olivia McDermott[2], and John Noonan[3]

[1] Lean BPI, Galway, Ireland
johnoshanahan@leanbpi.ie
[2] University of Galway, Galway, Ireland
[3] University of Limerick, Limerick, Ireland

Abstract. Existing research emphasises limited success rates for Lean implementation in Small and Medium Sized Organisations. The objective of this research was to test and validate the applicability of Design for Lean Six Sigma methodology in a case study within a micro enterprise. The DFLSS model of Define-Measure-Explore-Develop and Implement was utilised to redesign a new order entry process within the case study organisation. The results confirmed that utilising Define for Lean Six Sigma and the voice of the customer enabled a new order entry design that improved productivity, reduced nonvalue add steps and reduced order turnaround times while increasing revenue. The study demonstrates the applicability of Lean to smaller organisations and the effective application of the Define for Lean Six Sigma methodology.

Keywords: ME · DMEDI · Critical success factors · Lean implementation · Design for lean six sigma · Micro enterprises

1 Introduction

Small and Medium Enterprises (SMEs) which includes micro enterprises (ME's), which are family-run, are a vital sector of the Irish economy. They contribute significantly to Ireland's employment and Gross domestic product (GDP), making up over 90% of indigenous companies [1]. These businesses face various challenges, with many failures in the second generation (Groysberg and Bell, 2014). Stakeholders of family businesses must collaborate and exploit all available resources to maximise opportunities for multi-generational success. For enterprises to survive, they need to constantly adapt and improve to serve the needs of their customers and maintain competitiveness. Lean philosophy supports business improvement efforts by continuously identifying waste in processes and removing the identified waste from the system [2]. Since 2015, the Irish Local Enterprise Offices (LEOs), as part of their suite of business supports, have been running a successful Lean for Micro programme [3]. Microenterprises, businesses employing less than 10 people and with a turnover of fewer than two million euros [4], can

O. McDermott et al. (Eds.): ELEC 2022, IFIP AICT 668, pp. 318–328, 2023.
https://doi.org/10.1007/978-3-031-25741-4_27

benefit from the programme by adopting Lean business principles in their organisations to become more competitive [3]. Delivery of these programmes is through accredited consultants. They help form a network of small, often specialised businesses and promote economic growth. SME suppliers need to provide high-quality products or services at competitive prices to survive.

Adopting a Lean philosophy is beneficial to achieving this goal [5]. While the literature on Lean implementation in larger organisations has been extensive, the literature on Lean implementation in ME's has not been as thorough [6]. Despite Lean's reputation for vastly improving company operations, for the most part, only large companies have successfully implemented Lean and are reaping the benefits [7]. Lean adoption challenges in small businesses are unique and different from those faced by large corporations, according to research [8]. Due to many critical factors affecting Lean implementation, MEs lag behind large organisations in Lean implementation [9].

The objective of this research was to test the use of Lean methodology within a case study approach regarding the successful adoption of Lean practices within a ME. The case study was conducted through a LEO Lean for Micro consulting assignment. While engaged in Lean implementation, the researcher evaluated the use of Lean methods to achieve business results.

2   Literature Review

2.1   SME and Micro Enterprises in Context

While Lean is an established methodology for improving business performance, it is not a foregone conclusion that every Micro Business embarking on a Lean programme will succeed in its implementation and realise improved business performance [9].

SMEs are defined as companies with a maximum of 250 employees and an annual turnover of fewer than 50 million euros. SMEs are further broken down into small enterprises (less than 50 staff members and under ten million Euro turnover) and Micro-enterprises (less than 10 staff and under two million Euro turnover) [10].

Although these companies individually employ small numbers of workers, they collectively contribute to employment numbers and GDP. However, although the contribution Micro-enterprises make to economies worldwide, from a research perspective, the Micro Business sector is often overlooked [1].

The principle of Lean management is to eliminate waste to improve further the efficiency and quality of the business [11]. Lean production manufactures a wide range of products at lower costs and better quality with less input than traditional mass production. In their bestselling book, 'Lean Thinking' Womack and Jones define the five Lean principles (Value, Value Stream, Flow, Pull and Perfection) and suggest strategies for their implementation [12]. Organisations in many sectors have witnessed the positive impact that Lean can have on operational, financial, social, and environmental performance [13].

Micro-enterprises account for 91.8% of European enterprises, small-enterprises account for 6.9%, medium enterprises (employing 50 to 249 people) account for 1.1%, and large enterprises (employing 250 or more people) make up the remaining 0.2%.

There were an estimated 22.6 million small and medium-sized enterprises (SMEs) in the European Union in 2021, most of which were micro-sized firms [14]. The Micro-business sector is crucial to future productivity and employment growth [5]. However, we know little about these firms because they are often excluded from national and international surveys [15].

Within the E.U., 60% of all businesses are family businesses, their role in the E.U. economy is significant, no matter how big or small they are [14]. Family-owned businesses, where a family supplies a significant proportion of the enterprise's senior management and effectively controls the business' [16], account for a high percentage of employment, revenues, and GDP in many countries. Previous research suggests that 30% of family businesses survive past the first generation and that many small businesses fail shortly after the second generation takes control of the business [17]. This is a problem for business owners, their employees, society, and economies. In family-owned MEs, the owners can initiate change and ensure that the decisions are implemented to achieve the desired results; ownership gives them the power and freedom to explore and renew the business (Dolz et al., 2019). Nelson et al. [5] found that MEs have a high proportion of owner-managers and thus can influence Lean adoption more expediently and successfully in their businesses. Therefore, MEs' importance to the business infrastructure is greater than may be obvious at first glance [18].

2.2 Lean Implementation

Readiness factors are defined as 'essential ingredients which will increase the probability of success of any CI initiative before an organisation invests its resources heavily on the initiative' [19]. Nelson et al. [5] highlighted that in Lean deployment in M.E. is that resource issues such as time for training and time to implement Lean changes were cited as a challenge initially by the M.E.s; it was found that the changes once made and at a steady pace aided consensus, teamwork and engagement.

Different methodologies can be selected for Lean implementation. For example, lean has been incorporated with Six Sigma's DMAIC approach to reduce waste and variation by following the DMAIC problem-solving methodology to improve existing processes [20].

Design for Lean Six Sigma (DFSS) is a data-driven quality strategy for designing or re-designing a product or service from the ground up [21]. DFSS is an approach that improves quality by re-designing the product or service using the customer's voice or customer requirements [22]. Table 1 is adapted from the literature related to DFLSS structured methodologies. DFLSS can be utilised to ensure design quality and predictability during the early design phases of a process, and the approach employs a structured integrated product development methodology and a comprehensive set of robust tools to drive product quality, innovation, faster time to market, and lower product costs [23]. An example of different DFLSS methodologies is shown in Table 1.

Table 1. DFLSS methodologies described in the literature

DMAIC	Define, Measure, Analyse, Improve and Control	[20–24]
DMADV	Define, Measure, Analyse, Design, and Verify	[23, 25–28]
DMADOV	De sign, Measure, Analyse, De sign, Optimise, and Verify	
DMCDOV	Define, Measure, Characterise, De sign, Optimise, and Verify	
DCOV	Define, Characterise, Optimise, and Verify	
DCCDI	Define, Customer, Concept, Design, and Implement	
DMEDI	**Define, Measure, Explore, Develop, and Implement**	
DMADIC	Define, Measure, Analyse, Design, Implement, and Control	
IDOV	Identify, Design, Optimise, and Verify	
RCI	Define and Deve lop Requirements, Define and Develop Concepts, and Define and Develop Improvements	

3 Methodology

A case study approach was used and within that a DFLSS methodology. As part of the DFSS methodology, the DMEDI approach was utilised. DMEDI is "a creative approach to designing new robust processes, products and services [29]. Thus the difference between DMAIC and DMEDI is that DMAIC examines processes already in place, and DMEDI helps put a new process in place [30].

The case study methodology was applied because it enables more insight into the phenomenon under investigation [31]. In addition, the case study approach allows for the answer to the "how" and "why" questions as well as the recognition of contextual circumstances [32].

The Case study company, JFH Jewels is an online jewelry wholesaler based in Ireland. The business was in existence as a family run business for over 30 years. They had recently acquired a pearl jewellery manufacturing business as part of their growth strategy. Unfortunately, the acquired business had inefficient legacy systems. The Managing Director of JFH Jewels recognised the need to upgrade these inefficient processes and approached the Local Enterprise Office (LEO) for support. The LEO recommendation for JFH Jewels was to enrol in the Lean for Micro Programme, run by the LEO with support from Enterprise Ireland. Data for the Case Study was collected from interviews, existing company documentation, direct observation, participant observation, and physical artifacts.

Following the formation of the project team, an initial workshop was conducted, and the order entry process within the case study organisation was selected for improvement. The order workflow process was deemed fragmented and inefficient; it was agreed to develop a new order workflow process. The development of a stock management system was also included in the project scope, as there was no existing stock control system.

DMEDI was selected as a creative approach to designing new robust processes [22].

4   Results

Utilising DMEDI methodology as outlined in Table 2, various Lean Six Sigma tools or techniques were utilised to re-design the case study organisation's order entry process. First, the order entry process was defined and mapped, and data was collected around its current performance. Next, a Critical to Quality (CTQ) tree was utilised to establish internal and external customer needs. Subsequently, Quality Function Deployment (QFD) was utilised to design a new and improved process to meet the order entry process VOC and eliminate NVA waste from the process.

JFH halted production activities temporarily so that workers could absorb the new learnings implemented. During the implementation, the M.D. and office manager enrolled on a management development programme, which involved financial outlay and management time. New manufacturing equipment was invested in, and a barcode printer was required to integrate with the newly designed Sales rep app; this was purchased and allowed JFH jewels to take full advantage of the sales rep app. The new stock management system reduced inventory waste. The ordering app was integrated into the accounting software to cut out data entry steps and provide more detailed data for business development.

As a result of the newly designed and implemented order entry process, there was a reduction in order lead time from 48 h to 9.5 h, a reduction in order processing time from 20 to 10 min, a productivity improvement of 9.1 orders per hour inputted from a previous 7 orders per hour (Fig. 1). Staff numbers increased in the business from 3 to 5 full-time members as there was less non-value add work to be carried out and thus more opportunities to deploy staff into value add roles and increase sales. The invoice process time went from 3 min to 10 sec. Revenue increased by 70% due to the new, more efficient processes.

5   Discussion

Leadership and management, finance, organisational culture, and skills and expertise are the essential Critical Success factors for SMEs to adopt lean manufacturing. This study had a strong leadership ethos and committed management support from the outset. This is because implementing an idea within any organisation is founded on leadership and management commitment [33].

Financial Capacity was found to be a critical success factor in the DFLSS Lean implementation within the case study organisation as it involves acquiring new skills, investing in modern technologies and engaging with business advisers to help with the change process. The JFH jewels business invested in a training programme with the Local Enterprise Office, followed by work on the Lean implementation project. Funds were made available to develop technical solutions and to provide staff training.

Achanga et al. [33] were one of the few studies explicitly identifying the need for financial capability in SMEs as a critical success factor. Although other studies have discussed how Large enterprises (L.E.) can have better success with Lean deployment due to larger financial resources, people resources, training resources and allocation of employees to work on projects, all of which costs money in terms of labour costs [8, 34, 35].

Table 2. Overview of DMEDI methodology – Tools/Techniques

DMEDI	Phase deliverable	Tools/Technique	Application of Tools/Technique
Define	Define the purpose, structure, goals, and value. Identify benefits/challenges/risks	SIPOC	Agree project team and activities; scope confirmed to cover from materials to finished orders dispatch
		Project Charter	The Main goals were to implement lean systems in the order entry, production operations, stock control and invoicing processes
Measure	Understand Internal and External customer requirements	Critica lTo Qua lity (CTQ) Tree	Identify the needs of the internal customers (admin, operations and reps) and external customers (clients); these needs were translated into measurable process requirements. For example time to process an order in the field
		Voice of the Customer (VOC) and Quality Function Deployment (QFD)	Design factors such as ease of use, speed of use, relia bility, simplicity and scalability were identified with these tools
Explore	Explore a conceptual design of the new sales order workflow	Brainstorming/Affinity Diagram	At this stage, alternative solutions such as Microsoft forms, Jot forms, google sheets, web databases and custom systems were discussed
		Kaizen event	An outcome of the Kaizen event was to agree on the best coding system for finished products and raw materials stocks
		Pugh Matrix	The Mobile app solution for order entry was selected using the Pugh Matrix

(continued)

Table 2. (*continued*)

DMEDI	Phase deliverable	Tools/Technique	Application of Tools/Technique
Develop	Develop a comprehensive plan on how to organise and implement the new sa les order workflow	Develop User Story	The user story explained the order entry process, how ops processed the order, how the system handled automatic raw material stock control and how the invoices were generated
		FMEA Ana lysis	The FMEA was important to consider the impact of failure before rolling out the process; the main concerns were around the technology's robustness
		Prototyping	Built a working prototype in google sheets to demonstrate flow and provide users with an opportunity to identify changes needed
Implement	Implement the new process, validate the design, and establish control	Pilot	The pilots were run in pha ses, starting with sales, then ops and finishing with the finance side
		Control Plan	All data recorded with zero tolerance for discrepancies, the system was designed to be 100% effective
		Post Implementation	On going review of the workflow performance identified improvement opportunities; for example, the customer selection process was revised 3 times based on the post-implementation review process

Lean manufacturing implementation in MEs can be problematic. Typically, MEs employ staff with low skill levels and do not promote continuous learning and skill

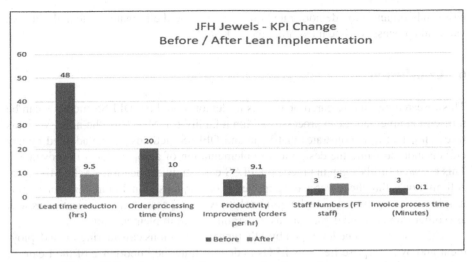

Fig. 1. KPI performance before versus after the new lean process design

development [33]. The research found JFH employees to be engaged in the Lean implementation process. This was demonstrated by the interest in the initial workshops and their engagement with project deliverables. The employees acquired new skills in workplace organisation, brainstorming, and visual management. They became skilled in using the technical tools employed in the Lean implementation, Dropbox, Evernote, Google Suite and Snagit, and in understanding how to operate the new Lean management system. A consistent vision and alignment of the Lean program with strategy is an explicit prerequisite for a Lean enterprise [36]. As part of their strategy, JFH management identified an opportunity to differentiate from competitors by being strategic and offering a 2-day lead time on hand-made jewellery; the employees embraced learning new skills and techniques to achieve this service level and provide JFH with a competitive advantage.

Utilising the DFLSS methodology, the M.D. communicated the company strategy and vision to the team members. By outlining the reason for the change and design of the new order entry process, the employees were made aware of the positive impact of Lean implementation and were more likely to support the change process. Lean's success depends on those who implement everyday practices [19]. The DFLSS methodology promoted employee collaboration on improvement plans and supported their input to new design layouts. In addition, the methodology aided employee involvement in continuous improvement, goal setting, problem-solving, and other daily management issues.

The researchers observed that the employees contributed suggestions for improvements which were taken on board and implemented. For example, the employees suggested an improved bar code printing system, which reduced rework in the process and freed employees to work on other tasks. The structured methodology aided employee involvement [37, 38]. The DFLSS methodology enabled the design of a new process with integration of the voice of the customer, both internal and external, as well as the designing of suitable KPIs to measure the design effectiveness. This experience of the case study organisation demonstrated how DFLSS could eliminate waste and improve value add processes while integrating the VOC [23].

6 Conclusion

This research met the research objectives to demonstrate how DFLSS methods can be utilised to implement Lean processes within a family-run ME. Thus the novelty of this research is that it demonstrates that Lean and DFLSS methods can be adopted by any organisation pursuing the design and implementation of an operational improvement. This research fulfils a gap in practical DFLSS case study applications in the ME arena. A limitation is that the research only applied to one organisation. Future research opportunities would be to carry out a longitudinal study on this case study organisation as well as o other similar-sized organisations undergoing Lean implementation.

This research can be leveraged by ME-type organisations considering Lean deployment and by Enterprise Ireland's LEOs to demonstrate the importance of the Lean for Micro program.

References

1. McDermott, O., Nelson, S.: Readiness for Industry 4.0 in west of Ireland small and medium and micro enterprises. College of Science and Engineering, University of Galway (2022). https://doi.org/10.13025/8sqs-as24
2. McDermott, O.: Barriers & enablers to lean six sigma in pharma. RAPS Euro Convergence 2021 (2021)
3. Lean Business Ireland: Lean For Micro. https://www.leanbusinessireland.ie/funding-supports-overview/are-you-a-local-enterprise-office-client/lean-for-micro/. Accessed 06 Feb 2022
4. Central Statistics Office: Small and Medium Enterprises - CSO - Central Statistics Office. https://www.cso.ie/en/releasesandpublications/ep/p-bii/bii2015/sme/. Accessed 09 Feb 2022
5. Nelson, S., McDermott, O., Woods, B., Trubetskaya, A.: An evaluation of lean deployment in Irish micro-enterprises. Total Qual. Manag. Bus. Excell. 1–20 (2022). https://doi.org/10.1080/14783363.2022.2140651
6. Alkhoraif, A., Rashid, H., McLaughlin, P.: Lean implementation in small and medium enterprises: a literature review. Oper. Res. Perspect. 6 (2019). undefined-undefined. https://doi.org/10.1016/j.orp.2018.100089
7. Shah, P.P., Shrivastava, R.L.: Identification of performance measures of lean six sigma in small- and medium-sized enterprises: a pilot study. Int. J. Six Sigma Compet. Adv. 8, 1–21 (2013)
8. Bhat, S., Gijo, E.V., Rego, A.M., Bhat, V.S.: Lean six sigma competitiveness for micro, small and medium enterprises (MSME): an action research in the Indian context. TQM J. 33, 379–406 (2021). https://doi.org/10.1108/TQM-04-2020-0079
9. Belhadi, A., Kamble, S.S., Gunasekaran, A., Zkik, K., Touriki, F.E.: A big data analytics-driven lean six sigma framework for enhanced green performance: a case study of chemical company. Prod. Plan. Control 1–24 (2021). https://doi.org/10.1080/09537287.2021.1964868
10. E.U. Commission: Commission Recommendation concerning the definition of micro, small and medium-sized enterprises (2003)

11. Liker, J.: The Toyota Way: 14 Management Principles from the World's Greatest Manufacturer. McGraw-Hill, New York (2004)
12. Womack, J.P., Jones, D.T.: Lean Thinking—Banish Waste and Create Wealth in your Corporation. Simon and Schuster, London (1996)
13. McDermott, O., et al.: Lean six sigma in healthcare: a systematic literature review on motivations and benefits. Processes **10** (2022). https://doi.org/10.3390/pr10101910
14. OECD: Entrepreneurship - Enterprises by business size - OECD Data. https://data.oecd.org/entrepreneur/enterprises-by-business-size.htm. Accessed 09 July 2021
15. Bourke, J., Roper, S.: Micro-Businesses in Ireland: From Ambition to Innovation. University College Cork, Cork University Business School (2019)
16. Central Statistics Office: Business Demography 2018 - CSO - Central Statistics Office. https://www.cso.ie/en/releasesandpublications/er/bd/businessdemography2018/. Accessed 30 Jan 2022
17. Miller, D., Steier, L., Le Breton-Miller, I.: Lost in time: intergenerational succession, change, and failure in family business. J. Bus. Ventur. **18**, 513–531 (2003)
18. Antony, J., et al.: A global study on the applicability of ISO 18404:2015 for SMEs: an exploratory qualitative study. TQM J. ahead-of-print (2022). https://doi.org/10.1108/TQM-08-2022-0276
19. McDermott, O., Antony, J., Sony, M., Looby, E.: A critical evaluation and measurement of organisational readiness and adoption for continuous improvement within a medical device manufacturer. Int. J. Manag. Sci. Eng. Manag. 1–11 (2022). https://doi.org/10.1080/17509653.2022.2073917
20. George, M.L.: Lean Six Sigma: Combining Six Sigma Quality with Lean Production Speed. McGraw-Hill, NY (2002)
21. Antony, J.: Design for Six Sigma: a breakthrough business improvement strategy for achieving competitive advantage. Work-study (2002)
22. Brue, G.: Design for Six Sigma. McGraw-Hill, London (2003)
23. Thomas, M., Singh, N.: Design for lean six sigma (DFLSS): philosophy, tools, potential and deployment challenges in automotive product development. In: SAE International, Warrendale, PA (2006). https://doi.org/10.4271/2006-01-0503
24. Chowdhury, S.: The power of design for six sigma (2003)
25. Chandan, G.K., Kanchan, B.K., Rajenthirakumar, D.: Lean start-up in market penetration using DMADV methodology: an empirical study. Mater. Today Proc. **63**, 328–334 (2022). https://doi.org/10.1016/j.matpr.2022.03.166
26. Cronemyr, P.: DMAIC and DMADV - differences, similarities and synergies. Int. J. Six Sigma Compet. Adv. **3**, 193–209 (2007). https://doi.org/10.1504/IJSSCA.2007.015065
27. Huang, C.-T., Chen, K.-S., Chang, T.-C.: An application of DMADV methodology for increasing the yield rate of surveillance cameras. Microelectron. Reliab. **50**, 266–272 (2010)
28. Byrne, B., McDermott, O., Noonan, J.: Applying lean six sigma methodology to a pharmaceutical manufacturing facility: a case study. Processes **9** (2021). https://doi.org/10.3390/pr9030550
29. Rai, S., Gurunatha, T.: Integrating LDP lean document production? Solution within the DMEDI methodology. Int. J. Perform. Eng. **6**, 547 (2010)
30. Fink, R., Bevington, N.: How caterpillar uses 6 sigma to execute strategy. Strateg. Financ. **91**, 25 (2010)
31. Yin, R.: Case Study Research Design and Methods. Sage, Thousand Oaks, CA (2016)
32. Yin, R.K.: Qualitative Research from Start to Finish. The Guilford Press, New York, NY, U.S. (2011)
33. Achanga, P., Shehab, E., Roy, R., Nelder, G.: Critical success factors for lean implementation with in SMEs. J. Manuf. Technol. Manag. **17**, 460–471 (2006). https://doi.org/10.1108/17410380610662889

34. Trubetskaya, A., Manto, D., McDermott, O.: A review of lean adoption in the Irish MedTech industry. Processes **10**, 391 (2022). https://doi.org/10.3390/pr10020391
35. McDermott, O., Antony, J., Sony, M., Healy, T.: Critical failure factors for continuous improvement methodologies in the Irish MedTech industry. TQM J. **34**, 18–38 (2022). https://doi.org/10.1108/TQM-10-2021-0289
36. Antony, J., McDermott, O., Powell, D.J., Sony, M.: Mapping the terrain for lean six sigma 4.0. In: Powell, D.J., Alfnes, E., Holmemo, M.D.Q., Reke, E. (eds.) Learning in the Digital Era. ELEC 2021. IFIP Advances in Information and Communication Technology, vol. 610, pp. 193–204. Springer, Cham (2021). https://doi.org/10.1007/978-3-030-92934-3_20
37. Al-Balushi, S., Sohal, A.S., Singh, P.J., Al Hajri, A., Al Farsi, Y.M., Al Abri, R.: Readiness factors for lean implementation in healthcare settings – a literature review. J. Health Organ. Manag. **28**, 135–153 (2014). https://doi.org/10.1108/JHOM-04-2013-0083
38. Antony, J., Palsuk, P., Gupta, S., Mishra, D., Barach, P.: Six sigma in healthcare: a systematic review of the literature. Int. J. Qual. Reliab. Manag. **35**, 1075–1092 (2018).https://doi.org/10.1108/IJQRM-02-2017-0027

Lean Implementation in a Painter/Decorator Micro Enterprise: A Case Study

Stuart Nelson and Olivia McDermott[✉]

University of Galway, Galway, Ireland
Olivia.McDermott@universityofgalway.ie

Abstract. This research demonstrates how Lean can be applied in a Microenterprise. Utilising a case study in a painter/decorator business, the study aims to show the benefits of applying Lean in a service organisation. The study also investigates how the Enterprise Ireland Lean program benefited the microenterprise case study. The results demonstrated that by utilising Lean tools, a new customer quotation process was designed with reduced the non-value add time to raise a customer quote. An enhanced online quotation process ensured a level-loaded, more value-added process. The study is the first published study of Lean in a painter/decorator and can be leveraged by similar size micro-enterprises to demonstrate the applicability of Lean. For academics and practitioners and informing government funding policy, this study demonstrates that Lean can successfully be deployed in Micro Enterprises. This study demonstrates that government support can aid Lean and enhance economic competitiveness. Further research opportunities are to compare and contrast Lean deployment in other sectors across the microenterprise space.

Keywords: Micro Enterprise · Lean · Enterprise Ireland · Lean for Micro · Painter · Decorator

1 Introduction

Organisations must strive to improve profits and increase their customer base in an increasingly globally competitive world. Micro Enterprises (ME) is defined as one with between 1 and 10 employees and less than 2 million annual turnover [1]. In Ireland, there are over 250,000 micro- enterprises employing just over 400,000 people [2]. The West of Ireland, in particular, have 20% of Irish gross industrial output for Irish-owned enterprises, with just under 14000 employees employed in the SME sectors [3]. Many Micro-Enterprises rely on self-employment and operations as their only source of income, and given the level of competition from large-scale industrial outfits, most MEs are finding it difficult to compete in terms of quality or price [4].

Lean is a proven method of reducing operating costs and removing waste from operations. Lean deployment has become common in many sectors, including manufacturing [5, 6], service sectors such as healthcare [7–10], public sector organisations [11], medical devices [12, 13], and pharmaceutical [14, 15] industries. However, these aforementioned

O. McDermott et al. (Eds.): ELEC 2022, IFIP AICT 668, pp. 329–337, 2023.
https://doi.org/10.1007/978-3-031-25741-4_28

sectors are typically larger enterprises and small and medium-sized organisations. The Irish government has supported all Irish businesses in recent years through the Irish Department of Enterprise. Funding and grants, as well as training courses with access to Lean consultants, have been provided to help train, mentor and implement Lean management[16]. This support has provided productivity improvements, Sales increases, improved product and service quality and increased employment across all sized enterprise sectors [17]. However, the impact of Lean on MEs is unknown, as are the specific challenges this Micro Enterprise size faces. Furthermore, limited literature exists on Lean applications in MEs globally and in Ireland [18–21]. This study explores a research gap and carries out a more in-depth analysis of the challenges and benefits of Lean deployment in MEs.

A case study around Lean deployment within a painter decorator ME in Ireland who participated in the Irish government Enterprise Ireland Lean program will be the main focus of this study. This study will provide detailed insight into Lean deployment within a single Irish ME to ascertain the challenges and benefits encountered. The main research questions that will be addressed are:

1. What are the reasons for and challenges to implementing Lean in the case study ME?
2. What are the main Lean tools and techniques used by the case study ME?
3. What benefits and results did the case study ME experience after using Lean tools and techniques?

The remainder of this paper is arranged further into five sections. Section 2 discusses a literature review of Lean and its applications and deployment in MEs. Section 3 presents the methods adopted in the study. The research findings and analysis based on the case study are presented in Sect. 4. Finally, the discussion and interpretation of the results are examined in Sect. 5, while the conclusions are presented in Sect. 6.

2 Literature Review

Lean mainly originated in LE's, and deployment of Lean initiatives has been more focused on LE's and then SME's rather than in micro organisations [19]. ME's vary in resources and capabilities in relation to SME's [22]. The owner of a micro-enterprise can be a manager driving the business as well as the delivery driver or someone who packs the delivery trucks [23]. MEs have been described as owner-managers [24]. Therefore the Leader/manager has much more of a hands-on role in Lean deployment than in other organisations. While there are many benefits to Lean deployment, smaller organisations such as MEs need government supports with Lean fundingtraining [25]. Irish enterprises are unique globally in that the state assists and recognise the competitive benefit of Lean and funds its implementation [21, 26, 27].

Lack of personnel, training and cultural issues are considered the biggest roadblocks to implementing Lean [5, 14]. However, these challenges are compounded in smaller organisations with fewer resources, such as ME's. Nelson et al. [21] highlighted that Lean deployment in ME is often resisted due to resource issues, time for training and time to implement Lean, but it was found that the Lean changes once made aided consensus, teamwork and workforce engagement. Nelson et al. [21] also found that MEs have a high proportion of owner-managers and thus can influence Lean adoption more expediently and successfully in their businesses. Therefore, SMEs' importance to the business infrastructure is greater than may be obvious at first glance [48]. Adopting Lean implementation in smaller enterprises is prescribed as starting with basic tools such as 5S, Kaizen and visual layouts and then deploying more sophisticated tools. Research conducted by Hu et al. [27] found that the most used tools by SMEs are the simplest and cheapest ones, such as value-stream mapping, 5S, Kanban and total productive maintenance [27]. There are many CSFs for Lean implementation for which leadership and management involvement and commitment are critical to the success of the lean program [28]. The CSFs of Lean deployment within SMEs include culture, financial resources, appropriate Lean expertise and training, and leadership commitment are important CSF's aspects for an SME to take into consideration when deploying Lean successfully [19]. ME's can often be due to their "micro" nature and lack of the necessary resources and culture to deploy these initiatives [29].

Through Enterprise Ireland (EI), Ireland has been supporting Irish enterprises with Lean introduction for several years. As a result, they set up a Lean for Micro Enterprises initiative in 2015. This initiative aimed to introduce ME's in Ireland to Lean concepts. The initiative's aim was that these ME's would garner an understanding of Lean and that the Lean tools and techniques could benefit process improvements, cost reduction, productivity improvements and, ultimately, competitiveness [29]. Since its inception, the Lean for Micro programme run through Irish Local Enterprise Offices (LEO's) has had over 800 companies have benefited from its expertise and principles [17].

3 Methodology

The case study methodology was applied because it enables more insight and understanding of the phenomenon under investigation [32]. Also, the case study approach allows for answers to the "how" and "why" questions of the research, as well as the recognition of the unique contextual circumstances [33].

A case study approach was used, and within that, Lean methods deployment. The painter/decorator ME business was started by its owner during a recession due to a dramatic slowdown in the construction industry in 2009. The owner grew the ME business from a one-person crew to a team of 10, amassing a vast range of painting and decorating skills and experience. Based in Ireland, the ME provides bespoke, premium painting and decorating services in the East of Ireland. The business offers several services, including free colour consultation by a professional designer with all interior work.

Along with hand painting and spray painting, the business carries out preparation work, such as Power Washing. They are also skilled in wallpaper hanging, hand-painting and spray-painting of kitchen units, floor sanding and lacquering. Quality control checks are carried out during and upon completion of all painting and decorating contracts, ensuring that the business and customer are satisfied with the work.

Building a professional operation in the painting industry is challenging due to competing with other businesses with fewer overheads, offering inferior services or products, or even operating on a cash basis. Thus the business is always seeking ways to improve business by reducing costs, ensuring a pipeline of work exists, and making the business profitable and sustainable. To this end, they sought to develop business skills by availing of any support and training they could access. Thus the business joined the "Lean for Micro" program run by their Local Enterprise Office (LEO). As a result, the case study ME was able to avail of the training and mentoring services offered by their LEO. The Lean program structured 2 days of training in Lean Thinking & Tools, followed by 5 × ½ days in company support.

During the Lean workshops, the ME owner realised that the problems in the business were not necessarily on the painting side of the business but on the planning and administration side. The business kept detailed spreadsheets covering all aspects of operations, including scheduling, leads, and scheduled jobs pipeline. During the first individual Lean coaching session, the Lean coach reviewed the level of detail and data that was being captured. Waste in terms of value add and Non- Value add waste was discussed and analysed. Problems in the current system were the time spent capturing and generating the data and spreadsheets, the level of detail, manual duplication, and the value of the data captured was analysed and mapped. Another, more urgent issue in the business was the time spent managing the sales process from inquiry to win or loss of the sale, and this was decided to be the focus of the first lean project.

Fig. 1. Current sales process

4   Results

Firstly a process map was carried out of the sales inquiry and customer quotation process. Next, a non-value add waste analysis (NVA) using the 8 wastes of Lean was carried out. The ME organisation's sales process started with a customer enquiry, typically through a social media channel (Fig. 1). These enquiries usually arrived in the evening with customers scrolling through social media and messaging to look for a quote. The ME owner would engage with the customer through chat/text and arrange a visit to measure. The ME owner would travel to the customer, measure, return home, prepare the quote, email to a client, and then follow up. Most of the quotation work took place outside office hours and the owners working day. The first step was to document and measure the process; each quote, including discussion, travel, measure and preparation, took, on average, 3 h.

There was a steady pipeline of enquiries, and on average, 12 quotes per week were generated with a success of win rate of 41.5%. The ME found that while the quote process was time-consuming, it generated work 41.5% of the time and kept the business profitable. However, there was still the fact that 58.5% of that time was nonvalue added work, and that approx. 17.5 h per week was used on non-value added and non-profitable work. In terms of Lean thinking, lost quotes were waste and needed to be addressed.

A root cause analysis was carried out regarding the ME's quotes that did not proceed and translate into orders. The top 2 reasons for quotes not going ahead were customers stating that the costs were too high and that they were not ready to have the work done. Upon discussing with lost customers why the cost was off-putting, customers stated that they did not think it would be so expensive to hire a painter/decorator compared to painting themselves. In terms of not being ready to take up the quote, customers cited the decision to get a quote as premature and stated they might come back on a future day. Thus based on the customer information, a brainstorming session to reduce the non-value add waste in relation to the quote process was discussed. The concept of BANT was introduced as a model for sales. BANT is an acronym for "Budget Authority, Need, Timing" [30] to establish the requirement by the customer for the painting job before committing to a resource-heavy site visit and a fixed visit quotation to improve the win rate.

A quote calculator was proposed to build an estimate from measurements provided by the customer. A quotation calculator or template was created, allowing a review of the services to be delivered; the room measurements could be added, along with a count of windows, doors, sills and radiators (Table 1). Now, everyone who enquired was requested to provide basic room measurements and the number of doors. Once provided, they would be entered into the calculator, and an estimate was provided to the customer. If the client was happy with the estimate, a visit was scheduled to measure and a fixed price quote.

Table 1. Quotation calculator template

Area	Selling Price (inc VAT)	Material used (L)	Cost Per L	Material Cost	Hours	Time Cost	Unit
Ceiling (2 Coats)	€ 13.14	0.25	€ 2.50	€ 0.63	0.33	€ 7.10	Metre Sq
Walls (2 coats)	€ 16.76	0.25	€ 11.00	€ 2.75	0.33	€ 7.10	Metre Sq
Single Doors (2 Coats)	€ 91.94	1	€ 11.00	€ 11.00	2	€ 43.00	Unit
Double Doors (2 Coats)	€ 183.87	2	€ 11.00	€ 22.00	4	€ 86.00	Unit
Single Doorframes (2 Coats)	€ 91.94	1	€ 11.00	€ 11.00	2	€ 43.00	Unit
Double Doorframe (2 Coats)	€ 113.98	1.2	€ 11.00	€ 13.20	2.5	€ 53.75	Unit
Skirting (2 Coats)	€ 14.20	0.25	€ 11.00	€ 2.75	0.26	€ 5.59	Linear Metre
Single Window Boards (2 Coats)	€ 27.67	0.5	€ 11.00	€ 5.50	0.5	€ 10.75	Unit
Double Window Boards (2 Coats)	€ 55.33	1	€ 11.00	€ 11.00	1	€ 21.50	Unit
Radiators (2 Coats)	€ 18.73	1	€ 11.00	€ 11.00	0.5		Unit
Sundries	€ 17.03	1	€ 10.00	€ 10.00			Unit

There were 3 advantages immediately from this improvement. Firstly the ability to provide almost instant estimates based on customer measurements eliminates waiting, transport and over-processing wastes. Secondly, by establishing their budget, customers have a very good guide price on the service and can decide whether it is for them. Thirdly many people never responded when measurements were requested from them, establishing, in many cases, the absence of Need & Timing on the customer side.

The final quote was presented in a format that could be completed with accurate measurements, the clients' details, special notes and photos. This was linked to the costing table in Table 1 above and gave the ME owner the ability to provide an instant quotation while still on site. This had multiple benefits, 1. Reduced time to generate a quote, 2. The client receives information immediately, 3. Decision makers are usually present during the quote visit. Thus non-value add waste was reduced. Moreover, a more streamlined level loading or Hejunka process was introduced.

The new process map is as follows in Fig. 2:

Fig. 2. New process for quotation with non-value add waste elimination and reduction

The overall improvements as a result of the new process for quotation are shown in Table 2.

Table 2. Process changes before and after lean deployment

Process Step	Change	% improvement
Quote generation	Reduced from 2 h to 30 min	75%
Quote sending	Reduced from next-day send to instant Send	100%
Win rate	Increased from 43% to 83%	48%
Time spent on quoting	Reduced from 30 h to 12 h per Week	60%

Based on the new qualification process - providing an estimated price before measuring and quoting- the number of leads going to quote decreased, but the win rate doubled, eliminating most of the waste. In addition, a pattern of "Click" was identified where people with no real intention to buy were eliminated from leads. As a result, the time to generate the quote was reduced significantly, and the time spent on quoting was reduced by 60%. This allowed the owner to concentrate on other value add work.

The "Estimator/Calculator" was integrated into a new website allowing clients to build their own quotes. The client portal was also developed to allow customers to add or remove options from the fixed price quote. Future projects will focus on 5S in the painter decorator vans, the offsite spraying process, and the set-up and breakdown of work on sites. In addition, the creation of the estimator tool has allowed other team members to be upskilled in the quotation and business development. Thus the owner has more time to focus further on growing the business.

Lastly, the owner stated, *"Lean has helped the business solve problems we know we had, but also many more we did not know existed. Usually, these hidden problems were explained by 'that is the way we have always done it!'".*

5   Discussion

The study demonstrated why a ME would deploy Lean to make a business more completive and efficient by removing nonvalue add waste. In particular, this case study demonstrated the amount of time spent on administration as non-value add work in the ME (RQ1). The challenge to deploying the Lean methods was taking the time to analyse the process and available data (RQ1). As found in similar studies on Lean deployment in

ME's lean can improve productivity and reduce non-value add activities, but resources to spend on the Lean initiative can be prohibitive to the success of Lean [20, 21]. In addition, many authors cite a challenge in Lean deployment with the lack of management commitment, particularly at the senior management level [27]. However, this case study aligned with the findings of Nelson et al. [21], where they studied the application of Lean in Irish ME's and found that ME's were more conducive to supporting Lean initiatives due to the owner-manager involvement and this active involvement promoted Lean success.

Simple Lean tools were deployed to initiate Lean in the ME, such as NVA waste analysis, process flow, Hejunka, brainstorming and root cause analysis (RQ2). Generally, the literature on Lean in ME's has observed that simple basic tools are utilised to start the Lean deployment in smaller organisations [12, 21]. Several benefits and results were observed in the case study organisation due to Lean deployment, such as increased order quotation response time, less administration by the ME owner in creating the quote and an overall reduction and elimination of non-value add waste (RQ3). This aligned with the Irish Enterprise Ireland's findings that their "Lean for Micro" program enhanced competitiveness and efficiencies in the ME's that participated in their program [16, 20].

The micro nature of the ME, with a small number of employees and owner involvement, aids in achieving consensus and engagement more expediently and enables rapid improvements. However, government support was instrumental in aiding and providing support and structure to the ME organisations [31].

6 Conclusion

The study is one of the first in-depth case studies looking at the experiences of Lean deployment in a ME. The study looked at several areas, including benefits, challenges, and types of tools utilised under the lens of government-sponsored and supported lean for the micro initiative. The authors argue that this study adds to the state of the art, can be utilised as a benchmark, and can inform further government policy and investment. In this study, the ME mentoring approach aided by an Enterprise Ireland consultant was instrumental to the success of the Lean deployment as it introduced Lean principles and translated it into action-based projects with clear linkages to the ME's strategy.

The practical implications of this research are that it provides evidence that Lean can be deployed successfully in ME's and identifies the importance of government support and mentorship, and this can aid ME's who are considering whether to embark on a Lean journey. From a theoretical implications aspect, this is one of the very few studies on Lean deployment in ME's at this level of case study analysis. The research emphasises the importance and success of government-aided support structures for Lean deployment and their role in improving economic competitiveness.

Future opportunities are to conduct further case study research on how the Lean journey has evolved in ME's who have deployed Lean for over 2 years. Expanding this research on Lean deployment in ME's to other countries could expand understanding of Lean in ME's given the place of the ME in global economies. Also, the impact of Lean as an enabler for Industry 4.0 and increased digitalisation in ME's is an opportunity for further study.

References

1. EU Commission: Commission Recommendation concerning the definition of micro, small and medium-sized enterprises (2003)
2. Central Statistics Office: Small and Medium Enterprises - CSO - Central Statistics Office. https://www.cso.ie/en/releasesandpublications/ep/p-bii/bii2015/sme/. Accessed 09 Feb 2022
3. Central Statistics Office: Business Demography 2018 - CSO - Central Statistics Office. https://www.cso.ie/en/releasesandpublications/er/bd/businessdemography2018/. Accessed 30 Jan 2022
4. Prasad, S., Tata, J.: Micro-enterprise quality. Int. J. Qual. Reliab. Manag. **26**, 234–246 (2009). https://doi.org/10.1108/02656710910936717
5. McDermott, O., Antony, J., Sony, M., Daly, S.: Barriers and enablers for continuous improvement methodologies within the Irish pharmaceutical industry. Processes **10** (2022). https://doi.org/10.3390/pr10010073
6. McDermott, O., Antony, J., Sony, M., Healy, T.: Critical failure factors for continuous improvement methodologies in the Irish MedTech industry. TQM J. (2022)
7. McDermott, O., Antony, J: Lean six sigma as an enabler for healthcare operational excellence in COVID-19. In: Six Sigma for Healthcare & Leadership. Purdue University Press Journal, Purdue University, Indiana (June 26–27)
8. McDermott, O., Antony, J., Douglas, J.: Exploring the use of operational excellence methodologies in the era of COVID-19: perspectives from leading academics and practitioners. TQM J. ahead-of-print (2021)
9. McDermott, O., et al.: Lean six sigma in healthcare: a systematic literature review on motivations and benefits. Processes **10** (2022). https://doi.org/10.3390/pr10101910
10. McDermott, O., et al.: Lean six sigma in healthcare: a systematic literature review on challenges, organisational readiness and critical success factors. Processes **10** (2022). https://doi.org/10.3390/pr10101945
11. Antony, J., Lancastle, J., McDermott, O., Bhat, S., Parida, R., Cudney, E.: An evaluation of lean and six sigma methodologies in the UK national health services. Int. J. Qual. Reliab. Manag. (2021)
12. Trubetskaya, A., Manto, D., McDermott, O.: A review of lean adoption in the Irish MedTech industry. Processes **10**, 391 (2022)
13. Slattery, O., Trubetskaya, A., Moore, S., McDermott, O.: A review of lean methodology application and its integration in medical device new product introduction processes. Processes. **10** (2022). https://doi.org/10.3390/pr10102005
14. Byrne, B., McDermott, O., Noonan, J.: Applying lean six sigma methodology to a pharmaceutical manufacturing facility: a case study. Processes **9** (2021). https://doi.org/10.3390/pr9030550
15. Duggan, J., Cormican, K., McDermott, O.: Lean implementation: analysis of individual-level factors in a biopharmaceutical organisation. Int. J. Lean Six Sigma. ahead-of- print (2022). https://doi.org/10.1108/IJLSS-10-2021-0184
16. Enterprise Ireland: Funding, grants and financial supports for entrepreneurs, companies and researchers - Enterprise Ireland. https://www.enterprise-ireland.com/en/funding-supports/. Accessed 23 Mar 2022
17. Lean Business Ireland: Lean For Micro. https://www.leanbusinessireland.ie/funding-supports-overview/are-you-a-local-enterprise-office-client/lean-for-micro/. Accessed 06 Feb 2022
18. Shah, P.P., Shrivastava, R.L.: Identification of performance measures of lean six sigma in small- and medium-sized enterprises: a pilot study. Int. J. Six Sigma Compet. Adv. **8**, 1–21 (2013)

19. Alkhoraif, A., Rashid, H., McLaughlin, P.: Lean implementation in small and medium enterprises: literature review. Oper. Res. Perspect. **6**, 100089 (2019). https://doi.org/10.1016/j.orp. 2018.100089
20. O'Reilly, S., Freeman, D., Dooley, L.: LSS implementation in micro enterprises: adoption of tools to support competitiveness. In: Emerging Trends in LSS. Purdue University Press Journal, Cork, Ireland (2021). https://doi.org/10.5703/1288284317326
21. Nelson, S., McDermott, O., Woods, B., Trubetskaya, A.: An evaluation of lean deployment in Irish micro-enterprises. Total Qual. Manag. Bus. Excell. 1–20 (2022). https://doi.org/10. 1080/14783363.2022.2140651
22. Ravi, A., Ramesh, N.: Enhancing the performance of micro, small and medium sized cluster organisation through lean implementation. IJPQM **21**, 325 (2017). https://doi.org/10.1504/ IJPQM.2017.10005234
23. Voss, C., Blackmon, K.L., Cagliano, R., Hanson, P., Wilson, F.: Made in Europe: small companies. Bus. Strateg. Rev. **9**, 1–19 (1998). https://doi.org/10.1111/1467-8616.00078
24. Gherhes, C., Williams, N., Vorley, T., Vasconcelos, A.C.: Distinguishing micro-businesses from SMEs: a systematic review of growth constraints. J. Small Bus. Enterp. Dev. **23**, 939–963 (2016). https://doi.org/10.1108/JSBED-05-2016-0075
25. Lande, M., Shrivastava, R.L., Seth, D.: Critical success factors for lean six sigma in SMEs (small and medium enterprises). TQM J. **28**, 613–635 (2016). https://doi.org/10.1108/TQM-12-2014-0107
26. Keegan, R.: Improving Competitiveness Using Lean Principles – The Irish Experience. Presented at the ICOPEV, Guimares, Portugale (2014)
27. Hu, Q., Mason, R., Williams, S.J., Found, P.: Lean implementation within SMEs: a literature review. J. Manuf. Technol. Manag. **26**, 980–1012 (2015). https://doi.org/10.1108/JMTM-02-2014-0013
28. Albliwi, S., Antony, J., Abdul Halim Lim, S., van der Wiele, T.: Critical failure factors of lean six sigma: a systematic literature review. Int. J. Qual. Reliab. Manag. **31**, 1012–1030 (2014). https://doi.org/10.1108/IJQRM-09-2013-0147
29. Enterprise Ireland: LeanStart - Enterprise Ireland. https://www.enterpriseireland.com/en/Pro ductivity/Lean-Business-Offer/Lean-Start.shortcut.html. Accessed 06 Feb 2022
30. Ekbote, B.: Dynamic sales forecasting method for increased accuracy. SSRN 3645032 (2017)
31. Bhat, S., Gijo, E.V., Rego, A.M., Bhat, V.S.: Lean six sigma competitiveness for micro, small and medium enterprises (MSME): an action research in the Indian context. TQM J. **33**, 379–406 (2021). https://doi.org/10.1108/TQM-04-2020-0079

Author Index

Printed in the United States
by Baker & Taylor Publisher Services